Occupy Pennsylvania Avenue

How Politicians Caused the Financial Crisis and Why their Reforms Failed

Kevin Villani

November, 2013

Abstract

This summary policy analysis provides a simple diagnosis of the sub-prime lending debacle and consequent systemic financial crisis: The Fed fueled an asset bubble, housing policy steered it to housing, and the extreme leverage required to fund political housing policy magnified losses instead of profits. The financial sector bailout, housing market and homeowner bailout, and fiscal and monetary stimulus were all more of the same. A financial sector meltdown was avoided, but at the expense of greater systemic risk prospectively. The Great Recession ended, but the recovery remains weak with economic costs in the aftermath many multiples those during the lending bubble and prospective economic risks are worse still.

The only relevant economic precept is the original – incentives matter. Understanding the financial crisis requires no more than an explanation of how politicians perverted them.

The simple prescription to avoid future systemic financial crises is to limit discretionary monetary policy, separate subsidy from finance, impose appropriate capital requirements, improve political oversight and re-introduce market discipline, the opposite of the Dodd-Frank legislation.

Kevin Villani, a former HUD and Freddie Mac Chief Economist and private sector executive, is currently an executive scholar at the Burnham-Moores Center for Real Estate at the University of San Diego and a consultant in La Jolla, Ca. (858 454 3833, kvillani@san.rr.com)

Table of Contents

Acknowledgements

Prologue

    The Current Housing Finance Policy Debate

    The Financial Crisis Inquiry Commission Report and Dissents

    The Fed's Monetary Policy

    "The *sine qua non* of the financial crisis was U.S. government housing policy." Wallison (pg. 44)

    F&F Agency Status and Bank Deposit Insurance: Housing Goals Trump Prudential Regulation

    F&F Inflate the House Price Bubble to Unprecedented Proportions

    The Origins of Political and Regulatory Intervention in US Markets: Why Us?

    The Solvency Crisis was Predictable and Inevitable

    Politicians could have easily prevented the Crisis

    The Intended Beneficiaries and the Vast Majority of Households are worse off

    Why the Correct Diagnosis Was and Remains Important

    The Policy Prescription: Competitive Markets

    Organization of the Book

Chapter 1: Original Sin; the New Deal to the Great Society: The Origins of Federal Financial Institutions 1913 to 1938 and their Role through 1968

    A. The Origins and Role of the Federal Reserve System

    B. Liquidity of Deposit Institutions

    C. Housing and Mortgage Market Distress

    D. The Consequences of Federal Institutions Through 1968

Chapter 2: the Great Society 1965-1968 to the National Home Ownership Strategy 1995-2000

A. The S&L Industry and Housing and Urban Development's Mission

B. The Early Origins of Federally Sponsored Mortgage Capital Markets

C. Speculative Trading of GSE MBS Promotes Agency Status and Wall Street Greed

D. The Implications of Government Backed Debt for Firm Behavior
  1. The Value of Government Backed Debt to Firms
  2. Moral Hazard: Going for Broke and Going Broke

E. Mission Regulation Undermines Prudential Regulation

F. Agency Status Crowds Out Private Portfolio Lenders and Mortgage Insurers

G. Housing Goals Coerce TBTF Banks and Solidify GSE Monopoly by the End of the Century

H. The Greenspan Put

Chapter 3: The Origins of Private Label Securitization and their Role in Meeting Housing and Home Ownership Goals 2000–2007

A. Prudential Regulation Trumps Market Discipline 1970-2000
  1. The Credit Rating Agencies
  2. Regulation and Risk-based Capital Requirements

B. The Origins of Private label Securitization (PLS) 1970-2000

C. Characteristics of the Borrower Pool 2000-2004 and 2005-2007

D. Determining PLS Net Capital Requirements Funding Sub-prime Mortgages 2000-2007
  1. Regulatory Arbitrage Enables Extreme Leverage
  2. Capital Requirements Using CDOs

E PLS and CDO Mis-Pricing

       1. Mis-pricing Senior PLS securities

       2. Mis-pricing PLS Equity

  F. PLS Funding of Bad Loans Generates Cash Profitability

  G. CDO Issuance and Ownership

Chapter 4: The Root Causes of the Systemic Financial Crisis of 2008

  A. The Subsidy-Fueled Mortgage Credit Bubble

       1. The Fed-Induced Housing Boom

       2. The Treasury ex ante Cost of Financial Sector Housing Subsidies

       3. The Housing Policy-Induced Lending Bubble

  B. Extreme Leverage Creates Moral Hazard

       1. F&F Follow PLSers: Go for Broke, then Go Broke

       2. FHA and the FHLBs also Go for Broke, then Go Broke

       3. Banks Go for Broke, then Go Broke

  C. The Consequences of the Credit Bubble: the House Price Bubble

       1. The Regional Land Use Restriction-Induced House Price Bubble

       2. The Magnitude and Distribution of Losses from the House Price Bubble Bursting

  D. The Systemic Financial Crisis of 2008: Financial Institution Insolvency Becomes Transparent

       1. The House Price Bubble Deflates: PLS Markets Crash

       2. The Financial Institution Solvency Crisis Becomes Globally Systemic

       3. Why didn't the House Price Bubble Burst earlier: the Role of the GSEs

  E. The Fallacy of Alternative Explanations

       1. The Fed's Spin

2. The Fannie and Freddie Spin

3. The Regulators' Spin

4. The Academic Economists' Spin

5. The Armchair Moralists' Spin

6. The Politicians' Spin

Chapter 5: Government Bailouts during the Aftermath: More of the Same

A. The Anatomy of Public Bailouts

    1. Casualty Insurance, Catastrophe Insurance and Emergency Assistance

    2. Endogenous Systemic Political Risk

    3. The Financial Sector Safety Net: The Source of Systemic Risk

B. The Great Depression and Great Recession: History Repeats Itself

    1. The Great Recession and the Great Depression

    2. Hoovers 'Laissez Faire" New Deal Intervention

    3. Roosevelt's "New" New Deal

    4. The Austrian Laissez Faire Response to Recessions and Depressions

    5. The Contemporaneous Competing System to Market Capitalism – Socialism/Communism

C. The Wall Street Bailout: Systemic Liquidity Support Becomes a TBTF Bailout

    1. Panics and Financial Sector Liquidity Support: Opaque Bailouts

    2. The Troubled Asset Relief Program (TARP): Crony Capitalism at its Worst

D. The Home Mortgage Bailouts and Housing Market Adjustment

    1. The Fed Attempts to Bail Out the Mortgage Market and Stimulate Housing

    2. The GSE Agency Bailouts: FHA/Ginnie Mae

    3. The Securitizer Lawsuit Investor Bailout

    4. The Servicer/Lender Lawsuit "Homeowner" Bailout

        5. The Refinancing Bailout

        6. The HUD Lender Lawsuits

        7. The Housing Industry Bailout: the Mortgage and Housing Market Adjustments Delayed

    E. Bailing Out the Economy: The Monetary and Fiscal Policy Bailout
        1. The Historical Context of US Macro-economic Policy: Cyclical and Secular Trends
        2. Government Spending and Regulation: the Stimulus and Beyond

        3. A National Infrastructure Bank, Once Again

        4. Monetary Policy: the Handmaiden of Fiscal Policy

    F. An Austrian Approach to the Aftermath

        1. The Austrian Prescription

        2. Is Laissez Faire Unfair?

Chapter 6: The Long Run Policy Prescription

    A. Are There Lessons from Mortgage Finance Systems in Other Developed Countries?

        1. Deposit versus Capital Markets: Regulation

        2. Savings for Down Payments and Borrower Underwriting

        3. Fixed Rate Mortgage Lending

        4. The Mortgage Interest Tax Deduction

    B. Separating Subsidy from Finance:

        1. The Future Role of HUD

        2. The Future Role of Fannie Mae, Freddie Mac, Ginnie Mae, the FHLBs and the FHFA

3. Privatize FHA

C. The Role of the Fed: Past, Present and Future

    1. Monetary Policy: Discretion, Rules or Metals?

    2. Moral Hazard Run Amok

    3. Eliminate the Consumer Financial Protection Bureau (CFPB)

D. Reform Bank Prudential Regulation: Keep it Simple

    1. Mitigating Moral Hazard: Regulating Federally Insured Banks in the US

    2. Rolling Back or Eliminating Bank Deposit Insurance

E. Mitigating Systemic Risk: Rely on Market Discipline

    1. Conflicting Incentives among Politicians, Regulators, Economists and the Public

    2. The Fed's Role as Systemic Regulator

    3. Regulating Firms: Mitigating TBTF and SIF

    4. Regulating Instruments and Markets

F. Restoring Mortgage Capital Markets

    1. Private Label Securities (PLS) and Private Covered Bonds (PCBs)

    3. Eliminating Regulatory Arbitrage within Banks and Between PCBs and PLS

    4. How Mortgage Markets Can Price Risk Efficiently

    5. The Implications for Fixed Rate Mortgage Lending

    6. The Transition to Private Securities

G. Sources and Uses of Funds for Mortgage Finance

    1. Sources and Uses of Funds for Home Mortgages 1960-2010

    2. Prospective Sources and Uses of Funds for Home Mortgages 2010-2030: Crowding Out

H. Final Comments: Restoring Economic Growth

Endnotes

Glossary of Abbreviations

References

About the Author

Acknowledgements

My two most dedicated readers of early drafts were Bob Buckley and Ken Thygerson, Bob to convince me of how crazy my ideas were and Ken the opposite. Mark Calabria of the Cato Institute provided encouragement and many helpful suggestions. While the conclusions are mine alone, their advice and encouragement was invaluable. Finally, I want to thank my mentor Pat Hendershott who started me on my writing career decades ago and re-started me about three years ago.

Prologue

The Current Housing Finance Policy Debate

Housing finance "reform" is once again on the front burner of Congress, although in truth it hasn't been off the stove for the last half century. Only a decade ago the unique US public/private hybrid was touted as the best system among developed market economies. A quarter century ago it failed systemically. That's happened in other countries as well, but only the US experienced two systemic failures in two decades.

The US has never seriously considered the alternative to a market system of housing finance, a state run system. Such systems are seemingly stable because the losses are opaque and isolated from main stream finance, mitigating systemic damage. The downside is that they don't necessarily encourage saving, they are extremely inefficient and stagnant, and they encourage borrower moral hazard as delinquencies are typically a multiple that of private lenders. The political upside is the ability to allocate mortgage credit; the downside is the political liability for failure. The primary advantages of competitive market systems are efficiency and innovation, which is both inherently destabilizing, and generally self-correcting to avoid systemic failure.

In theory a private-public hybrid could provide the best of both, what two cities New York – the financial capital - and Washington DC – the political capital have to offer. But former President Kennedy's quip characterizing Washington DC as having southern efficiency and northern hospitality is more apropos as the US system has enjoyed public efficiency with private instability, made systemic by pervasive public protection. That is because the political upside to a hybrid system is the ability to take credit for borrower and saver protections while using regulation to finance subsidies and extort political patronage from lenders when things go good while deflecting blame to their private "partner" when they don't. The US housing finance system worked demonstrably better for a century before federal politicians ever got involved.

The prescription for US housing finance should follow the diagnosis of the sub-prime lending debacle of 2000 through 2007. The two main competing diagnoses have followed political party lines, with Democrats generally supporting the narrative that markets failed with more government regulation the cure, and Republicans generally supporting the narrative that politically inspired regulation failed with political and regulatory reform and/or more market discipline the cure.

A decade ago the fix was simple: stop subsidizing borrowers and savers through finance by raising capital requirements. Housing goals for low-income and inner city borrowers could have been achieved as they had been historically with targeted subsidies transparently budgeted. The failure to do so cost trillions of dollars in *ex ante* subsidies and *ex post* losses. Unfortunately this simple fix may no longer be sufficient to restore the competitive market system due to the actions taken in the five year aftermath of the crisis that has increased the political risk of mortgage lending.

There are now multiple reform bills. The primary Corker-Warner bill in the Senate attempts to treat political protection of borrowers and savers as an actuarial rather than a political problem, a sure path to failure. The House Path Bill attempts to require private markets to determine capital requirements, but the most likely result is that GSEs will be replaced with TBTF banks. Reform in the context of continued deposit insurance requires setting and enforcing sufficient and consistent system-wide capital requirements. Nothing less will do and anything more will undermine this requirement.

The Financial Crisis Inquiry Commission Report and Dissents

The systemic financial crisis of 2008 that brought the world economy to its knees wasn't supposed to happen. It emanated primarily from the US mortgage capital market system, long touted internationally as the best model to emulate. This system had purportedly made home ownership affordable to as great or greater proportion of the populace than any other large developed market economy. When it failed spectacularly, politicians and regulators asserted "nobody could have seen this debacle coming."

By now, books on the causes of the financial crisis number in the hundreds and articles in the thousands. For example, the spring 2012 issue of the Journal of Economic Literature contained a survey article summarizing 21 of the most influential books and another summarizing 16 key scholarly articles. Other disciplines such as psychology, political science and sociology added to the inconsistent panoply of diagnoses, fostering a continuing controversy over the proper prescription. The financial system remains threatened and the recovery weak, with no consensus on future policies.

To provide this consensus, Congress established the Financial Crisis Inquiry Commission (FCIC) in May 2009, invoking the Great Depression-era Pecora Commission as precedent. As is customary, the Commission was bipartisan, with the Democratic majority appointing six members and former Democratic politician Phil Angelides as its Chairman and Republicans appointing four members. The Commission identified 22 specific causes to investigate, based primarily on the ideas and opinions floated up to that time.

Political commissions generally start with a point of view. The enabling Act's title, the Fraud Enforcement and Recovery Act (FERA) of 2009, is revealing: politicians implied that lenders had defrauded the American people, that the perpetrators would be arrested and that the money recovered! Invoking the Pecora Commission as precedent was also revealing as this Commission blatantly ignored the causes of bank failure during the Depression. Its real purpose was to provide the necessary publicity to get Congress to pass the long-stalled Glass-Steagall Act – the most consequential financial legislation prior to the most recent crisis - providing public deposit insurance and separating investment banking from commercial banking.

The FCIC spent tens of millions of dollars, had almost 100 staffers, held 19 hearings around the country, heard testimony from over 700 witnesses, and reviewed over a million pages of documents. But Congress did not wait for the FCIC Report, passing legislation with a party-line vote. The 2,300-page Dodd-Frank Wall Street Reform and Consumer Protection Act of 2010 may prove even more consequential than Glass-Steagall.

Given the broad scope the Commission was charged to investigate, the Report unsurprisingly concluded that there were multiple complex causes of the crisis but "Market failure" was the consistent culprit, occurring in virtually all home mortgage-related markets. The Democrats united behind their Chairman to issue the majority Report findings supporting the need for the recent Dodd-Frank legislation. It exonerated political housing policy and its primary implementers Fannie Mae and Freddie Mac (F&F), who were characterized as victims of private lenders, particularly private label securitizers (PLSers). This was completely consistent with Dodd-Frank, which codified more regulation for private firms while ignoring the baneful effects of housing policy.

The four Republicans filed two dissenting Reports. Three Republicans filed a dissent agreeing with the "multiple complex causes" narrative, narrowing the list of root causes from 22 down to only 10. The other Republican, Peter Wallison, challenged both his fellow Republicans and the conclusion of the Report. He argued that US housing policy, the Federal Reserve System's easy money policies, and the so-called global savings glut caused the US housing bubble to inflate. Bursting the bubble would cause a systemic financial crisis. In other words, politicians and regulators caused the debacle. By implication, virtually all the other purported causes cited by the FCIC Report were, in fact, consequences of political and regulatory distortions.

Most economists support the "multiple complex causes" narrative and the exoneration of political housing policy as well. The Wallison dissent directly challenged liberal orthodoxy and was almost universally reviled as an ideological defense of "free" or "unfettered" markets. Support came primarily from the Austrian School of economics, which is generally more sympathetic to free markets than to political alternatives.[1] In "The Global Financial Crisis: Causes and Cures" (2009), three Europeans with no obvious ideological bias, Jacobo Carmassi, Daniel Gros, and Stefano Micossi, blamed the Fed and regulators exclusively.

The majority Report criticizes the Fed in many ways, but exonerates the Fed's monetary policy, blaming the credit bubble on a global excess of savings. These commissioners are also sympathetic to political housing policy; they argue first that housing policy wasn't sufficiently comprehensive to apply to private label securitizers, who caused the crisis. Second, they claim F&F would have followed the same procedures regardless of the housing goals. Finally, prudential regulators blamed deregulation and a lack of authority. In fact, the Report is an in depth *description* of everything that happened – the purported multiple complex causes - without providing a convincing explanation of *why* all these events happened all at once.

The Report's defense of monetary policy doesn't withstand scrutiny. The Dissent is essentially correct regarding the central role of political housing policy, and regulators failed systemically while politicians failed to hold them to account. To the extent there were un-or under-regulated private markets, they performed as well as could given the multiple distortions they faced. Put differently, explaining these political and regulatory policies explains the multiple complex causes but not visa versa. This diagnosis is resisted most likely because it blames politicians and regulators, making the prescription politically problematic to implement.

The debacle was an entirely predictable consequence of several specific policies implemented by four politically powerful federal institutions or groups of institutions. Each was necessary and together more than sufficient to cause the debacle. The institutions were the Federal Reserve; the Department of Housing and Urban Development (HUD); the Government Sponsored Enterprises (GSEs), including F&F and the Government National Mortgage Association (Ginnie Mae), the institution that funded the insured loans of the Federal Housing Administration (FHA), and the financial regulators. These institutions have unique characteristics - a legacy of the US political system - that explain the failure of political oversight and the lack of public and market restraint.

The analysis in this book was written based on the author's experience working at and with the GSEs, the Fed, HUD, mortgage and commercial banks, PLSers, and investment banks. The analysis of the facts is generally consistent with a typical Austrian cycle of an excessive credit expansion, followed by an asset price bubble, inevitably leading to a financial sector crash. The Fed and GSEs fueled a mortgage credit bubble, as the outstanding stock of US household mortgage debt increased by almost $6 trillion, a 120% increase in aggregate first and second lien debt from 2000 through 2007. This fueled a housing price bubble of $6 trillion above the increase in physical housing stock and consumer price index (CPI) monetary inflation. When the bubble burst US home equity fell by $6 trillion by year-end 2009. By mid-2012 it had fallen by almost $7 trillion. About half of the drop represented negative mortgage equity, a direct result of the excessive leverage that fueled the bubble. That negative equity was the root cause of the globally systemic financial crisis.

The Federal Reserve's Monetary Policy

Housing prices are often cyclical and production is subject to booms and busts. The Federal Reserve System (Fed) historically took at least partial responsibility for these cycles, calling housing "the Handmaiden of Monetary Policy" in a 1972 study. The credit expansion described above led to an unprecedented housing construction boom that virtually doubled the mortgage stock, while the physical housing stock increased by only about 15%. This pushed prices up, particularly where "smart growth" policies limited land supply.

How big was the bubble in housing prices this past decade? From 1997 to 2002 real house prices rose 125% from their baseline trend, a historic peak over the last century. They typically peak there because by that point the pool of qualified borrowers that lenders can profitably finance is generally depleted and the Fed reverses course, ending the production boom and deflating the price bubble. But by the end of 2004 prices had risen by 2.5 to 5 times historic peak highs – based on the more recent baseline benchmark of 110% - and by mid-2006 by 5 to 10 times. Housing price bubbles fueled by a credit bubble always deflate, and virtually all agree that the collapse of house prices precipitated the sub-prime credit default debacle. Therefore explaining this house price bubble is essential to understanding the systemic financial crisis.

The Economist magazine warned almost from the beginning that this bubble would deflate, spreading great pain when it did. And there was plenty of evidence that credit losses would spread that pain to investors. But Fed Chairman Greenspan felt it was not the Fed's role to burst asset bubbles, even those that it inflated. Chairman Bernanke – who shared the Greenspan sentiment - blamed the bubble on a global savings glut, a hypothesis others have since refuted.

Bernanke's negative real interest rate policy for the first half of the decade was well intended – to reduce unemployment - and was repeated in the aftermath of the 2008 financial crisis. Low US interest rates also reflected the Chinese policy of accumulating US Treasury securities and later GSE securities, which contributed to making the crisis globally systemic. But the extreme zero rate policies, massive security purchases of US Treasuries, and risky mortgages dramatically redistributed wealth in the US, and posed extreme risk going forward.

U.S. government housing policy

The policy focused on "affordable housing" which led to several initiatives. F&F set out goals that required lenders to provide cheap home mortgage financing to borrowers with weak credit, questionable collateral, or both. These goals relied on public subsidies and coercion. During the Clinton Administration, the Department of Housing and Urban Development extended the affordable housing goals to private lenders with the same consequences. In addition, HUD extended liberalized underwriting standards and relaxed down payment requirements from banks and F&F to the entire home mortgage market. The Community Reinvestment Act (CRA) of 1977 also required banks to lend to applicants who did not meet normal standards of creditworthiness.

Banks needed approval pursuant the CRA to branch or merge. Such approval depended on "fair lending" by the banks, to extract subsidies from banks - especially those that were too-big-to-fail (TBTF) - because CRA approval was required to branch or merge. Starting in 1995, compliance with fair lending laws would be determined based on actual market outcomes - *disparate impact*, a legally dubious argument made by Patrick Duval of the Clinton Department of Justice (DOJ) and later by the Obama DOJ - rather than the intent to discriminate, making the CRA requirement much more binding.

Equally important, the policy sought to foster home ownership. In 1994, the Clinton Administration added a new home ownership goal of 70 percent, implying five million additional homeowners. The goal was ambitious. Homeownership rate remained stable at about 65 percent despite F&F's displacement of private lenders. In addition, affordable housing quotas were ratcheted up to between 50 percent and 70 percent (cumulatively, assuming no overlap) of all lending during the ensuing years. This, along with loan limits, facilitated the required bottom-up market expansion, creating a need for a substantial increase in borrower subsidies.

The required credit allocation was initially minor but was steadily increased during the Clinton Administration to take advantage of the newly acquired merger and acquisition authority under the Gramm-Leach-Bliley (GLB) Act of 1999, which was contingent on CRA ratings. Affordable housing advocates extracted over $4 trillion in bank CRA commitments by 2000 and tens of millions of loans were made to what by any historical measure were under qualified borrowers to meet these commitments. This housing policy was driving the unprecedented market expansion. F&F funded about half of all sub-prime borrowers directly and private label securities (PLS) the other half, with F&F providing as much as a third to a half of PLS funding as well. While not all sub-prime loans counted toward the CRA or affordable housing goals, they all promoted home ownership.

For the most part this political intervention was well intended, although there is plenty of evidence of political rent-seeking, e.g., the infamous "Countrywide 'friends of Angelo'" program that directly benefited key politicians. But intentions are irrelevant to likely consequences, whether intended or not. Defenders of housing policy attempt to isolate sub-prime lending as something independent of CRA and F&F specific lending quotas and hence political housing policy. Not all sub-prime loans were written specifically to satisfy CRA or F&F affordable housing goals – the specific research is inconclusive - but the number is much higher than affordable housing policy advocates will admit.

In sum, the political effort to deliver "affordable housing" contributed to the financial crisis. In perhaps the most comprehensive in-depth study of US housing policy to date, Oonagh McDonald, a British economist, Labor Party politician and financial regulator of the highest rank, *Fannie Mae and Freddie Mac, Turning the American Dream into a Nightmare*, (2012, p. 315), reviews the entire body of evidence and flat-out rejects the Report's conclusion, stating "The subprime mortgage market was more than a trigger. It was the root cause of the crisis..."

F&F Agency Status and Bank Deposit Insurance: Housing Goals Trump Prudential Regulation

The FCIC Report concluded that lenders made these loans not because they had to – which they did – but because they were "greedy" and the loans were profitable. There is a grain of truth to that otherwise misleading conclusion. They were profit motivated, and with sufficient leverage some of these loans were sufficiently profitable, at least early on. It would have been equally true and entirely consistent for Commissioner Wallison to have concluded that the root cause of the financial crisis was capital depletion. Opaque capital subsidies were required, as no direct budget funding was made available.

Financial market participants in well-functioning environments have historically imposed capital requirements on all parties to mitigate excessive risk-taking (moral hazard) and incentive conflicts. Two federal policies have long encouraged excessive leverage. First, debt costs are tax deductible whereas equity costs are paid after the issuer pays corporate taxes. Second, federal backing removes the risk premium from debt costs. As federal GSEs, F&F could issue debt at a slight premium over Treasury, despite limited capital and risky loans. Similarly, bank capital levels fell from about 16% prior to the introduction of federal deposit insurance to only 5% within a decade, where they remained for several decades.

F&F saved about $10 billion annually in taxes from 1970-2000, and cheap debt from low capital requirements saved them another $10 billion. During this period borrowers – many of whom met the affordable housing goals - captured about half the capital subsidy, while management, shareholders and politicians split the rest. Banks followed a similar route, though to a lesser extent due to their higher regulatory capital requirements.

Investors would have normally responded to the upward trend in house prices that started in 1997 by significantly raising the cost of debt and by requiring more equity capital from all parties. But not federal regulators. After the turn of the century, with the housing boom already several years in the making, F&F could maintain leverage about 100 to 1 – at least five times their likely private market limit - and still borrow at just above the Treasury cost of funds. During the next decade the total tax and debt value of the F&F capital subsidy grew to an average of about $50 billion annually

Unlike F&F, Ginnie Mae issuers had virtually no capital requirements. In addition, Ginnie Mae and FHA paid no taxes or dividends, made no political contributions, paid employees government wages, and expenses were government funded. So historically, F&F couldn't compete for FHA customers.

PLSers had to leverage commensurately to F&F or they would relinquished the conventional loan market. Fannie and Freddie capital requirements were transparent and set by politicians to finance political housing goals. However, insured banks could exploit inconsistencies in regulatory capital requirements and off-balance-sheet opportunities to achieve a similar leverage ratio and funding costs by securitizing pools of risky mortgages. The so-called "private" label securitization industry was no more "private" than the "privatized" F&F. It was built upon the foundation of publicly insured banks, conferring capital subsidies comparable to those of F&F. But securitization had the additional consequence of separating "lenders" into independent loan originators, loan brokers, loan servicers, PLSers, and investment bankers. These groups had little or no capital stake in the credit performance of the loans. Federally-insured banks and F&F funded most of the senior securities, while state & local retirement funds financed much of the mezzanine and subordinated debt, leaving taxpayers with most of the risk. Their capital subsidies averaged about $30 billion over the past decade, reflecting their smaller market share.

To compensate for this lack of lender capital, higher down payments from borrowers were necessary. But political housing goals encouraged both lower income-underwriting requirements and lower cash down-payment requirements. Home borrower equity – cash down-payment requirements – had fallen from 40 percent to 20 percent during the post World War II period. With federal and subsequently private mortgage insurance, these rates fell to 5 percent. But political housing goals encouraged both lower income underwriting requirements and lower cash down payment requirements - to the extent that both were largely inconsequential and hence often ignored in practice by lenders and regulators during the subsequent sub-prime lending debacle. Lower borrower and lender capital requirements are well documented, but most observers seriously underestimate the extent of capital depletion and the consequences of simultaneously depleting both sources of equity.

HUD knew from the very beginning – based on the experience of FHA in the 1960s – that affordable housing goals weren't without cost. It denied the need for borrower subsidies just as F&F denied the existence of capital subsidies derived from agency status, both bypassing the political budget process. But politicians recognized the value of capital subsidies. They openly prevented regulators from raising F&F capital requirements, recognizing it as necessary to fund housing goals.

The system thus worked in their interest so long as the surplus capital subsidy was sufficient to fill political coffers. This excessive surplus explains the ratcheting up of housing goals during the 1990s. In addition, a 2003 study by Fed economist William Passmore, which concluded that borrowers were receiving only a small fraction of the subsidy, helps to explain the housing goal expansion after 2003.. But with capital subsidies running out at the turn of the century, it wasn't at all clear how the bottom-up market expansion – as required by the combination of the home ownership and affordable housing goals - would be financed.

Prudential regulations that should have inhibited sub-prime lending due to the borrower's inability to pay - despite massive capital subsidies - actually encouraged it. In the most comprehensive critique of the US regulatory system to date, Barth, Caprio and Levine (BCL) in *Guardians of Finance* (2012) attribute the systemic financial crisis to "a colossal failure of regulation", a cause the FCIC Report describes but does not explain. We explain F&F regulatory failure as the primacy of mission over prudential regulation and bank regulatory failure as a combination of that and sheer incompetence with no political oversight or accountability.

F&F Inflate the House Price Bubble to Unprecedented Proportions

The perceived fallacy of the Wallison Dissent is that in the end only about a fifth of the total credit default losses were incurred by F&F. This number rises to a fourth when you take into account losses of private mortgage insurers and investors incurred from purchase money second mortgage financing down payments for first liens held or guaranteed by F&F. However, the story of F&F's central role – as well as FHA - is a bit more complicated.

The historically thin or non-existent profit margins of goal-oriented lending were easily offset by the bulk of bank and Fannie and Freddie business. Unfortunately, the dramatic market expansion of their share of lending magnified the severity of loss as they reached deeper into the loan pool. Perverse regulation, combined with the housing goals, created the incentive to "go for broke" – to take extreme risks with a high likelihood of failure borne mostly by taxpayers. This incentive was equally strong for PLSers, who gained conventional market share from F&F during the first half of the decade.

In spite of FHA's additional advantages over F&F agency status and PLS deposit insurance, FHA lost market share during the first half of the decade. By 2005 the FHA Commissioner - also the F&F mission regulator - weakened FHA requirements to regain lost market share to F&F, while simultaneously mandating that F&F maintain a 50% market share relative to PLS. So began the three-way race to the bottom, with PLSers, F&F and FHA all going for broke.

Hedgers and speculators began to show signs of doubt in 2002. By 2006, the entire market was bearish. Why did these sentiments not deflate the house price bubble sooner? The answer is that borrowers continued to pay – postponing defaults while increasing their ultimate severity - so long as they could refinance teaser rate mortgages, a scheme which required continually rising home prices. Private lenders cannot operate a loss-making business indefinitely. Over time as speculation scaled back, mortgage bank PLSers migrated to TBTF investment and universal commercial banks. Due to several regulatory distortions, these institutions faced no cash constraints. Thus, as a consequence of perverse SEC accounting regulations, participants in the loan process continued earning cash profits, encouraging PLSers to go broke in competition with F&F and FHA.

The primary difference between GSEs and PLSers is that PLSers - at least initially – were not viewed as TBTF. Speculators tried to stop them but stopped once they recognized the futility of betting against a GSE-inflated house price bubble. GSEs would continue to receive funding as too-big-to-fail (TBTF) government agencies, regardless of risk or loss and without facing a rising cost of debt. Additionally, the non-market domestic and international demand for GSE debt helped keep the housing market buoyant and the housing price bubble inflated for several additional years.

When the housing price bubble eventually deflated, it was the PLS market that investors dumped first. As mentioned previously, GSE debt was widely held by foreign central banks, on whom the Treasury was reliant for future funding. A bailout was therefore practically inevitable, making GSE debt an extremely secure asset. GSE activity initially made up the difference, but when F&F and FHA failed, the same incentive distortions encouraged them to keep operating, "going broke" well past the point of technical insolvency. Being quasi private, F&F were eventually put into conservatorship. The public FHA was thus the last man (or zombie) standing, propped up by the government-backed Ginnie Mae.

When house prices bean to deflate and defaults picked up, market prices for credit default swaps (CDS) on PLS rapidly reflected speculators' rational assessment of cumulative credit loss, as well as supply/demand imbalances in thin hedge markets. The so-called mark-to-market book values at regulated banks, investment banks, and their sponsored entities reflected regulatory-approved accounting entries of proprietary traders, who were earning huge bonuses based on inflated non-cash yields on these inflated book values. The price-disconnect between the regulated and transaction markets was not eliminated until regulated investors had to sell. The triggering event was the net redemption demands at the Bears Stearns sponsored hedge fund. When Goldman Sachs valued their assets at half their mark-to-market book value, all PLS prices in the market had to be revalued– by trillions of dollars –revealing a deep and widespread insolvency in the banking and investment industries. In the end it was CDS market discipline that finally ended the sub-prime lending debacle by bringing down seemingly TBTF investment bank Bears Stearns and later Lehman Brothers.

The root causes of the financial crisis were those events and actors contributing to the bubble inflating, not those triggering its bursting. The description of events by politicians and regulators rely on theories of irrational behavior that misinterpret the facts. Investors may not have been fully aware of the depth of the solvency hole, but they knew it existed and acted accordingly. The crash followed the normal pattern when any bubble bursts or any scheme collapses: The knowledgeable long-term players participate until just before the end, and then get out as quickly as possibly.

Of course, unlike PLSers the long-term investors in PLS did have much to lose and couldn't get out quickly. So why did they continue to buy in a bearish market when the sellers were obviously going broke? Most of this loss fell on TBTF commercial banks. Deposit insurance and the related regulations explain why they would go for broke but not why they would actually go broke funding these securities. The most plausible answer is that the demand for these securities was determined based not on a rational assessment of risk. Instead, demand was based on the dramatically increased need for high CRA scores at TBTF banks, the 1999 GLB Act, and the false assumption that the costs of CRA lending were low.

The Origins of Political and Regulatory Intervention in US Markets: Why Us?

How did the US – traditionally a market economy – come to transform a successful private housing finance system into one that depended almost entirely on political credit allocation and public regulation? The sub-prime lending debacle of 2000-2007 and the resulting systemic financial collapse of 2008 were the direct result of several "original sins" – so-called reforms enacted during prior "crises" which had nothing to do with the causes of those crises. These original sins caused the massive credit expansion, moral hazard, and credit allocation to unqualified borrowers which characterized the most recent crisis. The federal financial and bureaucratic interventions are relatively unique in some important ways from those of other market economies. They reflect the attempts by the progressive movement prior to and through the Great Depression to centralize power and the historic aversion of the states to which these responsibilities were specifically delegated. The biggest distinction between the US and Canada – which had no central bank and no bank failures during the Depression – was the high number of small undiversified US banks due to prohibitions on interstate – and in some cases intrastate - branching.

The bank-owned Federal Reserve is the oldest of our contemporary federal financial network of institutions, created in 1913 purportedly in response to the financial crisis of 1907 to provide systemic liquidity support. The S&L industry-owned Federal Home Loan Bank (FHLB) System was created in 1932 to provide a systemic liquidity substitute – really an *intermediary* as only the Fed could print money - for savings and loans and savings banks (S&Ls) who were at the time denied Fed access. The Glass-Steagall Act of 1933 established an independent federally *sponsored* deposit insurer - the Federal Deposit Insurance Corporation (FDIC) - to provide protection to "small" savers, as well as to separate commercial and investment banks. The National Housing Act of 1934 established the FHA to insure mortgages for new housing construction, as its sole purpose was to stimulate jobs. When that failed due to lack of investor demand for insurance, the Federal National Mortgage Association (FNMA) or Fannie Mae was chartered in 1938 to make a "secondary market" to provide "liquidity to the FHA loan market to promote their use.

The institutions that evolved reflected a politically expedient "second best" solution to the underlying political problem of decentralized power. All of these initiatives had good intentions. They all came with predictions of "unintended consequences." However, they also all overlapped and encroached on existing state responsibilities and the private sector. "Second best" does not necessarily imply better than nothing.

The Solvency Crisis: Predictable and Inevitable

The U.S. wasn't the only country to experience a housing boom and subsequent financial sector crisis. What distinguishes the U.S. from these other countries – other than it's size – is the dollar as the world's reserve currency, the prevalence of housing goals, universal deposit insurance, and dominant GSEs. The consequences became more systemic due to international distribution of private - mostly GSE- securities as close Treasury substitutes, held largely by political entities.

Public intervention in U.S. financial markets historically has two primary rationales: to protect and regulate and to "kick-start" a private market function. The political economy of regulation may be summarized as a cycle of misdiagnosis, mis-regulation, crisis, and repeat. The political economy of GSEs may be summarized as a cycle of adopt a "politically expedient" mission, "innovate," fail, and repeat. The lending debacle and financial crisis of the past decade was *entirely predictable because it had all happened before.*

The Fed fueled its first housing boom in the 1920s, shortly after it was created. The GSEs - primarily F&F - predictably channeled such a boom, as there was nothing new about their pro-cyclical mortgage funding. HUD's increasingly costly credit allocation mandates, particularly the new home ownership mandate of 70 percent, predictably raised subsidy costs until they swamped the available capital subsidies. Political credit allocation *always* comes at a taxpayer cost, however opaque.

"Regulatory arbitrage" - the term generally used to describe the phenomenon of minimizing tax and regulatory burdens, particularly capital requirements – was not new or unknown. Hendershott and Villani (1983) noted that the design and structure of U.S. mortgage finance institutions and instruments – financial "innovation" – had always reflected a response to taxes, laws, and regulation rather than market forces. Politicians and regulators determined the rules and market participants "innovated" to minimize their adverse consequences. As a consequence of this "regulatory arbitrage", deposit insurance predictably backed mis-labeled "private" label securities (PLS) leveraged at rates comparable to F&F. The Fed was well aware of the depth of regulatory arbitrage by 2000.

Securitization became a primary tool of regulatory arbitrage due to its opaque capital requirements. Virtually all "innovations" in securitization have been the result of regulatory arbitrage. Regulatory accounting rules governing securitization predictably accelerated non-cash and improbable income while deferring expense, allowing all participants to make cash profits in the loss-making enterprise until the end. There was nothing new as these are the same distortions that enabled the sub-prime lending debacle of the prior decade.

The Fed, particularly Chairman Greenspan and FRB St Louis President William Poole, had long predicted that the extreme leverage of F&F would eventually magnify losses, causing a systemic *solvency* crisis. Housing policy had already caused the systemic failure of S&Ls and the technical insolvency of Fannie Mae in the 1980s.

GSE securities and later PLS are marketable - traded at a narrow bid-asked spread - but they aren't liquid. This distinction was a root cause of the Orange County failure in the 1990s and played a large role in this crisis.

If politicians didn't see this crisis coming it is because they dismissed the consequences of past failure as "unintended", while clinging to myths of their own making. F&F primarily filled Democratic political coffers, but the housing boom broadly benefitted the housing, real estate, and mortgage lending industries, providing political benefits to both parties.

Politicians could have Easily Prevented the Crisis

Regulators have long recognized that in a heavily regulated and protected system it is up to regulators to establish sufficiently high borrower, lender and investor capital requirements to mitigate moral hazard and the relationship between and among these capital requirements. They further recognized that lobbyists would press politicians to force regulators to lower them.

The lack of sufficient lender capital was transparent at Fannie Mae and Freddie Mac but more opaque in the banking system due to complicated risk-based mortgage rules and all of the various forms and combinations of regulatory arbitrage. The simple regulatory fix for Fannie Mae and Freddie Mac was repeatedly proposed by their regulators during the sub-prime lending debacle – who unlike the bank regulators lacked the authority to do this on their own - but rejected on the same party line vote by Democratic politicians. For politicians to over-ride safety and soundness requests of prudential regulators was unprecedented, and requires explanation.

Politicians of both parties benefited from Fannie and Freddie political patronage, but the two Democratic politicians most directly responsible for implementing capital standards to achieve safety and soundness of all US financial institutions including Fannie and Freddie, Barney Frank as Chairman of the House Financial Services Committee and Christopher Dodd as Chairman of the Senate Banking Committee, were among the most vocal supporters of this ever expanding housing policy. Meeting regulatory capital requirements was mandatory, but providing capital was voluntary, based on the expected after tax returns and assessment of risk. Lending to meet housing goals never met these return criteria, so they had to know that Fannie and Freddie would have to significantly tighten underwriting guidelines and reduce credit losses to maintain profit margins in response to higher capital requirements. The conflict between the housing goals and capital requirements forced them to make a choice, and they chose the housing goals.

Regulators – including Republican appointees – also played a role. The Fed institutionally under Alan Greenspan had long argued that the capital requirements for Fannie and Freddie were too low, posing the largest systemic risk to the financial system. The Fed was also well aware of the problem with risk based capital rules and regulatory arbitrage in the banking system, having published an article on the topic in 2000. As the *de facto* systemic regulator Greenspan's successor Chairman Bernanke was arguably the one who should have pushed for eliminating regulatory arbitrage and fixing bank capital rules. As the primary regulator responsible for consumer lending, Bernanke was also responsible for limiting consumer "abuses" subsequently alleged as the reason borrowers took out loans they arguably couldn't repay, although with little or no equity they had little incentive to pay when the house price bubble burst. But Bernanke also supported the housing goals throughout the sub-prime lending debacle. Regulatory malfeasance especially of the Federal Reserve System better explains the failure to require sufficient bank capital.

HUD's powerful "mission regulator" John Weicher not only ratcheted up the goals but introduced new "market share" goals that prolonged the housing bubble, trumping HUD's roll as prudential regulator. The SEC also played a role, establishing capital for the large investment banks a small fraction of their historic market requirement. But all this fell within the oversight responsibilities of Congressman Frank and Senator Dodd, both of whom had long supported housing goals for banks as well as GSEs.

The Intended Beneficiaries and the Vast Majority of Households are worse off

Even in extremely competitive markets, some households will pay more than others for the same thing. Other households will pay the same price for something different. Federal interventions to eliminate these differences come at a high cost and are ultimately doomed to failure. The sunk cost of capital subsidies provided during the sub-prime lending debacle and aftermath are estimated at $1.5 trillion dollars. In spite of these subsidies, the deflating housing bubble quickly and predictably eroded $7 trillion in homeowner equity. At least half of this loss came from negative equity in mortgage loans. This left most subsidy beneficiaries worse off. Those who defaulted may have lived rent-free for an extended foreclosure period, but was it worth the grief? Those that continue to pay mortgage debts that exceed the value of their homes are subsidizing banks relative to the cost of rental housing.

In June 2012, a Fed release showed a 38% decline from 2007 through 2010 in the median net worth of U.S. households, from $126,000 to only $77,300, a level last seen in real terms in 1992. The mean household wealth fell only half as much as the median, an indication that higher net worth households had alternative assets. Current Fed zero interest rate policy has had a particularly devastating impact of on the elderly. The wealth decline has been reversed by creating a new asset bubble with additional wealth redistribution effects.

Who benefited from the boom/bust housing cycle? Huge political constituencies developed around the GSE originate-to-sell housing finance mechanism of mortgage origination and funding in the U.S. The mean household wealth fell only half as much as the median, an indication that higher net worth households had alternative assets. Delivering subsidies through finance requires generating and distributing "economic rents"- essentially unearned income redistributed through political means. This requires a form of uncompetitive crony capitalism that always favors politicians and other politically well-connected rent seekers. Those not politically connected get a smaller share of a diminished economic pie.

Why the Correct Diagnosis Was and Remains Important

There are two reasons why a correct diagnosis was important. First, the bailout policies in the aftermath would be structured to cover up rather than to re-cover. Second, the "reforms" would make matters a lot worse.

The financial sector bailout went well beyond liquidity and exacerbated the moral hazard that will generate future financial crises. Monetary and fiscal policies have exacerbated the fiscal debt crisis with little to show for it. The normal post-recession boost to economic activity was stifled. The prospects for economic growth are diminished. The risk to the economy was exacerbated due to the misdiagnosis of the financial crisis as a liquidity crisis and excessive government intervention in its wake.

Due to mark-to-market accounting, financial institutions reflected about half the negative equity loss within a year. The short and long run policies taken in the aftermath of the financial crisis during the first term of the Obama Administration focused on saving the banking system by keeping the house price bubble at least partially inflated, avoiding recognizing the other half of the loss in the protected banking system. To have done otherwise would have resulted in additional financial institution losses of potentially $1 to $2 trillion, which would have required another politically embarrassing bank bailout. Hence the financial bailout is simply more of the same policies that created the crisis in the first place. The risk to the financial system remains.

The policies leading up to and in the aftermath of the financial crisis all contributed to crony capitalism. GSEs garnered a market share of between 90% and 95% of residential mortgage lending, while the legal and regulatory retribution focused on private lenders. Fannie Mae and Freddie Mac were prevented from paying political rents directly as the U.S. Treasury pumped in several hundred billion dollars to plug their capital hole. But politicians demanded that F&F write down a like amount of mortgage principal, another huge taxpayer subsidy. At the end of 2011, politicians forced F&F to charge new borrowers a fee to finance the payroll tax reduction.

The public's historic tool to mitigate political rent seeking was constitutionally-limited government, long rejected by the progressive movement. Extending centralized authority, from the interstate and international transportation system to the financial pathways, was entirely within the context of the framers' limited government intent. Establishing rent-seeking federal tolls (mortgage borrower subsidies) was not. Establishing a central bank to provide systemic liquidity support- arguably - was. Unlimited printing of fiat money to fund domestic deficits and intergenerational income redistribution was not. Regulating interstate trade to avoid state rent seeking was. Using federal regulatory power to create and direct a crony capitalist economy dominated by rent generating TBTF financial firms was not. Centralizing political power reduces accountability, exponentially increasing the likelihood and systemic consequences of misuse.

Re-examining the causes of the Great Depression in 1963, the Austrian economist Murray Rothbard concluded:

"The guilt for the Great Depression must, at long last, be lifted from the shoulders of the free-market economy and placed where it properly belongs, at the doors of politicians and bureaucrats and the mass of "enlightened" economists. And in any other depression, past or future, the story will be the same."

Similarly, in his insightful 2009 paper on the financial crisis, economist Arnold Kling of the Mercatus Center concludes:

"In order to get policy right going forward, the historical narrative must be accurate. It will not help to airbrush out of history the role that regulatory policy played in setting up the crisis. It would be a mistake to create institutions with the presumption that regulators will correctly diagnose systemic problems, when the record shows that regulators were subject to the same cognitive shortcomings as private sector participants. Unless the United States comes to terms with the fact that the actions of policy makers and regulators contribute to financial fragility, it has little hope of moving in the direction of a less fragile system for the future."

Rothbard was correct - as is Kling this time around – but their advice was ignored. Politicians and regulators want taxpayers to believe two things. First, that the financial crisis had multiple complex causes mostly related to excessive risk-taking, conflicts of interest, and deregulation of the private sector, a view unconvincingly supported by the exculpatory 662 page summary Report of the Financial Crisis Inquiry Commission. Second, that public regulation is a Herculean task requiring the 2,313-page Dodd-Frank Act and tens of thousands of pages of additional regulation and thousands of additional regulators. This diagnosis and prescription are both wrong and part of a long historical pattern of political and regulatory covering up and doubling down.

History shows that this view is a recipe for subsequent failure, bigger in scale than the last. The response to the Panic of 1907 sowed the seeds to the financial failures of the Great Depression. The response to the Great Depression sowed the seeds for the systemic failure of the S&L industry in the 1980's. The response to S&L crisis sowed the seeds to the most recent systemic failure. Markets are forward-looking and dynamic; regulators are backward-looking and static. Markets reward going against the conventional wisdom; regulators maintain it regardless of the merits while promising reform.

The Policy Prescription: Competitive Markets

What distinguished the U.S. among competitive market economies is that sufficient political accountability to prevent misuse did not accompany the patchwork shift of political power from the states to the federal government. This is especially true for the financial sector. Competitive markets are forced to balance the interests of both borrowers and savers with the needs of financial intermediaries and adjust to changing risks as needed. Politicians, regulators and government-backed monopolists aren't accountable for their lack of restraint, calling on unsuspecting and defenseless taxpayers to make good on their promises *ex post* when they fail systemically.

What prescription follows directly from our diagnosis of the sub-prime lending debacle? Two words: align incentives. How can that be achieved? Three words: require sufficient capital. In one sentence: depend more on the judgment of competitive markets than that of politicians and regulators, however well intentioned. What is the blueprint? How do we make this happen?

To avoid credit bubbles, reduce monetary policy discretion. The Fed requires major institutional reform or a fresh approach. To avoid housing bubbles, separate subsidy from finance. Consumer regulation should be subservient to prudential regulation. To limit moral hazard and avoid financial crises, scale back and restructure deposit insurance and the safety net and eliminate the GSEs. Regulatory reform requires consolidation of agencies and political oversight to improve public accountability, eliminate regulatory arbitrage, and favor competition over TBTF crony capitalism. To enable mortgage capital market access, enact enabling capital market regulations. We must eliminate regulatory arbitrage while promoting competition and market discipline. To minimize borrower default and loss severity, restore traditional down payment and underwriting requirements.

There is nothing very radical or extreme about any of these recommendations. The U.S. housing finance system historically harnessed the power of market capitalism, driven by individual self-interest, while mitigating private incentive conflicts. The profit incentive, when not distorted by politicians, regulators, or bureaucrats, is generally consistent with the public interest. It is the U.S. housing finance system that produced arguably the best results internationally and historically, prior to the third largest social engineering experiment after Social Security and Medicare. The problems attributed to the private market reflect distortions from public policies; the purported benefits of public intervention would otherwise develop if valuable to market participants. The pejorative ideological labels, e.g. a return to *laissez faire* or unfettered free markets, are wildly inaccurate. The reform is more accurately characterized as *conservative*, i.e., a return to what works in other market economies and what historically worked in the US.

This prescription is easily designed. The major institutional reform of the Fed, the regulatory agencies, and HUD, as well as the required political restructuring to provide effective oversight, all reduce the opportunities for political rent-seeking. Without reform, the most difficult task will be finding the money to pay for housing in the future. Federal entitlements for retirement and health care mirror tenfold that of federal housing and mortgage entitlements. As with housing subsidies, they reduced or eliminated the need to save. Now the bill has come due. The issue going forward is not how to provide virtually every family access to homeownership and mortgage credit at a government-approved price. The question is how to deal with mortgage credit and housing scarcity.

Organization of the Book

This book doesn't exonerate the greedy people involved in the sub-prime debacle or their illegal activity. There are always some, but they are not the cause of the 2008 financial crisis. The book is about the distorted incentives facing private firms, individuals, public politicians, regulators, and bureaucrats. It focuses on the magnitude of these distortions, how they came about, and how they caused the crisis. The point isn't that F&F and credit rating agencies used bad models, although they surely did. The point is that by substituting a public monopoly opinion in place of the competitive market consensus, it was inevitable that things would go terribly wrong.

The analysis in this book was written and posted online six months prior to the publication of the Report and the Dissent. It was not influenced by either, but complements Wallison's Dissent and McDonald's subsequent support and goes beyond the FCIC Report in several ways. First, it traces political and regulatory intervention back to the creation of the Fed, finding precedents for all of the distortions that made this crisis inevitable. Second, it estimates the approximate value of the capital subsidies and cost of housing goals, making the net cost of housing goals to financial institutions more explicit. Third, it calculates the magnitude of the political and regulatory distortions to profit incentives and provides an incentive framework – going for broke and going broke – which explains the behavior of the parties to the mortgage finance process. While the GSEs led the disastrous housing policy in many ways, in the end they were also a victim of political housing policy and bank regulator malfeasance, going broke along with PLSers. Finally, it traces the actual losses and their ultimate incidence, revealing the magnitude of the wealth destruction and income and wealth redistribution that resulted.

Chapter 1 of this book traces the origins of the recent crisis back to the political compromises made during the creation of the key institutions - the Fed, the FDIC, FHA and Fannie Mae - as the federal government took power from the states. Chapter 2 describes the unintended consequences from 1968 to 2000, the rise of the GSEs to market dominance, and the increasingly disruptive role of CRA and of HUD's housing goals. Chapter 3 explains in detail how federal housing policy and regulation not only allowed PLSers to sustain a loss-making subprime lending business for the eight years from 2000 through 2007, but also encouraged them to do so by enabling huge up-front cash profits. Chapter 4 describes how Fannie Mae and Freddie Mac – and later in the game Ginnie Mae and FHA - kept the house price bubble inflating to systemic proportions in competition with PLSers, how it created the huge solvency hole that made this financial crisis systemic, and why only this explanation of the systemic financial collapse is credible. Chapter 5 explains how the emergency actions taken in the aftermath of the financial and economic crisis, not only put the future of the private housing finance system at even greater risk, but due to the unresolved issue of unrealized losses, the actions also threaten the entire financial system and economy as a consequence.

Finally, chapter 6 explains what works elsewhere in the world and how to restore the U.S. private competitive mortgage finance system. Solutions include mitigating housing credit allocation and housing booms by reforming or eliminating HUD and the Fed and relieving systemic risk by relying more on market discipline. This chapter also answers questions about how to fix the US regulatory apparatus and make it accountable for safety and soundness without dampening competition, as well as how to restore household savings to finance mortgage credit. This requires that virtually all of Dodd-Frank's provisions should be repealed, including the Consumer Financial Protection Bureau (CFPB), the Volker rule, the systemic risk regulator, orderly liquidation authority, derivatives regulation, and the securitization rules.

It is only human to believe that we can go back to the housing finance system of the past three decades, enjoying the benefits but this time without the costs. That system was always an illusion, but this time not one that can likely be maintained much longer. Pursuing this illusion will come at even greater cost to the public than in the past.

Chapter 1: Original Sin; the New Deal to the Great Society: The Origins of Federal Financial Institutions 1913 to 1938 and their Role through 1968

This chapter details the origins of federal financial institutions, each of which inserted a government monopoly in place of market activity. In the 25 year period from 1913 to 1938, a succession of progressive administrations——two Democrats (Woodrow Wilson and Franklin D. Roosevelt) and one Republican (Herbert Hoover)—created the Federal Reserve System ("Fed"), the Federal Home Loan Bank System (FHLB), the Federal Deposit Insurance Corporation (FDIC), the Federal Savings and Loan Insurance Corporation (FSLIC), the Federal Housing Authority (FHA) and the Federal National Mortgage Association ("Fannie Mae").

While each of these organizations was titled "federal," none were owned, directly controlled, or funded by the federal government. With the establishment of each entity, the combined wisdom and judgment of the marketplace was replaced by the decision making of politically-appointed bureaucrats, although the extent of political control and oversight would vary greatly among them and over time. They were all created in crisis environments, but not as specific responses to the immediate crises. Each entity had unique accountability mechanisms—or lack thereof—that reflected the political disagreements of the day regarding their intended role and likely outcome.

We are on the eve of the Fed's 100th anniversary and Fannie Mae's 75th anniversary, and only one of the original six entities is no longer independent (The FSLIC was merged into a single insurer, the FDIC, as originally intended). The others have spun their own histories as their roles evolved and as their powers and political influence expanded. Each agency played a role in the subprime lending debacle of the last decade. The ensuing systemic financial crisis was the bitter fruit of these federal seedlings. The agencies provided comfortable shade for the financial system for six decades, until they grew uncontrollably, resulting in financial disaster. Here is how it started.

A. The Origins and Role of the Federal Reserve System

The legislation that created the Fed was the result of five years of discussion following the banking panic of 1907 and the subsequent bailout orchestrated by financial tycoon J.P. Morgan. However, the debate started well before that. The financial panics argument—whether the government should provide systemic liquidity protection—dates back to Walter Bagehot's dictum in

1863 for the Bank of England to lend freely and without limit in times of crisis to avert panic. Unfortunately for those who support this myth, countries without central banks and without restrictions on bank branching did not experience panics. The existence of the Bank of England concentrated bank reserves, giving rise to the need for it to lend. Branching restrictions in the U.S. made the concentration of reserves even greater.[2]

The more fundamental issue was about money: should the government be allowed to create it? Historically, government typically expanded the money supply to finance a war. This is how the United States funded the Continental Army during the American Revolution. However, inflation was the inevitable result, and the U.S. Constitution banned States from issuing "paper" money. Beginning with the First Bank of the United States in 1791, a succession of central banks formed, each followed by increased boom-bust cycles and subsequent dissolution. By 1913, the focus of the central bankers was on systemic liquidity support.

Congress appointed a National Monetary Commission in the aftermath of the Panic of 1907, setting the precedent for Congress to respond to future crises. The Commission published numerous studies in 1910, providing a sense of legitimacy to the political pressure for a new central bank. The Federal Reserve was created in 1913 by the Glass-Owen Federal Reserve Act, sponsored by then Congressman Carter Glass, President Woodrow Wilson's former Secretary of the Treasury and then-Chairman of the House Committee on Banking and Currency. The charter reflected the "second best" nature of the political compromise. It was owned in part by private banks to satisfy banking interests and in part by the government to satisfy progressive political interests. It was a central bank headquartered in the nation's political capital of Washington, D.C. rather than its financial capital of New York, but power was also dispersed to a network of regional banks to address populist concerns with the concentration of power in finance.

When the arguably misnamed Currency Act was passed in 1913 establishing the Fed – misnamed and now referred to as the Federal Reserve Act because the newly created Fed had no power to issue fiat money - the *American Banker* (December 27, 1913) hypothesized that "from this time forward the financial disorders which have marked the history of the past generation will pass away forever." Soon thereafter, the Fed was accused of fueling the asset bubble of the 1920s. Housing production boomed as a result of the Fed's easy credit policies, then fell by over 80 percent from 753,000 units in 1928 to 134,000 in 1932. According to Johnson and Kwak[3] (p 30):

"Not only did the Federal Reserve's System encourage excessive risk taking by bankers, the safety net, it turned out, had gaping holes that could not be fixed in the intense pressure of a crisis. The result was the Great Depression."

This should come as no surprise. Rothbard (2012) traces the origins of the Fed back to decades of fighting between the Morgan and Rockefeller banking interests:

"In fact, as we have seen, the banks desperately desired a Central Bank, not to place fetters on their own natural tendency to inflate, but, on the contrary to enable them to inflate and expand together without incurring the penalties of market competition. As a lender of last resort, the Central Bank could permit and encourage them to inflate when they would ordinarily have to contract their loans in order to save themselves. In short, the real reason adoption of the Federal Reserve, and its promotion by the large banks, was the exact opposite of their loudly trumpeted motivations. Rather than create an institution to curb their own profits on behalf of the public interest, the banks sought a Central Bank to enhance their profits by permitting them to inflate beyond the bounds set by free-market competition."[4]

Milton Friedman and Anna Schwartz, in *A Monetary History of the United States: 1867-1960*, (1963) argue that the Fed caused the Depression by keeping the money supply too tight, resulting in deflation.[5] Current Federal Reserve Chairman and then-member of its Board of Governors Ben Bernanke publicly apologized to Milton Friedman on behalf of the Fed, agreeing that the centralized monetary authority was the cause of the systemic deflation that perpetuated the Depression.[6] That same year, Murray Rothbard disagreed with the monetarists, providing the Austrian school's explanation that deflation is not associated with depressions.[7] But both monetarists and Austrians agree that the Fed displaced the prior clearinghouses. These clearinghouses may well have avoided the problems created by centralizing this function in the Fed.

Economists are still debating the relevant causes of the Great Depression, but the central understanding is indisputable: The Great Depression was not caused by instability in unregulated financial markets. Unregulated private financial markets in the United States had previously produced regular but smaller and self-correcting financial downturns that were blamed—unfairly—for the Great Depression.[8] Rather, politically induced market distortions turned a recession into a depression and made it "Great."

Before the Depression, the Fed agreed for the need for an elastic currency, as the New York Fed had done to expand money under the leadership of Benjamin Strong. The Board of Governors in Washington prevented this, not out of a policy disagreement, but to seize control of policy in the wake of Strong's death in 1928.[9] In addition, labor market distortions stemming from the Wagner and Davis-Bacon Acts kept wages as much as 40% above market-clearing levels and the Smoot-

Hawley tariffs reduced the United States' international trade by more than half, both of which proved disastrous.

The Fed's fragmented structure, with regional banks controlled by bankers, a politically appointed board in Washington, D.C. and several regional Fed Bank presidents also appointed on a rotating basis, reflected industry resistance to the creation of a central bank. According to Strong, this resistance didn't start to soften until the Fed played a major role in funding the American involvement in World War I.[10]

In addition to its ability to create money for the economy, the Fed could freely create money for itself. In the 1960s, a populist politician named Wright Patman of Texas tried to subject the Fed to a budget approval process, but the move failed. Beyond that attempt, the Fed has had free rein to do just about anything it wants to do.

B: Liquidity of Deposit Institutions

The Depression era spawned numerous additional federal interventions in the financial system, including deposit insurance, mortgage insurance, mortgage discount lending, and market-making facilities. Many banks had liquidity problems early in the Depression and many—though not always the same banks—were technically insolvent. It was often difficult for depositors to discern the distinction between insolvency and illiquidity, and thus rational depositors would be first in line to withdraw funds. The Fed was charged to make the distinction between insolvent and illiquid banks, as it was chartered to provide sufficient liquidity to solvent banks only.

In their summary article "What Is Systemic Risk, and Do Bank Regulators Retard or Contribute to It?" (2003) George G. Kaufman and Kenneth E. Scott conclude:

"The evidence suggests that even during the Great Contraction of 1929–33 and at the height of the banking crisis and bank runs in Chicago in June 1932, liquidity problems and depositor runs rarely, if ever, drove economically solvent independent banks into insolvency. In those difficult times, at the margin, depositors and other banks were still able to differentiate economically solvent from insolvent banks rather quickly. Moreover, almost all the banks that failed during the Depression were small unit banks. Although in 1930, 1931, 1932, and 1933 the annual bank failure rate was 6, 11, 8, and 28 percent, respectively, the percentage of deposits in the failed banks was only 2,1, 2, and 12 percent of deposits in all banks. An analysis of this period concluded that "these failures occurred primarily because of adverse local business conditions rather than because of spillover from other failed banks outside their market areas"."

In sharp contrast to the experience in the United States, bank runs were not a problem in Canada. Banks could branch freely and, as a consequence, were well diversified, so no major bank failed.[11] Moreover, Canada had not established deposit insurance.[12] Jeremy Friedman (2008, pg 166) also concludes that, in the case of the U.S., the lack of deposit insurance was neither a cause of the bank runs nor of the Great Depression.

In fact, the large U.S. money center banks that engaged in both commercial and investment banking—i.e., universal banks—were even better diversified and generally remained both liquid and solvent, compared to the smaller commercial-only banks. Combining commercial and investment banking was common in market economies due to the potential synergies. Underwriting new securities sold through a bank's own sales force and making a secondary market in these and other securities as a broker (matching buyers and sellers) or as a dealer (maintaining a modest inventory for sale) proved to be stable and profitable for larger firms.

But U.S. Senators Carter Glass and Henry B. Steagall were much more concerned with the potential conflicts of interest between selling securities and taking deposits, and how that may affect the concentration of power on Wall Street. In 1933, Senator Glass became chairman of the powerful Appropriations Committee, giving him authority to oversee both banking and housing. The Pecora Commission was created specifically to cast these universal banks as villains, despite there being no evidence that risky investment banking activity was a contributing cause of the financial collapse or Great Depression[13]. After decades of failure, the negative press coverage of National City (later Citicorp) bankers during the Commission's hearings was sufficient to pass the Banking Act, known as the Glass-Steagall Act of 1933, separating commercial banking and deposit-taking from securities underwriting and market-making activity.

The fear of centralizing power in Wall Street money center banks made bank branching across state lines politically problematic. Not wanting to waste a crisis or the political momentum of the Pecora Commission, the framers of Glass-Steagall extended the prohibition against branching to federally chartered banks. As this would predictably exacerbate the problem of bank runs, it established the FDIC. Calomiris and White (1994) note that large banks opposed this cross subsidy to small, undiversified banks, as they were more likely to fail due to branching restrictions.

Glass was a fiscal conservative who opposed Franklin Roosevelt's New Deal, whereas both FDR and bank regulators had previously opposed public deposit insurance due to concerns of moral hazard. The result was to try to mitigate this risk by limiting insurance to small depositors and the federal role to sponsoring a self-funding enterprise.[14] The system was modeled after the deposit insurance system in Massachusetts. It was initially temporary but was made permanent in 1935.

The Hollywood version portrayed in Frank Capra's Christmas classic "It's a Wonderful Life" notwithstanding, most Savings and Loans institutions remained solvent during the Great Depression. Those that failed did so as a direct consequence of unemployment resulting from monetary and fiscal policies. Hence the S&Ls successfully resisted FDIC insurance, which they believed would have provided a cross-subsidy to the far-riskier small commercial banks funded with demand deposits, but were subsequently enticed to have their own deposit insurer, the FSLIC—which as noted was merged into the FDIC much later.

C. Housing and Mortgage Market Distress

While conditions in the banking industry during the Great Depression were terrible, conditions in the housing industry were arguably worse. Every housing program focused on new construction, as they had been in the previous century.[15] The rationale behind mortgage-finance-related legislation was to stimulate housing construction, and hence jobs, on the premise that the decline in construction was a consequence of banking problems. But housing production had boomed in the 1920s, and demand fell much faster than supply, due primarily to doubling up—conversion of large to multiple smaller units, etc. Vacancy rate rose by over 60 percent - from 8 percent to 13 percent - during this period.[16]

Prior to 1916, national banks and most state banks were prohibited from making real estate loans. Where authorized, the loan-to-value ratio was limited to 50% and the maturity to five years so loans could not fully amortize. Most borrowers took out second (and third) mortgages at higher interest rates.[17]

The savings-and-loan model of mortgage finance, patterned after the 200-year-old British system, worked fairly well in the United States until the Depression. The primary role of the government prior to the introduction of deposit insurance was to provide a fair and predictable legal system for contract enforcement. S&Ls grew *spontaneously* by providing a balanced approach to borrower and saver concerns. They protected savers by maintaining sufficient capital and encouraged high loan quality by maintaining sound underwriting and a substantial twenty percent down payment. The result was a century of remarkable industry success.[18]

No federal charters and hence no federal regulation existed at the time. State regulation evolved simply to ensure that S&Ls stuck to their charter limitations, and to monitor for fraud, of which there was little.

Borrowers repaid principal by contributing monthly to a sinking fund—a common practice of the time—effectively amortizing the mortgage principal and avoiding a balloon payment at maturity. Loans were rolled-over every five to ten years, at which time they were re-priced to the current market interest rate. So long as the borrower was current and the lender remained solvent, rollover was relatively automatic. Unlike bank deposits, S&L shares weren't callable, mitigating liquidity concerns. But no system could survive the systemic credit default debacle of the Great Depression unscathed, during which three in four home borrowers defaulted.

S&Ls relied on their commercial lines of credit for liquidity, but these lines mostly disappeared as banks failed and direct access to Fed discount lending was rejected (until 1989 when the FSLIC was merged into the FDIC banking regulator).[19] To address this problem, in 1932 the Herbert Hoover administration established an independent, federally-sponsored enterprise - the Federal Home Loan Bank system - to provide liquidity directly to S&Ls. They accomplished this by discounting home mortgages. This provided loan advances against mortgage collateral at less than par value - a "haircut" - and with full recourse to the borrowing institution. As Hoover said at the signing ceremony, the FHLB advance program was analogous to the Fed discount window, lacking the stigma of signaling distress, with a more liberal collateral requirement and significantly longer terms, both of which were at least partly intended to promote homebuilding and thus construction jobs.[20] The FHLB system had emergency authority to borrow up to $215 million from the U.S. Treasury— but notably not the Fed. The system generally relied on capital market access for funding.

FSLIC deposit insurance was optional for state-chartered S&Ls, but mandatory for federally-chartered institutions. The combination of federal charters and mandatory deposit insurance thus led to federal regulation.

High vacancy rates caused housing prices to fall by far more than the general monetary deflation. Politicians intervened to mitigate the impact of financial system distress on borrowers, as well as to stimulate housing production and jobs. The Homeowners Loan Corporation (HOLC) was established in 1933 and placed under the FHLB system to implement the government's Depression-era forbearance program for distressed but salvageable borrowers. One component refinanced creditworthy borrowers with a fixed-rate mortgage, replacing the rollover provision with a long term to maturity and replacing the sinking fund with a more portable amortization schedule. HOLC marked down the nominal loan balance to only 70 percent of the new, lower home price - with lenders taking the loss - and offered an interest rate slightly above their Treasury borrowing cost. Still, 20 percent of the borrowers subsequently re-defaulted. The re-pricing of mortgages at rollover reduced payments to reflect falling interest rates. HOLC remained profitable, in part, by requiring borrowers to pay a fixed rate while refinancing their own debt at lower rates. HOLC was liquidated in 1951 at a small profit, although, as with most government accounts, this calculation ignores indirect costs to taxpayers.[21]

FDR sought input from the National Association of Home Builders, the Mortgage Bankers Association of America, the National Association of Real Estate Boards, and the United States Savings and Loan League, among others, regarding ideas to stimulate housing demand. They enacting the National Housing Act of 1934, establishing the Federal Housing Administration (FHA) as an independent, federally-sponsored mutual mortgage insurance fund authorized to insure only long-term (up to 20 years), fully amortizing fixed-rate mortgages (FRM) with a maximum loan-to-value (LTV) ratio of 80 percent.

Private mortgage insurance was first offered in the U.S. in 1887 by the Title and Guarantee Company of Rochester, New York. Many other title insurance companies soon followed.[22] Private monoline mortgage insurers had previously insured loans with high LTV ratios, but they were inherently vulnerable due to their lack of diversification among other lines of insurance. They all failed as a consequence once the Great Depression hit. As the National Housing Act's stated intent was to promote homebuilding and construction jobs, activity was limited to new housing and the initial limit on the loan amount was more than three times the median home price.[23] Because portfolio lenders saw no need for default insurance on newly originated loans with a 20 percent down payment, FHA activity was minimal.

The National Housing Act also gave FHA the authority to establish private national mortgage exchanges to "make a market" for these FHA-insured FRMs and thereby promote their use. This followed the New York State law in 1911 allowing title companies not only to insure title and credit, but to buy and sell mortgages with this protection. However, there were no private takers for the charters to trade FHA loans. Instead, lenders originated mortgages as portfolio investments and S&Ls could now discount mortgages at the FHLB.

Undeterred, Congress established the Residential Finance Corporation (RFC) mortgage company in 1935with $10 million in capital to provide mortgages only for new residential construction by buying and selling FHA loans. In February 1938, after the RFC failed to stimulate housing production, Congress amended the National Housing Act to have the FHA create the National Mortgage Association of Washington (later changed to the Federal National Mortgage Association or "Fannie Mae") to replace the RFC Mortgage Company. The restriction to solely finance new construction was removed and the FHA loan limit was reduced to the median house price in 1938.[24]

The same conflicts between populist concerns with centralization and private control that shaped the Fed and FDIC charters were at play in the housing and mortgage sectors. The private lending industry strongly opposed the creation of what they recognized as a government housing bank. Fannie Mae's two main "special assistance" functions were financed directly by the U.S. Treasury, which also provided an emergency liquidity backstop similar to that of the FHLB System. To assuage these concerns, the bankers (mostly mortgage bankers) who used the facility became the owners of the third facility. To mitigate concerns of public credit allocation, this facility was explicitly limited to a purely secondary market broker/dealer function, requiring selling in equal proportion to buying. Further, it was limited to FHA insured loans, which had an insignificant market share at the time. Finally, dealer inventory had to be funded with "private" corporate debt, which required prior Treasury approval.

D. The Consequences of Federal Institutions Through 1968

The Great Depression marks the beginning of a cycle: a politically induced credit bubble, a crash, and then emergency intervention to alleviate the symptoms. The conventional wisdom says federal interventions restored the housing market in the wake of the Depression. While there is little merit in a separate liquidity facility without central bank access, the FHLB discount facility did no harm. It is unlikely that the FHLB, FHA or Fannie Mae stimulated many, if any, construction jobs in the post-Depression era, nor did Fannie Mae build a secondary market. By 1966, after almost three decades in operation, the secondary market "dealer" portfolio was about $2.5 billion. This reflected the post-war

Veteran's Administration,(VA), whose loans were made eligible for purchase after the war, as well as the FHA inventory, where there was little if any turnover.

After WW II, FHA essentially behaved like a private mortgage insurer, lending to good borrowers in good neighborhoods with low down payments. Hence, like the VA, it was primarily a middle-class, first time buyers program. Its market share remained below twenty percent as the home ownership rate rose. The economic conditions of the 1950s and 1960s were favorable to mortgage insurance, resulting in FHA's strong financial performance but also competitors. FHA's private competition was minimal at first as the first company to enter the market, Mortgage Guaranty Insurance Corporation (MGIC), wasn't formed until 1957 but by the mid-1960s there were multiple private insurers. The increase in home ownership occurred primarily in the suburbs, creating problems for the inner city that made mortgage insurance there problematic.

One later *ex post* rationalization is that FHA's long-term fully amortizing loan solved the problem of rollover balloon mortgages. Lack of amortization wasn't the problem because most mortgages had sinking funds. The rate adjustment at rollover wasn't the problem either, as rates were adjusting down during the Depression, making fixed rate mortgages more expensive than rollover mortgages. Only the liquidity of the rollover provision was potentially problematic. In theory, some current borrowers could have faced problems rolling over their loans. However, borrowers were mutual owners as well and hence had an equal say in making rollover policies. Additionally, liquid lenders had every incentive to roll over a loan for a current borrower rather than foreclose on an unsalable house, and the FHLB presumably provided the necessary liquidity beginning in 1932. Even in the event of lender insolvency, depositors and other creditors were better off with a paying loan. Thus the rollover problem, to the extent it existed, was with the way insolvent institutions were liquidated.

Whether it was deposit insurance that stopped the bank runs is debatable, but both federally sponsored deposit insurers remained solvent during their first 35 years of existence. The strategy of mitigating moral hazard by limiting the federal role to "sponsorship" was, however, an immediate failure. As early as 1933, when FDR re-opened banks, the markets perceived the federal backing of deposit insurance as complete.[25] Bank capital levels fell steadily from over 16 percent of assets to only 5.5 percent by 1945, where they stayed for over four decades before falling even further in response to risk-based capital requirements and off-balance sheet financing.

The home ownership rate rose from about 45 percent following World War II to about 65 percent by 1970. The Veterans Administration provided mortgage insurance to returning vets as part of the post-war G.I. Bill, thus many of the loans supporting this rate were made to returning war veterans. The idea was to help them achieve home ownership and promote domestic tranquility and housing production, in no small part due to a pervasive fear of a new depression. These loans were partly funded by Fannie Mae's special assistance function with Treasury borrowing and partly by private lenders.

The S&L industry that funded most home mortgages prior to the Great Depression continued to do so during the post-WWII era. Deposit insurance did not harm anyone; the insurance limits gradually rose from the initial $2,500 to $20,000 by 1969. This accelerated the trend of accepting deposits independent from mortgage lending and making deposits more liquid, i.e., more bank-like. At the same time, capital levels fell, likewise following the banking trend. In addition to deposit insurance and low capital requirements, S&Ls received a substantial tax break called the "Bad Debt Allowance," which permanently deferred about 60 percent of all taxes so long as they maintained about 80 percent of their assets in residential mortgages.[26] This tilted the playing field against commercial banks, who nevertheless had become players in the mortgage market. They raised their share of household mortgage debt to about 20 percent, a level not surpassed until the aftermath of the financial crisis during the next century.

Four months after the U.S. entered WWII, the Fed announced its commitment to maintaining the rate on U.S. Treasury Bills in order to fund the war effort. It maintained this commitment during the postwar years due to the fear of a return to deflation, despite the fact that inflation reached double-digit levels as wage and price controls were lifted. Monetary growth remained relatively uncontroversial and markets remained stable. This is partly in response to the Fed's regulation Q, which prohibited banks paying interest on deposits until the Korean War broke out in 1950.

The New York Federal Reserve Bank had by then taken over monetary operations as well as regulation of money-center banks, which were all located there. However, the Washington-based board retained control over monetary decisions. The other 11 regional banks were functionally—but not (yet) politically—obsolete, and desperately sought new missions to maintain relevance. The Fed had to raise interest rates to fight inflation, but the Treasury, which held all the cards, resisted. The result was the Treasury-Fed accord of 1951 in which the Fed would buy new issue securities at par but sell other securities at a discount, thereby raising rates. This was of course a charade as the Fed's losses would result in a smaller Fed dividend to the Treasury, but accomplished the Fed's goal of faux monetary independence.

The predicted unintended consequences of these federal enterprises were not realized in the two decades following WWII, as the U.S. emerged stronger than its competitors. Inflation remained low until two successive Democratic administrations with a strong Keynesian influence simultaneously financed a war and the Great Society with deficits and debt. This led to inflationary pressure that exposed cracks in the international monetary mechanism in the late 1960s and the federal government's housing finance structure.

Chapter 2: From the Great Society to the National Home Ownership Strategy

The mortgage markets took a radically different shape after the passage of the Housing and Urban Development Act establishing HUD in 1965 and the subsequent 1968 Act "privatizing" Fannie Mae. Prudential regulation became a tool for repressive controls and political housing goals, government sponsored enterprises (GSEs) crowded out private lenders, and lobbies coalesced around government intervention to extort subsidies through finance. By the end of the century the federal government determined both the pricing and allocation of about half of all mortgage credit, with virtually all sub-prime mortgages having been originated and priced in response to political and regulatory extortion. Trillions of dollars had already been lent to low-income borrowers but government housing policies extracted commitments amounting to about $5 trillion more in the next decade.

A. The S&L Industry and Housing and Urban Development's Mission

The public benefits provided to S&Ls in the wake of the Great Depression were not without costs. Due to deposit insurance, most withdrawal requests were generally met on demand. In addition, the commercial bank Regulation Q deposit rate ceiling authority was extended to S&Ls in 1965. This provided the benefit of protection from competition, but was very disruptive for several reasons. First, interest rates had become extremely volatile, resulting in investors making large fund withdrawals to take advantage of market rates. Second, the continued prohibition on interstate branching was an even bigger problem in the post-war period due to mass migrations from the industrial Northeast and Midwest to the Southwest and West, resulting in huge imbalances between savings supply and home loan demand.

Structurally, S&Ls were much riskier as regulated entities than they were before regulation due to their illiquidity and lower capital requirements. Credit risk was generally mitigated by requiring that borrowers put about 20 percent down or obtain private mortgage insurance (PMI). Federal regulation also became meddlesome in another important way. Virtually all state-chartered S&Ls responded to the extreme volatility of interest rates by only making loans with a variable rate, to avoid insolvency if rates rose. This made housing investment riskier and was thus opposed by the building industry. To prevent lenders from transferring these risks to households—risks generally the result of bad fiscal and monetary policies—erstwhile "prudential" regulators prohibited federally chartered S&Ls from making any loan other than a 30-year fixed-rate mortgage (FRM) in 1974. This policy was implemented at the behest of Democratic senator William Proxmire, chairman of the Senate Banking, Housing and Urban Affairs Committee. Given these circumstances, that rising interest rates would bankrupt the federally chartered S&L industry was entirely predictable – and thus preventable.

Lumping banking, housing, and urban affairs together is a conflict of interest, as demonstrated by Senator Proxmire's "housing" position on FRMs trumping his responsibility for the safety and soundness of the financial system. HUD was established as a separate cabinet department by the Lyndon Johnson Administration in order to give a greater priority to housing and urban issues. The administration thought this was necessary based on the mis-diagnosis that the urban riots of the 1960s were the direct result of poor quality housing. Politicians subsequently came to view home ownership as a source of political stability, as it required a significant investment in a fixed physical structure. Houses are usually financed with mortgages, so putting oversight of banking with that for housing and urban affairs didn't seem that far-fetched. Additionally, the 1965 HUD Act married the issues further by placing FHA's home mortgage insurance program under HUD supervision—but did not change its independent mutual charter. The Housing and Urban Development Act of 1968 gave HUD the mandate to "assist families with incomes so low that they could not otherwise decently house themselves." FHA became HUDs primary tool to implement its social mission. This started as early as 1965 with a request to Congress for forbearance for borrowers in default.

FHA continued to insure only fixed rate mortgages. This took on greater importance as a consequence of the continued reliance on fixed rate mortgages as inflation accelerated. The fixed rate mortgage only protected borrowers from inflation when it was unexpected. Lenders respond to expected inflation by raising the required mortgage rate. But by definition a fixed payment mortgage required paying now for inflation in the future. The rise in the required real – inflation adjusted – mortgage payment during the early years became known as the "tilt effect." HUD funded a study by the Harvard- MIT Joint Center for Financial Studies and published a subsequent book *Alternative Mortgage Instruments in an Inflationary Environment* in 1975 that suggested a variety of alternative mortgage designs that FHA could insure to address the problem. All had one thing in common, a lower initial payment resulting in either no amortization (i.e., an "interest only" loan) or negative amortization (i.e., a rising loan balance).

While these worked better in an inflationary environment, the credit risk increased if the inflation was less than expected. By the time these ideas worked their way through the HUD bureaucracy, inflation was already on the decline. But PMIs surpassed FHA in 1972, and FHA's market share fell by 75% by 1976, dramatically reducing its ability to cross-subsidize weak borrowers.[27]

HUD also inherited a mishmash of various federal programs, ranging from public rental housing to urban renewal. The initial political interest in housing during and after the Great Depression—when FHA and Fannie Mae were chartered—was entirely related to the short-term potential to create jobs and relieve cyclical unemployment. This was also true of the Depression era public housing programs.[28] The construction, management, and allocation of public housing, which had always been implemented to benefit builders and were generally rife with corruption, was no longer being built in 1965 and HUD wasn't involved in any major production programs.

Faced with steep budget deficits, the Johnson administration focused on ways to encourage off-balance-sheet financing of housing construction through public-private partnerships. Republicans, led by Senator Edward Brooke of Massachusetts, were convinced by academic studies on "housing needs" and lobbyists for housing producers that the urban problems were really housing problems. They worked to pass the Housing and Urban Development Act of 1968, which included as Title XVI "Housing Goals and Annual Housing Report." The federal government first became responsible for "housing goals" with the 1949 Housing Act, which established "a goal of a decent home and a suitable living environment for every American family." Such lofty goals were enacted into law without specifying a timetable for implementation or providing a budget with which to accomplish them.

Republicans have historically supported private sector incentives, including rental housing vouchers for existing private rental units, federal mortgage insurance, and tax incentives for privately built housing. But "Republican social engineering" isn't necessarily better than "Democratic social engineering," to borrow a phrase from historian and 2012 presidential candidate Newt Gingrich. By 1970, the still young HUD had already embraced bipartisan social engineering. As with Senator William Proxmire's committee, conflicts between promoting housing and urban development while simultaneously being the prudential regulator of a financial institution became evident almost immediately.

The problem of urban development, as many politicians and urban analysts saw it in the 1960s, stemmed from the 1956 Eisenhower initiative to build highways financed by the National Interstate and Defense Highways Act, a byproduct of which was that more affluent people moved to the suburbs while leaving poorer families behind. Most of the increase in home ownership financed by

S&Ls and others occurred in suburbs, leaving city administrations accustomed to cross-subsidizing municipal services in fiscal distress, creating a vicious cycle: as services declined, more affluent households moved out of cities. Policymakers needed to figure out how to promote home ownership without provoking urban flight. One tool now available to HUD was to promote both housing and urban development with mortgage insurance targeted to inner cities.

Private mortgage insurers, bankrupted by the Great Depression but reincarnated in the 1950s, were reluctant to insure politically motivated HUD loans due to the risk. But FHA (and the Veteran's Administration) had several financial advantages over PMIs as a consequence of federal sponsorship. First, FHA paid no taxes, whereas PMIs were subject to state, local and federal taxes – although they received a federal tax break similar to that provided to S&Ls to incentivize reserves. Second, the mutual policyholders—the mortgage borrowers—were much less likely to be aware of – and thus require – dividends than shareholders. Third, FHA generally had a lower capital requirement. Fourth, taxpayers paid FHA's administrative expenses. In return, HUD asked it to take greater risks in pursuit of its housing and urban mission to subsidize certain risks.

With cities in turmoil, many lenders and insurers—including FHA—"redlined" certain neighborhoods as too risky to lend or insure: often these lines were drawn around neighborhoods with well defined race and ethnic characteristics. Using race or sex to discriminate is a violation of federal statutes, which the Department of Justice (DOJ) is responsible for enforcing. But borrower-underwriting criteria are highly correlated with race—and to a lesser extent sex —and race is often highly correlated with neighborhood, i.e., inner city collateral risk. In that context, historical redlining is a legitimate and appropriate device but widespread use makes it self-fulfilling, as the lack of finance will contribute to urban decay. Contrary to some narratives, FHA, not the private sector, created mortgage redlining.

As with most products, the additional costs, such as those associated with verification of minimum standards, would be addressed by raising the price of that product. But with insurance, adverse selection occurs when lenders or insurers attempt to accept more risk with higher losses offset by charging all borrowers a higher rate premium. Unfortunately, the best of the more risky borrowers find cheaper loans elsewhere, leaving inadequate premiums to cover losses on the insured loans. This is what happened to FHA with its inner city lending programs of the 1960s that had been instituted to eliminate redlining: they resulted in actuarial insolvency. As with the cities they were trying to help, their ability to cross-subsidize was limited.

In the end, FHA did not help urban development, but instead undermined neighborhood stability. In 1998, the late Gale Cincotta, a long-time community activist, in testimony before a subcommittee of the House Financial Services Committee, told the subcommittee that FHA had to change its abusive lending practices: "We have been fighting abuse, fraud, and neglect of the FHA program that has destroyed too many neighborhoods and too many families' dreams of homeownership for more than 25 years... The FHA program has a national default rate 3 to 4 times the conventional market, and in many urban neighborhoods it routinely exceeds 10 times. In addition, the FHA program is hemorrhaging money." In 2009 Beryl Satter observed in the NAACP's *The Defenders Online* "The 1970s FHA-HUD Scandal... bore well over the lion's share of responsibility for the decayed buildings and vacant lots that scar urban minority communities."[29]

B: The Early Origins of Federally Sponsored Mortgage Capital Markets

The influence of the numerous Depression-era federally sponsored enterprises was virtually inconsequential until the 1968 Housing and Urban Development Act, which shaped the federally sponsored mortgage capital markets during the last quarter of the 20th century. One of the most consequential aspects of the HUD Act was the so-called "privatization" of Fannie Mae's "secondary marketing" facility. This was driven by nothing more than myopic political expediency as President Johnson's "guns and butter" strategy ratcheted up the normal pressure for budget accounting gimmicks. Politicians had previously tried to get Fannie Mae mortgages off the budget with the 1964 Housing Act. The 1964 Act provided authority for Fannie Mae to issue off-balance sheet participation certificates on pools of mortgages by treating the securitization as a "sale of assets" rather than a "financing," but they continued to borrow from the Treasury instead.[30] So the 1968 Act established the Government National Mortgage Association—"Ginnie Mae"—with the sole purpose being to "manage and liquidate" the Treasury-financed FHA/VA-insured Fannie Mae portfolio of about $4 billion as quickly as feasible. This would move them off the budget to reduce the reported deficit – which was, at the time, about twice this amount and had been generally viewed with alarm. In addition, Fannie Mae issued debentures to repay the Treasury $216 million for its preferred stock that had capitalized the entity.[31]

Arguably, the newly-chartered Ginnie Mae should have been given the $2.5 billion corporately-financed "dealer" portfolio to liquidate as well. Unfortunately, that portfolio was already off-budget and would have had to be put back on until it was sold: the exact opposite of what the Act was trying to accomplish. It was more expedient politically to simply give the "company" to the mortgage bankers, an industry virtually created by Fannie Mae and holders of nominal "stock" issued in return for a fee for using the Fannie Mae secondary market facility as a consequence of the 1954 reorganization Act.[32]

The mortgage market was still plagued by the restrictions on bank and S&L branching across state lines. S&Ls had previously addressed the problem created by branching restrictions by using mail advertising and higher rates to compete for deposits across states and regions, but deposit rate controls put a stop to this in the 1960s. Additionally, there were increasingly numerous state laws and regulations inhibiting issuing and trading securities across state lines. Mortgages were being actively sold as whole loan transactions in significant volume, typically with recourse to the seller or with the seller retaining a junior participation. These restrictions took on increasing significance in the 1970s as household wealth began to shift from retail savings to wholesale retirement savings in life insurance annuities and private pensions—capital markets.

Prior to the Depression, several companies offered "participation certificates" or PCs backed by a pool of mortgages that reflected the same risk structure as whole loan sales. In other words, the seller bore the first loss and the investors purchased a senior participation. This was more convenient than buying individual mortgages, but their sale was subject to state laws and was illegal in several states. Moreover, the issuer retained the right to substitute collateral with the same principle amount, a practice exploited during the Depression as issuers often substituted inferior collateral.[33]

In 1970, Sherman Maisel, a Berkeley professor and Fed Vice Chairman at the time, promoted the concept of a security that could be issued and traded nationally to improve capital market access. Federal government and agency issues had a federal preemption from the conflicting state, local and federal laws and regulations that otherwise would have, among other things, required separate security registrations in all fifty states for each security offering. Maisel tried to persuade the recently privatized Fannie Mae to create mortgage backed securities (MBSs) backed by pools of FHA insured (and VA guaranteed) loans that could be traded nationally. When they refused, he proposed this to Ginnie Mae – an activity that went well beyond its "management and liquidating" charter.

The government did not want these securities on its balance sheet, as that would have defeated the purpose of the Fannie Mae privatization and the Ginnie Mae liquidation, so these securities needed to be considered as a sale of the underlying assets. Government sponsored enterprises were exempt from many security laws, but any such entity would not be exempt from the federal law that taxed mortgage revenues as profits before distribution of interest to security holders. To get around this, HUD lawyers found an old but limited "grantor trust" statute that avoided corporate tax. Thus each security was to be considered a separate corporate entity. The IRS allowed a minor exemption—the guaranteed advancement of the typically delayed FHA insurance reimbursements in the event of borrower default—but the grantor trust vehicle prohibited Ginnie Mae from guaranteeing credit risk. Investors hated the idea of uncertain monthly cash flows for 30 years, but the IRS ruling allowed no alternative. The Ginnie Mae PC – meaning pass-through, not participation — trust certificate had no capital, relying on the implicit federal backing of FHA. As securitization was legally and financially an asset sale no subsequent substitution of assets was allowed.

Soon after Ginnie Mae introduced the PC, the newly privatized Fannie Mae—limited to the broker-dealer role in FHA loans—was totally superfluous. The stock that had little value when privatized now became virtually worthless. In retrospect, had the Ginnie Mae security been anticipated and authorized by the 1968 Act, this corporate-funded broker-dealer facility would likely have been liquidated as well. Instead, the mortgage banking industry lobbied for new legislation providing conventional loan authority. This push represented an unprecedented intrusion into private lending, allowing mortgage bankers to compete directly with S&L portfolio lenders even though the charter restriction limiting activity to a broker-dealer function remained. S&Ls had no use for such a secondary market facility, but they did not want to lack an authority given to mortgage bankers so, having lost the political battle to prevent Fannie Mae from acquiring conventional loan authority, they successfully lobbied for the Federal Home Loan Mortgage Corporation (Freddie Mac). Freddie was authorized by the Emergency Home Finance Act of 1970 to deal in conventional mortgages, without the explicit charter restrictions but with the explicit promise that if this broker-dealer function became a commercial failure, the corporation would be liquidated.

It wasn't long before Fannie Mae's new private shareholders, the mortgage banking industry, recognized that uncontrollable growth financed with cheap debt benefited them directly, which far outweighed their indirect risk and return as Fannie Mae's shareholders. So they immediately turned the Fannie Mae secondary market facility into a portfolio-lending government-sponsored housing bank serving their interests, despite the unambiguous charter limitations to the contrary and ostensible Treasury Department control. They also realized that Fannie Mae could offer higher prices for mortgage purchases if it took more risk, for instance by financing purchases with cheaper short-term debt. By 1980, Fannie Mae's retained portfolio exploded to about $100 billion. HUD, its erstwhile prudential regulator, wasn't about to blow the whistle, especially not while politicians stood on the sidelines cheering them on. The securities disclosures continued to warn investors that the U.S. Treasury would not back defaults on the underlying mortgages and securities, but public regulation eliminated any investor concerns.

Likewise, when Freddie Mac realized that S&Ls had no use for a broker-dealer in conventional loans, it closed its Automated Mortgage Market Information Network (AMINET) broker-dealer. Then-CEO Thomas Bomar recommended liquidating the young agency in 1972, as former chairman Preston Martin had promised Congress during his testimony regarding the agency's creation. Instead, they found a new mission and in the mid-1970s they began purchasing loans with at least 20 percent down payments. Those with a loan-to-value greater than 80 percent had to have private mortgage insurance – at the time down to 75 percent. This fortuitous requirement was imposed by James van Horne, then-CEO of Investor Mortgage Insurance (IMI) and past aide to the Senate Banking Committee, as his reward for shepherding the Freddie Mac bill through Congress. Freddie Mac followed Fannie Mae's lead as a federally sponsored, quasi-public, and subsequently privatized housing bank engaged in funding mortgages with the full support of its regulator, the FHLB Board.[34]

Freddie Mac initially limited its activity to fixed rate loans, allowing S&Ls to reduce interest rate risk by selling them while maintaining adjustable rate loans on which they could still earn a reasonable spread. Shortly after Ginnie Mae introduced its PC, Freddie Mac securitized conventional mortgages by issuing *participation* certificates, also called PCs as Freddie Mac initially purchased only senior 95 percent participations. Freddie Mac was tax exempt by charter and not subject to double taxation, so it provided a complete guarantee of the pool of loans with the underlying credit risk of conventional loans privately insured. But unlike early PCs, it didn't allow asset substitution. In spite of Freddie Mac's status as a public entity, its disclosures warned that the U.S. Treasury did not back defaults on the underlying mortgages and securities.

Unlike debt financing, securitization passes on the interest rate risk to investors. GSE securitization exposed investors only to the residual default risk as a pool insurer, i.e., beyond the private mortgage insurance coverage. Consequently, the public's risk exposure to securitization in the 1970s through the 1980s was minimal. GSE securitization benefited mortgage borrowers by alleviating regional credit shortages due to branching restrictions, increasing the overall availability of funds. Securitization also reduced rates somewhat in credit-short areas while raising them in credit-surplus areas. But this capital market access rationale became obsolete by 1990 with the phasing out of bank branching restrictions and other legal and regulatory obstacles to private capital market access. The new Real Estate Mortgage Investment Conduit (REMIC) legislation of 1986 also enabled private-label MBS without being subject to taxes at the pool level.

Securitization had the additional potentially negative consequence of separating "lenders" into independent loan originators, loan brokers, loan servicers, and investment bankers that had little or no capital stake in the credit performance of the loans. Moral hazard is inherent in the originate-to-sell model but FHA and Ginnie Mae minimized it in three ways. First, FHA maintained local underwriting offices. Second, Ginnie Mae required an "excessive servicing fee," postponing some of the origination profit to the end of the loan which was lost in the event of default due to foreclosure expense borne by the servicer.[35] Third, Ginnie Mae had full recourse, which cross-collateralized all securitizations, thereby putting an MBS originator's entire profitable loan servicing business and capital at risk for a failure to perform on any individual pool. Freddie Mac was historically more protected against this moral hazard by dealing with better-capitalized portfolio lenders who "participated" in the loss rather than mortgage brokers and bankers.

There are tremendous scale economies to servicing loans. Servicing contracts were long term with a fixed fee, so most of the net revenue came later in the contract if defaults were avoided. There were no scale economies or barriers to entry for loan originators, resulting in "cut-throat" competition to originate loans, as described by the head of the Mortgage Bankers Association in 1945. This competition generally resulted in mortgage bankers originating at a loss of a percentage point or two, offset by the long-term profitability of the servicing contract.

This practice of selling at a loss resulted in both Generally Accepted Accounting Principles (GAAP) and tax accounting issues, as the loss came up front and the taxable revenue later. Mortgage bankers lobbied for the ability to "book" the value of the servicing contract so that the balance sheet would allow borrowing to fund the business. Put another way, they counted expected – unearned – revenue as a currently held asset, appearing to be more financially sound, in order to borrow against it. Within a few years, the IRS caught on and started taxing this value up-front. After that, there was no GAAP or tax penalty to selling the servicing contracts, so servicers with a massive nationwide platform came to dominate. Origination could be done with in-house loan officers, independent loan brokers, or both. The effect of these moves was consolidation. For comparison, the top 20 mortgage bankers were independent in the early 1970s; by 1980, 17 were owned by large banks or S&Ls. Moreover, since branching restrictions did not apply to mortgage banks, they were more likely to operate regionally or nationally.

Securitization also required a uniform contract mortgage rate to facilitate the pooling of homogeneous loans into a Ginnie Mae security with a coupon rate reflecting the rate on the underlying mortgages. To achieve this, the FHA Commissioner set a maximum ceiling mortgage coupon rate for FHA loans that would be the lowest yield required during the pooling period, hence the coupon rate that all loan originators used. Since private investors funded the loan, it did not affect the lender's required yield or the borrower's required cost. The borrower was charged "points" up front to make up the difference, but assuming the borrower wasn't already at the maximum loan-to-value ratio, she could borrow the additional points by increasing the loan principal. This faux consumer protection allowed the FHA Commissioner to take political credit for lowering mortgage rates, but borrowers who prepaid were actually worse off as a result of the points, whether paid up front or financed.

The independent Federal Home Loan Bank (FHLB) System also contributed to capital market access, borrowing wholesale to lend directly to S&Ls by discounting loans. The FHLB Board in Washington, D.C. regulated the FHLBs with three politically appointed directors generally supportive of a "housing" mission. The FHLBs funded these loan advances with short-term debt to reflect the maturity of advances—essentially collateralized by the mortgages—and, like Freddie Mac, they specifically disclosed that the U.S. Treasury did not back the advances. The FHLB became the relief valve, providing S&Ls with funds for housing when deposit rate ceilings combined with rising interest rates to cause fund outflows, a process called "disintermediation."

Fannie Mae, Freddie Mac, the FHLBs, and Ginnie Mae (which funds FHA) are often referred to collectively as the "mortgage GSEs." Their financing is all off budget and exempt from the control of the Federal Financing Bank, historically the Treasury's agent for that responsibility. Housing promotion agencies —HUD for FHA/Ginnie Mae and Fannie Mae; the FHLB Board for the FHLBs and Freddie Mac—are responsible for approving their financing. During the 1970s, Freddie Mac and Ginnie Mae were funded with MBS. Fannie Mae and FHLBs were funded with debt. The debt didn't trade much, as there was little reason to trade it, but active trading did develop for GSE MBS.

C. Speculative Trading of GSE MBS

The political *ex post* rationalization for securitization is that it converted inherently illiquid mortgage loans into "liquid" mortgage backed securities. The reality is that GSE MBSs became a trading vehicle for speculation—much of it otherwise illegal—and the profits from this trading was a major factor in converting investment banks into highly leveraged hedge funds issuing bank-like deposits in the shadow banking system.

This enduring political fiction continues to be the primary political and economic GSE rationale. The financial press has always used the terms "liquidity"—the ability to sell quickly for cash at par value—interchangeably with the term "marketability"—the ability to sell with a low bid-asked spread at whatever investors think the security is worth. Cash managers buy government securities to invest cash balances and sell (or issue short-term debt such as commercial paper) when they need cash. Marketability, as measured by the bid-asked spread, does improve with the volume of trades, but this had never previously been a concern to long-term investors in bonds or mortgages and hence long term debt rarely traded.

Unlike government bonds or highly-rated corporate bonds, the cash flows of pre-payable and, in the 1970s, generally assumable (by a subsequent house buyer) fixed-rate home mortgages were extremely difficult to predict. Hence, there were reasons to trade MBS based on different prepayment and assumption views, or changes in projections over time. GSE MBS were priced off the Treasury yield curve for comparable maturity or comparable "duration" securities, as duration is a more precise measurement than maturity for measuring the price sensitivity to changing interest rates. Prepayment was projected based on experience and, because FHA had the most comprehensive existing database, it became the standard and "100 percent FHA" became the unit of measure. Then "put" option models were used to price the likelihood that prepayment would occur earlier than the standard—when rates declined—and "call" option pricing models were used to price the risk that it would occur later— that homeowners wouldn't move when rates rose or, if they did, the buyer would assume the below market rate loan. In 1986, Salomon Brothers introduced the concept of "option adjusted" yields on MBS that subtracted the imputed option price from the yield. This prepayment option spurred the early development of derivative securities. An individual MBS could be unbundled and re-packaged in all sorts of ways. Interest only (IO) and principal only (PO) strips became two of the most common early derivative securities.

As interest rates became more volatile in the 1970s, there were both premium and discount pools to trade. There is nothing inherently wrong with speculative trading, which arguably made the options price more efficient. But the implicit option premium is taken into current income with no regard for the cost of the residual risk, which is often called "tail risk" because it often comes at the end.[36] The "tails" could be quite long and the perception of higher yields created by the options premium encourages speculation, especially if the tail risk will be borne by others.

Because they trade so frequently, speculators are often called "traders" or, more specifically, "proprietary traders" that speculate rather than market-make. The political fiction that GSE securities were liquid because they were traded essentially allowed regulated investors authorized to *invest* only in "liquid government securities" to engage in speculative GSE MBS trades. Consequently, the investment banks all came up with competing strategies as to how to speculate. These trading strategies generally allowed traders to write "out of the money" options using GSE and derivative securities in an opaque way, treating the entire trading revenue in the form of option premium as profit.

Speculating in tail risk was particularly attractive to money managers who were typically otherwise prohibited from doing so. Whether the *ex ante* "option premium" in the quoted yield is sufficient to cover the *ex post* cost of the tail risk is another related issue. That most investors in risk-free securities apparently believed that the higher-quoted yield on GSE securities implied a higher realized yield suggests that *ex post* yields on GSE securities were generally lower than on an otherwise comparable non-callable portfolio of U.S. Treasury securities, because they paid too much up front.[37] The perception of higher yields would drive the subsequent global demand for GSE securities by otherwise risk-averse investors in a later era.

Investors initially hated the idea of uncertain monthly cash flows for 30 years. Bill Simon, the Salomon Brothers partner and later Energy and Treasury Secretary, tried to convince Ginnie Mae to issue bonds to reduce uncertainty, but the IRS ruling allowed no alternative so he ignored them. But in 1977 a Salomon Brothers trader Bobby Dahl and investment banker Steve Joseph, brother of Fred Joseph who was CEO of Drexel Burnham, issued the first private mortgage backed security for B of A. The security could only be sold in only three states due to the previously discussed restrictions and even though B of A got the loans off its balance sheet, freeing up capital, the B of A MBS was a bust. But the experience convinced Simon to make Dahl head of a new Mortgage Securities unit and Dahl moved Lewis Ranieri from the utility bond trading desk to the new unit as his MBS trader.

Ranieri at first wanted no part in the move but GSE MBS issuance and speculation-driven trading volume skyrocketed due to the risk and uncertainty. Investment banks historically had two trading (market-making) desks, government and corporate. It was the lawyers at and advisors to the Wall Street trading firms that made a judgment that Ginnie Mae, Fannie Mae and Freddie Mac securities could all be traded on the government desk, removing a potential obstacle to trading. The judgment that such securities would be backed by the government in the event of default - in spite of the specific disclosures to the contrary - reflected their federal sponsorship with their regulatory and tax exemptions of a public entity. As volumes soared, the market itself became "too big to fail" and, as with deposit insurance, there was no denying the implicit government backing, removing any pretense of market discipline. Within four years Ranieri's trading desk was making more than all the rest of Wall Street combined.[38]

By the 1980s, proprietary trading to execute "risk-controlled arbitrage" strategies were marketed mostly to stockholder-owned and mutual thrifts as part of their "go for broke" survival strategy, often camouflaged as "hedging"—i.e., using instruments and strategies to reduce portfolio risk. After the S&Ls went broke, the investment bankers turned to cash managers of state and local governments.

In 1994, Orange County, California, one of the richest counties in history, was forced to declare bankruptcy. Its investment manager, Robert Citron, had collected all the cash accounts that numerous local governments held in their local bank accounts to meet the public payroll and deposited them at Merrill Lynch. He then leveraged them with loans collateralized by securities – repos - and invested them directly in supposedly "liquid" risk-free GSE securities that were, in fact, derivative securities employed in "risk-controlled arbitrage" strategies largely designed by Merrill Lynch. He was considered a hero for years as the higher earnings from this speculation allowed local politicians to keep taxes down. But he was essentially "playing the yield curve" by investing in long-term securities as well as speculating by earning excess "quoted yield" that reflected not higher expected returns, but rather the "option premium" for prepayment risk and other derivative trading strategies and accepting tail risk. When GSE MBS prices subsequently plummeted as interest rates rose, the tail wagged; past gains were wiped out, bankrupting Orange County and severely wounding San Diego County finances.

Orange County blamed its demise on Wall Street greed. Citron and other cash managers obviously had no business transferring taxpayer bank accounts to the shadow banking system and then speculating with options trading. Whose responsibility was it to stop them? The answer, in this case, is that politicians who provided oversight took responsibility when the bets paid off and Wall Street investment banks took the blame when they didn't, a political lesson that didn't go unnoticed.

Wall Street loved the trading of GSE MBS because they profited handsomely as the market-maker. Whereas speculation had historically been reserved to individuals and hedge funds, speculating in GSE MBSs enticed investment banks to do so for their own account, establishing "proprietary trading desks"—essentially in-house hedge funds. Hedge fund managers generally keep 20 percent to 25 percent of the return over a benchmark as a management bonus with no downside risk, creating an incentive conflict to load-up on tail risk. Hedge fund managers are also expected to contribute their own personal funds to mitigate moral hazard of excessive risk taking at someone else's expense.

Proprietary trading began at investment banks when the banks were all partnerships where partners had historically waited a lifetime to receive the bulk of their compensation. Arguably, partners could mitigate traders from taking tail risk at the partnership's expense. There were some losses considered huge at the time, such as those of Howie Rubin at Merrill Lynch, but these were generally viewed as aberrations. Nevertheless, proprietary traders eventually demanded and received annual cash bonuses just like hedge fund managers, often on unrealized profits. This undermined the partnership structure. When Salomon Brothers—the premier fixed income trading house—cashed-out by selling the firm to the commodities trading firm Phibro in 1979, the partners of other firms took notice. Virtually all the Wall Street firms had sold out or converted to stock by 2000, with only Goldman Sachs retaining some partner equity. Because all the firms were now owned by shareholders and many investment bank CEOs now rose from the proprietary "trading" ranks, limiting or deferring bonuses wasn't a competitive strategy. Wall Street had become greedier, and mortgage securities had become even more complex, both as an outgrowth of speculating in GSE—now "agency"—securities backed by fixed rate pre-payable mortgages.

By the end of the century, the largest investment banks had portfolios approaching or exceeding a trillion dollars of mostly hedge fund— that is, proprietary trading—account balances with some private equity fund and real estate assets. But these banks were able to fund their portfolio by borrowing over an extremely short term using a variety of instruments such as commercial paper and overnight repurchase agreements. A repurchase agreement, or "repo," is essentially an overnight or very short-term loan at a slight haircut to the trading or market value of the collateral. Repo's were provided with GSE MBS as collateral on essentially the same basis as for liquid government securities based on their marketability. In fact, their entire funding structure assumed that "marketable" dealer inventory and internal hedge fund assets were "liquid," ignoring the distinction between immutable liquidity and ephemeral marketability. The too big to fail investment banks essentially had commercial bank, hedge fund, and private equity fund assets and near-money liabilities without bank regulation or a systemic liquidity backstop.

The separation of commercial from investment banking required by Glass-Steagall was gradually phased-out through regulatory forbearance in the 1980s and 1990s, and finally eliminated with the repeal of the Gramm-Leach-Bliley Financial Services Modernization Act of 1999. The Financial Crisis Inquiry Commission (FCIC) Report (Chapter 4: Expansion of Banking Activities: "Shatterer of Glass Steagall) follows the conventional wisdom that this "deregulation" was a major cause of the financial crisis. But the crisis had nothing to do with commercial bank underwriting or broker/dealer activities, which was the original separation required by Glass-Steagall. Funding hedge funds with near money was something altogether different, as discussed in later chapters.

D. The Implications of Government Backed Debt for Firm Behavior

The role of investors in any security has historically been to assess and price risk. For riskier and presumably "high yield" assets - those with a greater variance in returns - lenders will generally target a higher return on equity (ROE) to compensate, and vice versa for less risky assets. Hence, according to the Modigliani & Miller (M&M) Irrelevance Theorem,[39] leverage shouldn't affect total issuer financing costs (debt plus equity) because investors will always price the total risk the same no matter how it is allocated. An implied corollary when financing something like a multiple credit tranched private label securitization, i.e., debt with varying levels of subordination, for example, is that the issuer's total debt and equity cost would be the same no matter how the subordination is structured because the price and yield of each class would reflect the risk.

But two federal policies have long-encouraged excessive leverage that represent exceptions to the M&M Theorem. First, debt costs are tax deductible whereas equity costs are paid after the issuer pays corporate taxes. Second, federally sponsored deposit insurance, introduced in the United States during the Great Depression, removed the risk premium from deposit rates so that yields don't properly reflect risk.

The tax wedge would drive capital levels toward zero but debt costs would rise such that total funding costs would still reflect total risk. Because extreme leverage exposes debtors to moral hazard – that the equity investors will take risks *ex post* greater than whatever risks debt investors' price *ex ante* - debt investors impose a minimum capital requirement to mitigate this conflict. The federal guarantee of debt encourages extreme leverage - with or without the tax wedge – but without the debt investors' capital requirement. And with so little equity the debt holders would be quickly exposed as well. Extreme leverage causes borrowers and lenders to behave in an extreme manner, going for broke and then going broke.

1. The Value of Government Backed Debt to Firms

Mortgage GSEs issue securities slightly above the government's cost of funds due to their market-anointed agency status. Commercial banks, mutual savings banks, and S&Ls—particularly those that are TBTF—can also issue government-insured liabilities (deposits) at an all-in-cost slightly above GSEs because they have a so-called "dueling charter."[40] That explains why bank capital levels fell from about 16 percent—with shareholders on the hook for more as needed—to only 5 percent within a decade of enactment, with no shareholder recourse. Capital levels remained near that level for several decades thereafter, reflecting the regulatory minimum.

So banks, Fannie, Freddie, and the rest of the GSEs can borrow at low rates *no matter how much capital they have or how risky their loans are.* This arrangement gives new meaning to the term "limited liability company:" from the debtors perspective, there is no bankruptcy risk; from the equity investors perspective, however, there is extremely limited liability as deposit insurance eliminated creditor capital calls, never a feature of Fannie or Freddie. This is the source of moral hazard: shareholders are incentivized to maximize both leverage and loan risk.

Comparable federal policies exist for home mortgages. Home mortgage interest is tax deductible as is corporate debt. Home borrower equity—cash down payment requirements—similarly fell from about 40 percent first to about 20 percent during the post WWII period and subsequently to about 3 percent (or less) with federal mortgage insurance, the equivalent of deposit insurance for investors. Hence mortgage insurance creates the same moral hazard as deposit insurance.

How much could the agency status of Fannie and Freddie distort (lower) the yields on, for example, "risky" mortgages as compared to the yield requirements of a hypothetical uninsured private lender? Suppose that the private lender would need 10 percent equity capital to get a AAA credit rating and financing cost equivalent to Fannie and Freddie—assumed to be 5 percent for illustrative purposes—on all of the remaining 90 percent debt that finances a pool of sub-prime mortgages. If we assume that a lender targets an average 15 percent ROE after tax, it would have to earn 25 percent before tax (at an assumed 40 percent combined corporate federal and state tax rate).

The average return on assets (ROA) is the net yield—the promised yield after subtracting average servicing costs and credit losses over the life of a pool—less debt financing costs. The ROE is the ROA divided by the ratio of equity to assets, or equivalently multiplied by the leverage ratio. For example, at a leverage ratio of 10 to 1 (10 percent equity to total assets) a 2.5 percent ROA would generate a 25 percent before tax ROE. Now suppose Fannie and Freddie can fund the same assets with leverage ratio of 100 to 1 based on the government's equity capital implied by agency status. The leverage reduces the required ROA to .25 percent to achieve the same ROE, giving Fannie and Freddie a 2.25 percent lending advantage – a lower loan rate by that amount - over the private lender. Forgone taxes provide half Fannie's and Freddie's capital subsidies (the difference between the 25 percent before-tax and 15 percent after-tax ROE) and the government's opportunity cost for bearing the risk of this highly leveraged lending strategy without compensation for its implied equity provides the other half (the difference between 15 percent cost of equity and 5 percent cost of debt).

That's the simplified version of the methodology for calculating the total value of Fannie's and Freddie's capital subsidies. In fact, Fannie Mae and Freddie Mac targeted an average 15 percent after-tax ROE, which is fairly typical at commercial banks as well.[41] The bank capital subsidy due to deposit insurance can be calculated in a similar manner, but with somewhat less leverage and a somewhat higher all-in cost of funds. The FHLB subsidy is the same as for Fannie and Freddie. Ginnie Mae received an even bigger capital subsidy than Fannie and Freddie, funding at the U.S. Treasury rate (on an "option-adjusted" basis, to reflect prepayment risk). Ginnie charges only six basis points (.06 percent of principal) annually for agency status conferred on Ginnie Mae mortgage backed securities, just enough to cover administrative costs, so FHA captures the full Ginnie Mae subsidy and, when combined with the FHA subsidy, is larger than the Fannie and Freddie. So FHA can offer the lowest mortgage rates, followed by Fannie and Freddie, then banks.

CBO pioneered the first official calculations of the F&F subsidy cost to taxpayers in a study by Marvin Phaup in 1996.[42] The first difference from the methodology above is that the CBO didn't measure the tax savings from equity, so Phaup's methodology generates about half the savings. The second difference is that CBO calculated the present value the savings from new business—i.e., the annual addition to the stock, which requires estimating the life of the securities—whereas this methodology estimates the annual subsidy based on the outstanding stock. This avoids problematic estimates of mortgage life, but ignores the fact that subsequent subsidies are locked in once a security is issued because there is no withdrawing the guarantee. While estimates vary widely, using this methodology and ignoring annual variation, the average annual capital subsidy due to agency status for mostly "prime" loans was in the range of $10 billion in tax savings and another $10 billion from the cheap debt over the last three decades of the 20th century, give or take a billion dollars.

An equivalent model for computing the amount of implicit government capital to the "pool-insurer" model above is the "options-writer" model, which provides somewhat different insights. The pool-insurer model measures the capital inadequacy of low-risk government pool insurers and the option pricing model does the same for writing "way out of the money" options, in finance parlance, "put" the loan back to the government at par in the unlikely event default costs exceed insurance coverage or the private mortgage insurer defaults. Hence, the final outcome for such options is likely one of two extremes: the options remain out of the money and the government never pays, in which case all of the premiums—the interest savings on their debt and tax savings—become profit; or, the much less likely event, the options come into the money and the government pays heavily. This options concept illustrates the accounting illusion of recording revenue as profit before the option expires, which in the case of mortgage securities is when the last mortgage in a pool is paid off or matures. The two models are reconciled by considering the "tail risk" of the first "pool insurance" model as functionally equivalent to the risk of a "way out of the money" put option. But the options writer has to have substantial and credibly permanent capital to pay such distant future claims when the bet loses. That requires diversification of uncorrelated business lines as a source of payment or taxpayers.

Fannie Mae and Freddie Mac used all of their substantial political clout to squash Phaup's 1996 CBO report, but to no avail (Morgenson and Rosner, 2011).[43] So Fannie and Freddie resorted to Plan B: they rolled out their own academic economists to argue that the "true cost" was negligible, i.e., the market price was just wrong.

In 2002, Joseph Stiglitz and Jonathan and Peter Orszag used the options based approach in a research paper financed and published by Fannie Mae. They argued that the exposure to a severe macro-economic shock of ten-year duration would cost the government only $2 million for every trillion dollars in GSE assets with their current risk-based regulatory capital requirements. In short, three economists including a Nobel winner and future OMB Director essentially found the government's GSE holdings to be risk-less.[44] In a later analysis using the same approach, Deborah Lucas and Robert L. MacDonald (2006) concluded that the value of the options for the year-end 2004 outstanding debt and MBS was less than $8 billion cumulatively over ten years.[45] That is, Stiglitz et al. estimated a premium of only $10 million and Lucas and MacDonald $8 billion for an option that was exercised a few years later for hundreds of billions of dollars at a taxpayer expense over and above the prior tax and credit subsidies.

The Treasury maintains a budget for tax benefits. It includes such things as the annual cost of the home mortgage interest deduction. As discussed in more detail later in chapter 6, it also maintains a budget for credit guarantees, although this calculation woefully underestimates the true cost. But the GSEs are not included in either of these budgets.

2. Moral Hazard: Going for Broke and Going Broke

The originate-to-sell mortgage capital market model, the predominant model of mortgage funding in the US since the demise of the portfolio lending S&Ls, has inherent latent conflicts of interest between unrelated parties that increase potential investor risk. In addition to assessing and pricing risks, the role of "at risk" investors at the end of the chain is to mandate that all the parties in the chain adopt mechanisms to deal with these agency conflicts. The legal contracts merely backstop the trust in long term relationships, historical precedent, and capital. Insufficient regulatory capital requirements that allow extreme leverage encourage firms to "go-for-broke." When they finally do go broke, regulatory failure to shutter these firms allows them to continue going broke past the point of insolvency.

The main parties in the originate-to-sell chain of finance are the borrower, the originator, the third party mortgage insurer (if any), the packager/securitizer and guarantor (if applicable), the credit rater (if rated), the investor, and ultimately, for most of the mortgage market, the taxpayer. Secondary mortgage markets, which preceded the creation of GSEs and "asset sale" securitization by a century, had historically addressed possible conflicts of interest in a number of ways. Wholesale market investors relied on legal contracts spelling out the representations and warranties of the loan originating seller. In addition, they employed numerous other mechanisms, often in combination, including: buying only senior participations, right of put-back, requiring private mortgage insurance, and later requiring a third party guarantee or "pool insurance" on mortgage pools financed with securities.

But all of this comes down to requiring capital – an ongoing stake in the relationship. The basic moral hazard is caused by extreme leverage. Using such extreme leverage generates extraordinary expected returns at very low margins. This is a good deal for shareholders as long as risks are well diversified so that a relatively minor adverse event doesn't result in insolvency. This creates an incentive to "go-for-broke" by taking even more risk because there is even less to lose and more to gain if insolvency can be averted. But if credit costs reduced the net portfolio yield by only one percent the extreme leverage would multiply the loss to equity holders commensurately.

Shareholders who believe that the government will bail them out even in this event are even less risk-averse than those expecting liquidation. For example, because Fannie Mae had been allowed to operate indefinitely while insolvent, F&F shareholders may have had a reasonable expectation of such treatment, but accounting rules adopted in the late 1990s made their insolvency somewhat more transparent. Those banks that were considered TBTF also had a reasonable expectation of operating while technically insolvent based on their experience with Latin American loans in the 1980s, and investment banks based on the experience with the bail-out of the Long Term Capital Management hedge fund in the 1990s.

At extreme leverage ratios, e.g., 100-1, technical insolvency becomes increasingly likely. Once technically insolvent, there is an incentive for managers to go beyond "broke", looting the firm of cash in all manner of ways before the operation is shut down. This is what S&Ls were accused of doing (discussed below), taking advantage of delayed recognition of insolvency, using regulatory-facilitated leverage to go-for-broke, then going beyond broke, and magnifying the subsequent losses of the shareholders and creditors!

E: Mission Regulation Undermines Prudential Regulation

What did taxpayers get in return for providing these capital subsidies? Housing goals!

As a result of the 1968 Act, the Secretary of HUD had to report annually to Congress on the progress toward reaching a congressionally determined annual production goal from 1970 through

1979 that was based on a timber industry forecast of the number of trees the industry would need to plant to meet lumber demands. As the Secretary lacked the command and control tools of his/her soviet counterparts the delivery of the annual report was inevitably a surreal scene: year after year, the HUD Secretary traipsed up the Capitol steps with a 3" binder to report on why the industry failed to meet the production goals, and year after year, Congress made the Secretary promise to do better the next year. Democratic administrations typically used this opportunity to plug for more money for public construction, while Republicans used it to advocate for greater tax incentives for private sector production, but—regardless of which party was in power—meeting housing goals became the agency's political mission.

A key player in developing the goals for the 1968 Act was Leon Weiner, an East Coast housing developer who was at the time president of the National Association of Homebuilders (NAHB), which represented primarily single-family builders. In 1974 Weiner became president of the National Housing Conference, a group formed in the Depression to promote public housing, something the 1968 Housing Goals had avoided doing. During the election of 1980 Weiner approached President Carter with a promise: Weiner could deliver the campaign support of developers and building contractors if Carter agreed to support a presidential Housing Commission—without input from OMB or Treasury to avoid imposing fiscal reality on the promise of future funds for public housing construction. This commission would be sure to confirm sufficient "housing needs" to justify a massive construction program. When President Carter agreed, another ten years of housing goals were imminent, but this time the HUD Secretary was to have the tools necessary to meet them.

However, the day before President Carter signed the legislation authorizing the President's Commission on Housing in the Rose Garden, the Reagan campaign upstaged the event with a press release asserting that if elected Reagan would form a Housing Commission. This was intended as a forgotten campaign tactic, but after his inauguration Reagan named Samuel Pierce as HUD Secretary; from his first day, Pierce was deluged with requests from Republican supplicants seeking appointment to the Commission, so there was no avoiding it. While the result was likely to be quite different than that of a Democratic-appointed commission, Republican support for the original annual housing goals made this Commission a dangerous undertaking.

The White House quickly took control of appointments to the Commission, being sure to name people it felt it could trust to stick relatively closely to market principles. It was, after all, a Presidential Commission. In order to ward off the repeat possibility of "Republican social engineering" the Commission's chairman, William McKenna, appointed a sub-committee to produce a Commission "mission statement"—and named Maury Mann, a former deputy OMB Director under President Nixon, to chair it. The sub-committee met in private; when the first meeting in Washington, D.C. was leaked to the "affordable housing" lobby, lobbyists showed up in force but were repelled. The first order of business at the next meeting of the full Commission was to adopt the mission statement, which promised to adhere to "market principles," with the objective of nipping potential Republican social engineering financed with opaque subsidies in the bud.

The Commission recommended phasing out the GSEs, relying instead on private capital market access, but by this time the GSEs were already too politically powerful. It also recommended phasing out FHA, as had the Ford Administration. But - as will be discussed in detail below - the S&Ls were phased out instead. During the ensuing Reagan and George H. W. Bush years, the Treasury Department was the major instrument of housing policy. Homeowners got the mortgage interest deduction while rental housing received a variety of tax deductions and credits.

Budget support for home ownership has been infrequent and negligible. Tax support - the mortgage interest tax deduction (actually the failure to tax imputed rent, done only in Belgium, the Netherlands and Switzerland)—was inadvertent but politically difficult to reverse. But the anti-urban bias reflected in homeownership support policies was diminishing during the 1970s and 1980s for several reasons. First, the rise of condominium ownership reduced, and eventually virtually eliminated, the physical distinction between owner and rental housing, with urban apartments historically typifying the latter. Second, the tremendous tax advantages to owner (relative to rental) housing in the 1970s were largely eliminated by the 1981 Economic Recovery Tax Act; subsequently, depreciation of rental housing accelerated, while disinflation reduced the relative value of the owner subsidy.

During the 1970s, HUD looked to Fannie Mae—primarily a single-family lender—to promote housing goals. Conflicts between Fannie Mae's private and public roles were evident from the very beginning. Nixon fired Fannie's first CEO, Ray Lapin, and replaced him with a politician, former Republican Congressman Oakley Hunter. In 1981 Hunter was replaced by David Maxwell, HUD's general counsel from 1970-1973 who leveraged that position into the CEO of Ticor Mortgage Insurance from 1973 to 1981 (Ticor mortgage insurance slipped into bankruptcy five years later.)[46] Fannie Mae became technically insolvent under Maxwell's watch, which did not stop him from receiving a severance package in 1991 estimated to be about $30 million—huge even by "private sector" standards at the time, and enough to attract the attention and anger of Congress.

HUD Secretary Patricia Harris was nominally responsible for prudential regulation of Fannie Mae from 1976-1979, but virtually no resources were devoted to that effort, even as Fannie Mae dramatically increased interest rate risk. Secretary Harris was more interested in having women and minorities appointed to Fannie Mae's Board of Directors, something strenuously opposed by then Chairman Hunter, than their financial risk. Secretary Harris soon discovered she had no direct authority in that regard, but she did have leverage as the 1968 Act had given the Secretary authority to impose "affordable housing goals" reflecting its housing and urban mission. In 1978, she proposed that 30 percent of Fannie Mae loans had to go to low-income and central-city households. The opposition was overwhelming—1,217 comments were filed against it, while only 16 were filed in support—so much weaker, non-binding goals were ultimately put into effect. No such goals were adopted for the public FHA insurance fund for which Harris was responsible or the then-public Freddie Mac regulated by the FHLB Board.[47]

Political concerns with discrimination beyond that based on reasonable borrower underwriting criteria or property value were legitimate in the 1960's, and resulted in the Fair Housing Act of 1968. The Equal Credit Opportunity Act of 1974 was more specific as to what criteria a lender could and could not use to determine borrower and property qualification for a loan. Strictly interpreted, these laws didn't require lenders to make unsound or unprofitable loans. By the mid-1970s, it was possible to conclude that competition alone had already adequately addressed the problem.

Urban areas still got relatively less home mortgage credit than suburbs in the early 1970s; lenders argued that this was only prudent given the risk. The Community Reinvestment Act (CRA) of 1977 purportedly reflected a concern that local bankers were not lending "enough" in their communities or neighborhoods, which were typically characterized by ethnic and/or racial concentrations. Economists have since provided *ex post* "market failure" rationalizations for housing goals. Because older inner city neighborhoods often had a much higher percentage of African Americans—and, later, other racial minorities—the implicit concern of regulators and economists was with illegal racial discrimination. The *ex post* theory behind these goals was that there was a sufficient supply of creditworthy borrowers in those areas, but that lenders were blinded by prejudice and would not extend credit. Because incomes were also generally much lower in older inter-city neighborhoods, and the risk of a systemic decline in property values much greater, it was generally difficult to distinguish illegal racial profiling from legal credit discrimination. Lenders argued that they were just being prudent, as required by regulation.

The evidence favors the lenders' explanation. Delinquency and default rates for approved borrowers were higher, not lower, than the average for all borrowers. Rates and fees may have been somewhat higher, but the return on equity was generally lower. The banks were essentially being asked to succeed where FHA had failed during the prior decade, when it resorted to redlining to mitigate risk.

Politicians, regulators and many economists still viewed the mortgage markets as if Frank Capra's depiction of a Depression-era S&L in the film *It's a Wonderful Life*—in which residents of Bedford Falls depend only on savings & loan owner George Bailey to determine whether or not they get credit, and at what price—were a documentary reflection of the market of the day. The reality of the home mortgage market was quite different than that implied by political legislation or the economic models on which such legislation relied. Home mortgage lending was characterized by cut-throat competition. Instead of community bankers, the market was already being dominated by the originate-to-sell model, even within the banking and S&L industry. Mortgage banking consisted of two very different functions: origination and loan servicing.

Competition in the mortgage banking industry was cut-throat because little capital was required to originate and therefore the barrier to entry was low. One way to keep costs down was to rely on independent mortgage brokers. Because there were no scale economies to origination a firm with a single loan officer could originate loans. The independent mortgage broker got paid on commissions, so his incentive was most often diametrically opposite that of the investor. He was generally not concerned with the lender's yield or the long-term credit performance of the loan, and would shop the loan to the cheapest lender to increase the likelihood of closing the loan. One mortgage banker, Angelo Mazolo (the CEO of Countrywide) took a different approach. He avoided the conflict of interest between brokers and commissioners by bringing all the loan brokers in house, paying them a salary and bonus instead of commissions. But his subsequent scale increased investor competition for the loans.

By the end of the 1977, there were literally thousands of potential loan brokers who would profit from originating and selling loans originated in older inner-city neighborhoods so long as they could be underwritten to the standards of the most liberal investors nationwide. FHA was one among many ways to finance them. Local branch offices of banks were rarely responsible for mortgage lending in any event, so the decision generally was not made locally. Moreover, banks decided whether to sell or to hold mortgages for portfolio independently, in competition with other investors. So while there was plenty of competition to make good loans, this was unlikely to be reflected in the portfolio of any "community" banker or lending practice of any bank branch.

But Senator Proxmire, then Chairman of the Senate Committee on Banking, Housing and Urban Affairs, promoted the Home Mortgage Disclosure Act (HMDA) of 1975 on the premise that local branches should lend more locally and that more data couldn't hurt. Opponents didn't see it that way: since HMDA did not require collection of data on lender risk, the HMDA data could only show the existence of "disparate impact"—that minorities and urban areas received less credit than their proportion of the population—without providing any insight into whether that impact was driven by prudence or discrimination. As it was already known that rates of credit denial showed "disparate impact" on minorities in urban areas, it was widely suspected that the true motive for collecting more data under HMDA was to eventually use it as a club to allocate credit.

As late as 1992 the Boston Federal Reserve Bank—whose president, Richard Syron, would later become CEO of Freddie Mac—argued that discrimination persisted, and this produced political pressure for compensatory credit allocation to minorities.[48] While most academics treated this as serious research, the lending industry viewed it as a political foundation for credit allocation. The study alleged discrimination based on differences due to one credit factor only, the applicant's debt to income ratio. Lenders and regulators recognized that there was much more that went into the lending decision, e.g., the stability of income and the historic track record on repayment, to name just a few underwriting criteria.

Subsequently Deputy Attorney General of the Department of Justice Deval Patrick argued in 1994 that any final lending distribution that contained racial disparities—disparate impact—relative to population (racial being the only kind of disparity he was interested in) should be assumed to be a violation of federal law unless the lender could prove otherwise. As Federal Reserve Board Chairman, Alan Greenspan argued that banks should discriminate on the basis of risks and price accordingly as they had always done. An article by Joanne Pierson "Navigating the Shoals between Alan and Deval" captures the essential conflict between prudential regulation and credit allocation.[49] Such "proof" of non-discrimination would be difficult at best to produce, since the disparity itself is considered proof of racial prejudice which is impossible to analyze or disprove. Furthermore, the cost of a legal defense is generally crippling. The alternative to litigation is to err on the side of leniency and sign DOJ quota agreements when required to do so.[50] This was called "confiscation by consent decree" at the time and later in a related context "extortion by consent decree."[51]

HUD was charged with enforcing laws prohibiting racial discrimination in addition to the DOJ. Moreover, while the government's direct lending programs had been scaled back to minimize budget impact, HUD had the capacity to direct credit to worthy borrowers who would otherwise be discriminated against through FHA, which it administered. But politicians and bureaucrats understood that failure to extend credit was most often might not be due to prejudice, but rather a sound appraisal of risks. In FHA's case, pricing additional credit risk was also actuarially difficult, because adverse selection was a major obstacle to raising borrower rates to cover the extra risk. Moreover, HUD was more directly responsible for FHA actuarial soundness than for Fannie Mae and not at all responsible for the soundness of the recently privatized Freddie Mac.

FHA passed all their capital subsidy on to borrowers but there was no such requirement for Fannie and Freddie, who had strong incentives to retain it for shareholders and management or spend it on political patronage. Estimates vary widely on how much of the Fannie and Freddie subsidy got passed on to borrowers. The early studies beginning with Hendershott and Villani (1975), and Kane and Foster (1986) and Hendershott and Shilling (1989) concluded that Fannie and later Freddie were only passing through a fraction of their capital subsidy to reduce mortgage rates. Hendershott and Shilling found that borrowers of conforming conventional loans paid .25 percent less than borrowers of otherwise comparable loans.[52] Federal Reserve economist William Passmore (2004) estimated the Fannie and Freddie passed on only 7 basis points (.07 percent).[53]

One thing was certain: Fannie and Freddie only passed on to borrowers enough to maintain a monopoly, passing the surplus on to shareholders, managers and politicians. How much were these groups able to extract from Fannie and Freddie due to the status in the market their agency status granted? Management compensation was commensurate with Wall Street—and the risk managers assumed was much lower. The GSEs made excellent returns for their shareholders for decades. And according to Gretchen Morgenson and Joshua Rosner, politicians received largess from the two firms worth hundreds of millions of dollars (2011). All together, Dwight M. Jaffee and John M. Quigley (2008, p 122) estimate that 50 percent of the value of agency status went to these three groups—in other words, they received as much of the value of agency status as homeowners themselves did. So in 1992 transparent explicit housing policy goals focused on both Fannie and Freddie to force a larger borrower subsidy.

The (ironically named) Federal Housing Enterprises Financial Safety and Soundness Act (FHEFSSA) Part 2, Subpart B required Fannie and Freddie "to provide ongoing assistance to the secondary market for residential mortgages (including activities relating to mortgages on housing for low- and moderate-income families involving a reasonable economic return that may be less than the return earned on other activities)." The act established three specific housing policy goals:

(1) the Low- and Moderate-Income Housing Goal, to assist households with income at or below a geographic area's median income,

(2) the Special Affordable Goal, to assist households with incomes at or below 60 percent of the area's median income, and

(3) the Underserved Areas Goal, to benefit households in low-income census tracts.

Implicit in the legislation's language specifying that return "may be less than the return earned on other activities" is the acknowledgement of higher credit losses not actuarially paid for with higher mortgage rates, especially for the second and third goals. The term "secondary market" first used in conjunction with the 1938 Fannie Mae "secondary market facility" was by now a euphemism for wholesale portfolio lending.

A major change came in 1994, when President Bill Clinton directed HUD to boost the homeownership rate to an "all time high by the end of the century." HUD responded by requiring that Fannie and Freddie direct at least 30 percent of their loan financing to households whose income was at or below the area median. HUD Secretary Henry Cisneros, in the National Homeownership Strategy of 1995, set an additional goal to raise the homeownership rate to 70 percent. The U.S. homeownership rate had increased from about 45 percent after World War II to about 65 percent by 1975, where it remained for two decades in spite of the tremendous expansion of the GSEs. That is, even with mortgage credit generally available with low or no down payment, and often underwritten at a below-market teaser interest rate, and with no evidence of qualified borrowers systematically being denied credit, the homeownership rate had not risen during the quarter century of GSE expansion. Hence, reaching Cisneros's 70 percent target would seem to require major outreach and, presumably, additional larger subsidies to expand the market from the bottom up.

By 2000, HUD had increased the percentage of Fannie and Freddie's financing required to go to households at or below an area's median income from 30 to 42 percent, supporting the Low- and

Moderate-Income Housing Goal. HUD further required that one-third of that money be directed to those households with less than 60 percent of the area's median income, supporting the Special Affordable Goal.

The Federal Savings and Loan Insurance Corporation (FSLIC) was abolished by the Financial Institution Regulation and Reform Enforcement Act (FIRREA) Act of 1989, and the FHLBs who also served S&Ls exclusively should have suffered the same fate. Instead, they found a new mission: lending to banks. Within little more than a decade banks accounted for about two thirds of their membership. What did they offer banks? Cheap money often collateralized with junk-level collateral. Rather than reject collateral outright, the FHLBs would simply require more than enough to cover their risk. The more they required, the less coverage was offered for FDIC-insured liabilities in the event of a bank failure. Hence the FHLBs continued to exist only to facilitate regulatory arbitrage. For political cover, 10 percent of their profits were set aside for an "Affordable Housing Program" with grants disbursed by a 15 member advisory council.

The social lending goals made explicit for the GSEs what was implicit in the goals for other originators: the desire to require lenders to extend credit to low-income households without adequate compensation. Contrary to the 1970s theory that prejudice was to blame for limited credit for lower-income households, the fact is that credit was constrained because too many of these borrowers defaulted, reducing the profitability of lending to them. Policymakers wanted this lending to continue nonetheless, but would not budget subsidies to cover the losses or to make home-buying more affordable for these borrowers. Instead, they implied that the cost of the subsidy was to be financed out of the "franchise value" of the lenders conferred by public protection.

The justification for imposing binding quotas on banks is the same as for GSEs: to share the capital subsidy with creditworthy mortgage borrowers. But withholding permission to branch or otherwise engage in profitable business is perverse. Moreover, while the risk of extorting more than the subsidies are worth is the same as for Fannie and Freddie, the consequences of doing so with the providers of the nation's payment mechanism are orders of magnitude greater. Commercial banks have special government charters and deposit insurance due to their key role in the payments mechanism, so banks will seek regulatory protection from regulators in return for these subsidies, most easily provided by encouraging them to be "too-big-to-fail" (TBTF). Politicians were playing a dangerous game that was clearly not in the public interest.

F. Agency Status Crowds Out Private Portfolio Lenders and Mortgage Insurers

Thrift institutions specializing in mortgage lending—S&Ls and savings banks—had been the backbone of the mortgage-lending industry for the century prior to GSE securitization, rather than diversified commercial banks. Deposit rate regulation introduced for demand deposits at commercial banks in the 1950s (Reg Q) was extended to S&Ls in the 1960s. Thrifts were granted regulatory authority to encroach upon what had historically been banks' turf by offering money market accounts in the 1970s, and they had the competitive advantage of being allowed to pay interest. But rates were still capped, and when market rates rose in the late 1970s, Merrill Lynch developed a form of cash management account that paid market interest rates while providing check-cashing privileges. This extended the payments mechanism further to investment banks and, ultimately, other "shadow" banks. Money-market funds became a boom industry when interest rates rose and deposit institutions were "disintermediated" by deposit outflows. Advances from the FHLB helped maintain thrift liquidity, but deposit rate ceilings channeled a significant share of conventional mortgage funding to Fannie and Freddie.

Once privatized, Fannie and Freddie dropped any interest in being mere secondary market facilities. They spent lavishly on politicians to maintain their legal and regulatory advantages in the conforming loan market, fearing the competition of retail portfolio lenders and private label securitizers. Ultimately they prevailed against both. Because agency status trumps deposit insurance—a consequence of more liberal capital requirements—Fannie and Freddie determined both lending rates and loan quality in the markets in which they operated. Banks and others funded the non-conforming (i.e. not eligible for Fannie and Freddie purchase) "jumbo" loan market. FHA undercut them all with Ginnie Mae financing, assuring a virtual monopoly in its allocated market segment.

High mortgage rates due to a significant inflation premium and the tax deductibility of home mortgage interest led to rapidly rising house prices relative to inflation during the 1970s. Kevin Villani (the author) held a conference on this issue in April 1980 and published the proceedings (with John Tuccillo) *House Prices and Inflation*, which described why house prices wouldn't go back down.[54] Credit risk ceased to be a problem as a consequence of this inflation but this was replaced with interest rate risk. The luncheon speaker, Fed Board of Governors member Henry Wallich, titled his luncheon address "The High Cost of Trying to Help Housing" that addressed the unintended negative consequences of implicit housing subsidies creating a house price bubble.

As a result of the sharp increase in short-term interest rates in the late 1970s and early 1980s, federally chartered S&Ls became technically insolvent – a consequence of the Fed regulations limiting them to FRMs. While Salomon Brothers would later introduce an interest-rate swap for fixed-rate loans that were already underwater—the first "derivative"—this invention did not come in time to save the S&Ls. In 1982, Freddie Mac introduced the "Guarantor" program; this program essentially sold government backing for portfolio mortgages to thrifts for a small fee, allowing those thrifts to get regulatory capital relief by treating their mortgage portfolio as government securities. This "regulatory arbitrage" was a harbinger of things to come, but Freddie Mac's capital relief was not enough to save the S&L industry.

Fannie Mae's strategy of borrowing short and lending long made it deeply insolvent as well[55]—a problem which became increasingly obvious to investors as rates stayed high throughout the early 1980s. [56] But its implicit government backing encouraged investors to continue to finance it, and regulators at HUD with implicit political approval encouraged it to grow out of its problem covering past losses with future profits rather than embarrass politicians with a public declaration of insolvency. Fannie Mae decided to load up on credit risk in the mid-1980s, the revenues from which were intended to cover the interest rate bets. This backfired as credit losses soared. But Fannie Mae's disclosure requirements at the time were minimal, and a government agency doesn't have to stop issuing debt until HUD or the Treasury Department says so.

Had this same political forbearance been extended to the S&L industry, the arguably could have survived as well. But whereas politicians had allowed Fannie Mae to "grow out" of insolvency, they couldn't wait for both Fannie Mae and S&Ls to do so. They had to pick a winner.

In 1981, Fannie and Freddie had a combined seven percent market share, a $65 billion portfolio, and $21 billion in MBS pool guarantees. A decade later, their market share had grown to almost 30 percent, their portfolio to almost $155 billion, and MBS guarantees to $715 billion. The thrift industry was largely gone, replaced by the GSEs; the few remaining large thrifts were indistinguishable from commercial banks. Meanwhile, the shadow banking industry spawned by deposit rate ceilings had grown in size to rival the commercial banking industry, and subsequently became a source of funds for mortgages.

The prevailing view of why the S&Ls failed in 1989 is much the same as that for sub-prime lenders several decades later: deregulation and greed. Of course moral hazard was a problem, as the industry was highly leveraged, and many economists argued that this caused the industry to "go for broke" as a result. Some economists even argued that the cause of the systemic failure was that S&Ls purposely tried to "go broke," with management "looting" the already failed and sure-to-be-closed thrifts.[57] This theory even resulted in the jailing of 1980s poster-boy Charles Keating of Lincoln Savings and Loan in Phoenix who among other things was charged with transferring assets out of his S&L after it was technically insolvent but still in operation What enabled looting of insolvent institutions was FHLB Board regulatory policy to keep "zombie" S&Ls open to avoid the loss to the insurance fund, with academics and other rent-seeking political appointees in charge. But the government spent an unprecedented amount on "looting" prosecutions in the search for scapegoats in the wake of the savings and loan debacle, with little to show for the effort.[58]

The S&L deregulation started with the prohibition on deposit rates, without which S&Ls were unable to meet withdrawal demands. By the early 1980s, virtually the entire S&L industry was underwater, and the reason was entirely political. As already noted, federally chartered S&Ls were forced into an interest rate maturity mismatch by Senator Proxmire's Banking Committee. That refused to allow S&Ls to invest in anything other than fixed-rate mortgages. State-chartered S&Ls had issued mostly adjustable-rate loans, minimizing the maturity mismatch.

The industry subsequently did "go for broke" as predicted, but this too was at least partially caused by explicit federal policy. The Federal Deposit Insurance Corporation increased the deposit insurance coverage maximum from $40,000 to $100,000 even while capital requirements were lowered. The Garn-St. Germain Depository Institutions Act—passed in 1982—is cited by some as Reagan-era deregulation which caused the thrift industry's failure.[59] In fact, Garn-St. Germain was an attempt to diversify out of the politically risky mortgage market into commercial real estate and high-yield bond investments. S&Ls utilized them as desired: the share of S&L assets in home mortgages plunged from 73 percent in 1981 to 57 percent in 1985. Most S&Ls chose commercial real estate, but the market was far too small relative to the magnitude of the funds S&Ls needed to redeploy, leading to extensive overbuilding. The real estate cycle was amplified by the stimulus provided by the Economic Recovery Tax Act of 1981—stimulus subsequently reversed by the Tax Reform Act of 1986.[60] Defaults on commercial mortgages played a significant role in subsequent failures due to the politically induced property bubble bursting.[61]

A few S&Ls chose to redeploy into high-yield bonds. Realized losses from bond defaults played no role in the subsequent failures, but regulatory enforcement of mark-to-market accounting for loans held for investment did.[62] FIRREA reversed Garn St Germaine, requiring an orderly liquidation of the bonds. But the FIRREA Conference Committee had noted that bonds held for investment should be held at book value, as was required at the time under generally accepted accounting principles. Otherwise the liquidation which predictably would force bond prices down would force capital write downs at a time when there were no markets, causing institutions to fail and market prices to collapse. But regulators at the FHLB of San Francisco ignored this provision, requiring the bonds to be marked to market during the forced liquidation down to a level of about half their *ex post* realized value—a level that essentially implied a 100 percent default rate with normal recoveries from bankruptcy.[63]

In any event, these powers had come too late as the S&Ls were already technically insolvent. These events validated the prediction of numerous congressionally mandated study commissions spanning four decades: that political distortion of this industry would eventually but inevitably lead to systemic failure.[64] Politicians nevertheless claimed they didn't see this failure coming and blamed greedy thrift owners (in spite of the fact that most thrift institutions were non-profit mutual institutions) and their managers (of which courts subsequently found virtually no evidence of guilt).

Private mortgage insurers fared no better in competition with FHA than S&Ls did in competition with GSEs. HUD has never required FHA to pay a dividend, and FHA pays no income tax either, two huge subsidies over PMIs even if run in an "actuarially sound" manner as defined by the government. As with the S&Ls, the PMIs were only able to compete in that segment of the market from which FHA was restricted by law or regulation, but unlike S&Ls they had benefited from the growth of Fannie and Freddie who required PMI coverage. The HUD report on the future of the FHA written in 1974 at the tail end of the Ford Administration, argued that with the reincarnation of the PMIs this government-sponsored fund was no longer needed. That report was never sent to Congress, however, and a new report was written in the early days of the Carter Administration that argued that FHA was the proper tool for addressing "under-served" markets, whatever that might mean.

The only "under-served" borrowers were those with weaker credit. PMI competition eliminated the ability of FHA to cross-subsidize - what FHA called "cream-skimming." Had they attempted to price for risk the resulting adverse selection would have bankrupted the general insurance fund, just as it had the special insurance fund the prior decade, if not for the massive Ginnie Mae subsidies and other advantages of government ownership discussed above. And as with Fannie and Freddie, the government made no serious attempt to estimate these subsidies until the 1990s, and what estimates it eventually made were relatively low. Nevertheless, after the housing price bubble of the late 1970s deflated the FHA insurance fund had lost about $6 billion.[65]

In 1978, Ginnie Mae proposed issuing a conventional pass-through security for mortgage bankers to complement Freddie Mac's conventional participation certificate for savings and loans. Their reasoning was that since Ginnie Mae didn't guarantee the credit risk in any event, there was no additional risk to the government. Of course, the markets did not see it that way, and the idea was eventually dropped in the face of bureaucratic opposition.[66] Had the proposal been implemented, it likely would have put an end to Fannie and Freddie and removed the veil of privatization—and the market distortions that came with it – as FHA and Ginnie Mae had no private shareholders to satisfy or politicians to satisfy.

Even with the rate advantage provided by Ginnie Mae, FHA still had to compete with the PMIs on down payments. As the down-payment requirements for PMI-insured conventional loans remained relatively constant (between 5 percent and 10 percent), the FHA minimum down payment had been lowered from 20 percent to 5 percent in 1950 and 3 percent in 1961. FHA covered a lender's entire loss, the Veterans Administration covered the top 20 percent, and PMI covered the top 25 percent—but these differences were generally insignificant: in practice, very few loans resulted in losses greater than 20-25 percent unless they had been fraudulently underwritten to begin with.

Low down payment loans require much more careful underwriting. Both FHA/VA and the PMIs maintained local underwriting presence and rigorous underwriting guidelines to compensate for low down payments. FHA and the PMIs both "assure" risks with *ex ante* risk mitigation measures to minimize the potential for moral hazard associated with insuring borrowers with little or no equity at stake and "insure" remaining risks through diversification and capital adequacy. The fundamental principle of insurance is that the remaining credit risk can be diversified and actuarially priced based on the uncorrelated nature of default risk among the individual loans in a pool. Further, PMI, FHA, and the VA all had to meet statutory capital requirements (set by state insurers, HUD, and the VA, respectively).

Since mortgage insurance is written in nominal terms, falling home prices present a systemic risk; generally rising prices increase borrower equity and reduce default risk, while generally falling house prices have the opposite effect, especially if the loans are without recourse to the borrower's other sources of wealth. The difference between mortgage loan insurance and mortgage pool insurance such as that provided by Fannie and Freddie is that the option is not very far out of the money as it is first loss. As most PMIs were historically monoline companies like FHA, the risk of falling house prices was hard to capitalize and hence the risk threatened solvency. Just as the deflation that raised the real payment burden, combined with systemic unemployment, bankrupted private insurers in the Great Depression, the inflation of the 1970s, combined with FHA, bailed them out.

An alternative theory to insurance is that each borrower has a "put option" to default when house prices fall sufficiently to erode borrower equity. In 1984, Chet Foster, then chief actuary of FHA and Robert Van Order, an economist at HUD and later Freddie Mac were the first to discuss borrower default as a "put option" in 1986.[67] Their concept was that without recourse, borrowers would default at will when homeowner equity turned negative due to falling house prices. However, throughout the 1980s and 90s, there was little evidence of the "put" option motivating so-called "strategic" defaults when a borrower's equity became negative, and so private mortgage insurers continued to insure.

House prices were relatively stagnant in the 1980s so there was neither inflation to reduce default nor deflation to cause it, but down payment requirements and underwriting guidelines had become more liberal during the prior inflationary decade. Credit risk did pose a concern to insurers. The PMIs raised premiums numerous times, but in order to prevent what would have otherwise been overwhelming adverse selection they also significantly tightened underwriting guidelines. They completely stopped insuring investor loans; loans with cash-out refinancing; loans with deep buy-downs; and loans in regions with a weak economy due to a systemic risk factor, e.g. the oil patch.[68] Even these steps didn't save every PMI, but the industry as a whole survived the decade.

FHA's strategy throughout the 1980s was generally the opposite that of the PMIs. FHA first lowered insurance premiums, and then, when it subsequently raised them, allowed borrowers to finance the higher premium in the loan amount, resulting in negative borrower equity at origination. Moreover, by 1988–1989, investor loans and loans with an initial loan-to-value ratio above 95 percent accounted for more than half of FHA's business. The combination of adverse selection and systemic risk left the fund technically insolvent and clearly actuarially unsound. It would require a legislative bailout in the form of the 1990 Cranston –Gonzalez National Affordable Housing Act.

But the availability of mortgage insurance meant that credit risk was not a big concern of investors by 1990. The FHA fund was bailed out, protecting Ginnie Mae. And the losses investors (mostly Fannie and Freddie) bore due to PMI failure were minimal. Investors were protected.

One drawback to private mortgage insurance was that premiums were not tax deductible until 2008, whereas the interest on a second mortgage used for a down payment was. Second mortgages became even more popular in the 1980s when interest on consumer loans was no longer deductible. The subsequent growth of the market for second mortgages and home equity loans would play a big role in supplanting the PMIs in a later era.

G. Housing Goals Coerce TBTF Banks and Solidify GSE Monopoly by the End of the Century

Banks and Fannie and Freddie were generally profitable in the 1980s and extremely profitable in the 1990s. This was not a reflection of the profitability of meeting housing goals, but of the way in which they were able to exploit franchise value to cover the costs. By the end of the 1990s, these goals had led to the growth of sub-prime mortgages- establishing both their quantity and their price – that was responsible for subsequent decline in profitability and ultimately losses.

With thrift competitors largely out of the way by the end of the 1980s, Fannie and Freddie focused on eliminating competition from private label securitizers as well. The PLS subsidy is derived from deposit insurance so it is calculated the same as for banks and S&Ls, but historically with less leverage.

PLS had the potential to be more innovative than the government sponsored agencies. In 1983, First Boston purchased a firm with the technology to originate mortgages straight into private label securities. Fannie and Freddie strongly opposed extending their regulatory exemptions to private-label competitors issuing Real Estate Mortgage Investment Certificates (REMICS), and flexed their political muscle to stop it from occurring. Fannie Mae, in particular, was known to be quite vindictive in kneecapping potential Wall Street competition. By the early 1980s Fannie and Freddie were both the biggest customers of the Wall Street investment houses and their biggest competitors. Fannie and Freddie had monopoly power, like the U.S. Treasury, and could negotiate low underwriting fees, but Wall Street firms earned lucrative underwriting fees on sheer volume. Similarly, the bid-asked spread was much narrower for Fannie and Freddie than for corporate securities, but this could be made up with speculation—driven trading volume. Underwriting spreads were more lucrative for PLS, but the investment banks were leery of losing a sure thing with Fannie and Freddie for the potential profits of private securitization.

At the end of the day, agency status still trumped private-label securitization, especially if exploited with risky strategies. During the 1990s, private label securitizers found ways to exploit the credit rating dependent risk-based regulations and the moral hazard of deposit insurance expanded across the financial markets, but they didn't compete directly with Fannie and Freddie business.

Hence from the shareholders' perspective, Fannie and Freddie were quite successful during the 1980s and 1990s, consistently generating returns on equity in the 25–30 percent range and often higher. Reflecting these high returns, Fannie Mae's stock price quintupled between 1990 and 2000. However, the Fed's Passmore, in 2004, concluded that these earnings were roughly equal to the value of the subsidy they received. Including the tax subsidy would reveal that Fannie and Freddie generally lost money but for their agency status and resulting capital subsidies. These subsidies allowed any individual lending line to do slightly better than breaking even—extreme leverage would take care of the rest. Internal Fannie and Freddie studies of the 1980s and 1990s concluded that, by using a highly leveraged strategy, they could operate some programs at close to break-even rates and still generate a reasonable ROE. That said, Fannie Mae's "Community Homebuyer Program" still consistently lost money.[69] Lending to lower-income households with little to no down payment, especially those in inner cities, was known to be especially risky, and default rates for such mortgages for Fannie and Freddie in the 1990s were about 50 times that of prime loans.[70] The risk to lending to borrowers with a lower credit score was likewise about 50 times greater.

While the 1992 FHEFSSA allowed Fannie and Freddie to earn "a reasonable economic return that may be less than the return earned on other activities" it did not specify what this meant in practice. If they only needed an average .25 percent ROA to achieve their ROE targets, for example, the Act's wording could reasonably be interpreted to allow them to target a .125 percent ROA (i.e., a mark up of .125% over their cost of funds) for affordable housing goal program—bringing them as close to breaking even as possible. Moreover, charging higher rates for sub-prime lending was not feasible for several reasons. First, adverse selection would quickly set in: higher rates would produce disproportionately riskier loans. Second, charging higher rates to sub-prime borrowers was viewed by regulators as "predatory."

But Fannie and Freddie were wholesalers—their yield reflected the price paid for loans. If they had to immediately sell these loans, the price would reflect a discount to the purchase price to reflect the added risk. At the same time, the originating broker may have charged more in origination fees or excess yield. So it is entirely possible that a goal-qualified borrower could be getting a rate well below-market relative to risk but still be paying more than other borrowers. However, in addition to rules and regulations regarding up front fees and excess yield spread, intense competition among originators for loans sold to Fannie and Freddie presumably minimized this practice.

The historical approach was to cross-subsidize loss lending for affordable housing goals with profitable prime lending. But by the end of the century, Fannie and Freddie had captured the entire prime market within their limits, which amounted to almost half the total mortgage market. Their borrower rates were only slightly better than competitors' (Passmore argues the difference was down to .07 percent by 2000), so raising the cost to prime borrowers would result in a loss of market share. Fannie and Freddie had two choices: first, push more risk down to the PMIs; or second, further exploit their agency status to increase the capital subsidy, primarily by switching from MBS to portfolio loans financed with debt. They did both.

Fannie and Freddie's influence with PMIs was limited to loans, so they bullied the PMIs into insuring loans with only 3 percent down in 1998, and in 2001 pushed them to insure loans with no down payment. In addition, both firms introduced their own versions of automated underwriting, which imposed weaker credit standards on lenders for loans the PMIs had to insure. By 1999, ninety five percent of all loans sold to Fannie and Freddie were underwritten by their automated systems, bypassing the lender and PMI in the risk evaluation process.[71] Given that PMIs relied almost exclusively on Fannie and Freddie business at this time, they had no choice but to accept the additional risk.

In 1991, guarantees accounted for about eighty five percent of Fannie and Freddie's stock of business, with only 15% held in portfolio. By 2002, this had fallen to about fifty five percent, with 45% held in the portfolio, about one and a quarter trillion dollars. The potential interest-rate risk this represented was enormous. Both firms had similar risk management strategies. In the early 1980s—while still public—Freddie Mac set up a broker dealer called the Securities Sales and Trading Group (SS&TG) to make a market for its securities, and this group took on the responsibility for "hedging" as well. But from all appearances, it also underwent the same metamorphosis as investment banks did during this period, engaging in proprietary trading—essentially a hedge-fund activity. Fannie and Freddie's net income from proprietary trading exceeded their net guarantee income for the 1980s and 1990s. As credit and interest rate losses remained low, profits from proprietary trading, interest rate and credit risk were able to subsidize the cost of meeting the affordable housing goals during this period.

The pool of borrowers targeted by bank CRA quotas overlapped significantly with the borrowers targeted by HUDs housing goals for Fannie and Freddie. F&F maintained their capital advantage over banks when making mortgage loans, but banks had many other profitable lending opportunities and profit sources that would allow them to cross-subsidize this competition.

The role of the CRA and HUD in loan originations not intended to be funded by Fannie and Freddie is perhaps the most controversial aspect of the conclusion that housing policy was the subsequent root cause of the financial crisis. In her landmark book, Oonagh McDonald (2012) devotes her first 24-page chapter entirely to the role of CRA. She reviews all the databases of mortgage market research, concluding that "the HMDA data did not serve a useful purpose throughout their history…").[72] As a consequence, she finds the economic studies using HMDA data to be seriously flawed. Fears of HMDA and CRA opponents were essentially confirmed when prudential regulators used poor grades on CRA assessment reports to withhold approval for branching applications in return for meeting credit quotas under CRA. This was particularly ironic as the inability to branch had given rise to the need for deposit insurance and regulation in the first place.

Some aspects of the story McDonald tells are comparable to the story of Fannie and Freddie's role over this period. For example: banks, like Fannie and Freddie, were highly profitable during the 1990s, earning record profits from 1991 through 2001—largely due to the strong economy and capital subsidies. But banks were also much more diversified than Fannie and Freddie, so their profitability did not mean CRA lending was profitable, just that it was more easily cross-subsidized.

President Clinton personally takes credit for the changes he made to the CRA, which resulted in a tenfold increase in CRA commitments from 1977-92 to 1993-2000.[73] Two things account for the ability of consumer groups to extort more out of banks under Clinton. First, CRA reports were confidential until 1989, when the FIRREA made public disclosure a requirement. Having CRA reports on hand gave consumer advocacy groups tremendous lobbying power to use when banks needed discretionary regulatory approval. Second, the Reigle-Neal Interstate Banking and Branching Act of 1994 phased-out legal prohibitions against banking and merging across state lines, giving rise to a surge in merger and acquisition activity as well as branch openings.

Affordable housing advocates primarily used the CRA to extract subsidies from banks—especially those that were too big to fail—because CRA approval was required to expand, acquire, merge or branch. Between 1977, when the act was passed, and 1991, community groups had negotiated a total of $8.8 billion in CRA qualified lending agreements; between 1992 and 2007, by contrast, ACORN and other groups negotiated $4.6 trillion in CRA related commitments. This five-hundred-fold increase was reported both in Wallison's *Dissent* and McDonald's book, but ignored in the 2011 FCIC Report. And CRA lending was by no means limited to meeting the requirements of just these agreements. No bank entering into these agreements could know that all its competitors were employing the same market share expansion strategy—and hence that, as with commercial real estate in the 1980s, the market impact could be devastating.

Data showed that CRA loans had higher rates of delinquency and default—even controlling for race or neighborhood—so banks knew this strategy would have associated costs. Detailed Fed studies showed that CRA loans during the 1990s had higher delinquency rates and were, at best, marginally profitable.[74] But for the most part, these studies only tracked the loans held for investment after they met the CRA assessment need. As banks are most likely to "keep the best and sell the rest," this modest difference proved nothing. Moreover, as servicing defaults is expensive, they are likely to sell "servicing released" to the buyer of the loans. Hence Fed studies of the historical cost of CRA based on retained loans or loans serviced illustrate only that the banks kept the best.

McDonald rejects the argument that sub-prime lending was somehow independent of CRA lending. There is no way to tell from the data how many of these loans counted for CRA qualification at some point; it is possible that virtually all of them did. Moreover, in any event, HUD extended liberalized underwriting standards and relaxed down payment requirements from banks and Fannie and Freddie to the entire market, in recognition that all sub-prime lending served the general housing policy goal of home ownership.[75] The banks were essentially being asked to succeed where FHA had failed during the prior decade when it resorted to redlining to mitigate risk.

Banks' willingness to enter into loan agreements of this magnitude reflected the size of the "economic rents" politicians could collect for prudential regulators allowing banks to do what was in the interest of both the bank and the regulators anyway. From 1982 to 2001, the number of banks was cut in half while the total number of branches doubled. Community action groups also extracted huge fees for the services they would provide to find the borrowers. Even politicians got sweetheart loans in what the loan originators referred to as the "Friends of Angelo" program, which they justified as "nothing special"—an accurate characterization in the context of the trillions of CRA loan commitments being similarly negotiated with political leverage.

The percentage increases in lending to minorities during the 1990s as a result of the CRA are truly astounding. In spite of this political success in 2000 Congress directed the Fed to study the profitability of CRA lending—apparently under the impression that banks were "preying" on low income borrowers by charging higher rates, earning obscene profits to boost their generally high overall profits. The standard they set for "predatory" lending was "higher rates than other borrowers"—not higher rates than other borrowers *of equivalent risk*. Furthermore, this standard failed to acknowledge the differences in rates among different loan types, e.g., whether a loan was fixed or adjustable, and the consequences of the slope of the yield curve for such comparisons. While there was no systemic evidence that even that low standard was met, lenders got the message not to price risk.[76]

The Fed in particular promoted CRA as a useful tool in credit allocation, arguing that such loans would not otherwise have been made. It has since been the most vocal regulator defending these policies. But its studies of CRA profitability are seriously limited and flawed because these studies fail to recognize that loans could be bought and sold to meet CRA criteria. Attempts to argue that sub-prime lending was an independent phenomenon from meeting CRA assessment criteria are equally flawed because they ignore the same factor: loans could be originated by or sold to the bank that needed to meet an assessment criterion, then re-sold either to Fannie and Freddie, another bank, or into a pool to be securitized. There has never been a shred of evidence to suggest that banks were motivated to hold CRA loans (and other sub-prime loans generally) because the potential yield warranted the risk. Clearly, it did not.

In fact, CRA loans had higher default rates, and as a consequence they likely cost banks more in servicing costs (although the data on this point is scant). As with Freddie, they could only be sold in the marketplace at a discount to the acquisition price—the exception, of course, was if loans were instead sold to another bank willing to take a loss in order to fill a need for a CRA accreditation. Banks used their mortgage banks to generate these loans, which in turn often used independent loan brokers to originate them. All of the loans involved in the July 2012 settlement of the Wells Fargo discriminatory pricing suit, for example, were originated by independent brokers.

By the end of the Clinton Administration, the government controlled not only Fannie, Freddie, and the TBTF bank lenders reliant on regulatory discretion, but FHA/Ginnie Mae as well. Even as expanding demand for Fannie and Freddie kept demand for PMI high, FHA—and its financing arm, Ginnie Mae—maintained their monopoly on the market segment Congress had allocated to them, between 15 and 18 percent of the entire mortgage market throughout the 1990s. With the beneficial economic environment and the benefit of the combined subsidies given to FHA and Ginnie Mae, the cohort of FHA loans written between 1991 and 1999 were profitable. Like the banks and Fannie and Freddie, FHA entered the great housing boom of the 2000s in good financial shape.

As S&Ls gradually disappeared during the 1990s, the FHLBs expanded, virtually tripling total membership. Banks now found ways to exploit the regulatory arbitrage of FHLB advances, requiring more excess collateral the greater the credit risk to raise cheap money at the FDIC's expense. FHLB debt outstanding more than tripled from $132 billion in 1995 to $438 billion by the end of the decade. Some of this debt financed traditional advances, but the FHLB also used some of it to buy mortgages without recourse—placing it in direct competition with Fannie and Freddie.

The FIRREA transferred the authority to regulate the FHLBs to the Federal Housing Finance Authority (FHFA), whose board was a political entity consisting of four presidential appointees and the HUD secretary. This arrangement and the fact that the regulator was within HUD made HUD the *de facto* prudential regulator. Not surprisingly, the additional risk FHLB took on during the 1990s, and the additional growth funded by its expansion, facilitated an expansion of its mandate to promote affordable housing.

When Clinton announced his seventy percent home ownership goal in 1994, the homeownership rate was 64 percent—about where it had been for three decades - but maintaining this level in the face of changing demographics and wealth characteristics required underwriting and down-payment requirements to be liberalized to their logical limits. By 2000, it was up marginally to 68 percent. Over that period, the GSEs expanded by 60 percent and added a trillion dollars of mortgage credit. By how much Fannie and Freddie actually promoted home ownership is difficult to say but, the "mission" Fannie and Freddie had been assigned *ex post facto*—to promote homeownership—generally provided good political cover.

But when housing prices started rising in 1997 there were still trillions of dollars committed to financing low-income households by banks—with trillions more committed as a result of HUD, Fannie and Freddie, and FHA policy. It was generally up to the secondary marketing arm of the mortgage banking subsidiaries to originate these loans while minimizing funding costs. At what cost would these commitments be funded? What investors would fund them? Chapter 3 describes how private securitizers of sub-prime loans exploited regulation to compete with Fannie and Freddie and FHA directly during the 2000's, and chapter 4 describes how Fannie and Freddie, FHA and the

FHLBs responded—leading to the sub-prime mortgage debacle that brought down the global financial system.

H. The Greenspan Put

The 1990 recession officially ended in March 1992 (although that was not announced until after the November presidential election). In response to large proposed increases in government expenditures, the republicans picked up 54 seats in the 1994 mid-term elections, controlling the House for the first time since 1954. The economy continued to grow as the US fiscal deficit shrank and was eventually eliminated.

The financial markets had remained very stable since Greenspan's bailout in the wake of the 1987 stock market crash until the Russian default of 1998, which reverberated through global financial markets. Long Term Capital Management (LTCM) was a hedge fund established by former Salomon Brothers proprietary trader John Meriwether to take advantage of what it perceived to be small anomalies in prices of fixed income securities. To do this, it employed massive leverage, sometimes exceeding 1000 to 1, mostly funded with bank repos. While known for having two Nobel Prize winners in Finance on its board and massive modeling capacity, LTCM turns out to have been doing no more than playing the tail risk – betting against an unlikely "black swan" event. The fund failed spectacularly.

Timothy Geitner, then the President of the New York FRB (later to become Secretary of the Treasury and the systemic financial crisis manager) organized a bailout by arm-twisting the TBTF banks and investment banks to socialize the loss by committing $300 million each of their own firm's capital to the bailout. The CEOs, some of whom may have been conflicted as they had personally invested significant sums in LTCM, agreed to contribute their stockholder's capital, but not their own. Lehman, the weak sister at the time, was only asked to pony up $100 million, and Bear Stearns, which was not exposed, notably refused to contribute anything to the bailout fund.

In the immediate aftermath of the LTCM crisis, banks significantly raised haircuts and stopped financing much of their repo activity. This forced a widespread de-leveraging by hedge funds that depressed asset prices and slowed asset backed securitization until significant de-leveraging had occurred. The Fed's role in the aftermath was to flood the market with liquidity and keep interest rates extremely low.

The LTCM bailout and subsequent comments about the Fed's role in the aftermath of a bubble created in investors' minds the perception of a "Greenspan put," a bailout in the event of trouble that many believe exacerbated subsequent moral hazard.[77] Essentially the Fed's thinking was that an immediate hit to the banking system's capital was better than the prolonged uncertainty of a bankruptcy proceeding.[78] The trade-off is the long term economic cost of subsequent moral hazard behavior engendered by a short term bailout. The bailout of LTCM in 1998 arguably (it is hard to know for sure) prevented a more systemic problem to avoid the economic consequences of the aftermath, but whether the precedent was worth the subsequent moral hazard created is questionable.

Chapter 3: The Origins of Private Label Securitization and their Role in Meeting Housing and Home Ownership Goals 2000–2007

As part of a larger government housing policy, the CRA and GSE affordable housing goals sought to stimulate demand for mortgage securities by CRA-regulated banks and GSEs by a combined total of roughly $10 trillion, about half the total mortgage market, during the last decade. As home prices rose, qualifying borrowers would normally have been the first households rationed out of the market. Chapter 2 showed how the government directs investment decisions for F&F – who can fund about 99% of their mortgages at a cost slightly above the Treasury borrowing rate due to their agency status with implicit debt guarantees - and banks - who can fund about 96% of their mortgage acquisitions at an all-in cost that is slightly above the risk-free rate due to deposit insurance

Politicians, regulators and most economists accept the outdated conventional wisdom that rational at-risk investors were still making investment and pricing decisions for the so-called *private* label mortgage backed securities (MBS) market, but F&F and banks were the dominant price-setting investors. The private label securitizers (PLSers) – issuers of private label securities (PLS) - were also largely subsidiaries of regulated commercial or investment banks originating to meet the needs of these regulated investors, so security pricing and capital allocation not longer reflected the underlying fundamentals of borrower mortgage credit characteristics.

To some extent the advent of PLS reflected the ongoing GSE-driven trend to separate mortgage origination and servicing from portfolio investing. The ability of the originator-securitizer to exploit regulatory distortions to strip out cash profits up front while leaving investors with subsequent losses – the cause of the sub-prime debacle of the 1990s – remained a major motivation. But the biggest motivation was the need to find the cheapest funding source for the huge increase in CRA and housing goal driven demand. PLS was the cheapest funding mechanism available due entirely too regulatory arbitrage that lowered capital requirements for pools of first mortgages relative to funding whole loans on the balance sheet funding.

Most of these loans could qualify for CRA accreditation prior to securitization and F&F affordable housing goals after securitization. That's the reason F&F provided between a third and half of the funds for PLS to meet the increased commitments and goals discussed in chapter 2. As a result, political and regulatory policy determined demand and pricing as effectively for PLS as for CRA-driven bank and F&F investments.

Moreover, securitization removed the loans from the direct view of bank examiners and auditors who required reserves up-front whereas investment accounting postponed any expected losses. Other regulatory distortions helped make PLS securitization profitable even when securitizing loans sure to subsequently default, in particular present value accounting which accelerated expected income so PLS funded loans could be profitably originated even if subsequent losses were expected, shifting the ultimate incidence of losses from originator to investor.

The political and regulatory distortions were so great and generally so complicated that even many market participants didn't understand how they were driving behavior. No subsequent analysis has adequately explained them. Weak borrowers were able to employ almost infinite leverage. Lenders made the loans because they were able to do the same. The normal market constraints had all been trumped by political goals, regulators and regulations.

The topic is best approached in steps and from different perspectives. But the focus remains on how regulations distorted capital requirements and returns on equity, motivated largely to fund political housing goals but also reflecting gross regulatory incompetence. It is a story of unintended but inevitable consequences of political failure to fund their policy goals transparently and provide proper regulatory oversight. The story is hard going at times, but the conclusion is irrefutable: *this was no private market failure*.

A: Prudential Regulation Trumps Market Discipline 1970-2000

To summarize the prior discussion of the M&M Theorem, market discipline is imposed *ex ante* by creditors and investors who make independent assessments to estimate the distribution of potential returns and losses. The consensus of market assessments determine each firm's capital and leverage structure which are then reflected in the loan price and the interest rate. Two well intended regulatory interventions, the public certification of credit rating agencies and the adoption of ratings in bank risk based regulation, which was intended to complement market discipline, trumped it instead. In hind sight, government sanction freed PLSers from the discipline that the markets would have imposed by delegating it to private for profit raters without the regulatory oversight that certification implied.

1. the Credit Rating Agencies

Government bonds are relatively simple for investors to understand and evaluate. They are generally treated by regulators as risk-free despite the historical pattern of explicit or implicit government default (by inflating away the real bond value).

Traditionally, corporate bonds were also relatively simple as only large, stable, well capitalized companies could issue bonds with a statistically estimable default risk. Two bond ratings agencies have operated since the nineteenth century and began rating corporate bonds in the early part of the 20th century: Moody's in 1909 and Standard and Poor's predecessor in 1919. The third, Fitch, is only a few years younger founded until 1924. Historically, rating agencies were publishing companies, which sold their opinions to investors. Moody's was bought by the publisher Dun & Bradstreet in 1962 and S&P was bought by McGraw Hill in 1966. [79]

Investors could usually confirm a rating's accuracy by reviewing a simple transparent balance sheet of a large company, and by monitoring the stock, including short positions. At large, investors concluded that investment grade rated bonds were fairly reliable. Occasionally companies would fall below investment grade, a so-called "fallen angel", but this could take decades. By 1970, despite more than half a century of selling dependable opinions, only about ten percent of corporate bonds were publicly registered and rated. Most of the remaining were privately placed with life insurance companies who still made decisions based on what was "prudent". Such bonds rarely traded among long term investors. Life insurance companies had no reason to sell.

Beginning in 1975, with the SEC adoption of Nationally Recognized Statistical Rating Organizations (NRSROs), risk regulators began moving away from what was "prudent" and toward greater reliance on risk-based ratings given by Moody's, S&P, and Fitch, the only raters recognized at the time. Within two decades virtually all securities were publically placed and rated. This SEC policy had an enormous impact on the way markets evaluated risk. Prior to the SEC designation, the rating agencies either didn't rate weak companies or rated those without a sufficient track record as "below investment grade (BBB)". As a result, such companies typically relied on banks for financing. Subsequent to the adoption of NRSRO regulation, Michael Milken of Drexel Burham Lambert started issuing bonds that were rated junk when issued. This method of finance effectively replaced bank loans for riskier companies which were more highly leveraged. These events converted published "opinions" into a legally approved sanction and created a three-tiered new-issue market of senior investment grade (AAA/AA), mezzanine investment grade (A/BBB) and below investment grade (BB/or below). The Secondary Mortgage Market Enhancement Act (SMMEA) of 1984 extended the NRSRO designation to privately issued MBS, which unlike junk bonds didn't have a market-based tracking mechanism.

But regulators created a huge incentive conflict with certification. Now that ratings were virtually mandatory, all investors would be required to pay for them. But under pressure from unions who mistakenly believed that requiring issuers to pay rather than investors would improve the net yield on public pensions and raise their retirement benefit, the SEC required that issuers had to pay for the rating.[80] This was disastrous for investors. Issuers could shop among raters until it got a favorable opinion. The raters and all their employees made out well, reaping in a few short bubble years what historically was a lifetime of normal earnings. Regulators forced investors to accept bad models. Whether or not intentional, bad models offered good political cover for the raters' conflict of interest.

2. Regulation and Risk-based Capital Requirements

The SMMHA went beyond the NRSRO designations to improve the regulatory environment for private MBS, enabling federally chartered institutions to purchase investment grade PLS without limit. It pre-empted state laws and regulations so that state chartered and regulated financial institutions of all types could do the same, and removed state registration requirements. In addition, the Fed had extended the privilege of pledging MBS as margin collateral to PLS the year before. All this paved the way for a truly national market as initially sought at the creation of the Ginnie Mae PC.

But the real damage done by the raters came later. Bank regulators became increasingly reliant on ratings and subsequently embedded them in the Basel I risk-based capital rules in 1988 which govern commercial bank capital and GSE regulators followed suite. Rules for commercial banks set the basic capital requirement at 8% tier one capital, only half of which had to be equity. On balance sheets, commercial bank deposit funding required a 50% risk weighting (4% capital) for whole mortgage loans. This was predicated on the historical experience of well underwritten borrowers having a 20% down-payment or private mortgage insurance (PMI). But rules were even more favorable for investment grade securities: a 20% risk weighting (1.6% capital) for AAA and AA rated securities, a 50% risk weighting for A, a 100% risk weighting for BBB, and a 200% risk weighting (16% capital) for below investment grade BB securities.[81] F&F risk based capital requirements for senior AAA and AA rated securities were the same as for banks.

Some people, most notably former FDIC Chairman William Isaac, strongly opposed risk-based capital rules based on credit rating agencies, as did the Shadow Regulatory Committee of market-oriented economists, arguing that the rules would replace bank due diligence.[82] In contrast, the Fed strongly supported a rules based approach. Isaac correctly anticipated that the regulations would transfer responsibility for credit risk evaluation from the loan officer and investor to the ratings agencies. Investors in investment grade securities ceased doing independent due diligence and began purchasing securities depending entirely on the ratings that were provided by the rating agencies. As a consequence, investment grade securities were priced based on these ratings and their regulatory status at a slight discount to Treasury securities (reflecting only the difference in the rating). By substituting prudential market leverage with regulatory compliance, regulators effectively determined all of the components of loan pricing and even became indirectly responsible for that as well. The collective wisdom of the marketplace was replaced by a federally sanctioned private for-profit regulator.

The premise of the capital regulations was that a portion of an investor's money was being spent on the ratings process and due diligence rather than being spent reviewing a larger volume of individual securities. You couldn't afford to do both. For example, "prime" money market funds invested in AAA rated 30 day paper yielding a few basis points more than similar funds invested only in Treasury paper. The expense of re-evaluating the quality of these credits would have more than wiped out the yield advantage, which explains why they subsequently were so exposed to the collapse of Lehman brothers.[83]

The reliance on ratings provided a particularly big savings for more complicated mortgage backed PLS which came along about a decade later. Armed with the assumption that the ratings accurately reflected risks, all investment grade PLS were considered to be commensurate with the risk of similarly rated corporate securities, a logical inference of consistency, and they essentially became a homogenous commodity with corporate bonds. Spreads on investment grade securities narrowed to reflect the absence of due diligence costs as well as the risk-based ratings. For example, a bank only needed to earn a return on assets (ROA) of 40 basis points (.4%) to earn a 25% return on equity (Table 4 below). Thus, the combination of both the mandatory credit rating and risk-based capital market rules determined security prices and indirectly the prices and borrowing rates for PLS mortgage loans as well.

These regulations had the biggest impact on the demand for AAA rated corporate securities – especially for very short term securities such as commercial paper. In the 1990s Citicorp introduced and sponsored Structured Investment Vehicles (SIVs) to take advantage of low yields in the commercial paper market. These SIVs bought short term loans and leases and financed them in the commercial paper market. In order to be marketable, they needed a "liquidity guarantee" which generally amounted to a "put back " –a return of the loans to the sponsoring bank at par in the event new commercial paper could not be sold when the old matured, resulting in a loss to the liquidity provider if the securities lost market value. An SIV could purchase virtually any supposedly "liquid" but really just marketable asset by holding a "cash reserve", typically around one percent, even less than the Basil I requirements. The sponsoring bank was not required to capitalize the liquidity guarantee so long as it rolled over a one year term.

These regulations created a whole new market structure and pricing mechanism for regulated securities. To meet the greater demand, which was stimulated by removing the cost of due diligence, issuers were now able to create pools of mortgages, bundle them into a series of both investment grade and below investment grade tranches, and then sell them to investors. This effectively removed all of the risk and stake which originators had in any part of the MBS. The result was the development of private label securitization (PLS).

B. The Origins of Private label Securitization (PLS) 1970-2000

Banking, like insurance, is based on risk diversification. When Lloyds of London first began insuring commercial shipping in the 1600s, it sold shares in each voyage for each ship to individual investors. Using the *law of large numbers,* the benefits of risk diversification, by insuring many voyages, soon became obvious to Lloyd's investors. However, a larger portfolio increased the difficulty of scrutinizing each of the individual investments by a firm as diverse as Lloyds. The same trade-offs still apply today: some investors purchase participations in the risk of individual loans they evaluate; others prefer to purchase shares of an undivided pool of loans (or the equity or debt of the investor) and rely on diversification.

Capital market funding for home mortgages dates back several hundred years to mortgage bonds issued in Northern and Central Europe, and much of Northern Europe still relies on "covered bond" financing by large banking institutions. These bonds are securitized debt obligations of the issuer, providing the benefit of diversification, but they also specify particular assets available to the bondholder as collateral in the event that the issuer defaults. Because these claims are senior to other claimants in bankruptcy, the subordination risk for others, potentially including depositors and deposit insurers, is greater. The history of mortgage bond financing in the US dates back to the late 1800s. These bonds were generally backed by thinly capitalized issuers and conflicts arose between the interest of issuers and that of investors. These are sometimes referred to as principal (in this case issuers) agent (investors) conflicts or simply "agency conflicts." Defaults were fairly widespread and the market for such bonds eventually dried up.

The main parties in the contemporary originate-to-sell chain of finance are the borrower, the originator, the third party mortgage insurer (if any), the packager/securitizer and guarantor (if applicable), the credit rater (if rated), the investor, and ultimately, for most of the mortgage market, the taxpayer. Secondary mortgage markets, which preceded the creation of GSEs and "asset sale" securitization by a century, had historically addressed possible conflicts of interest in a number of ways. Wholesale market investors relied on legal contracts spelling out the representations and warranties of the loan originating seller. In addition, they employed numerous other mechanisms, often in combination, including: buying only senior participations, right of put-back, requiring private mortgage insurance, and later requiring a third party guarantee or "pool insurance" on mortgage pools financed with securities.

When Robert "Bobby" Dall of Solomon Brothers attempted to recreate the mortgage bond market by issuing mortgage backed bonds in the 1970s beginning with the first issued by a name investors recognized, Bank of America, conflicts arose again. Even though the Bank of America had legally sold the loans to a Trust and as Trustee had no legal obligation to compensate investors for default, it bailed out the investors when fraud was suspected in order to protect its long run reputation. In addition to legal and regulatory obstacles, credit rating agencies' treatment of the bonds also discouraged issuers from issuing bonds with this structure by requiring that collateral be posted at market value in order to support the par value of the bonds. This resulted in as much as 100% over-collateralization when interest rates rose and prices fell, which happened with increasing frequency during the 1970s and early 1980s, discouraging mortgage backed bond (MBB) financing.

For most of US history, capital market financing was treated as debt for accounting purposes while the issuer funded the equity. Capital was required of all participants but mainly the issuer. But securitization was initially created for the Ginnie Mae pass-through certificate (PC), primarily issued by thinly capitalized mortgage bankers, with government FHA insurance and a Ginnie Mae guarantee in lieu of private capital. Freddie Mac later pioneered the Freddie participation certificate and, working with Salomon Brothers and First Boston, Freddie Mac issued the first collateralized mortgage obligation (CMO) in 1983. It was the first MBS that divided the cash flow into different tranches for different investors and was based on duration (interest rate maturity) since Freddie Mac already guaranteed the credit risk. As a consequence of CMOs, not all investors had to accept the uncertain cash flows for the entire 30 year life of the PC mortgage pool since some mortgages were paid off earlier than others. This didn't incur tax difference at the pool level due to Freddie Mac's tax exempt status. The CMO left a residual, or "equity tranche," held by Freddie Mac.

Imperial Savings of San Diego issued a number of innovative collateralized bond financings during the second half of the 1980s, all motivated by tax or regulatory arbitrage. The first was a collateralized mortgage backed bond for mortgages that had an average interest rate below the market rate and therefore the loans were worth less than par value. The issue was structured as a debt financing using GAAP rules (and at the time different from regulatory accounting principles or RAP) in order to avoid selling the loans at a loss and the resulting capital hit. But the transaction was structure to meet the test for a sale of the underlying loans under the rules governing income taxes so that the sale of assets would accelerate the loss and hence the tax deduction. Borrowing costs were below the all-in cost of deposits – the interest paid plus the administrative expense of, e.g., maintaining bank branches - due to over-collateralization, which left less collateral available to the FSLIC in the event of liquidation.

Using the same over-collateralization approach once again, Imperial Savings issued a collateralized loan obligation (CLO) backed by commercial loans which were purchased wholesale. The collateral still had to be marked to market, resulting in excess collateral when rates rose because the collateralized debt was not similarly marked to market. To address this issue, Imperial got the rating agencies to rate the next CLO obligation based on the projected cash flow of the underlying collateral. Shortly thereafter they used the same over-collateralization technique to fund a portfolio of high yield low-grade "junk" bonds with triple AAA securities - a collateralized bond obligation (CBO). These CBOs and CLOs were the precursor to what would later be called collateralized debt obligations (CDOs), all of which would be rated based on projected cash flow and overcollateralization.

These issues worked as expected for purchasers as well as for the FSLIC, which put Imperial into conservatorship – and four months later in receivership - as a result of rejecting the capital plan required by FIRREA in 1989. The bond holders were paid in full due to the excess collateral, leaving less collateral resulting in a loss for the FSLIC.

The Tax Reform Act of 1986 brought changes in the laws that govern securitization by permitting REMICs (introduced in chapter 2) for mortgages. "REMICs" were first issued in 1987 and are sometimes also called collateralized mortgage obligations. Whereas Ginnie Mae pools were put into a

"Grantor Trust," PLS pools were put into a special purpose vehicle (SPV) with the same objective. SPVs didn't issue securities comparable to corporate equity in the M&M sense, so those rated below investment grade were generally considered "equity" and those rated above as debt.[84] The REMIC changes in the laws governing securitization for mortgages in 1986 were followed in the early 1990s with Financial Asset Securitization Investment Trust (FASITs) for non-mortgage assets that essentially ended grantor trust prohibitions on managing cash flows for virtually any types of loans so long as they all got passed through to some investor.

The intent was to foster private securitization by facilitating management of the underlying credit risk. The particular goal was to allow credit "tranching," .e.g. into more senior and correspondingly subordinate securities. Starting in the late 1980's numerous variations ensued. Most of the MBS and derivative securities used decades later were incubated during this period of experimentation. These innovations mitigated some of the most extreme drawbacks of securitization but still didn't address the inherent issues of originator moral hazard or uncertain monthly cash flow.

PLS debt investors implicitly relied on ratings agencies to determine the appropriate level of equity subordination; those who invested in senior securities implicitly assumed that there was sufficient subordination of mezzanine and subordinate securities. Investors in mezzanine securities assumed that the levels of subordination were comparable to that of similarly rated corporate securities. A typical simple multi-class credit-tranched security might be structured with 90% senior (AAA/AA) securities, 8% mezzanine (A/BBB) securities and 2% subordinated (BB/non-rated NR) retained equity. Complexity increased immediately with the creation of many different structures, some with a hundred or more different classes of security, to take advantage of investor misconceptions and hence mis-pricing of risk.

PLSers in the US sought "asset" sales treatment to avoid the capital requirements, but sales treatment didn't allow retaining much of the subordinated residual equity interests, so others would presumably provide the required capital. However, selling PLS equity was difficult and expensive due to the obvious conflicts of interest between the originator and investor, a conflict mitigated in GSE securities with federal guarantees and servicing contracts). Because retained equity interests were subordinate, their cash flow was deferred and the "residual" value depended entirely on expectations of default performance over the life of a set of pooled mortgages. That is, the 2% residual may have been worthless based on a slightly more pessimistic default projection. In fact, PLSers would sometimes create such worthless interests based on overly optimistic default assumptions and give them away to charity to get sales treatment - removing the loans from their books while getting a charitable tax deduction to boot!

PLSers tried to minimize their funding costs in two ways. First, they used deposit insurance to re-leverage subordinated equity securities using the techniques described below. Second, they pushed the credit rating agencies to meet the test for asset sale treatment with a minimal amount of equity and to minimize the more expensive mezzanine tranche as well. This function was entirely new to rating agencies who were now hired and paid by the firms being rated, representing a major conflict of interest. And it was not easy as subordination levels weren't nearly as transparent as they were for companies. The inevitable result was regulatory shopping by PLSers among the approved raters to negotiate the best security structure and rating possible.

Financial firms are required to keep (at least) two sets of books: one that follows generally accepted accounting principles (GAAP) and one for tax (if they are diligent they would keep a third set that reflected the underlying economics of risk and return, which is often not reflected in the previous two). Banks and thrifts were also historically required to keep a third set that followed regulatory accounting principles (RAP), which was later combined with GAAP by FIRREA in 1989, with subsequent exceptions. The accounting rules were relatively malleable when it came to securitization. For example, when securitizing recently originated loans, one would want to get "sales" treatment for GAAP and RAP to free up capital and book the gain, while getting a "financing" status for taxes to defer the tax on the profit. When securitizing a portfolio of underwater loans, one would want to do the opposite to avoid reporting a loss publicly and reduce current taxes, as in the Imperial Savings case reported above. Consistency was generally not required.

The total equity of a securitization depended not only on how the sold tranches were leveraged, but also on how the retained interests were leveraged. RAP determined the amount of equity needed to fund residual interests for loans originated in a bank or thrift. After RAP converged to GAAP in 1989 this allowed banks that securitized to consider the assets as sold for both GAAP and RAP.

The case of Superior Bank of Illinois, owned by the Pritzger and Dworman families who were also owners of the Hyatt hotels and NY real estate developers, best illustrates the potential for extreme leverage provided by regulatory arbitrage that bank securitization and "asset sales" accounting treatment produced. In 1993 they purchased the sub-prime lender Alliance Funding Inc. The sub prime loans were originated and securitized in the bank, which was treated as a sale according to GAAP. RAP followed the GAAP sales treatment, in spite of a small but still significant residual retained interest. Thus, these risky residual equity interests were funded almost entirely with insured deposits according to risk-based capital rules for normal loans. [85] Residuals that reflect the 100 to 1 leveraging were funded by a bank already leveraged 15 to 1, providing total potential leverage of 1500 to 1 or, alternatively, a capital requirement of only .07% for the first loss on the underlying mortgage loans. Superior bank didn't have much "skin in the game" and soon failed.

To prevent such obvious abuse, the rules for RAP were subsequently changed such that the securitization of loans that originated in a bank would receive "financing" capital treatment. Alternatively, a regulatory capital requirement of 100% of the retained portion was imposed if the residual interest was less than the required capital on the entire pool. "Purchased" interests had a lower capital requirement than "retained" interests, however, and invited temporary "parking" of retained interests which were recorded as sold with an unrecorded repurchase agreement in order to get the lower capital requirement for a purchased interest. Investment banks were more than willing to provide a parking place ion return for the securitization fees. But parking was illegal even if difficult to trace and, eventually, not worth the risk.

That pretty much ended commercial bank PLS issuance as a means to finance balance sheet assets because a similar 100% capital requirement was not imposed on the retained interests of other securitizers, e.g., finance companies that funded retained interests with equity and high yield "junk" bonds. So in the 1990's banks spun out their mortgage banking divisions as finance companies or as free standing mortgage banks with warehouse lending provided by the bank and permanent funding provided by PLS for the investment grade securities. The retained equity interests were funded by capital by issuing stock as well as by high yield bonds. Often some or all of the stock of all these entities were owned by the same corporate parent.

The first big sub-prime mortgage lending boom occurred in the mid 1990s. Loans were provided to people with generally bad credit but substantial down-payments, initially 20% to 30%. The loans typically were not eligible for sale to the GSEs because of the borrowers' low credit scores, but the loans didn't require private mortgage insurance due to the low loan-value ratios (often based on inflated appraisals). Originators chose private securitization over internal bank funding because the rating agencies dramatically under-estimated the default risk and loss severity, thereby enabling excessive amounts to be financed in the investment grade tranches with only a small retained equity strip. In addition, following "present value" GAAP accounting rules as dictated by the SEC, these firms booked large current profits based on projected lifetime revenue of the residual interests discounted at a relatively low interest rate which was also specified by the SEC.

Finance companies went public based on these reported book profits. The SEC-inflated reported profits enabled lenders turn these book profits to cash, raising both equity and debt in the high yield (junk) bond market relatively cheaply in order to fund residual interests of only 1%-2% of the pool, thereby achieving about 50/100 to 1 leverage. Some of these lenders converted to a real estate investment trust to avoid paying taxes on the investment earnings of the retained interests (and potentially on the operating profits as well).[86] Not all investors were fooled by SEC accounting, however, and recognized the pyramid scheme, profiting at the expense of those on the bottom of the pyramid. Speculators, some of them former investors, subsequently shorted the market to restore discipline and end the boom. Within a few years realized credit losses proved the fallacy of SEC-dictated financial disclosure and virtually all the publicly traded companies filed for bankruptcy within a few months near the end of 1998.

The managers all made huge sums by starting companies and taking them public, and many investors, particularly those who never believed in the business model, made a lot of money as stock prices ran up in reaction to the high reported profits. Only those investors that got in late and holders of high yield bonds lost out. Some of these sub-prime lending operations then migrated back to the TBTF commercial and investment banks. In spite of the universal failure of the issuers, Fannie and Freddie weren't involved and speculators were able to burst this bubble before it caused widespread systemic damage to the broader financial system.

Thanks to Fed economist David Jones (2000) the Fed knew all about all these forms of bank regulatory arbitrage by the end of the decade. But rather than sound an alarm, Jones was relatively sanguine about the process. Kling (2009, p. 25) summarizes Jones conclusions as: "The Basel risk buckets were arbitrary; the risk classifications may have been overly conservative for certain types of loans; Regulatory Capital Arbitrage (RCA) enabled banks to reduce the capital requirements for these loans; RCA was difficult to stop politically, and; RCA did not necessarily harm safety and soundness if it kept banks competitive in markets *to make low-risk loans*" (emphasis added).

C. Characteristics of the Borrower Pool 2000-2004 and 2005-2007

The elections at the end of the century technically brought the end to President Clinton's National Homeownership Strategy of 1995 but this was quickly replaced by President Bush's Ownership Society, which was in many ways indistinguishable. The new millennium began with a strong housing market, three years into a boom in production and prices. Though the popping of the dot-com bubble and the 9/11 terrorist attacks produced a minor recession right as the millennium began, people showed increasing confidence in investing in real estate and, specifically, in their homes.

But the borrower pool became increasingly risky. Aggregate default risk analyses made on a few marginal borrowers – the "crème de la crap" according to one analyst - during prior normal times were applied to the weakest borrowers en masse during an unprecedented housing bubble. Down payment requirements were lowered to negligible levels to meet housing goals.

Even with continued low long term interest rates, few if any of these remaining marginal borrowers could afford much if any down payment - and had little incentive to invest very much late in a housing bubble in any event - so they would have to borrow the money. Down payments on subprime loans for home purchases fell from a reported 10 percent in 2003 to zero from 2005 through 2007 and some of those loans could negatively amortize after closing.[87] Reported down payments on Alt-A pools for home purchases declined from 10 percent to 5 percent during the same time period (Alt-A loans are considered to be of higher quality than subprime, but the borrowers lack complete documentation of income and assets, employment, and/or appraisals on refinancing.) Further, many notionally five percent down payments were so-called "3/2 down payments" where borrowers report that a "gift" will appear at closing to cover the 3 percent share, when in fact that money often comes from an unrecorded loan or a loan that was recorded after the mortgage credit check was complete.

Mortgage insurers had been the traditional gatekeepers preventing excessive lending, particularly during a boom. Private mortgage insurance was historically required on all GSE loans with less than the required 20% cash down-payments, and generally was used on loans purchased by non-GSE investors as well. Subprime loans represented a huge potential business for private mortgage insurers, who would agree to cover defaults in exchange for homebuyers paying the insurers actuarially fair premiums, but the fraction of these loans that qualified for PMI coverage was small. In addition, for many of the rest the insurers and their state regulators likely knew that there was no actuarially sound price at which the risks of the subprime loans being originated in the early to middle part of the last decade could be insured. Moreover, the PMIs were well aware that house prices revert to the mean, having been burned before. So the PMI market share continued shrinking over this period, becoming insignificant during 2005 through 2007 when down payments evaporated.[88]

So if private mortgage insurance was not available and state regulators were bypassed, how were borrowers able to secure subprime loans? The main answer is "purchase money" second mortgages that provided cash for a down payment to secure the primary mortgage. That is, insured low down payment first mortgages were largely replaced by "qualified" first mortgages with an LTV of 80% or less with a simultaneous piggy-back purchase money second.[89] As evidence, the seconds' share of originations more than doubled from the 2001–2003 time period to the 2004–2007 time period.

About 28 percent of subprime loans and 42 percent of Alt-A loans originated in 2006 had piggyback seconds that were reported to the first lien holder.[90] Some lenders were interested in the combined LTV (CLTV) even though their loan had an 80% LTV or less because purchase money seconds weren't underwritten like insured loans. But in practice it was impossible to monitor as the title search was done before loan closing and the so-called "silent" second could be recorded after closing the first loan. Anecdotal evidence suggests the widespread use of silent seconds during this period: including unrecorded "silent" seconds could easily double the percentages of loans funded with purchase money piggy-back second mortgages.

About half of Alt A and 40% of sub-prime were for purchase, the rest refinancing. Many households refinanced and the percentage of refinancings with over 5 percent cash take out doubled from 2002-04 to 2006-07.[91] MPS report an average LTV of about 80% for refinancing for both Alt A and sub-prime. But many households took seconds – and thirds – to cash out equity gains as the bubble progressed. Goodman et al (2010) estimates that well over half of the sub prime and Alt A loans had seconds that averaged over 20%. That suggests that there was virtually no cash equity for Alt A or sub-prime lending on home purchases, and little left after refinancing even as house prices rose.

Even with little or no down payment, most subprime and Alt-A borrowers could not afford to pay the normal principal, interest, insurance, and taxes, let alone a mortgage insurance premium. Instead, they borrowed at a "teaser" rate typically at least 2 percent less than the fully indexed mortgage rate, expecting to roll over the loan with a new teaser when the old teaser expired, cashing out any gains to that point. In the aggregate, this was a pyramid scheme.

Relaxed lending standards allowed mostly sub-prime homebuyers to buy houses with little or no down payment, and either flip them to reap tax free capital gains or cash out by refinancing. If prices fell before they sold, they could default, most often without recourse. Low or no down payment loans with teaser payment rates often resulted in current ownership expense well below the cost of renting, and ongoing tax benefits were minimal because many of these buyers didn't pay income tax, and many others took the standard deduction. Homebuyers weren't irrational and most weren't "victimized" during the housing boom and lending bubble, they just had more to gain and less to lose. This made such loans extremely risky, so how did they get funded?

One answer is bad or historic but inapplicable risk models. The risk of second mortgages depends on several factors. There are basically three categories of second mortgages: home equity lines of credit (HELOCs): closed end second mortgages (CESs); and piggy-back second mortgages, i.e., those originated at the time of a home purchase.

Home equity loans became popular after the interest deduction was removed for consumer credit in the 1980s. They were a typical bank product because only banks had the liquidity to offer a line of credit and the interest rate was adjustable. The historical default experience of the 1980's and 1990's had been extremely good because most borrowers still had substantial residual homeowner equity and banks underwrote the borrowers carefully.

CES were also typically used as a way to tap into home equity without refinancing the first mortgage, although traditionally the CLTV had been limited to 80%. Hence they were less favorable in a falling interest rate environment when the benefit of cash-out refinancing outweighed the transaction costs of a second mortgage.

Purchase money seconds were different than home equity loans or lines of credit. Historically sellers would sometimes provide this financing to facilitate a sale (and sales were occasionally structured in a way to postpone capital gains taxes due on sale). The seller, who had intimate knowledge of the property and local market, could rely on the lender to underwrite a sound prime first lien loan. Sometimes the seller wanted the second as an investment. There is a secondary market for these seconds made up of investors who historically purchased them at a discount typically of about 25% and financed the purchase with equity.

For conventional loans, the anecdotal evidence suggests that seller financing had largely evaporated: sellers selling at the peak realized that their entire capital gain could be eviscerated when house prices started to decline. With FHA, the "seller" was cashed out up-front by the government.

The credit risk of piggy back seconds and cash out refi CES are orders of magnitude greater than traditional HELOCs, especially when combined with low sub-prime credit scores. But Countrywide classified all of its second mortgages as prime HELOCs, undoubtedly originated to close first liens. At any rate, the expected losses as house prices revert to the mean should be orders of magnitude greater for HELOCs as well.

That was not as obvious to the rating agencies that rated piggy-back purchase money pools based on the historical experience of HELOCs and CES. This resulted in a financing cost on the pool of second mortgages of only about 1% above the rate for first lien PLS as discussed below, well below market. Mortgage insurance costs are imposed on the whole loan, or the entire purchase price in FHA's case. So paying a 1/2% to 1% insurance premium could be the same as paying 5% to 10% on a second mortgage, over the base rate financing cost of the first, with a loan to value ratio (LTV) of 80%. Moreover, this PMI cost was not tax deductible until 2008. So purchase money seconds could finance down payments more cheaply than an insured high LTV loan.

Piggy back second mortgages paved the way for PLS funding of the first mortgage, but PLS accounted for only a tiny share of second mortgage funding, so risk modeling doesn't explain mis-pricing of these seconds. As discussed in chapter 4, these seconds were funded mostly by banks and CRA is the most likely explanation for this mis-pricing.

D: Determining PLS Net Capital Requirements Funding Sub-prime Mortgages 2000-2007

In spite of the PLS failure of the 1990s, none of the bank capital rules which allowed regulatory arbitrage were changed. In fact, SIVs expanded to include the purchase of long term PLS securities on the assumption that they were not just marketable but liquid. Citicorp, a TBTF universal bank, was the sponsor of 6 out of the 16 total created SIVs and these were largely repositories of the sub-prime mortgage securities being issued by Citi's investment bank. They also extended regulation – and by implication implicit protection – to investment banks. Essentially PLSers built upon all of the past regulatory arbitrage techniques – all still available - to fund the huge increase in mortgage demand represented by political housing goals.

1. Regulatory Arbitrage Enables Extreme Leverage

The type of institution that issued PLS would determine how they were financed. There were basically four charters: stand alone finance companies like Ameriquest, finance companies with a captive bank like Countrywide (which owned a bank), commercial (universal) banks, and investment banks. As in the prior decade, finance companies would use third parties as warehouse lenders, securitize and fund retained interests with a combination of debt and equity. Those with a bank had several advantages, including favorable warehouse lines and a place to fund PLS rejects ("lame loans" mostly lame for documentation reasons). Banks had these advantages plus the ability to fund on the balance sheet with FHLB advances or off the balance sheet with sponsored SIVs. Investment banks had the biggest leverage advantage for retaining subordinated interests as a consequence of the SEC capital requirements being only a fraction that of bank risk-based capital requirements.

Investment banks had historically employed modest leverage to finance their highly "marketable," i.e., supposedly readily saleable dealer inventory. Hedge funds and other assets comparable to those of private equity funds now made up the bulk of the balance sheet and arguably shouldn't have been leveraged much, if at all. But the market determination of the leverage available to these investment banks and their investors was replaced by SEC regulation as they went public and expanded dramatically. In April 2004 the SEC voted to designate the five biggest non-bank investment banks and subprime securitizers (Goldman Sachs, Morgan Stanley, Lehman Brothers, Merrill Lynch and Bear Stearns) as "consolidated supervised entities" and lowered their minimum capital requirements, based on computer model simulations of the 1988 Basel I Capital Accords, recognizing a fait accompli.[92]

As a consequence, these investment banks had dramatically greater leverage during this bubble than in prior decades, even as their assets became much less marketable. By year end 2007 the book capital-to-assets ratio for Goldman Sachs, Lehman Brothers, Merrill Lynch and Morgan Stanley averaged 3.33%, barely more than half the 5.88% average of commercial bank capital.[93] And, as with the GSEs and commercial banks, book leverage ratios understated the extent of investment bank over-leveraging due to the various accounting gimmicks that were used to move assets off the balance sheet (e.g., Lehman's 105 accounting rule that hid $50 billion in assets) and onto off-balance sheet sponsored hedge funds with an implicit put-back to the sponsor.

Although the entire market for PLS grew exponentially from 2002 through 2007, the Wall Street market share fell marginally from 32% to 27%. The bank share also declined as the finance companies Ameriquest and Countrywide became the number 1 and 2 security issuers by 2005.

The negotiations to structure a PLS took place almost exclusively between PLSers and the credit rating agencies. Bank regulators weren't involved and the SEC was only involved in the registration process. Investor prices and demand were exogenous, so investors weren't involved. So PLSers negotiated the structure of PLS in such a way that maximized the total amount raised from investors and that increased the value of retained securities. This process was designed to fully exploit low bank and investment bank regulatory capital requirements and other sources of regulatory arbitrage.

Exhibit 1 below, Risk Profile of Subprime Mortgage Loans, illustrates a typical structure of a simple MBS, collateralized debt obligation (CDO), and CDO squared structure. A subset of a mortgage pool with low down payments and high borrower credit risk - sub-prime mortgage loans - is put into a standard PLS structure (MBS, referred to as mortgage bonds in this exhibit). Then the investment grade securities are re-securitized into a high grade PLS CDO – labeled an asset backed security (ABS) in the exhibit - and a mezzanine ABS CDO. This process is then repeated with the second CDO (CDO squared) that produces more in the senior and junior tranches. This is actually a simple version of what became very complex securitization structures.

One can calculate the *net* capital requirements of the main structures based on this exhibit taking advantage of the capital arbitrage opportunities discussed above, then compare: on versus off balance sheet bank SIV financing for PLS debt; equity interests being retained by a commercial or investment bank PLSer or sold to a hedge fund; whole loans to PLS, CDOs and CDOs squared; and combinations of these alternative capital structures. [94]

In what follows, we make some assumptions reflecting a typical security. Table 1 calculates the total net regulatory capital requirements for this simple PLS. The first column shows the credit and risk rating for each tranche and the second column shows the Basel I capital requirements discussed above. The third column indicates the percentage of the mortgage pool put into the various tranches illustrated in the exhibit. The fourth "Balance Sheet" column is the product of columns two and three, the total capital needed to support investments in each tranche when financed on a bank balance sheet, and the last column if financed off-balance sheet by an SIV (we assume all investment grade securities purchased by an SIV have one percent reserves, i.e. required capital).

Exhibit 1

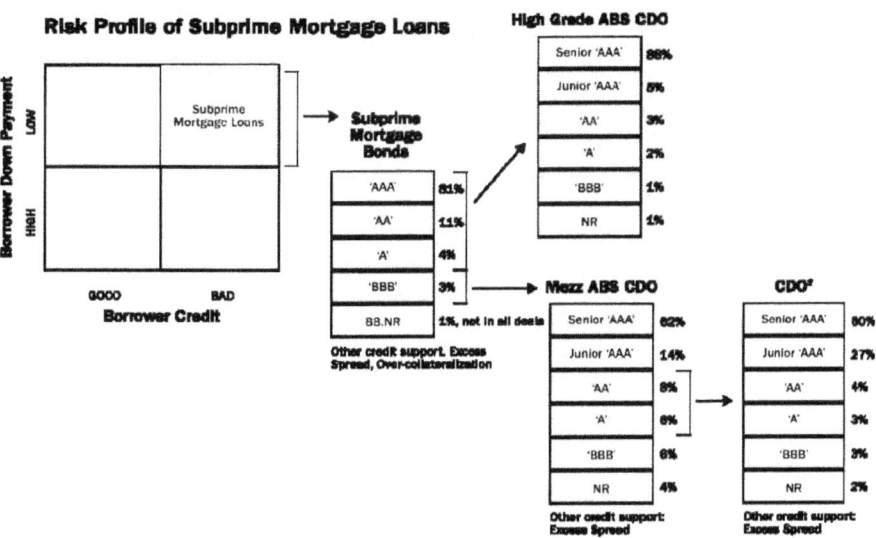

Source: UBS, "Market Commentary," December 13, 2007.

Looking at the commercial bank Total line, we see that a bank could reduce the 4% tier one capital requirement of holding whole loans in portfolio to only 2.45% by securitizing them and implicitly retaining all the securities. This clearly indicates that for comparable risk, the risk based capital rules favored PLS over balance sheet financing even with the 100% capital rules for retained interests, which in this security only applies to the NR, ½ % of the total. SIV off-balance sheet regulatory arbitrage reduces the bank capital requirement to only 1.57%. Moreover only half of tier one capital had to be equity; as with finance company PLS the prior decade banks could use preferred stock and subordinated debt to double their leverage.

	Table 1 Bank Securitization		Commercial	
rating weights	risk-based capital 100%=.08	% of Pool	Balance Sheet	SIV
AAA 20%	0.016	81	1.30	0.81
AA 20%	0.016	11	0.18	0.11
A 50%	0.04	4	0.16	0.04
BBB 100%	0.08	3	0.24	0.03
BB 200%	.16	0.5	0.08	0.08
NR all	1	0.5	0.50	0.50
Total		100	**2.45**	**1.57**
Investment Bank Securitization				
BB na	0.02	0.5	0.01	0.01
NR na	0.04	0.5	0.02	0.02
Total			**1.90**	**1.02**

The bottom two rows of the table assume that the below investment grade residual interests are funded not by a commercial bank but rather by an investment bank PLSer with leverage provided largely with commercial paper purchased by money market funds in the so called "shadow" banking system and with commercial bank repos. Assume that the 1% below investment grade in the PLS exhibit, the subordinated equity, is divided equally between the BB and the first loss NR (non-rated) security. If default experience is much better than assumed, the NR "residual" gets all the benefit; if any worse, the BB quickly moves from second to first loss position as the NR loses all value. We assume for illustrative purposes that the BB securities can be conservatively financed by using a repurchase agreement with a 25% haircut and that the total investment bank leverage for the retained interest is, estimated conservatively, 25 to 1, i.e.; a 4% capital requirement.

Investment bank leverage of equity reduces the capital requirement from 2.45% to 1.90% (and only 1.72% (not shown) by retaining the BBB and financing them by using a repo with a 25% haircut). Employing both forms of arbitrage, an investment bank PLSer selling investment grade PLS to an SIV, reduces the total net capital requirement from 1.57% to only 1.02% - only a quarter of that required by the Basil risk-based capital requirements for bank financing of whole loans.

While investment bank leverage at 30 to 1 represents the biggest regulatory distortion, it is not the most important one because bank risk-based capital requirements applied to 200 times more (99.5%)

of the total PLS financing in this example. Overall, low investment bank capital requirements shifted about a third of PLS issuance to investment banks, but with commercial banks still providing almost all the funding while keeping the loans hidden from regulators. Hence blame "Wall Street."

These net capital requirements of only about 1% to 2% are only examples of an almost infinite number of combinations, but they are fairly representative of a PLS transaction during the sub-prime lending bubble. The primary point is that the capital requirements were comparable to those of F&F and made them competitive with F&F (see H&V, 2012). But even this minimal capital was often an illusion.

2. Capital Requirements Using CDOs

Much has been made of the complex multi-layered CDOs that financed most PLS from 2005 through 2007. Investment banks used CDOs extensively, often repeating the process multiple times. For those interested in how the capital requirements for CDOs are calculated, refer to the box below.

Capital Requirements from repeating the CDO process

Calculating the percentage of the pool follows the tranching in Table 3. The third column shows the percentage of high grade CDOs from the re-securitized tranches. Columns 3 and 4 refer to the high grade CDOs and 5 and 6 to the mezzanine CDOs. The 3rd and 5th columns show the percent of the PLS going into the tranche from the exhibit (junior AAA is treated as just AAA for simplicity), and columns 4 and 6 give the actual distributions of the re-securitized securities (the product of the percentages and the 96 senior and 3 mezzanine allocation, respectively). The 7th column shows the net percentage of the underlying pool which ends up in the specified ratings basket. The 8th and 9th columns shows the net capital requirement if financed on balance sheet and with SIV financing.

		Table 2 Capital Requirements Using Collateralized Debt Obligations						
		% of High Grade Pool	Net High Grade	% of mez grade pool	Net Mez Grade	% of Total Pool	Balance Sheet	SIV
AAA	0.016	93	89.28	76	2.28	91.56	1.46	0.92
AA	0.016	3	2.88	8	.24	3.12	0.05	0.03
A	0.04	2	1.92	6	.18	2.10	0.08	0.02
BBB	0.08	1	.96	6	.18	1.14	0.09	0.01
BB	.16	0	0.00	0	.0	0.50	0.08	0.04
NR	1	1	0.96	4	.12	1.58	1.58	1.58
Total		100	96.00	100	3.0	100.00	**3.35**	**2.60**
		Investment Bank Securitization						
BB	0.02	0.5					0.01	0.01
NR	0.04	0.5					0.06	0.06
Total							**1.76**	**1.05**
		CDO Squared						
		% of CDO Squared	CDO Pool	CDO 2 Cap Required		% of Total Pool	Capital Required	SIV
AAA	0.016	87	87.30	0.010		91.93	1.46	0.92
AA	0.016	4	5.22	0.004		3.14	0.05	0.03
A	0.04	3	3.12	0.002		2.11	0.08	0.02
BBB	0.08	3	2.10	0.002		0.97	0.09	0.01
BB	.16	0	0.66	0.030		0.50	0.08	0.04
NR	1	2	0.60	0.020		1.59	1.58	1.59
Total		99	99.00	0.068		100.24	**3.35**	**2.61**
		Investment Bank Securitization						
BB	0.02	0.5					0.01	0.01
NR	0.04	0.5					0.06	0.06
Total							**1.75**	**1.05**

> The CDO squared structure is shown in the bottom of the table. The calculations follow those for the CDO, with new percentages for the baskets from the exhibit. CDO squared structures reallocate only 14% of the CDO, without increasing leverage at the investment banks.

Table 3 shows the net capital requirements for CDOs and CDO squared using the same method as in Table 1. CDO and CDO squared structures, putting slightly more in the top and bottom categories, would have been counterproductive for commercial banks because it would raise their capital requirements (from 2.45 to 3.35 for on-balance sheet financing and from 1.57 to 2.65 for off), reflecting their 100% capital requirement for NR retained interests. CDO and CDO squared

Table 3

Collateralized Debt Obligation

Net Capital Requirements

Financing For Investment Grade	On BS	SIV
Commercial Bank CDO	3.35	2.60
Commercial Bank CDO Squared	**3.35**	**2.61**
Investment Bank CDO	1.76	1.05
Investment Bank CDO squared	**1.75**	**1.05**

did marginally improve investment bank leverage from 1.90 to 1.75 without using SIV financing, but not with it. These relatively minor differences in leverage, in spite of the high and duplicative costs, suggest that CDO issuance was not driven by the PLSer's desire to increase leverage. In fact, the CDO structure more than tripled their first loss "skin in the game."

But complexity wasn't the motivation either, as many analysts alleged. To understand what motivated CDOs we need to understand securitization profitability, which was determined by yield requirements. These yield requirements were in turn determined by almost entirely by bank capital regulations.

E. PLS and CDO Mis-Pricing

The government-induced distortions described above made the M&M Irrelevance Theorem irrelevant: the highest value PLS structure was the one that took maximum advantage of regulatory and tax arbitrage and other government distortions to issuer and investor incentives. This is primarily due to the mis-pricing of senior debt reflecting risk-based capital requirements. But distorted incentives facing managers of public pension funds caused junior tranches and equity interest to be mis-priced as well.

1. Mis-pricing Senior PLS securities

Low AAA yield requirements were the result of regulations that created a global shortage of AAA securities.[95] Some of this demand came from global money market funds. Hedge funds and pension funds were attracted by the low haircuts banks required for repo funding and hence the extreme leverage. The global payments imbalance also created demand for virtually riskless US securities with a slight yield advantage over US Treasury securities. CDOs were created to meet this regulatory-driven demand for AAA and to a lesser extent AA rated securities.

As illustrated in table 4, a typical CDO structure raises the total AAA proportion from 81% in the MBS up to 92% of the pool, with the PLS AAA senior to the CDO AAA, and up to 95% including AA, which also enjoys the 20% risk weighting. In total 98.5% of PLS and CDO securities in this example could be leveraged under the risk based capital rules on bank balance sheets, consistent with the findings of Pinto (2011, p 147, footnote 387) that the CDO squared structure typically brought AAA/AA financing up to 98% of the total mortgage pool.

The rise of credit default swaps (CDS) also kept CDO prices from rising significantly. A CDS is just an insurance contract between two parties. Generally the CDS writer guaranteed the value of the security for a period of one to five years in return for an insurance premium. The guarantee of a "credit event" isn't based on ultimate credit loss, but a variety of events that can require the writer to pay the difference between the par and market value of the security or to buy the security at par. The market value of CDS outstanding doubled during 2005, doubled again during 2006, and then increased four-fold during 2007.[96] These were being written and purchased almost entirely within the regulated financial system and AIG wrote credit default swaps (CDS) out of a thrift subsidiary in order to insure them. The purchasers were allowed by the Fed to reduce required regulatory capital but the writers weren't required by the OTS and its parent US Treasury to post a commensurate amount, so this market, like the others, was entirely driven by regulatory arbitrage.

Not surprisingly, this risk mis-pricing caused PLSers to increasingly re-securitize into CDOs in order to boost current profits as the bubble continued to inflate. CDO issuance rose from 30% of the market in 2002, to 60% in 2003, and 80% ($154 billion) by 2004. Senior CDO AAA/AA securities were vulnerable to the crash because they were based entirely on mezzanine PLS. Spreads on CDOs widened gradually and progressively during the 2005-2007 bubble, reflecting growing investor concern with this risk. But this didn't represent a switch from regulatory to risk-based market pricing. Recall that with a 1.60% capital requirement, AAA/AA CDOs priced at 30 basis points over the insured cost of bank funds generated a 24% ROE, so an additional 30 basis points with this leverage represented a significant yield sweetener. As yields on mezzanine PLS widened relative to similarly rated debt, issuers increasingly relied on the senior CDO AAA/AA market where the much smaller yield premium would attract global investors.

CDOs doubled, and CDO squared tripled, the up-front fees and cash profitability of ratings agencies and investment banks. But they could not have generated these fees unless this process also improved the profitability of the issuer and mortgage lender. Low yield requirements with high leverage often allowed the loan originator to charge the borrower a premium over what was needed in order to sell the loan to investors Using an old rule of thumb (based on mortgage life) for every 20 basis points in extra coupon yield, a lender could strip out a point premium for the loan broker. They were more profitable for loan servicers who generally booked a gain on the sale for the 50 basis point mortgage servicing rights contract (MSRs). In addition, a PLS issuer could book a profit on the excess spread, or interest only (I/O) strip security, using a discounted present value accounting method to value the expected excess yield over the life of the loan.

2. Mis-pricing PLS Equity

As we noted in chapter 2, the ability to leverage excessively with fixed cost government backed debt doesn't raise equity costs because equity investors can go for broke. The pool of funds readily seeking go for broke opportunities expanded rapidly during the sub-prime lending bubble.

During the early stages of the bubble the below investment grade and lower rated CDO interests were largely funded by hedge funds who were able to further leverage these investments using bank repo's, . Whereas the first loss was funded by equity and junk bond markets in the 1990s, hedge funds financed a lot of the mezzanine debt and retained interests at much lower yields than the risk warranted due to several incentive distortions.

Managers that funded mezzanine and some subordinated interests received annual cash performance bonuses with no claw-back provisions and hence had an incentive to go-for-broke. In the first assessment of hedge fund returns, former hedge fund manager Simon Lack calculates the weighted average long run net of costs and fees return to be about zero or slightly positive, depending on whether one uses more pessimistic or more optimistic assumptions.[97] This was a shock to many given the outsized returns often reported and most analysts explain the flood of money into hedge funds as herd behavior chasing yields, a form of irrational exuberance. But the more robust explanation is politically distorted investor incentives.

In spite of this distortion favoring managers over investors, hedge fund assets approximately doubled during the boom from 2000 to mid 2004 and then doubled again during the bubble from mid-2004 through year end 2007.[98] Most of the asset increase during the bubble apparently came from state and local pension funds that also faced go-for-broke incentives due to their public risk for private profit incentive structure. The higher the assumed rate of return, the more politicians can pay on state and local employee pensions without raising taxes. Mutual insurance companies have faced this problem for well over a century when advertising the costs and benefits of guaranteed annuities. In response, the NYS regulator held the assumed rate of return at 2% for most of the last century, with any additional returns payable as an "unexpected" dividend. Paying additional pension benefits for "extraordinary" investment performance with their taxpayers on the hook for any shortfalls resulted in both pensioners and pension managers taking more than prudent levels of risk.

Recent analysis in an article by Howard Bornstein, Stan Markuze, Cameron Percy, Lisha Wang, and Moritz Zander entitled "Going For Broke: Reforming California's Public Employee Pension System" suggests that the proper assumed rate for government guaranteed pensions should be about 4% (consistent with a calculation by me published in 2005).[99] California, like most state and local governments, assumed a return of about twice that. Hence the managers had every incentive to go for broke by investing in hedge funds and hedge fund managers had an incentive to go for broke investing in risky mortgage securities, the more leverage the better. Banks provided significant leverage for these investments, thereby magnifying the effects of moral hazard.[100]

Investment banks also had incentives to mis-price equity risk. Investment banks were historically funded by partner equity and retained annual management bonuses in the firm, until retirement, to mitigate the agency conflict between traders and investors (which is common among hedge funds). But by the time of the housing boom the firms had virtually all gone public, with partners cashing out from the sale of stock to private investors, which were largely sovereign (government sponsored) wealth funds.

During the later stages of the bubble investment bank PLS issuers "parked" them in their proprietary trading accounts, and booked large profits due both to cheap debt and inflated assumed yields that were further magnified by extreme leverage. They were supposedly marked to market, but because there was no organized market for these securities, SEC rules allowed the "traders" to book nominal values and yields based on "projected" cash flows. Because these residual cash flows are subordinate to more senior debt, the most junior securities often wouldn't start generating cash for years, giving wide latitude to the forecasting models.

Present value accounting allowed PLS securitizers and proprietary traders to accelerate gains and investor accounting to defer losses, so annual all-cash bonuses, with no claw-back provision, posed an extreme moral hazard to shareholders. Shareholders faced agency conflicts in attempts to reign in securitizers and traders, but the fundamental reason they didn't is because the firms' extreme leverage allowed them to share in the gains. Investment bank securitizers, traders, and shareholders all had the incentive to go-for-broke at the expense of investors and ultimately taxpayers.

Investment banks began by expanding from underwriting PLS to buying the loans and in some cases the issuer, and issuing their own securities. These PLSers relied increasingly on their own "sponsored" hedge funds to fund the riskiest mezzanine and subordinated interests both because sponsorship was extremely profitable and because, over time, independent hedge funds became more reluctant to do so. As with bank SIVs, these managed fund assets were only nominally off balance sheet with an implicit put back to the originating sponsor. When the major potential conflict of interest between securitizers and "sponsored" asset managers became overly apparent, PLSers relied increasingly on their own "proprietary trading desks" to fund the increasingly hard to sell mezzanine and subordinated securities. These "proprietary traders" were engaged in the same activities as hedge funds, but with the investment bank's capital.

Large loan originators publically traded as finance companies also retained residual interests. They faced the biggest incentive distortions.

The nation's largest sub-prime lender Countrywide was the leader in originating and servicing loans with little or no down payment using "piggy back" purchase money second mortgages, which they also securitized with PLS. This gave them enormous leverage with private mortgage insurers and F&F, both of whom they could now bypass. Countrywide exploited the competition between PLSers and F&F more than any other sub-prime lender. It sold 20% of its originations to F&F in 2004, down from two thirds the previous two years, as it ramped up PLS for first and second mortgages. Countrywide also pressured the insurers to enter into "re-insurance contracts" that left the insurers with virtually all the risk and Countrywide with as much as 40% of the premium, in what is now being investigated as a "kick-back" scheme.

In relative terms, Countrywide may have set the record for going broke the most, surprising as it was not a regulated bank or investment bank, but it did have "friends of Angelo." Countrywide bribed F&F executives and politicians with its "friends of Angelo" program to get low F&F guarantee fees and favorable political treatment.[101] The CEO Mazolo cashed out his stock before the bubble burst, realizing a $100 million profit. Bank of America bought the company and indemnified Mazolo, protecting his gains from any claw-back in spite of illegalities. B of A is now expected to lose about 8 times its purchase price, an insolvency that would have brought it down had it not been TBTF.

F. PLS Funding of Bad Loans Generates Cash Profitability

Sub-prime loans originated during the housing boom could only be considered marginally profitable by using extreme regulatory leverage and exogenously priced cheap debt to generate an expected return of a few basis points over break-even to generate a sufficient expected ROE. This attracted equity investors who were already attempting to go for broke with even a slight chance of success even though there was more downside risk than up-side potential for the go-for-broke strategy, and the pool of even marginally qualified borrowers soon dried up. But the ability to strip out profits up front in cash meant that borrowers, lenders, securitizers and equity managers – hedge funds and proprietary traders – all had the incentive to keep the process going well after they were already broke, i.e., originating and securitizing mortgages that would most assuredly default when the house price bubble deflated.

The projection of returns that more than broke even depended on many questionable assumptions. The two most important were that home prices would continue rising and that first lien mortgages with down payments financed with a second lien - purchase money seconds - would perform as well as those which were privately insured or had cash down payments of at least 20%. These assumptions became increasingly unrealistic, but even if PLS securitizers projected default rates on the underlying loans that would wipe out not only the value of their retained interests but also that of the investors in many of the sold securities, *they* would remain profitable as long as the credit ratings, and therefore yield requirements, didn't change.

As long as the housing price bubble continued to inflate and the borrowers remained marginally qualified even with continually rising house prices PLSers could continue to securitize even loans that almost assuredly would default when the bubble burst. Rising house prices allowed borrowers to continually re-financing before the teaser rate would reset. Mortgages with teaser rates enhanced PLS profitability by raising future cash flow projections even if borrowers couldn't afford the coupon rate and hence would never pay it. This also benefited lenders who received all pre-payment fees as well as the ratings agencies

This wasn't particularly new. The regulatory accounting distortions behind the sub-prime lending debacle of the 1990s weren't corrected, and were of even greater consequence in the next decade. PLSers were allowed to earn cash profits making bad loans. Rising house prices delayed default recognition but holders of retained interest still had to generate the cash to finance larger retained interests that were required by CDOs. Now PLSers had more alternatives to turning these book profits to cash than borrowing in the junk bond and equity markets. Investment banks could fund freely in the commercial paper markets. And, the I/O security structure was changed to trigger cash distributions to the issuer who held the retained I/O strip, increasing losses to more senior bondholders when prices subsequently fell.[102]

This hypothetical but representative example illustrates how they generated profits regardless of future credit loss projections, a bit tedious analysis but hopefully worth the effort.

Table 4 Return on Assets to Achieve a 25% Return on Equity

Rating	Bank INV		ROE 25% ROA	weighted	SIV/F&F	ROE 25% ROA	weighted
AAA	0.016	81	0.4%	0.324	0.008	0.2	0.162
AA	0.016	11	0.4%	0.044	0.010	0.25	0.028
A	0.04	4	1.0%	0.04	0.010	0.25	0.010
BBB	0.08	3	2.0%	0.06	0.010	0.25	0.008
BB	0.01	0.5	2.5%	0.00125	0.010	0.25	0.001
NET ROA		99.5		**0.47%**			**0.21%**

Table 4 above shows the required return on assets to generate the targeted return on equity based on risk-based capital requirements. Column 4 shows the minimum ROA for each rating and column 5 shows the weighted average ROA to achieve a 25% before tax ROE, with the weights in column 3 from the securitization structure in Exhibit 1 above. Using bank financing for investment grade securities and investment bank financing for those below, the net required ROA is only 47 basis points. If we assume that F&F purchase the AAA PLS (and uses preferred stock sold to banks with a 1.6% capital requirement for half its capital) and an SIV purchases the rest of the investment grade securities (columns 6 through 8), then a net ROA target of only 21 basis points will achieve the 25% target ROE *for all investors in the securitization.* These ROA requirements are close to break even, and with extreme leverage the slightest miscalculation of credit default costs will magnify losses instead of gains.

Table 5 illustrates the consequences of hypothetical regulatory-determined yield requirements for potential PLS profitability. The hypothetical securitization of a pool of 7.25% coupon mortgages with a $100 principal, a 50 basis point sub-prime servicing fee, and a 25 basis point default risk premium to cover credit losses leaves a net of servicing and credit coupon of 6.5%,.[103] This is based on the typical senior/sub structure illustrated in the exhibit with capital requirements calculated as in Table 1 without resorting to the more highly leveraged SIV off-balance sheet financing or CDO restructuring illustrated in Table 3.

The upper portion of the table shows the ratings (column 1), tranche size as a percent of the pool from the Exhibit 1 (column 2), and the assumed yield requirements (column 3) consistent with the ratings and market interest rate assumptions. The premium or discount (column 4) is the present value difference between the net mortgage yield (net of costs and fees) and assumed yield requirement for this tranche assuming a five year mortgage pool life (ignoring monthly payments and principal amortization). Column 4 presents the present value of the retained excess spread or interest only (I/O) security,

Table 5   Securitization Profitability

Mortgage Backed Security					
	MBS (%)	Rate (%)	Premium or Discount	Value of Excess Spread	Value Including Residuals
AAA	81	4.75	$107.63	$8,717.97	$8,717.97
AA	11	5.2	$105.60	$1,161.57	$1,161.57
A	4	5.8	$102.96	$411.86	$411.86
BBB	3	6.5	$100.00	$300.00	$300.00
BB	0.5	10	$86.73		$43.37
NR	0.5	25	$50.25		$25.12
Total				$105.91	$106.60
	ROA@3%	ROE@2-1	ROE@20-1	ROA@3%	ROE@20-1
BB	7%	14%	140%	10%	200%
NR	22%	44%	440%	32%	640%

which reflects the difference between the net 6.5% coupon and the weighted average yield on the investment grade securities of 4.95% in this example, an excess spread of 1.55%. The net value (columns 5 & 6) are the share of MBS financing multiplied by the premium/discount value (the product of columns 2 and 4). Column 5 Total is the net value (per hundred dollars) when equity is retained (5.9% of the par value (i.e., total cost) of the pool) and column 6 is when equity is sold (6.6% of par). Only slightly higher gains can be recorded by selling retained interests because of the high assumed investor required yields of 10% for BB and 25% for NR securities.[104]

The hypothetical yield requirements are driven by bank risk-based capital requirements. For example, an ROA of only 1/2% for AAA securities would generate a before tax ROE of over 30% based on a 20% risk weighting and .016 capital requirement. BBB securities held by a bank have an 8% capital requirement or 12.5 to one leverage, so a (net of credit loss) average ROA of 2% implies a before tax ROE of 25%. For BB rated securities the capital requirements are double, so the ROA would also have to double, i.e. rise to 4% to achieve the same projected ROE. That represents an increase in required yield of only 2% from 6.5% to 8.5% (conservatively assumed to be 10% in Table 4.) These are typical of the calculations bankers make when pricing loans.

The accrued return on equity for the retained interests depends on the hedge fund or investment bank's financing cost (here assumed to be 3% as it is short term and fully collateralized) and the leverage ratio. We illustrate a 2 to 1 leverage ratio for an independent hedge fund. But much higher leverage was generally possible and a 20 to 1 ratio for an investment bank proprietary trading desk is conservative. Even at a low assumed yield of only 10% on the BB and 25% on the NR securities, the ROAs are 7% and 22%, and the ROE ranges from 14% for BB and 44% for NR securities, by using hedge fund leverage, to a range of 140% to 440% with investment bank leverage. At the higher assumed yields for BB (13%) and more typical NR (35%) securities shown in column 5, the investment bank ROE soars to 200% for BB and 640% for NR securities. Note that NR would generate a 22% to 32% ROE even if held by a bank with the 100% capital requirement.

CDO and CDO squared structures don't increase the gain on sale very much when below investment grade securities are retained because there is less to sell. So the motivation created by the CDO structure is that investors would pay a sufficient premium for the AAA (and AA) securities over BBB relative to risk due to their excessively low capital requirements, slightly raising the total value of excess spread based on the same assumptions as in Table 4, while retaining 50% to 150% more. As the boom progressed, distributions on this security became a significant source of cash for PLSers. As a result of CDO AAA pricing, the excess spread averaged about 2.5% during 2006 (Ashcroft and Schuermann, 2008, pg 31), over 60% more than in the above example not using a CDO, with profits commensurately larger.

The only thing that would change in the above analysis when funding purchase money seconds with PLS is the third column of Table 1: the percentage of the pool rated senior AAA/AA would fall well below 92%, due to the additional risk, with a commensurate rise of mezzanine and subordinated debt. If we assume, for example, that the tranche weightings were a much more restrictive AAA 50%, AA 15%, A 15%, BBB 15%, BB 4.5% and NR ½ %; then the cost of second mortgage financing would rise by only about 100 basis points (1%) over and above the cost of the first mortgage (based on the yield structure in Table 5 below, which is independent of the collateral being financed). Ratings were in fact in this range, the result was a substantial advantage for piggy-back second mortgage financing over PMI or FHA insurance. PLS financing accounted for less than ½% of second mortgage financing overall, although as much as 6% of those originated in 2006 and most were undoubtedly backed by piggy-backed purchase money seconds.[105]

Actual credit losses were orders of magnitude greater than those implicitly projected in the required security yields. But those making the projections all gained. Investors and tax payers, who relied exclusively on regulators, bore the losses.

G. CDO Issuance and Ownership

By the time of the 2008 crash, banks financed about $1.25 trillion of off balance sheet entries with commercial paper (much of which funded PLS). In addition, banks may have funded as much as another quarter of AAA securities indirectly with repos for hedge funds and other investors. Banks also funded about 20% of the below AAA tranches directly, and perhaps another 30% indirectly with repos or off balance sheet.[106] Large banks dominated funding for CDOs which, in turn, funded the BBB securities (FCIC, 2010, p 155). About half of the CDO AAA securities were directly funded, largely with bank repo funding, by the FHLBs and investment banks (Acharya and Richardson, 2009, p. 202). Between a third and a half of the all AAA PLS (and, some say AAA CDOs) were bought by F&F and thus their cost structure dominated pricing for this tranche. And regulated investment banks and hedge funds investing public pension money dominated the pricing of mezzanine and subordinated securities. So the entire funding cost for sub-prime PLS was determined by risk based capital requirements, SEC capital requirements, and credit agency regulatory distortions with only a minor contribution due to agency conflicts of public pension hedge fund investing.

Figure 1 below, from Cordell et. al. (p. 38), illustrates how the junior securities from a total issuance of $3.8 trillion of PLS from prime and Alt A loans and $2.5 trillion of PLS sub-prime "home

Figure 1
Transformation of Mortgage Loans to CDO²s 1998 – 2007

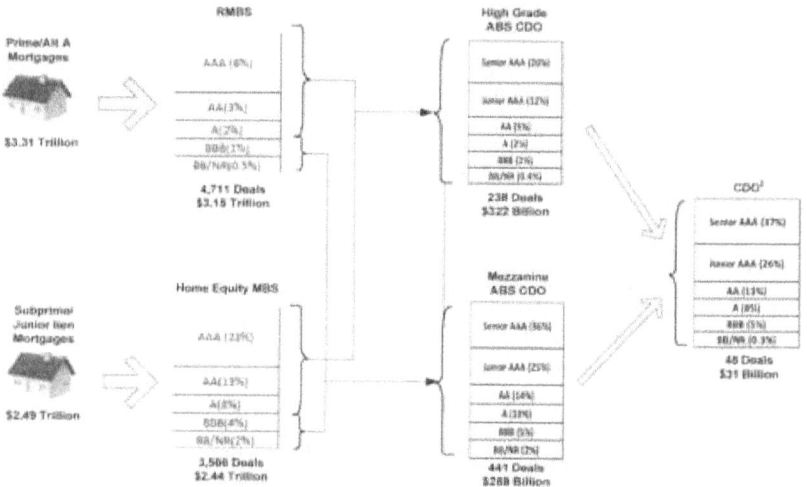

Note. This figure shows the total dollar amounts and counts for the various sources of mortgages, mortgage-backed securities, CDOs and CDO²'s that made up the mortgage market from 1998 – 2007. CDO = Collateralized Debt Obligation; RMBS = Residential Mortgage-Backed Securities; HEL = Home Equity loans; ABS = Asset-Backed Securities. Subordination levels are in parentheses.

equity" loans was transformed into $641 billion of structured finance (SF) ABS CDOs. The term 'home equity' here refers to sub-prime first liens generally. Total CDO issuance rose to $250 billion in 2005 and $521 billion in 2006. From 2004 through 2007 PLSers issued $1.4 trillion in CDOs, with most using the CDO squared structure to increase the total volume of AAA/AA securities.

Figure 2 below, from Cordell et al (p.39), shows that over two thirds of the CDOs were backed by sub prime (called home equity) loans during the peak years 2006-2007.

Figure 2

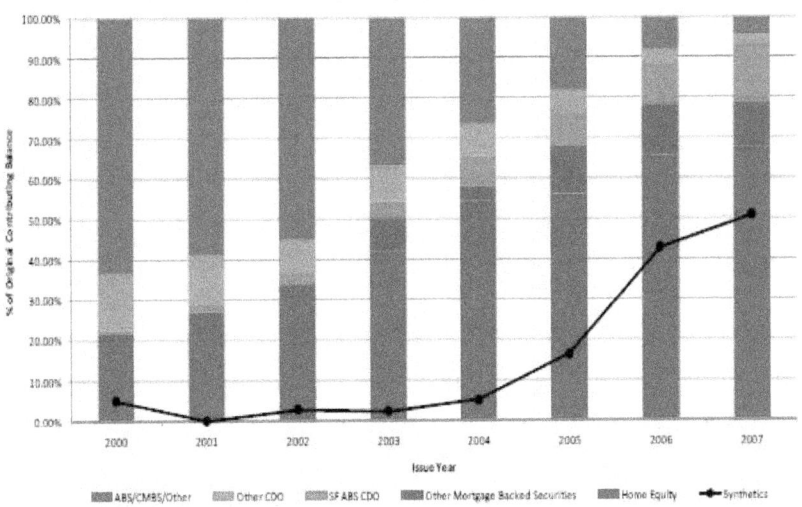

Original Asset (Collateral) Composition of Structured Finance ABS CDO

Note: This table summarizes shares of assets for structured finance ABS CDOs by five asset categories in the bar charts, and also includes shares of synthetic collateral in the line plot. Synthetics = Credit Default Swaps, Home Equity = Home Equity Mortgage-Backed Securities, SF ABS CDO = structured finance asset-backed security collateralized debt obligations, ABS = asset-backed security, CMBS = commercial mortgage-backed securities, Other = all remaining asset collateral within the SF ABS CDO

This strongly suggests that the biggest rating agency failure was in regard to sub-prime loans, which was further compounded by rating mezzanine PLS as AAA CDOs. This makes sense, as the rating agencies, like everybody else but for the long term investors, got paid up front and hence had the incentive to keep going well past the point where investors would go broke, which required their otherwise inexplicable optimism.

Who owned PLS? Table 6 below, from Acharya and Richardson (p. 203), illustrates who owned the mortgage stock in 2008 when the financial system crashed. F&F apparently bought only PLS AAA securities because the CDO AAAs didn't qualify for the housing goals, a lucky happenstance as all the AAA/AA CDOs were subordinate to the AAA/AA PLS. This implies that the AAA/AA CDOs ended up in the non-GSE financial system. Banks owned about a quarter of senior AAA PLS tranches (mostly CDOs) and about 20% of subordinate tranches directly. Investment banking PLSers funded over 27% of the Mezzanine PLS and 20% of the retained interests. Other private investors, mostly hedge funds and finance company PLSers, held about 10% of the mez and 40% of the

Table 6: PLS Ownership

	Privately Issued Senior AAA PLS	Privately Issued AA/Mezzanine PLS	Other (Retained Interests)	Total	Total share
Banks	383	90	0	473	21%
GSEs	308	0	0	308	14%
Inv'nt Banks	100	130	24	254	12%
Guarantors	0	100	0	100	4%
Insurance	125	65	24	214	10%
Foreign	413	45	24	482	22%
Other	307	46	49	402	18%
Total	1636	476	121	2233	!00%

retained interests. Foreign investors – mostly banks - were relatively large players in senior AAA CDOs (25%), mez (10%), and retained interests (40%). US banks also repo funded an additional 25% held by broker-dealers.[107] Some of this was funded off-balance sheet with commercial paper, which continued to rise. Finance companies such as Countrywide that issued PLS probably account for the "other" holdings.

Including the possibility for falling house prices, an inevitable and obvious forthcoming event to many observers by the end of 2004, would have increased the cumulative loss projections and forced recognition of losses on existing PLS and halted new issues. But international lenders generally didn't know the extent of loan risk or leverage in PLS, and had no reason to distrust the SEC certification of the credit rating agencies. Thus, when American investors began to demand additional yield, or lower prices, relative to similarly rated investments, particularly on AAA/AA CDO backed by mezzanine PLS, foreign invertors were drawn in without much thought given to the potential risk. The state owned German Bausparkassen savings banks are prime examples.

As shown in Exhibit 2 below, total PLS and CDO issuance continued to grow from 2003 through mid 2007, before plummeting during the second half of 2007 and shutting down entirely by the end of 2008.[108] The reasons for the magnitude of this rise and fall are at the root of the sub-prime debacle, explained in the next chapter.

Exhibit 2

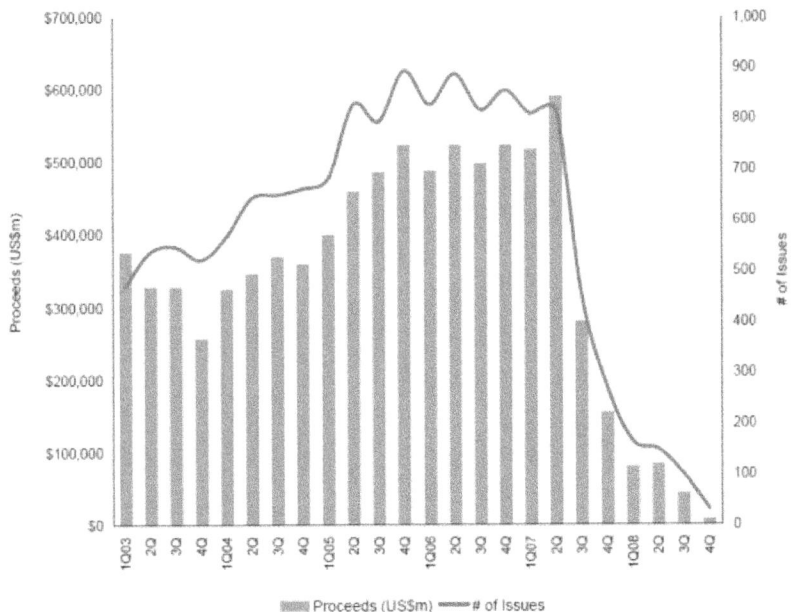

Quarterly Residential ABS, MBS & CDO Volume

The agency conflicts inherent in PLS were latent and manageable prior to investor and borrower capital depletion and the implementation of political housing goals. All the parties could be held accountable under both the legal arrangements and could have expected performance behavior. I spite of all these and other previously mentioned political and regulatory distortions that exacerbated incentive conflicts, the sub-prime lending debacle described in the next chapter may arguably have been averted if the state-regulated PMIs had remained as the gatekeepers. The subsequent plethora of lawsuits discussed in chapter 5 represents the dissolution of well-functioning market constraints and accountability as a consequence of the extreme leverage enabled by regulatory malfeasance and encouraged by housing policy.

Chapter 4: The Root Causes of the Systemic Financial Crisis of 2008

The US – like all market economies - has always experienced boom-bust cycles in interest sensitive sectors, non-residential as well as residential housing. As capital flows freely across open market borders, it is not at all surprising that such cycles occurred approximately simultaneously in other market economies. Booms generally turn to bust eventually. The US sub-prime lending debacle is credited with causing the global financial crisis due to the magnitude and duration of the bubble in house prices to historic levels, the depth of losses to systemic proportions and the global breadth of the incidence of loss.

The US was unique in two ways: its use of financial sector housing policy and its multiple overlapping financial sector regulatory structures. The unique nature of US politics created the Fed, FDIC and Fannie Mae as hybrid structures resulting in multiple overlapping levels of prudential regulation without effective political accountability. By the end of the century early fears of federal credit allocation were realized as federal financial sector housing policies prospectively added about 20 million sub-prime borrowers to home ownership housing demand, most but not all explicitly linked to CRA lending quotas or F&F affordable housing quotas. No subsidies were explicitly budgeted, the assumption being that banks and F&F could afford to make the loans required to meet these goals by using extreme leverage with federal backing.

Extreme leverage made funding these housing goals with PLS seemingly marginally profitable in the 1990s. But house prices were only rising gradually and from a low base, so defaults eventually accelerated, and the shorts brought the market to a complete collapse. PLSers were again active within a few short years, and this time, the borrowers were even worse, with both weak credit and less or no equity. So how were they able to get funding while memories of the last debacle were still fresh? The regulatory distortions to investor incentives were even worse, as regulatory capital rules facilitated booking phantom profits and hence capital, which was then converted to cash so that lenders had "no skin in the game. The cash kept the PLS funding machine going, leading to even greater cash profits in the short run.

But as long as house prices continued inflating borrowers could refinance, postponing and exacerbating subsequent investor losses. Real house prices doubled before peaking. There were two necessary conditions, which together were sufficient. First, the Fed flooded the market with cheap credit that political housing policy directed to generally un-or-under qualified home mortgage borrowers using federally backed credit. Second, state and local governments implemented "smart growth" policies limiting housing production, causing the excess demand to dramatically inflate the value of land and existing housing.

Such asset price bubbles always burst, *always*! Speculators shorting the market would have normally burst the asset price bubble by the end of 2002, and certainly no later than the end of 2004, but federal backing of the debt provided immunity from the shorts. Continued easy money that GSEs – particularly F&F – channeled to housing allowed this bubble to continue inflating well past the historical breaking point to systemic proportions when the pool of qualified borrowers was depleted. FHA and the FHLBs played a supporting role, coming in at just the right time as PLSers were exiting. Funding the price bubble with publicly backed debt made the resulting solvency crisis extremely deep and global.

Political housing policy clearly "pushed" all the GSEs, the PLSers and the banks into the market to fund generally un-or-under qualified borrowers through porous regulatory barriers while implicit GSE and PLS (FDIC) capital subsidies totaling about $10 billion per trillion dollars – well over $150 billion annually and cumulatively over $1.5 trillion dollars for the decade - "pulled" them in. All the GSEs competed with PLSers and banks by increasing both leverage and loan risk, but F&F and the FHLBs also cooperated by meeting F&F and FHLB housing goals by purchasing privately originated CRA whole loans and AAA PLS backed by pools of sub-prime loans.

These subsidies were supposed to make sub-prime lending profitable, but the net credit loss far exceeds the value of the subsidy to borrowers – cost to taxpayers - by trillions of dollars. Hence the political myth that lenders and investors were attracted to these loans by expectations of extra profits at the borrower's expense – predatory lending - is far fetched. Extreme leverage made this high risk strategy profitable to the people on the front end originating loans during the first half of the decade. PLSers and F&F at first competed to "go for broke" funding pools of sub-prime loans likely to default and hence unlikely to be profitable even with extreme leverage. As the risks increased and the rise in house prices slowed, they eventually competed to "go broke" while technically insolvent, looting their firms and funds - and ultimately taxpayers - causing the lending bubble of 2005-2007 to continue inflating. FHA and the FHLBs provided most of their support at the peak, helping sustain and extend the price bubble. The *ex post* losses resulting from this moral hazard were several times greater than the *ex ante* capital shortfall.

This was no private market breakdown based on irrational exuberance as the entire market operated free of normal market constraints in the short run on the false premise of prudential regulation. Regulatory malfeasance was so widespread it is hard to pick a winner. But the risk-based capital rules – especially for second mortgages and AAA CDOs – are the biggest contributors to the debacle. Banks also went for broke providing second mortgage financing in lieu of cash down-payments, providing both PLS and F&F a way around the private mortgage insurers who were the traditional gatekeepers: direct bank funding of about a trillion dollars of second mortgages enabled both PLS and F&F funding of the first liens. Bank funding of CDOs – mostly funding first mortgage liens - also kept the PLS machine humming from 2005-2007.

The result was a typical Austrian cycle of credit expansion causing an asset price bubble and subsequent financial sector crash. The Fed provided the money and GSEs fueled a mortgage credit bubble as the outstanding stock of US household mortgage debt increased by 120%, almost $6 trillion. This fueled an asset price bubble in housing of $6 trillion over and above the increase in the physical stock and general monetary inflation. US home owner equity then fell by $6 trillion by year-end 2009 and by mid 2012 almost $7 trillion in homeowner equity had been wiped out, about half of which represented negative mortgage equity, the cause of the systemic financial crisis.

The political narrative that as of mid 2008 nobody could have seen this crisis coming and then when it hit it took incredible political action to mitigate the damage done by the unregulated private sector is entirely false and misleading. Even market participants who recognized the credit bubble as a form of pyramid finance had the incentive to stay in the market until just before the crash. Understanding what was known or knowable at the time provides a clearer explanation of the unfolding crisis.

Part A puts the magnitude of this bubble in historical and international perspective, describes the Fed's role in the bubble and reviews the measurable *ex ante* Treasury costs of capital subsidies to fund housing policy without the benefit of hindsight regarding future losses. Part B explains the extreme moral hazard of excessive leverage motivating the GSEs - F&F, FHA, the FHLBs - and TBTF banks that continued to expand, inflating the bubble to systemic proportions. Part C explains the consequences of the credit bubble raising house prices, mostly due to the influence of regional restrictions on housing supply and house prices, allowing about three fourths of the benefit of lower mortgage rates to be captured by land and existing housing owners and smart growth politicians and regulators. It then compares the up-front subsidy costs to the ultimate actual and projected credit losses readily predictable the time of the 2008 financial crisis and their distribution through the financial system. Part D explains how and why this bubble finally deflated and the market crashed, distinguishing between the causes and the consequences of the resulting PLS crash and financial crisis. Part E explains the fallacy of competing explanations as all of the other purported causes of the financial crisis were symptoms of out of control Fed monetary and political housing policy facilitated by chronic and systemic regulatory malfeasance and smart growth regulations.

A. The Subsidy-Fueled Mortgage Credit Bubble

The Fed's low interest rate policy fueled an asset price bubble, which political housing policy diverted to the housing sector. The result was an unprecedented bubble in house prices.

1. The Fed-Induced Housing Boom and Asset Price Bubble

By the end of 2002, the run-up in U.S. house prices had reached an historic peak in real terms. Not all asset price inflation is caused by a bubble in credit expansion, but asset bubbles of this magnitude historically are and this case was no different. The housing boom would normally have turned to bust due to rising interest rates and the lack of qualified home buyers, but the Fed kept interest rates extremely low, fueling the continued rise in housing demand. Real interest rates were a historic negative levels based on CPIU inflation of the time. Moreover, a strong case can be made that monetary inflation was much higher than implied by this construct of the CPI due to the growth in productivity during the first half of the past decade that lowered many prices, causing what would otherwise been a mild and beneficial deflation.[109]

Figure 1

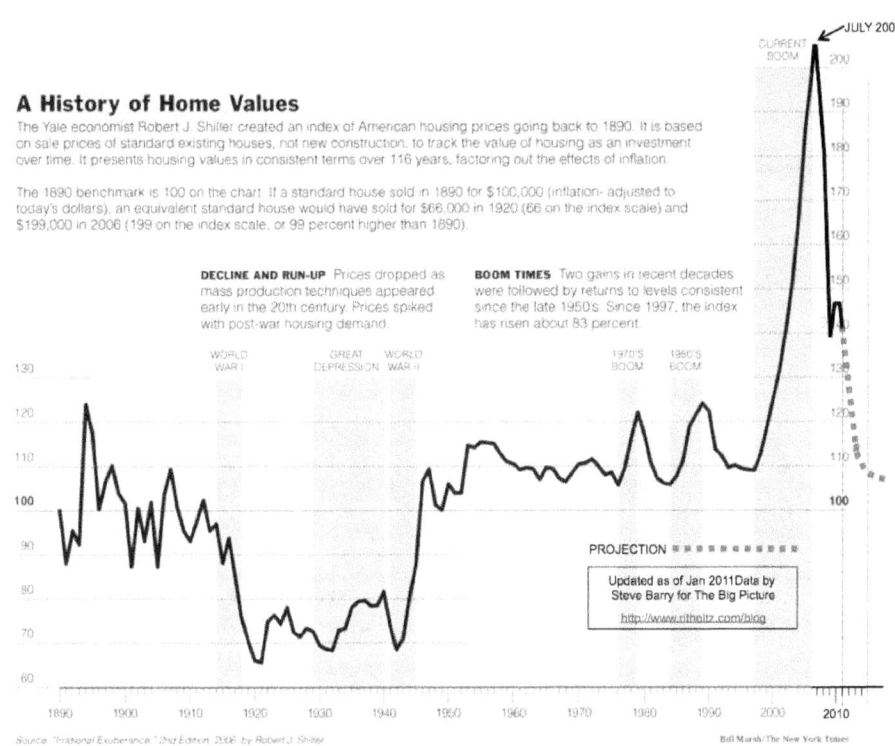

Why was this low interest rate policy implemented? Raising the specter of another Great Depression after 9/11/2001, then Fed Board Member Bernanke urged Chairman Greenspan to lower interest rates and keep them low. As a result, the Fed Funds rate was held to only one percent through mid-2004.

In *Getting off Track* (2009) Stanford professor John Taylor, author of the Taylor Rule, summarizes his research on the latest housing boom and price bubble. Had the Fed followed this rule, it would have started raising interest rates by the beginning of 2002 and the bust would have followed the historical pattern. By holding down the fed funds rate for another two and a half years it deviated from normal policy more than at any time since the end of the 1970's. The chart below illustrates the rise in interest rates had the Fed instead followed the Taylor Rule.

Figure 2

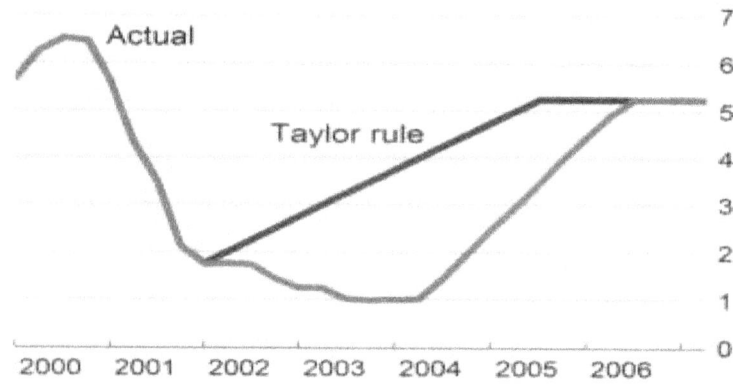

FIGURE 1. Chart from *The Economist*, October 18, 2007

What would have happened had the Fed followed the Taylor rule? Using his macro-model, Taylor simulated the consequences for the housing boom of the tighter monetary policy implied by the Taylor Rule, shown below. The housing boom and resulting price bubble would have ended in late 2002 in this simulation, following the historical pattern. Instead by the end of 2004 the US house price bubble was inflated to about five times the historic maximum, so by this account the Fed added about 2&1/2 years to the bubble.

Figure 3

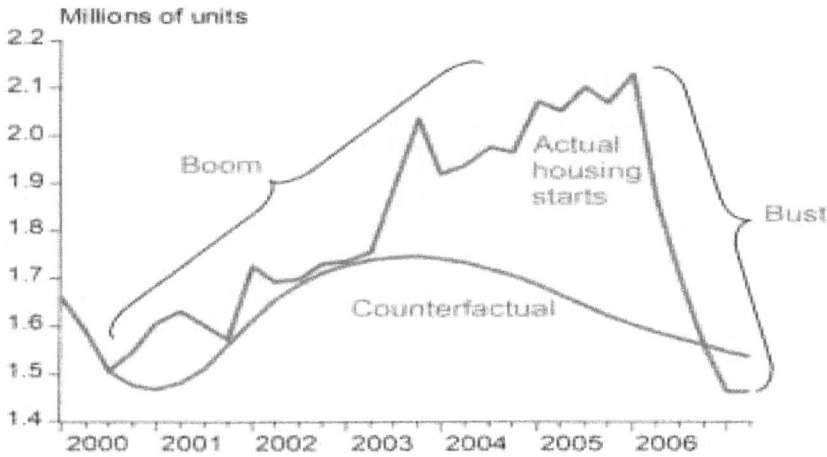

FIGURE 2. The Boom-Bust in Housing Starts Compared with the Counterfactual

As the housing boom and bubble subsequently developed, Chairman Bernanke developed the position that monetary expansion and the associated housing bubble was beyond the Fed's control, driven by a global savings glut.[110] The first FCIC dissent of the three other republican commissioners cites the evidence of the housing bubbles in Europe and Australia as evidence of a common cause. These are all countries that allow capital to flow freely, so it is not surprising that all would have easy money policies simultaneously with the US to minimize interest rate differentials. Taylor also debunks Fed Chairman Bernanke's excuse of a global savings glut: global savings had been on a downward trend for about 25 years (see figure below from the IMF study in 2005).

The Taylor Rule also applies to central banks in other countries that have always watched the Fed and often followed its lead. Hence the boom in other countries is also easily explained: our biggest export is the Fed's easy money policies: when Fed Chairman Arthur Burns "primed the pump" prior to the 1974 election campaign, for example, the subsequent inflation spread world wide. Some other countries followed the Fed's interest rate lead this time as well rather than the equally applicable Taylor Rule to avoid unwanted capital inflows, with a similar housing bubble resulting. Those that followed the Fed instead of the Taylor Rule this time had a similar housing boom; those that didn't follow the Rule didn't. The dollar is the world's reserve currency and the Fed is the leader, not the follower.

Figure 4

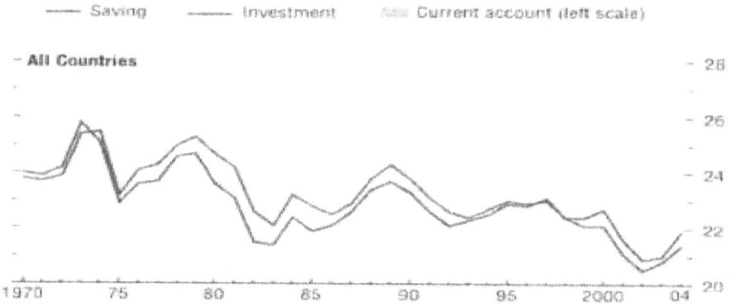

Figure 2.1. Global Saving, Investment, and Current Accounts
(Percent of world GDP)
Global saving and investment have been trending downward since the early 1970s. They reached historic lows in 2002, and have recovered modestly since then.
Saving
Investment
Current account (left scale)
All Countries
28
26
24
22
20
1970
75
80
85
90
95
2000
04

China ran trade surpluses so it had a glut of savings, which rather than spend it exported to the US, but that doesn't explain the Fed's easy money policy. China doesn't determine US monetary policy. In fact, as shown in Exhibit 1 below the US was pulling in almost the entire available savings surplus globally to fund the US housing boom.

Exhibit 1

The US current account deficit from 2005 to 2009 absorbed all the surplus saving from China, the rest of Asia, and the Middle East

Cumulative current account balances, 2005–09

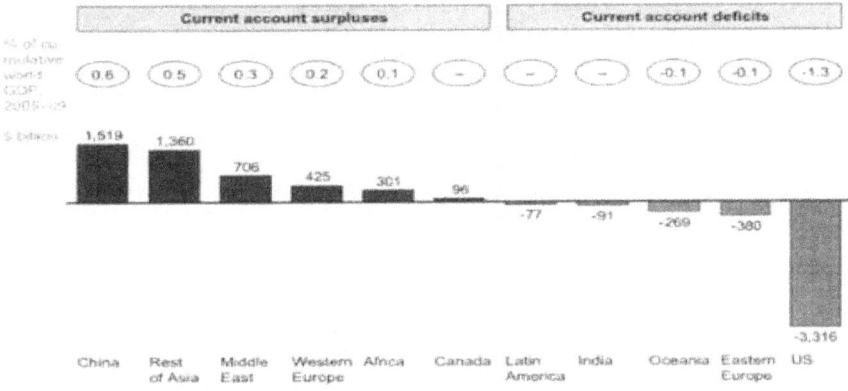

SOURCE: McKinsey Global Economic Growth Database; McKinsey Global Institute

One can provide various defenses for Fed actions taken and critiques of the alternative analyses. But the fact remains that domestic savings didn't fund the boom and the Fed chose not to mitigate the effects of foreign inflows. The international monetary mechanisms of the past two centuries had dissipated. China chose it's own, to purchase unlimited dollars at a fairly constant exchange rate to stimulate domestic employment. To avoid the US deflation that all prior monetary mechanisms would have required and the potential unemployment that goes along with it, the Fed printed money to accommodate the Chinese demand. Other countries intervened in currency markets to mitigate the effects of the Fed's beggar thy neighbor policies, spreading the credit expansion globally, particularly in Europe (see Jacobo Carmassi, Daniel Gros and Stefano Micossi, 2009, p. 979). The resulting housing boom maintained employment levels until the credit and house price bubbles began deflating in 2007.

The European Central Bank (ECB) may have followed the Fed's lead, but it was the creation of the euro at the beginning of the decade along with the ECB that created a "GSE effect" (below) in the poorer European countries. Interest rates in Spain, Ireland and the other poorer southern European countries plummeted to German levels, so the combination of low rates and even lower rates in poorer countries fueled a real estate boom. [111]

What motivated the Fed to start this cycle? Kling (p. 39) cites Krugman's column intended as a joke that stated:

"To fight this recession the Fed needs more than a snapback; it needs soaring household spending to offset moribund business investment. And to do that, as Paul McCulley of Pimco put it, Alan Greenspan needs to create a housing bubble to replace the NASDAQ bubble."[112] But maybe he was not joking. Rickards (2011, p. 181) notes that as colleagues at Princeton in the late 1990s Krugman collaborated with then professor Bernanke and fellow Princeton professor at the time Vice Chairman of the Fed Alan Blinder to diagnose the "Japanese disease" and should the need arise in the US to formulate such policies to stimulate household consumption while keeping the dollar cheap to maintain competitive parity with China.

2. The Treasury *ex ante* Cost of Financial Sector Housing Subsidies

In addition to cheap credit provided by the Fed and low underwriting and down-payment constraints provided by political housing policy, taxpayers provided a carrot to accompany the credit allocation stick by providing enormous additional capital subsidies to further reduce interest rates below their risk-adjusted level. The magnitude of these subsidies depends on the difference between required and market capital levels. With the benefit of hindsight, we could simply calculate the amount of capital that would have absorbed the *ex post* credit losses and still left financial institutions well capitalized but this is misleading because high initial capital requirements would have prevented the resulting moral hazard. Without exploiting that advantage, we could simply determine a more modest *ex ante* capital standard based on past experience with mortgage risk, part art and part science.

Start with F&F, taking into account the new high risk strategies adopted during the last decade. Total F&F mortgage loans and guarantees outstanding averaged roughly $5 trillion for the decade 2000-2009, about half funded with debt and half funded with MBS. As PMI had historically covered virtually all the credit risk, the difference between the .45% capital requirement for MBS and the 2.5% capital requirement for debt primarily reflected the remaining un-hedged interest rate risk. If we conservatively assume they operated on about one fourth the market required capital for less risky loans during the last decade, i.e. that MBS guarantees should have required 2.0% capital instead of

.45% and debt 10% capital instead of 2.5%, this implies a weighted average capital shortfall of about 5%, i.e., that 5% their total mortgages were funded with debt instead of equity, a very conservative estimate relative to market capital of 16% for banks prior to deposit insurance (and as we will discuss, woefully inadequate relative to their true risk).

From the prior example in chapter 2, the estimated annual savings on $250 billion (5% of approximately $5 trillion on average) of implicit equity capital is 20% or $50 billion, based on a before tax ROE of 25%, an after tax ROE of 15% and a funding cost of 5%. Again, the subsidy is half tax and half the difference between debt and equity costs. To put the $25 billion debt savings in perspective, the Congressional Budget Office (CBO) reported that the GSE funding advantage resulted in a $19.6 billion annual combined subsidy for F&F in 2003, when the outstanding debt and MBS were about 20% below the decade average. The CBO calculation ignored the tax savings, the other half of the subsidy so this estimate is consistent with theirs.[113] Hence the total F&F capital subsidy implied by our methodology was about $50 billion per year or about $500 billion for the decade.

This represents a $30 billion annual increase from prior decades, due both to their larger portfolio and higher risk profile. How far does a $50 billion annual capital subsidy go? That's just enough to lower the rate charged on all 12 million subprime loans made by F&F during the lending bubble by 1% (100 basis points) for an average $417,000 mortgage and assuming other borrowers, shareholders, managers and politicians got nothing. Put somewhat differently, as required capital is lowered from 5% (20-1 leverage) to 1% (100-1 leverage) the required return on assets (ROA) to achieve the targeted 25% return on equity (ROE) is lowered from 1.25% (25%/20) to .25% (25%/100). At this leverage ratio and ROA there is little margin for error.

These imputed market capital requirements assume the same difference between credit risk in MBS and interest rate risk for debt. The market distinction may well be different and also vary over time and by mortgage maturity. For the last decade the credit risk assessment would probably be much higher and the interest rate risk much lower than in prior decades. In addition, the interest rate risk for adjustable rate mortgage pools funded by PLS is obviously less than for fixed rate pools. For the purpose of illustration, we simply calculated the consequences of a 5% additional capital requirement: to put that in perspective the Dodd-Frank Act discussed later proposed issuers put up 5% capital in addition to the capital required by purchasers.

Calculating Ginnie Mae capital subsidies using the same F&F methodology of $10 billion per trillion securities outstanding – equivalent to issuers maintaining 5% capital - implies an average Ginnie Mae subsidy of about $20 billion annually from 2000-2009 on $2 trillion of Ginnie Mae PCs. FHA nevertheless operates in the red, with an implied subsidy of about $5 billion. The FHLBs would add another $5 billion with most of the benefit passed on to sub-prime bank lenders (and their borrowers) and most of the loss transferred to the FDIC over and above the direct bank capital subsidies.

Table 1   Capital Subsidies

	Total in billions $	market-reg cap	Missing Capital	ROE-Debt	Tax Savings	Debt Savings	Annual Savings	Decade Savings
F&F	$5,000	5%	$250.00	20%	$25.00	$25.00	$50.00	$500.00
Ginnie Mae	$2,000	5%	$100.00	20%	$10.00	$10.00	$20.00	$200.00
FHA			$25.00	20%	$2.50	$2.50	$5.00	$50.00
FHLBs	$500	5%	$25.00	20%	$2.50	$2.50	$5.00	$50.00
Total							**$80.00**	**$800.00**
Banks	$4,000	5%	$200.00	20%	$20.00	$20.00	$40.00	$400.00
PLS	$3,000	5%	$150.00	20%	$15.00	$15.00	$30.00	$300.00
total	$14,500		$750.00		$75.00	$75.00	**$150.00**	**$1,500.00**
					$75.00			

PLS securities outstanding averaged about $3.0 trillion during the sub-prime lending debacle. From the prior example, that saved $150 billion (5% of 3.0 trillion) of implicit equity capital and the 20% reduction in the cost of funds would represent about $30 billion in annual savings, again half tax saving and half reflecting the difference between debt and after tax equity borrowing costs.

Insured depositories – mostly banks – held about $4 trillion in home mortgages during 2000-2007. Using the same methodology as for F&F, and assuming a 100% risk weighting instead of 50%, the missing capital is about $200 billion and the capital subsidy to mortgage investment was about $40 billion annually or $400 billion for the decade.

So the rough tally is that the US Treasury delivering about $80 billion to the GSEs in tax and "user fee" savings through "agency status" and about $70 billion annually to the banks (over FDIC fees charged) due to their "dueling charter" providing deposit insurance to fund mortgages. The GSE quotas and subsidies were about the same as the Bank/PLS quotas and subsidies, another term for "economic rents." That's $150 billion annually combined or about a trillion and a half dollars for the ten years ending in 2009 that was *potentially* available to lower mortgage rates. As noted previously in chapter 2 and discussed later in chapter 6, the tax savings is indisputably quantifiable and inexplicably ignored. The credit premium represents a foregone "opportunity cost" to taxpayers for which they are none the wiser until there is a loss. The Treasury maintains a budget for both estimates (using questionable methodologies) but they don't include GSEs.

The extent to which the Treasury cost accrues to the benefit of home-buyers depends on the ability of others to capture the value. This occurs in two stages: first, in loan rates being lowered by less than the subsidy cost and second by house prices rising in response to the increase in demand, discussed below. A gross approximation of this interest rate pass-through historically is 100% for Ginnie Mae/FHA but only about 50% for Fannie and Freddie (and probably bank customers as well, in competition with F&F), with the other half captured mostly by shareholders, the rest by managers, regulators and politicians. This changed dramatically during the last decade as owners of land and existing housing and the associated regulatory and political rent seekers captured a disproportionate share of the subsidy, and housing goals left little or nothing for the traditional rent-seekers, as discussed in Part C below.

3. The Housing Policy-Induced Credit Bubble

The first sub-prime lending debacle of the 1990's collapsed when PLSers could no longer issue junk bonds or equity to generate cash as speculators shorted the market. This didn't happen in the next debacle until about a decade into the bubble, after real house prices reached a peak of over 125% above their long run equilibrium level, five times more inflated that any house price bubble in the prior 120 years (see Figure 1 above) and eight times the more recent peaks. Had it followed this historic pattern, the bubble would have begun deflating in mid-2002.

Even with the Fed's cheap money policy, there are two reasons to believe that the housing boom and price bubble would have peaked by about 2002 and no later than late 2004. First, based on historical trends, purchasing housing at the peak of a bubble was not a good investment, and by mid-2004, there seemed to be few prospective U.S. borrowers left who had not already purchased a home but who had sufficient cash for a down payment (or were privately insurable) and who met normal underwriting criteria. Households that had money to invest had already purchased by then, leaving behind only un-or-under qualified borrowers. Second, lending to such households at the peak of a house price bubble was extremely risky. So what was different this time? As discussed in chapter 3, lending quality collapsed as lenders turned their attention to providing credit to ever less worthy borrowers while relaxing and eventually eliminating down payment requirements.[114]

The Wallison Dissent has an earlier version of the house price inflation graph presented above and the figure below linking the inflation in house prices to the increase in housing demand financed to meet the various housing goals.[115] The correlation is striking but not surprising.

Exhibit 2

Federal housing policy expanded demand by strongly supporting sub-prime lending generally and by setting goals for specific bank CRA and GSE affordable housing goals.

By the end of the century the historical distinction between banks and other federally insured depository institutions had largely faded, replaced by the distinction between the four TBTF commercial/universal banks – now Wells Fargo, B of A, JP Morgan Chase, and Citi Group - and all the rest of the federally insured depository institutions (hereafter all referred to as banks). The TBTF banks got that way largely by merger and acquisitions, so they accounted for most of the CRA lending commitments. Of the $4.5 trillion in CRA commitments made between 1992 and 2007, $3.8 trillion came due between 2000 and 2007, the majority by the TBTF banks active in M&A. Over the same period 2000-2007 GSE holdings of home mortgages also about doubled, increasing by about $2.5 The outstanding stock of US household mortgage debt increased by almost $6 trillion, a 120% increase in aggregate first and second lien debt, about half directly related to affordable housing goals, so it was political credit allocation that was fueling the construction boom and house price bubble during this period.

B. Extreme Leverage Creates Moral Hazard

There are two distinct time periods to the sub-prime lending debacle. The first from 2000 to 2004 was a typical the Fed-fueled housing boom. As noted in Calem, Nakamura and Wachter (2011, pp. 89-93) the homeownership rate peaked in mid 2004 but the house price bubble didn't peak for another two years (three in California).[116] Mortgage underwriting and down payment requirements became even looser, allowing homeowners to continue to do cash-out refi's and investors – many posed as owner-occupants – to finance multiple houses. The second from 2005-2007 aided the sub-prime housing policy creating a lending and price bubble that caused most of the subsequent credit loss when it burst.

As noted above, pursuing a high risk strategy with a thin interest rate margin and little capital provides little margin for error. The greater the risk, the more firms and their managers go for broke as described in chapter 2, and when they go broke they will keep on going broke until an external force, usually speculators or ultimately a bankruptcy court, forces them to stop. Only an end to the house price bubble could have stopped the PLSers, for the reasons discussed in the last chapter. Unlike the sub-prime lending debacle of the prior decade, this time the GSEs competed vigorously. Eventually all the GSEs and TBTF banks competed with PLSers by going beyond go for broke strategies; when they went broke the GSEs kept on going long past the point of technical insolvency, allowing the PLSers to do the same.

Chapter 3 discussed the motivations and incentives facing PLS issuers and investors. These three sections describe the motivations and incentives facing the GSEs - F&F, FHA/Ginnie Mae and the FHLBs - and bank issuers and investors, respectively.

1. F&F Follow PLSers: Go for Broke, then Go Broke

As the affordable housing goals ratcheted up during the first half of the decade the lending margins continued to be squeezed and F&F profits continued to fall: their after tax return on equity fell from an average of 25% to 30% or more in prior decades to only 15%. Moreover, while F&F didn't accelerate income the way the PLSers did, they were able to defer loan losses as a result of rising house prices. But even this understates the decline in profitability of their traditional funding and guarantee business because as much as 75% of their profits were now derived from proprietary trading so the ROA and hence ROE on the traditional business was negligible.[117] In response to this declining profitability, F&F had already deviated from their historical low-risk patterns during the prior decade by ramping up their portfolio lending and hence their interest rate risk while simultaneously abandoning the strategy of avoiding credit risk.

By the first half of the last decade this was not enough to stay competitive with PLSers or FHA/Ginnie Mae, so they doubled down. They increased their interest rate and credit risks, both without a commensurate increase in expected return as compensation. To achieve ROE targets, there was not much else they could do but further increase their leverage to levels approaching 100-1 (with preferred stock, which they counted as capital but banks bought with a 20% risk weighting or only 1.6% capital). F&F managers were clearly going for broke with a highly leveraged strategy by this time in an attempt to save the franchise and shareholders didn't have much choice but to let them try.

F&F continued to purchase their own MBS funded with debt in an attempt to take on greater interest rate risk. The percent of mortgage portfolios funded by debt doubled from 10 percent in 1997 to 20 percent in 2003 (HHS, p 4). In addition, AAA/AA PLS securities counted toward their affordable housing goals – and sometimes were pooled to order – so F&F at times purchased as much as half the market of newly issued PLS for this purpose, assuming all the interest rate risk and the residual credit risk of highly rated securities.

The additional risks had initially proven costless, but reported profits were down for the first half of the decade, performance was weak and Freddie Mac's stock was flat while Fannie Mae's stock price fell by about 50%, all reflecting the lack of profitability of their formerly *core* business and their increasing risk. If the high risk strategy was paying off, why were profits so meager? Raising borrower yield requirements with competition from PLS and FHA/Ginnie Mae would have made adverse selection worse, so they either had to accept thin projected margins with huge downside risk or lose market share. That left shareholders with virtually no chance for profits and massive downside risk of bankruptcy unless bailed-out and resurrected, given a second life. Managers and shareholders obviously had no choice but to go for broke whether or not they recognized the strategy as such at the time and had to make optimistic default assumptions to justify the thin projected margins.

Perhaps in anticipation, management at both Fannie and Freddie attempted to capture a bigger share of the dwindling "excess profits" - economic rents - from agency status for themselves by manipulating earnings to increase their bonuses, resulting in the two biggest GAAP corporate accounting scandals ever in 2003-2004.[118] Their prudential regulator OFHEO responded after the fact to restrain them by imposing an additional 30 percent capital requirement in 2004.[119] As expected, the surcharge raised their cost and caused their share of the sub-prime market to fall, quickly rising to the prior level as soon as the audited accounts were finally released in 2006 and the surcharge requirement was lifted.

Unless margins improved, F&F would clearly go under when credit losses caught up to them. But the internal documents show a policy of regaining the market share lost to private securitizers, which their "mission regulator" John Weicher – who was also the FHA Commissioner - required beginning January 1, 2005, auspiciously the beginning of the sub-prime bubble. F&F were to "meet the market," which he defined as funding at least 50 percent of total affordable housing goal–qualified originations. Exhibit 3 from Thomas and van Order illustrates the resulting turn-around in market share.

Exhibit 3

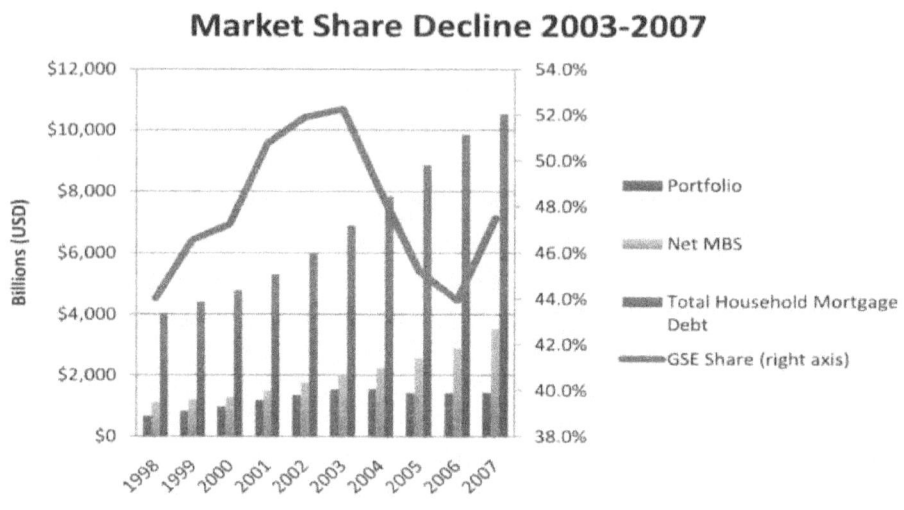

Source: Federal Reserve, Enterprise Monthly Funding Summaries

Weicher, who by his own admission apparently did not see problems with the subprime lending bubble until it was already bursting several years later, accelerated the affordable housing lending goals as well. In 2004 he increased the goals for each subsequent year, driving them to 56, 27, and 39 percent of acquisitions and guarantees by 2008.[120] Most of the high-risk low-yield lending can be attributed directly to the increase in affordable housing goals. By mid-2008, 54 percent of Fannie's portfolio and 51 percent of Freddie's were to below-median-income households, 26 percent and 23 percent were to households with below 60 percent of median income, and 39 percent and 38 percent counted toward the "underserved areas" goal.[121]

Subprime lending had grown from a niche market earlier in the decade to almost 40 percent of the stock by 2008, accounting for most new loans written during the bubble years of 2005, 2006 & 2007.[122] Pinto and Wallison estimate that by year-end 2008 private-label MBS had funded 7.8 million subprime loans and Fannie and Freddie about 12 million. Low-documentation and no-documentation loans became common, with a stunning 80 percent of Alt-A's being low or no-doc. Most of the loans used teaser rates to underwrite borrower income.

In fact, there is ample evidence that the senior credit risk officers at both F&F realized they were entering a new period of much riskier loans in an increasingly risky environment and pressed for restraint. F&F CEOs might have been expected to resist these goals as too risky, but in the wake of the prior accounting scandals F&F were no longer infallible and politicians took the unprecedented step of having two new politically beholden CEOs installed, neither of whom was inclined to violate the new HUD market share mandate.[123]

The new F&F CEOs continued the go for broke strategy, but by the beginning of 2005 the bubble had progressed to where PLSers were well past going for broke based on any reasonable estimate of future credit losses, essentially now going broke and looting their firms. Rather than appeal the new mandatory market share mandate to follow PLS into bankruptcy, these two CEOs did the same thing. They subsequently justified their actions as motivated by the pursuit of housing goals and they opposed increasing capital specifically because that would have lowered the projected return on equity on these loans well below their target ROE.[124] Modeling falling house prices would have done the same.

The FCIC report states: "In 2005, Freddie Mac CEO Richard Syron fired Dave Andrukonis, Freddie's long time chief risk officer. Syron said one of the reasons that Andrukonis was fired was that Andrukonis was concerned about relaxing underwriting standards to meet mission goals." Moreover, his replacement "repeatedly made the case for increasing capital to compensate for the increasing risk," but his position was dropped from the senior management team,[125] thus paving the way for Syron, a former public servant with no business experience, to earn a combined $23.5 million in 2005–2006 and an additional $18.3 million in 2007 as the company hurtled toward bankruptcy and federal conservatorship. The pattern of ignoring the loud warnings of the chief risk officer — paving the way for similar compensation — was virtually identical at Fannie Mae. The two CEOs walked away with about $100 million looting insolvent firms, taking what would later prove to be taxpayer money,

This strategy stood little chance of benefitting shareholders unless they were bailed out, and they were subsequently shocked when forced to accept conservatorship that wiped out shareholder value. But there was no manager claw-back as the federal government indemnified them and no firings as more than four years after insolvency there were over 90 F&F executives still making over a million dollars a year, so going broke was clearly a rational management strategy.[126]

The role of the Bush White House is perplexing. On the one hand, it inherited the homeownership policy and embraced it, promoting an "ownership society." On the other hand, it supported the OFHEO regulator when he imposed an additional 30 percent capital surcharge requirement, which transparently inhibited such lending. Bush supported both the prior head of OFHEO Armando Falcon Jr. appointed in 1999 by President Clinton and his replacement James Lockhart in 2005 in proposing higher F&F capital requirements, always rejected by democrats in Congress along strict party lines. But when in February of 2003 Falcon issued a report citing the systemic threat posed by F&F, the President caved to Wall Street demands for Falcon's resignation.[127] When the Senate finally passed legislation to increase F&F capital requirements, the Bush administration opposed it.[128] Thereafter neither Falcon nor his successor reigned in the HUD mission regulator, which the Bush White House could have and should have done.

2. FHA and the FHLBs also Go for Broke, then Go Broke[129]

FHA's share of home purchase mortgage originations dropped from about 14 percent in 2001 to just below 5 percent in 2005. Over 14 percent of FHA borrowers were low income and a like amount high income, as FHA was an inherently middle class program geared to first time buyers. Given the historically central role of the FHA in low down payment lending and the fact that the F&F mission regulator was also the FHA Commissioner this decline was more likely a consequence of ratcheting up F&F affordable housing goals than a HUD policy for FHA to exit the market. Freddie Mac and Fannie Mae programs to meet their housing goals targeted traditional FHA borrowers, which meant taking business from FHA. FHA's market share declined in census tracts with median credit scores in the bottom quarter of the distribution from just over 40 percent to around 15 percent and lenders attributed almost two-thirds of the FHA decline to F&F.

Private lending to meet CRA quotas also came at the expense of the FHA, but by implication much less so. Only 7 percent of subprime lending went to low- income households and four times that much went to high income households as sub-prime lending focused on higher risk borrowers.

In response to F&F and PLS competition, FHA continually lowered its down payment requirements along with its underwriting standards. FHA Commissioner Weicher announced the proposal for a Zero Down Payment mortgage to promote home ownership at the National Association of Homebuilders Convention in January of 2004. About half of FHA loans had a nominal down-payment of only 3% or less and another quarter had LTVs between 95 and 97 percent during the bubble.

As small as the down payment requirements were, over have of all FHA borrowers didn't provide the cash to meet them. During the bubble these were provided mostly by sellers - builders for new construction. In other cases the funds were provided by non-profit organizations, who often received seller kick-backs to finance the contributions. The purchase price was inflated relative to value, increasing the effective LTV relative to the nominal LTV such that about three quarters of FHA borrowers during the bubble years 2005-2007 likely had negative equity at closing. As both F&F mission regulator and FHA Commissioner, Weicher had the two GSEs in a race to the bottom.

Low down payments and weak underwriting can generally be managed in isolation, but not both simultaneously. FHA didn't begin collecting borrower credit scores until May 2004, but once they did the data revealed that over half of FHA borrowers during this period had subprime credit scores. In the 2005 book of business, for example, about 60 percent of FHA borrowers had FICO scores under 640.

FHA also made administrative changes in 2006 – at the peak of the house price bubble - to regain lost market share. As you would expect of a government-run insurer, FHA processes hadn't kept pace with technology. For example, FHA required lenders to submit loan files by mail, whereas private lenders sent doc's electronically. Now FHA went to the other extreme, allowing "higher-performing" lenders to self-approve FHA insurance endorsements. FHA had also maintained a variety of property inspection requirements that went beyond the requirements of other market participants, but now simplified FHA's appraisal process. To regain market share, the new FHA Commissioner Brian Montgomery explained in mid-2006: "FHA reform is designed to give homebuyers who can't qualify for prime financing a choice again."[130] This contributed to the race to the bottom between FHA and F&F as PLSers had already peaked by then and would soon be in decline.

From 2002 to 2007 the delinquency rate of FHA mortgages actually exceeded that of subprime. As with PLS and F&F, it is the combination of poor credit quality with low or no down-payment that resulted in tremendous losses. As Table 2 (in Calabria, 2011) illustrates, when low equity is combined with weak credit, defaults skyrocket. Note that the table is normalized so that a loan with a credit score between 680 and 720 and a LTV between 71 and 80 percent equals "1." Other figures are either fractions or multiples of this number. Loans with a FICO below 620 and down-payments of less than 10 percent display default rates 20 times that of the base group.

Table 2
Default Rates

		Loan to Value Ratio			
		<70%	71-80%	81-90%	91-95%
Credit Score	<620	1.0	4.8	11	20
	620-679	0.5	2.3	5.3	9.4
	680-720	0.2	1.0	2.3	4.1
	>720	0.1	0.4	0.9	1.6

While the debate about the proper methodology for calculating FHA's subsidies parallels that of F&F, CBO analysis concludes that this subsidy was about $5 billion annually during this period. But even when combined with Ginnie Mae subsidies about four times that of FHA, this was not enough to maintain the FHA reserves, with losses of over $25 billion projected on sub-prime loans made during the bubble.

The FHLB story is similar, but on a smaller scale. The FHLBs took any mortgage collateral and eliminated their risk by increasing the over-collateralization requirement, so lenders had the incentive to supply the worst, loans rejected by F&F and even PLS, most likely sub-prime. From 2000 through 2003 FHLB debt grew by about 15% to a half trillion dollars. By 2005 it had grown another 25% to $620 billion dollars. Then during the peak bubble years of 2006 and 2007 it grew by 40% to $867 billion and continued growing in 2008 to over $900 billion.

The explanation isn't difficult. PLSers were already going broke by 2005 so when PLS sources of funds starting drying up in 2006 those that owned banks like Countrywide used FHLB advances to fund what they couldn't sell to F&F. The FHLB allowed them to keep looting their firms because they passed the expense entirely along to the FDIC by requiring sufficient excess collateral. The FDIC complains that when Countrywide spin-off Indy Mac failed, for example, the FHLB had priority access to about *two thirds* of the collateral due to extreme over-collateralization – about double - because the mostly sub-prime loan quality was so bad, leaving the FDIC with deep losses of over $9 billion for a bank only about three times that size. Obviously these loans were way under-reserved, an FDIC regulatory and accounting failure. So the FHLBs were also going broke but in this case looting the FDIC!

In addition to purchasing whole loans, the FHLBs also purchased PLS to meet their "affordable housing" goals. Based on the marks as of 2008, only four of the 12 FHL banks met minimum capital requirements.

3. Banks Go for Broke, then Go Broke

During the 1990s federally insured depository institutions held basically two categories of conventional first lien home mortgages: jumbo loans – those not eligible for F&F purchase; and CRA qualified loans. The jumbo loans were generally profitable due to their 50% risk weighting under the risk-based capital rules and the higher spreads due to the inability of F&F to compete. The CRA loans were valuable for their regulatory leverage that provided significant franchise value, so if they broke even that was more than sufficient.

All four of the largest TBTF banks owned mortgage banking companies that originated through in-house and external broker networks or purchased their mortgage loans, as well as PLS issuing subsidiaries. They also had large servicing platforms that mostly serviced loans originated by the corporate mortgage bank, but servicing contracts were also bought and sold, and loans could be sub-serviced for a fee as well. In general the mortgage bank and mortgage servicing subsidiary was each a separate profit center of the bank. It remained more profitable to sell qualifying loans to F&F. The rest had historically been retained in portfolio, but PLS became a preferred method of financing sub-prime loans due to the significantly greater leverage available. Many other banks had a similar system, depending on their size.

CRA goals didn't necessarily change the system very much. The mortgage bank would originate and "sell" CRA qualified loans to the parent bank, generally retaining servicing. But the loan could be re-sold subsequent to CRA certification - as this generally was not tracked – and once again the decision would be whether to sell to F&F or fund with PLS. If it was a first lien with an LTV of 80% or less it was a pretty safe bet that the F&F bid would represent the best execution, especially if it also qualified for one or more F&F affordable housing goals, as the 1992 GSE Act required F&F to support bank CRA lending.

The $4 trillion in new CRA commitments banks entered into to take advantage of merger and acquisition opportunities required that they unleash their mortgage banking subsidiaries to produce CRA-qualified loans, the more the better. Mortgage bankers have never been known for their self restraint, historically provided by the market's willingness to fund, in this case distorted by regulation. So they went for broke.

In 2008 commercial banks held 2.7 million in "junk" mortgage loans that generally qualified under the CRA lending requirements.[131] But the $4 trillion in CRA commitments far exceeded the bank net increase in direct first lien mortgage holdings, suggesting that after they were used for CRA accreditation the banks sold a lot of the first liens to F&F or funded them with PLS, retaining the seconds. As the loans needed to meet CRA quotas became increasingly risky, banks had a greater incentive to save the best and sell the rest.[132] PLS offered the best permanent funding alternative for those loans that didn't meet the F&F loan limit because virtually all loans originated to meet CRA requirements likely had a combined LTV (CLTV) above 80% and during the bubble years of 2005-2007 the vast majority had a CLTV of closer to 100%. These loans generally didn't qualify for PMI, so purchase money piggy-back second mortgage financing substituted for the borrower cash down payment.

From year end 2000 to year end 2007 the stock of mortgages grew by 120 percent. Bank holdings increased by about 100%, from $2.5 to $5.0 trillion, so the bank share fell by only 3% from 32% in 2000 to 29% in 2007. The PLS share doubled from 10% to 21%, so on first blush it would appear that F&F lost market share to PLS, while banks held their own. But the PLS and F&F loans were virtually all first mortgage liens. The stock of second mortgages had expanded dramatically, to over a trillion dollars by year end 2007, and these were held almost entirely – over 90% - by banks.[133]

So the first question is, why did the banks hold most of these much more risky second liens? The most likely answer is due to CRA regulations. Second mortgage loans had a 100% risk weighting, except when combined with a first mortgage lien, in which case it was only 50%. That not only doubled the ROE, but that and retained servicing of the first probably continued to allow the loan to count for CRA. That would explain why the four CRA-driven TBTF banks hold a disproportionate 45% of the stock of second mortgages.

Why banks purchased almost a half trillion dollars of PLS also requires explaining. The first part of the answer is that they had the highest promised yield relative to their risk-based capital weighting – only 20% for AAA/AA CDOs. The second part of the answer is that they could use PLS backed by loans that would have qualified for CRA. [134] The third answer is that much of this was purchased by off balance sheet sponsored SIVs, further lowering the capital requirement – at least until they were put back to the bank sponsor when SIV financing dried up. So the combination of these three incentives was quite powerful. Bank funding of second mortgages and CDOs – largely off balance sheet - and their provision of under-priced CDS insurance gets significant credit for enabling both PLSers and F&F to go for broke, and then to go broke.

Home mortgages accounted for only about a quarter of bank assets at the end of 2007, and second liens only about 8%. But that represents a significant risk to total bank capital. If bank mortgage experience was anything like the experience of first and second lien PLS implied by PLS prices in 2008, the valuation of bank mortgage assets would probably have implied widespread insolvency, especially among the TBTF banks. As Wallison points out, first and second lien losses were the two largest categories of bank loss, over $100 billion for first liens and over $83 billion for second liens in the stress tests required in the spring of 2009 for the 19 largest banks.[135] But PLS had to be marked to market, whereas loss recognition on these portfolio loans could potentially be delayed until they were in default, and sometimes much longer.

TBTF banks are large complex organizations. Their boards of directors should have realized the risk posed by their highly leveraged strategies, but it is unlikely they understood their consequences any better than the directors of the investment banks until it was too late. Former Treasury Secretary and investment banker Robert Rubin, for example, who was compensated an estimated $100 million as a Citicorp director in charge of risk management oversight at this time, was apparently unaware of the risks.[136]

C. The Consequences of the Credit Bubble: the House Price Bubble

There are three economic certainties. First, credit bubbles always lead to asset bubbles. Second, asset bubbles always burst. Third, when a credit-financed asset bubble bursts a financial crisis ensues. By the end of 2007 the *relative* value of the housing stock had inflated by about $6 trillion, about the amount of the additional credit provided to finance it. This purely illusory wealth would predictably be destroyed when the asset price bubble burst, with great pain when it did.

The Fed's post 9/11/2011 low interest rate strategy was followed by most OECD countries, and most experienced a credit-fueled bubble in housing prices. These asset price bubbles were the source of various degrees of stress in the banking system of these countries, but none leveraged the increase in housing demand to the extent of the US. The relative impacts on house prices and housing production varied widely, reflecting differences in credit policies and mostly politically-induced supply restrictions. Similar variations were observed between states, regions and localities in the US.

Section 1 explains how the credit bubble inflated the house price bubble, by how much, where and why. Section 2 describes the amount and allocation of the loss between households and lenders/investors and among financial institutions when it belatedly but predictably deflated.

1. The Regional Land Use Restriction-Induced House Price Bubble

Not every rise in house prices is necessarily a bubble about to burst. As we discussed in chapter 2, the secular increase in nominal inflation increased the before tax mortgage rate in the 1970s, but because the nominal rate was fully tax deductable by homeowners the after tax real rate declined. This produced a dramatic rise in homes relative to other forms of real estate or other assets. In the bubble of the last decade the Fed lowered financing costs resulting in an across the board bubble in real estate prices. But the bubble in home prices was greater than the bubble in commercial property, reflecting the GSE credit bubble with subsidies attached.

Some analysts were reluctant to call the rise in housing prices a bubble, attributing it to a secular increase in housing demand. Adam J. Levitin and Susan M. Wachter review the various demand side theories including irrational exuberance, but come down on the side of the credit bubble due to a falling mortgage rates relative to interest rates generally.[137]

There is no disputing the Fed and GSE credit bubble. How much did these interest rate subsidies delivered by GSEs and banks improve housing affordability? That depended on the extent to which the increase in demand resulting from reduced underwriting and down payment requirements and subsidized interest rates inflated housing prices.

Houses aren't mobile, so international bubbles aren't relevant to domestic prices and production. But one house is a substitute for another in a local market whether or not occupied by goal qualified households and regardless of whether funded by PLS or F&F. A house purchased by a sub-prime borrower may equally be purchased by a prime borrower, and a house purchased by a goal-qualified borrower may equally be purchased by a non-goal qualified borrower, so it is the politically-induced expansion of aggregate market demand that expands production and/or inflates costs and house prices.

Trillions of dollars of cheap mortgages with little or no borrower equity didn't quite achieve the 70% home ownership goal as the home ownership rate peaked at 69% in 2004 and remained there after that until the bubble burst. But between the end of 1994 when the home ownership goal was announced and the end of 2006 when the housing production boom ended, this increase in the homeownership rate to 69% reflects more than 4 million additional households who had achieved homeownership, mostly younger first time homebuyers. For the previous 15 years prior to the homeownership goal, single (one to four) family housing starts averaged less than 1 million units a year. From 1995 through 2004 they averaged 1.3 million units and in 2005-2006 they averaged 1.6 million units, so over the 12 year span of the home ownership goal 4.2 additional 1-4 family units were added.

Multifamily housing starts (5 or more) averaged 340 thousand from 1980 through 1994, but only 294 thousand from then on through 2007, including the three years of the single family housing bubble.[138] That is roughly a 40 thousand unit shortfall per year for 13 years, or 520, 000 units for the period, about two full years of production. So the decline in multifamily was much less than the increase in single family: the construction boom produced a surplus of about 3.7 million units overall relative to the historic trend.

But about 75% of the additional credit financed an increase in real (inflation-adjusted) house prices. Why did this demand drive price as well as quantity? The first FCIC dissent also focused on the regional nature of the house price bubble, particularly in California, Nevada, Arizona and Florida. Demographics pressure on housing demand and land-use restrictions limiting supply obviously contributed to the house price bubble being higher and lasting longer in some states and regions than others.

Sometimes called "smart growth," excessive land use policies such as urban growth boundaries, building moratoria, inexplicably high taxes in the form of "impact fees," and excessively large minimum lot sizes raise land prices and limit the expansion of residential construction. The result is a smaller increase in production and a larger increase in land and hence house prices.

Smart growth policies were implemented in California and Florida, where demographic pressures were greatest, as well as in the Northeast the Northwest. In contrast, the country's three fastest-growing metropolitan areas with a population of more than 5,000,000: Atlanta, Georgia, and Houston and Dallas-Fort Worth, Texas, were far better able to accommodate the higher demand for growth without raising prices as a result of more relaxed land regulation.

This is illustrated by developments in the nation's 50 largest metropolitan markets. Between 2000 and 2007, house prices increased an average of more than $275,000 compared to incomes (house price to household income ratio) in the 10 markets with the greatest price escalation. Among the

Table 3

Excess Price of the Housing Stock and Excess Mortgage (From 2000)

By Average House Price Increase	Number of Excessive Land Use Planning (Smart Growth) Markets	Estimated Excess House Prices over 2000 Average Price/Income Ratio	Rise in Aggregate House Value Relative to Average Price/Income (in Billions)	Rise in Mortgage Exposure Relative to Average Price/Income (in Billions)	Share of Excess Mortgage Escalation
Highest 10	100%	$277,400	$3,400	$3,060	64%
Higher 10	100%	$135,900	$1,020	$920	19%
Middle 10	50%	$76,500	$520	$470	10%
Lower 10	10%	$32,000	$190	$170	4%
Lowest 10	0%	$5,200	$30	$30	1%
Total Major Metropolitan	52%	$134,100	$5,160	$4,650	98%
Other Areas			$110	$100	2%
United States			$5,270	$4,750	100%

Notes: Assumes excess mortgage exposure is at the same ratio as aggregate value increase. Detailed metropolitan area excess housing value estimates are available at http://www.demographia.com/db-overhang.pdf

second 10 markets with the greatest price escalation, prices rose $135,000 relative to incomes. By contrast, in the markets with the least price escalation, house prices increased by only $5,000. What the 20 markets that had the most price escalation have in common is excessive land use regulation.[139]

As in the OECD countries, this additional demand pushed housing prices upward relative to production where supply was the most constrained. For the US, real housing prices peaked at about the beginning of 2007 at about 70% above the level at the start of the decade, based on an average of three measures.[140] From 2000 to 2007 the nominal dollar value of the single family housing stock increased by slightly more than 70%, over $8.5 trillion according to the Fed Flow of Funds data.[141] But the number of residential housing units increased by only 11% according to the Census Bureau.[142] So even assuming the new additions to the stock were roughly comparable to existing units and remodeling and upgrading just about offset depreciation, we can assume a real increase in the physical stock of only about 10%-15% and a total inflationary price increase of about $7.0-$7.5 trillion, only 15% of which represents underlying monetary inflation as reflected in the GDP deflator. From 2000 through 2007 the value of the housing stock rose by $5.3 trillion more than the amount that would have maintained a constant cost to income ratio, even though incomes had been rising. So both indicators imply that about 75% of the increased purchasing power due to cheap credit was captured by owners of existing land and houses and rent-seeking politicians and regulators associated with the smart growth process.

About 83% of the reduction in housing affordability occurred in the 20 major markets with the greatest house price escalation, which account for only 26% of the housing stock. Assuming the same proportion of that was financed, 83% of the rise in the mortgage stock financed this regulation-induced price bubble. When house prices fell, the loss in value for these metropolitan areas slightly exceeded the prior gain.[143] Land prices had inflated rapidly all during the boom, falling as much as 90% when the bubble deflated, mostly in smart growth regions.[144]

But it is equally true that two cities with a historically elastic housing supply, Las Vegas and Phoenix, also had rapidly rising – and subsequently rapidly falling – housing prices. Gerardi, Foote and Willen review all the economist theories as to why this was or was not a housing bubble.[145] The bottom line is that housing markets are sufficiently numerous and diverse that statistical evidence can be found for just about any hypothesis so long as you ignore the elephants in the room.

2. The Magnitude and Distribution of Losses from the House Price Bubble Bursting

Had the supply of land and houses – including labor and building materials - been perfectly elastic, housing production both in terms of the number of units and size would have increased as a result of the Fed and housing policy-induced increase in demand, but the house price bubble would have been avoided. The economic cost of building houses earlier and bigger than otherwise is roughly comparable to the cost of the distortion caused by the deductibility of mortgage interest, i.e., the value added reflects the cost before including the subsidy. The long term economic consequences would be reflected in the decline in the productivity of the capital stock.

Smart growth policies limiting supply converted the increase in demand to a house price bubble that housing policy leveraged. It is the deflation of the price bubble financed almost entirely with mortgage credit that resulted in negative mortgage equity subsequently leading to delinquency and default and caused the financial crisis, a classic case of Ponzi finance.

As previously noted, all homeowner equity nominally rose by almost $6 trillion from 2000 to 2006, and 7.5 trillion from 1997 to 2007. If house prices reverted to the mean – as they always do eventually - then the $6.0-$6.5 trillion inflation gain in the value of the housing stock since the 1990s would be reversed.

It soon was, as predicted. The Fed's Flow of Funds data show that US home owner equity then fell by $6 trillion within three years by year-end 2009 and by mid 2012 almost $7 trillion in homeowner equity had already been wiped out. That the loss of homeowner equity exceeded the inflationary bubble even before house prices reverted all the way to the mean is most likely because households had been encouraged to reduce saving, borrowing to consume homeowner equity to "stimulate the economy." The increase in consumption due to the wealth illusion further reduced capital accumulation, productivity and long term growth.

The reversal of wealth represented the reversal of net illusory gains. The previously paid economic rents collected by participants in the political housing process represent additional dead weight loss.

The magnitude of the wealth creation and destruction created a lot of winners and losers, but the massive size of the program makes calculation of the net wealth destruction and income and wealth re-distribution extremely opaque and difficult to measure. The net wealth gain is reflected only in the small increase in the housing stock. The housing and mortgage related industries were all beneficiaries, but only temporarily. Those who owned and sold land at inflated prices were net winners. All those who purchased housing and continued to pay mortgages with negative net equity – mostly those that were the intended beneficiaries of political housing policy - were *net losers*. Those that defaulted but lived rent free through an extended foreclosure process may have come out financially ahead, but it was likely not worth the hassle for many.

While cheap credit may have funded the entire house price bubble, lenders and their creditors wouldn't bear the entire loss because many households still had equity in their homes and many others would pay even if they didn't. But even if only half of the loss in homeowner equity was passed on to lenders, that still represented a potential net lender/investor loss of $3.5 trillion due to default, pain enough to destroy the financial system and severely impair the global economy. And that loss was predictable in mid-2005 as a consequence of the prediction of the house price bubble bursting, and certainly in 2007 when it already had started deflating. Political and regulatory policy in fact attempted to shift as much of the loss to households as possible to avoid a more politically embarrassing transparent public financial sector bailout.

To our knowledge there has been no attempt to determine the actual cumulative home mortgage credit loss, over and above the subsidy cost, of financial institutions in spite of the best efforts of the Fed to keep the house price bubble inflated. This is necessary in order to understand the depth of the opaque financial institution capital solvency hole that existed in 2007 and 2008 leading up to the crisis that had motivated go for broke and go broke behavior as well as the political and regulatory policy then and since, discussed in the next chapter. This section attempts to extrapolate a ballpark estimate from the various piecemeal financial disclosures and announcements and reports through mid 2012 that we are aware of, a tedious effort as with the calculation of capital subsidies, with more art than science relegated to the box below.

The Mortgage Credit losses Reported by Financial Institutions

Table 4 below taken from Acharya and Richardson (p. 209) shows the ownership of the entire $10,636 trillion stock of first and second liens as of 2008, from which we extrapolate to determine the approximate incidence of reported credit losses. Note that GSEs are considered the investor for whole loans financed with debt, but not for MBS. As we know, they bear the uninsured credit risk for both (beyond losses to second lien holders or mortgage insurers) so their share of ownership by that credit risk benchmark is 55% (41% + 14%).

Table 4: The Ownership of the Mortgage Stock 2008

In billions of dollars

	Non-Securitized First Liens	Non-Securitized Second Liens	GSE MBS	Total PLS and CDO	Total share	
Banks	2020	869	852	473	4212	40%
GSEs	444		741	308	1493	14%
Inv'nt Banks			49	254	303	3%
Guarantors		62		100	162	2%
Insurance			856	214	1070	10%
Foreign			689	482	1172	11%
Other	461	185	1175	402	2268	21%
Total	2925 28%	1116 10%	4362 41%	2233 21%	$10,636	

Table 5 below is intended to ballpark total sub-prime default related credit losses and the incidence of these losses in financial institutions. The totals in the last row reflect *ex post* credit losses reported by financial institutions on first lien loans and securities (column 3) mortgage insurance companies (PMIs and FHA in columns 4 & 5) and second lien loans and securities (column 6). Column 7 allocates the PLS losses to financial institutions according to their ownership reported in Table 5 (chapter 3), so column 8 totals losses reported by financial institutions. The Table is structured this way so we can use a combination of financial reports and securities data mostly focused on actual *ex-post* credit losses and extrapolate to fill in the blanks.

We have the best actual credit loss data on structured finance (SF) CDOs. Cordell, Huang and Williams (2012) estimated that losses on SF CDOs (financing mostly PLS BBB securities) issued during the housing boom years 2000-2004 will average about 30% (with lower PLS tranches wiped out).[146] They estimate the of the total ABS CDOs issued during the bubble years 2005-2007 with a principal balance of $641 billion, actual credit losses had already or soon would reach 65%,. More specifically, losses on senior/junior AAA CDOs are 44%/83% for 2005, 67%/94% for 2006 and 76%/93% for 2007 with most classes below this a total loss.[147] Total *ex post* CDO credit losses were estimated to be $420 billion in mid 2012.[148]

Table 5

		Total Sub-prime Credit Losses			in billions of dollars		Total
	First Lien LTV<=80	Mortgage Insurance			Seconds	on bal-sheet	Total
			PMI	FHA		securities	on BS
GSE	F&F	300	30*		120*	50	350
	other	5		25			30
Finance	Bank	80			310	322.5	712.5
	other	40			150	272.5	522.5
PLS	CDO	420	10		20		
	non-CDO	150					
	Retained	75					
	Total PLS	625			20	645	1615
Total		1050	40	25	500	1615	

Next we extrapolate other PLS losses in the third column. The extent of default for AAA/AA PLS isn't yet known but the pattern of actual losses on CDOs by vintage explains the pattern of AAA PLS market prices. As of March 2009, market prices of AAA PLS ranged from 80% of par for PLS issued in the first half of 2006 down to 40% of par for issues in the second half of 2007, with MtM losses of between $158 Billion and $473 billion.[149] But by 2012 the prices of the remaining AAA PLS being traded had largely rebounded.[150] F&F had still marked down their non CDO AAA portfolio by about $50 billion in late 2012. F&F owned one third of the total PLS, and these mark-downs have withstood the test of time, so extrapolating from F&F mark-downs total non-CDO PLS losses are estimated at $150 billion.

As CDOs were derived from investment grade PLS, CDOs bear the loss over and above a total loss on subordinated interests and second liens, so lower PLS tranches are assumed to be wiped out. We estimate that of the $121 billion "other" securities in Chapter 3 Table 6 $75 billion are the retained interests: that's just over 1% of all PLS issued so it could well be more. Total PLS losses on all first and second mortgage pools are thus estimated to be $645 billion in column 7.

Only about $30 billion of piggy-back second mortgage PLS were issued. But the $338 million pool called GSAMP 2006-S5 issued in mid 2006 by Goldman Sachs discussed in the last chapter is illustrative of default expectations. These loans were all piggy-back purchase money second mortgages and the pool was issued at the house price peak. About half the securities issued against the pool were rated AAA, and only 20% were rated below investment grade. For the Goldman Sachs PLS second mortgage issue discussed above, the AAA rating dropped to the lowest investment grade rating of Baa within months after the issue and was rated junk about a year later, in 2007 before the PLS market collapsed. So parenthetically we estimate a two-thirds default with 100% severity and net $20 billion of the PLS loss on seconds in column 6, hence a total for first lien pools of $625 billion in column 3.

Our next best credit loss data comes from specific public filings by Fannie Mae and Freddie Mac. The reported credit losses by F&F on loans of about $260 billion net of all private mortgage insurance reimbursements from 2006 through 2011, which we extrapolate to $300 billion through 2012 in addition to $50 billion in PLS mark-downs.

Industry sources indicate that the total of all PMI claims paid to date are at most about $30 billion, with another $10 billion in the pipeline. Based on F&F data on insured loans, we attribute about $30 billion of that to loans sold to F&F, and $10 billion to loans financed by PLS in the 4th column. Projected FHA sub-prime credit losses are reported in the fifth column as $25 billion based on their financial disclosures.

Private mortgage insurers were the traditional gatekeepers for conventional loan financing at banks and F&F, bearing first loss on high LTV loans as FHA/VA did for Ginnie Mae securities.

Insurance reimbursements traditionally covered virtually all F&F credit related losses. But $30 billion represents only 10% of F&F losses on first mortgage liens in this debacle, and if anything the reimbursement estimate is high and the net loss estimate low, so how did this ten to one loss ratio of PMI to F&F get reversed?

One answer is that early on F&F had been leading the way in bullying the private mortgage insurance companies to raise LTVs insuring loans with only 3% down in 1998, and in 2001 loans with no down payment while lowering underwriting standards, as PLSers later did.[151] In addition, they both introduced their own versions of automated underwriting, imposing weaker credit standards on lenders for loans the PMIs had to insure.[152] But the PMIs clearly resisted sub-prime, so F&F agreed to take more credit risk by negotiating insurance coverage down to only the legal minimum 80% LTV in many cases. But this only reduced PMI payouts to F&F by at most about $7 or $8 billion dollars.

It was the extreme loss severity that caused F&F credit losses on insured loans. Fannie Mae reports the net recovery on REO as a percent of their original first lien loan balance as 87% for 2005, 83% for 2006, 78% for 2007, 68% for 2008, 55% for 2009, 57% for 2010 and 55% for 2011. If we assume a three year lag between origination and REO disposition, that implies a net loss on loans originated in 2005-2007 of 45% of the loan amount on average, an extreme experience. Even if we assume they were all at the maximum LTV of 80%, this implies an average loss severity of over 55% of the initial home value on these loan cohorts. For every dollar of PMI loss insuring the loss from 95% down to 80% of the initial home price, F&F would lose more than twice that from 80% down to 45%. This average loss severity is roughly consistent with the bursting of the house price bubble. Of course all houses weren't financed at the peak, but the costs of foreclosure and repossession can easily account for the difference.

If we assume that on average F&F losses were twice that of the PMIs on insured loans, then PMI losses should have been $150 billion, so this still only explains about one fifth of the reversal. The remaining $120 billion can only be explained by F&F bypassing the PMIs. The PMIs only insured about 7% of Freddie Mac loans and about 15% of Fannie Mae loans during the sub-prime lending debacle. That's consistent with their reported data that the rest had an initial LTV at or below 80%. Freddie Mac reports an average initial LTV of 70%, i.e., a 30% down-payment, Fannie a somewhat higher LTV, with both reporting the LTV rising only slightly as the boom turned to bubble. But we know that equity is not from cash down payments from household savings. The data cited earlier in chapter 3 for all sub-prime and Alt A indicated that sub-prime and Alt A purchase mortgages originated during the sub-prime boom and subsequent bubble had virtually no cash equity and refinancings averaged an 80% LTV at best – before including seconds - so more than half of these loans would have required either mortgage insurance or seconds.

PMI resistance primarily drove the riskier uninsured purchase money piggy-back seconds business. Both Fannie Mae and Freddie Mac had programs for buying first liens with piggy-back seconds. In 2001, Fannie Mae introduced a program to buy the seconds only, as well as both first and second loans as a package, with the added benefit of counting one household twice toward their affordable housing goals.[153] But this activity was relatively minor. Fannie Mae reports a combined LTV (CLTV) that would include seconds, but the numbers appear way too low. Industry estimates indicate that about 25% of F&F loans have seconds not reported at the time of purchase. Those loans are orders of magnitude more likely to default than loans with borrower cash equity of 20% or more, with a much higher loss severity.

This implies that for every loan in default with PMI, F&F had four loans in default without it. Hence the credit losses on second mortgages related to first liens held by F&F are estimated to be $120 billion in the 6th column. So we note the indirect losses attributable to first liens held by F&F as $30 billion for PMIs and $120 billion in seconds held by others that are not included in the F&F reported losses because the incidence lies elsewhere, primarily with banks.

To complete the calculation of losses on first liens, we assume that banks held about 40% as many first liens as F&F (including MBS) with the same default frequency and loss severity. This may be biased downward because some of these loans had a higher LTV, but that would only affect the relative allocation of loss between first and second mortgages, not the bank total. But we assume a much higher loss ration for "other" as this most likely reflects a higher percentage of lame loans that didn't make it into PLS.

Assuming the same two to one ratio, non PLS second mortgage losses related to PLS would have been about $280 billion ($310-$20 PLS-$10PMI), and second mortgage losses related to first liens held in portfolio would have been about $60 billion, implying total losses on second mortgages of $460 billion ($280 + $120+$60). We assume that the seconds held by finance companies largely reflects PLS purchase money piggy back activity, so we attribute a disproportionate (one third) share of this loss to them. This implies a total bank loss on second mortgages of over $300 billion, roughly 30% of their total holdings that also include less risky home equity loans.

> This brings the total loss in the last row to $1.615 trillion. The total in the bottom row shows the losses by origin, i.e., whether first or second lien, how financed, etc. The totals in the last column reflect where the loss was reported by financial institutions. GSE "other" are losses reported by PMIs and finance "other" are losses reported by non-bank financial institutions. We allocate the PLS security losses to financial institutions based on the distribution of ownership in Table 6 (chapter 3) In this way the CHW data for credit losses in CDO securities is consistent with ultimate losses reported by financial institutions.

The total loss of over $1.6 trillion is the same as the total financial institution losses reported by Blundell et. al. up to mid-August 2009 of $1.6 trillion, which included mark to market losses, a forecast of future losses. The major trend from 2009 through 2012 was to increase actual credit losses while reversing mark to market losses as the security balances declined due to default.

This analysis was tedious and at best imprecise, but does suggest several broad conclusions: First, the losses were recognized quickly after the financial crisis of 2008 – about half of the losses cited above by year end, mostly due to mark to market accounting - suggesting that the approximate magnitude of the deep solvency hole should have been recognizable at that time.

Second, the losses could have been much greater. By the end of 2011, CoreLogic estimated that negative mortgage loan equity was still three quarters of a trillion dollars, about half on loans with seconds, and an additional trillion if prices reverted all the way to their long-run mean, validating our prior ballpark estimate of potential additional lender losses due to the decline in homeowner equity equal to those already reported.[154]

Third, Fannie and Freddie account for more than half of the mortgage stock of the time but less than a third of the losses either directly or indirectly. Direct losses for F&F and FHA are much less than for banks in part because F&F were forced to transfer taxpayer costs from agency status to deposit insurance due to their 80% LTV limit. The major regulatory barrier was that Fannie and Freddie couldn't use present value accounting the way that PLSers did.

Fourth, banks were able to use PLS regulatory distortions to transfer about 30% of the total loss out of the federally backed system, a good portion of which likely fell onto state and local taxpayer backed retirement funds invested in PLS directly or through investments in hedge funds. As banks funded the investment bank and finance company PLSers, some of that loss reverted back to banks as well.

Fifth, regulatory distortions shifted both the incidence of loss and the way losses were reported. Losses on bank first liens were a fraction of their total loss, explaining why searching for CRA costs there is relatively fruitless.

Sixth, the taxpayers bear much of the loss as consumers of financial services, as it reflected the moral hazard of taxpayer backing. As of 2012, F&F have required an additional capital infusion of about $200 billion, wiped out book capital of about $90 billion and reduced cumulative earnings by about $100 billion since 2000. Unlike with F&F, Treasury only temporarily recapitalized the banks, until private capital could be found. This was raised on the promise of future franchise value to be provided to the new investors, largely economic rents delivered through protection, particularly for the TBTF banks.

Seventh, the households targeted by political housing policy were, on the whole, left worse off than before the entire policy was implemented.

D. The Financial Institution Solvency Crisis Becomes Transparent

The political and regulatory spin is that events in unregulated derivatives markets caused a systemic liquidity crisis that spilled into the unregulated shadow banking market, causing widespread panic leading to a systemic financial crisis. This description essentially ignores the sub-prime lending debacle, a house price bubble and the resulting solvency hole, absolving the Fed, housing policy and regulators. That description of events relies on un-provable theories of irrational behavior that make little sense and have little proof. The actual story of the 2008 financial crash is an unsurprising dénouement. When viewed out of context it provides good copy for made for TV movies, which is not the case with the portrayal of the root causes of the financial crisis.

The Fed can mitigate the negative consequences of systemic attempts by solvent borrowers to rapidly de-leverage by providing systemic liquidity support, but the Fed has neither the direct tools nor the authority to address systemic insolvency. Moreover, to recognize the crisis as such would have shifted the blame from private actors and markets to politicians and regulators. Hence as the solvency hole was revealed politicians and regulators maintained the pretence of a liquidity crisis and market failure while trying as best they could to fill the solvency hole made with their complicity, i.e., to cover up and double down by generating future economic rents to cover past losses.

1. The House Price Bubble Deflates: PLS Markets Crash

Most private subordinated debt became more difficult to sell due to rising market pessimism as the bubble in house prices started selectively deflating in 2006, causing delinquencies to soar. When investor purchases of mezzanine and subordinate sub-prime MBS slowed the nation's largest sub-prime lender American Home Mortgage was forced to hold more securitization interests on its balance sheet. Unlike Countrywide, the second largest sub-prime lender by then, they didn't own a bank and had to rely on equity and debt markets for funding. When they could no longer raise cash in the market by borrowing against illusory earnings they eventually had to file for bankruptcy in August 2007. This marked the beginning of the end of the sub-prime lending debacle.

By late 2006 all the less regulated debt and equity markets were betting against the house price bubble continuing. By 2007 even those hedge funds that were long, mostly representing public pensions, began experiencing withdrawals. By August 2007 the highly leveraged Bear Stearns sponsored hedge fund supposedly invested only in low risk super-senior AAA PLS had been losing investors to redemptions due to rising market pessimism. As the pyramid scheme started collapsing, investors hastened their exit.

The role of speculators is to hasten an inevitable collapse. Since CDOs were the largest market for mezzanine investment risk on PLS, that was a good instrument to short. Synthetic CDOs were created to facilitate taking a bearish position, some using credit default swap. So the synthetic CDO and the CDS markets provided the best reflection of the relative bull/bear sentiment. The ABX index was purportedly an index of trading prices for asset backed sub-prime mortgage securities, but actual trading was so thin that the index mostly reflected the cost of CDS. This insurance was in great demand due to the massive over-exposure of investors to sub-prime PLS; demand for CDS exploded during the subprime bubble years 2005 through 2007, increasing ten fold (market value) to 15 fold (notional value). It became in short supply when AIG suddenly backed out, causing CDS prices to skyrocket during 2008 – when market prices rose by about 60% - as the shorts used it to bet against the CDO market. This drove the ABX index down sharply all year.

Figure 5 below taken from Acharya and Richardson (p. 209) illustrates market prices of AAA CDOs. House prices had plateaued or even started down in most states by the time the index was introduced in 2006, and by June 2007 the resulting credit losses due to falling house prices were becoming highly predictable. These market prices in the ABX CDO market – clearly a thin market - reflected both speculators' rational assessment of cumulative credit loss as well as the dearth of shorting instruments - whereas the so called mark-to-market book values at regulated banks and investment banks and their sponsored entities reflected regulatory approved accounting entries of proprietary traders earning huge bonuses based on inflated non-cash yields on inflated values (chapter 3). The price-gap between the regulated and transaction markets didn't begin to close until regulated investors had to sell. The triggering event for this was the net redemption demands at the Bears Stearns sponsored hedge fund. Goldman Sacks gave a market price of 50 cents on the dollar - based on the price of credit fault swaps - for their assets held and financed at par, and when Merrill Lynch seized $400 million of repo collateral based on this mark that summer, it received actual bids of only 65 cents. The fund couldn't meet collateral calls and redemptions and as a result failed, taking Bear Stearns along with it soon thereafter.

Figure 5

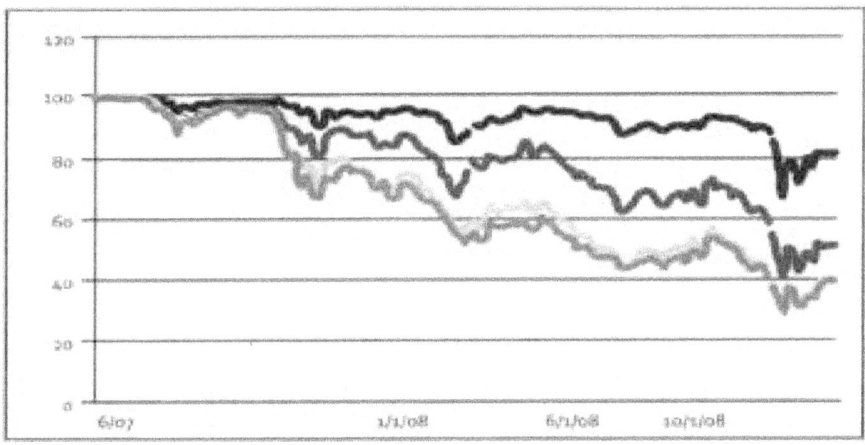

Figure 4. Prices of Subprime AAA Tranches, 2007-2008

The top line represents the prices of the ABX index of AAA-rated tranches of subprime mortgage-backed securities (MBS) issued in the first half of 2006. The second line represents prices for AAA MBS tranches issued in the second half of 2006. The third line represents price of AAA MBS tranches issued in the first half of 2007. The bottom line represents prices for AAA MBS tranches issued in the second half of 2007. The period shown is 1 June 2007 – 31 December 2008. The ABX index reflects the prices of twenty representative tranches.
Source: Markit.

The price of AAA CDOs reflected new issue "trades" at par until the Bear Stearns sale in August of 2007: then prices plummeted quickly reflecting the cost of CDS, a more accurate reflection of ultimate credit loss. All PLS prices in the market had to be remarked– by trillions of dollars –not as a consequence of illiquidity but reflecting a deep and widespread insolvency in the banking and investment banking industries as estimated above. The house price bubble deflated and as discussed in chapter 3 when it did the PLS new issue market crashed precipitously, revealing the breadth and depth of the widespread insolvency.

2. The Financial Institution Solvency Crisis Becomes Globally Systemic

In 2008 the magnitude of the financial institution solvency hole was more easily discerned than the incidence, and bail-out policies were opaque, so the solvency of financial institutions around the globe was called into question. Commercial bank capital and safety in particular was being questioned by large institutional customers. Large US based international commercial banks virtually stopped freely lending to one another in the Fed Funds market.[155] In addition, the internationalization of bank regulatory requirements resulted in heavy concentrations of US originated toxic but investment grade rated sub-prime mortgage securities - mostly AAA/AA rated CDOs - in numerous large international and foreign banks.[156]

By September 2008 Lehman Brothers still had $600 billion of short term debt obligations that it could no longer roll over backed by an incredibly illiquid and increasingly unmarketable portfolio at virtually any price. The precipitous drop in market values of sub- prime related securities had largely shut down the repo market by then.[157] In addition, the collapse of market prices caused Lehman Brothers book capital to virtually evaporate.[158] The impending downgrades of their credit rating made further issuance of their commercial paper problematic.

Most analysts agree that the Lehman Brothers default in mid September 2008 was the trigger and the loss of confidence in "near" money in the shadow banking system was the cause of the systemic contagion that brought credit markets crashing to a virtual standstill.[159] If not "too big," Lehman Brothers was "too systemically integrated" to fail, at least without severe market disruption. But Lehman's bankruptcy isn't the only potential cause. Kane cites sharply deteriorating consumer confidence and the Presidents televised address on September 24th.[160] Taylor argues that the perception that policymakers didn't understand what they were doing and the uncertainty of the proposed bailout actions precipitated the crisis.[161] Had the Fed not bailed out Bear Stearns the market may not have anticipated a Lehman bailout and Lehman might have recapitalized, postponing its insolvency and shifting the blame elsewhere. The specific triggering event isn't very important in any event, as the solvency hole was deep and the crash was unavoidable by then.

While the full extent of financial firm insolvency was not initially recognized, there were no buyers to set a floor under CDO prices, which generally could no longer be leveraged very much, if at all. Insolvent firms were also illiquid and unable to borrow. In the ensuing systemic rush for liquidity, sellers overwhelmed buyers for all but risk free liquid US Treasury securities.[162] Investors sold their most liquid assets first to raise the most cash, simultaneously minimizing the hit to earning and capital of selling risky assets at fire sale prices. Many economists view the rising spreads on these assets that resulted from this selling as evidence of a rising credit risk premium, hence "irrational" selling, but cash was the best life raft for underwater firms.

The SIV and repo market was never structured to survive a systemic rush to liquidity, and investors in cp and repo never intended to make hard discretionary credit assessments. That doesn't mean that panic had spread to a concern with the credit quality of all assets. It does suggest that the Fed failed to see the systemic liquidity crisis coming and had to play catch up.

The price decline of short term liquid assets caused some money market funds to "break-the-buck" (fall below par). At the time of the Lehman Brothers bankruptcy, the money market manager who was the most vocal opponent of purchasing any commercial paper had over 1% of *his own fund,* the Reserve Primary Fund, invested directly in Lehman Brothers cp, and this fund is illustrative of the impact the failure had on the shadow banking system. The Reserve Primary Fund, almost $100 billion, had 1.2% of their holdings invested in Lehman Brothers CP. Redemptions skyrocketed to take advantage of the par guaranty within minutes of market opening after the 2am Sunday night Lehman Brothers bankruptcy filing, to $5 billion in the afternoon and to $25 billion overnight, shutting down the fund.[163] Investors in this fund eventually received over 99% of par value over the next two years, but the damage to the payment mechanism had been done.[164]

So the precipitous decline in PLS prices revealed a solvency crisis in the shadow banking market, causing liquidity demands to skyrocket. The Fed immediately moved in to guarantee this market to minimize the impact on the real economy. All of this spilled over into other markets as investors sold any marketable assets to get liquid. The dramatic drop in the price - alternatively increase in yield - didn't necessarily reflect a precipitous change of credit risk premium of that magnitude so much as the initial attempts to de-leverage in what was a very thin and extremely over-leveraged market.

The solvency crisis became international because many foreign banks had purchased PLS, based entirely on the risk-based ratings and regulatory capital requirements, and international bank regulators were clearly concerned with mark-downs of these securities as well. Total foreign holdings of PLS totaled almost a half trillion dollars (Chapter 3, Table 6) and these took an immediate price hit of over a hundred billion dollars. Investors globally, including many central banks, treated GSE securities as higher yielding equivalents to Treasury securities, funding over 20% of the stock when the market crashed (see Exhibit 4 below). F&F had promoted their securities to investors globally for at least three decades, and the Chinese central bank alone held over a half trillion dollars in GSE securities in late 2008. The view of foreign investors was that if the US government could default on GSE debt, it could default on Treasury debt as well. As the Euro zone vividly illustrates, that becomes a self-fulfilling prophecy as the credit premium in debt yields rises, making default more likely. So guarantees were liberally provided, moral hazard be damned

Exhibit 4

Foreign commercial and central banks fund US home mortgage market

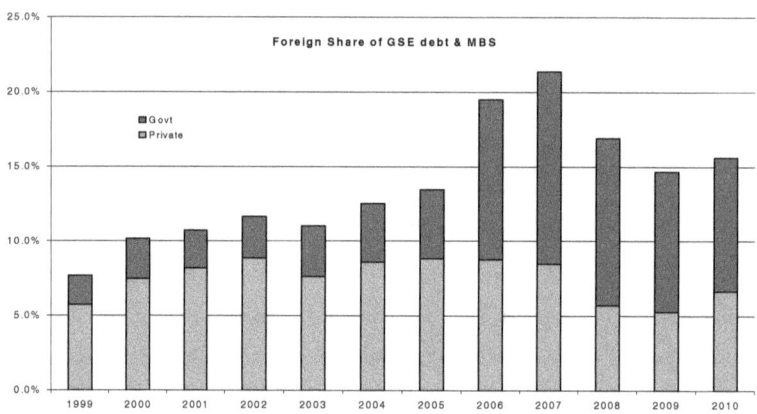

3. Why didn't the House Price Bubble Burst earlier: the Role of the GSEs

The notion that "nobody" thought that house prices could fall – a black swan event - isn't correct. While a failure to model reversion to the mean is an incredibly common human error it is not one generally made by speculators.[165] Even Taleb, the author of *The Black Swan* (2005) repeated warnings about the coming crash and eventually shorted the market himself.[166] The financial markets were well aware of the risk to financial institutions posed by falling house prices. Housing booms always run out of qualified buyers and turn to bust eventually.

Numerous industry publications questioned the PLS pool insurers' ratings and their ability to pay as early as 2002, but investors accepted their AAA rating until the ratings agencies down-graded them beginning in June 2008, well after the risks to their capital had been exposed. By mid-2004 the

168

shorts had started seriously betting against the housing market.[167] By 2006 hedge funds *on net* were speculating against the house price bubble, making securitization more difficult.[168] Goldman, the only investment banking firm that still had significant partner ownership, began shorting the market at this time to hedge the firm, a source of its subsequent legal and regulatory as well as public image troubles as it still simultaneously created and sold PLS.

The PLS funded sub-prime lending debacle of the late 1990's ended well before the losses became systemic. In chapter 3 we argued that PLSers wouldn't stop this time until well after house prices stopped rising, precipitating defaults and causing long term investors to bail out. It was cheap credit that kept the bubble inflated, but market speculators had stopped PLSers in the previous decade before the bubble inflated to systemic proportions. With "market" sentiment turning bearish in 2004 and pervasively bearish by mid 2006, why didn't speculators stop them much earlier? What was different this time? First, housing quotas had been ratcheted up, bringing GSEs into the sub-prime lending business. Second, bank regulator distortions actually got worse, allowing TBTF banks even greater regulatory arbitrage opportunities in pursuit of CRA credits to facilitate expansion.

The explosion of government credit and resulting house price bubble was too obvious to hide from market participants. Investors may not have been fully aware of the depth of the solvency hole, but they knew it existed and acted accordingly. Two things were obvious to market participants by the fall of 2008. First; the US financial markets were way over-leveraged, and second; the financial system was deeply insolvent, both as a result of political housing policy, excessive Fed credit expansion, mis-regulation and the house price bubble.

But a short position is relatively expensive to carry and has unlimited down-side risk when prematurely taken. As we observed in the prior decade, long investors will participate in a pyramid (sometimes called Ponzi) scheme fueling a bull market and frustrating the shorts on the expectation that they can exit before it collapses. What we observed in late 2008 was what usually happens when any asset bubble bursts or any pyramid scheme collapses, including that of Bernie Madoff, when the end nears. The knowledgeable long term participants have every incentive to stay in until just before the end, then to get out quickly. The rational investor response at that point was to rapidly deleverage, even if that meant selling PLS at what may have appeared at the time to some to be fire sale prices. This caused PLS markets to crash. The recent adoption of mark to market accounting rules accelerated the widespread reported losses making the deep financial institution solvency crisis more transparent earlier than otherwise, and the need for liquidity depressed the prices of even quality assets, worsening the solvency crisis.

It was obvious that PLSers were clearly going for broke during the first half of the past decade as they had in the prior decade, and that by 2005 PLSers were going broke. But they would not run out of cash so long as house prices didn't fall due to present value accounting. Betting specifically against PLS was a losing bet so long as borrowers didn't default. House prices were held up by mortgage refinancing – postponing defaults - until house prices stopped inflating in 2006-2007. We know from past experience that PLSer going broke and subject to bankruptcy when they did couldn't keep the house price bubble inflating that long on their own, so what did?

F&F and FHA/Ginnie Mae continued to compete with them as they went broke by doing the same thing. Betting on a credit-induced failure or debt default directly against F&F stock was a purely political gamble, and betting against their debt and securities an even bigger political gamble because the GSEs were correctly perceived to have no bankruptcy constraint. F&F stock prices fell but their security prices didn't - reflecting their agency status. Whether F&F (and to a lesser extent FHA and the FHLBs) knew it or not, their massive market presence late in the bubble kept the house price bubble rising at least several years longer than it otherwise would have, which kept sub-prime borrowers and the PLS market from crashing earlier as well. This increase in GSE activity as PLS originations collapsed confounded the shorts and comforted the longs, prolonging the bet on the bubble. The longer the bubble remained inflated, the worse the crash would be.

When the house price bubble eventually deflated, it was the PLS market that investors dumped first as ownership of GSE debt by foreign central banks on whom the Treasury was reliant for future funding made a GSE bailout a virtual certainty. GSE activity initially made up the difference and when F&F and FHA did fail, the same incentive distortions encouraged them to keep operating while "going broke" well past the point of technical insolvency. Being quasi private and subject to financial disclosure, F&F were eventually put into conservatorship, so the public FHA was the last man (zombie) standing, propped up by the government-backed Ginnie Mae. While PLS and GSE funding both contributed to funding the systemic bubble, GSE funding gets credit for continuing to inflate the bubble to systemic proportions. The loans originated during 2006-2007 subsequently accounted for about two thirds to three fourths of all the losses on sub-prime mortgages.

E. The Fallacy of Alternative Explanations

Credit bubbles cause asset bubbles that cause financial crises when they burst. This bubble was worse than most and generated numerous alternative explanations. But in the end it wasn't much different than Charles Kindleberger describes in *Manias, Panics, and Crashes, A History of Financial Crises*, (1978).John Kenneth Galbraith reached the same conclusion in *A Short History of Financial Euphoria" (*as cited by Kling, p. 33): "All innovation involves, in one form or another, the creation of debt secured in greater or lesser adequacy by real assets. . . . All crises have involved debt that, in one fashion or another, has become dangerously out of scale in relation to the underlying means of payment." This time the mania was political housing policy.

Most of the alternative explanations assume that the bubble was unforeseeable, and then proceed to explain why. But according to the Economist back in the summer of 2004, "the first law of bubbles is that they inflate for a lot longer than anybody expects …The second law is that they eventually burst." The Economist followed this on June 16th, 2005 with: "In come the waves: The worldwide rise in house prices is the biggest bubble in history. Prepare for the economic pain when it pops." Economists apparently don't read the Economist, Kindleberger or Galbraith. According to Galbraith's son economist James K Gailbraith in late 2008 only about a dozen of the nation's 15000 economists saw this crisis coming. [169]

With the benefit of hindsight, the sub-prime lending debacle obviously fits the classical debt bubble pattern. But knowledge of a solvency crisis resulting from the bubbles bursting in 2006 was in fact widespread as of 2008, although estimates of its depth continued to increase. By the time the FCIC Report was released in 2011 the depth of the solvency crisis was easily determined and the implications for the solvency of the financial system in 2007 obvious.

How a solvency crisis could *grow this deep and widespread* before being exposed is what needs to be explained, and *only* that. Political housing goals, regulatory distortions and malfeasance, and political "smart growth" policies are each necessary and taken together are sufficient conditions to provide the only explanation of the go for broke and go broke behavior - particularly by GSEs not subject to market constraints - described above that made the losses so deep. There were numerous symptoms – effects rather than causes - discussed in this and prior chapters, e.g., complex CDOs and credit rating agency malfeasance, but none of these are *independent* of these three root causes, public policy failures all. There is no alternative explanation for why all of these other events occurred simultaneously.

In contrast to the 662 page FCIC Report, our explanation of the 2008 financial crisis is only six pages. While this crisis varied in the particulars, it fit the historical norm. Our discussion of the fallacies of alternative explanations below is almost three times as long, a topic that most of the remaining chapters are devoted to as well. What are these fallacies and why do they persist?

A half century after the assignation of President John F. Kennedy a majority of the American people still do not believe the simple narrative that he was killed by a left wing communist sympathizer. The dozens of complex counter-factual alternatives generally relate to right wing conspiracies.

Ultimate proof of the role of housing policy, the subsequent performance of loans that were used to qualify either for CRA and/or GSE housing goals, is locked in federal vaults were it will undoubtedly remain. Even this ignores the role of home ownership goals. But the attempt to maintain credible denial is totally undermined by the alternative offered of a purely private market failure. The only thing not known with certainty is the apportionment of relative blame between housing goals and regulatory malfeasance. The solution is the same in either case, more reliance on market mechanisms and discipline.

Support for freer markets finds surprisingly little sympathy among the economics profession. Many of these 15000 economists were also regulators or political administrators with a responsibility to see the crisis coming and act accordingly, and the flow of economists between academia and regulatory agencies or politically appointed administrators and advisors is fairly fluid. Almost all professors work directly for public universities, and the so-called private universities are dependent on federal largess and the regulation that goes with it. For the most part, the explanation for the persistence of these fallacies is the same as that of the financial crisis, mis-aligned and distorted incentives and rent-seeking. Market capitalism is definitely not politically correct.

1. The Fed's spin

The Fed and regulators could have stopped the lending bubble at any time by enforcing prudential lending guidelines and imposing effective capital requirement. Why didn't regulators stop the bubble much earlier? Fed Chairman Alan Greenspan had denied the existence of a housing bubble much less one of the Fed's and F&F's making, and as late as early 2006 under Bernanke's watch as Fed Chairman two Fed of New York economists presented a paper asking the question "Is there a Bubble in the Housing Market Now?" – concluding there was not. The Fed was in good regulatory company: Kling (p. 18) cites an FDIC paper prepared in 2004 that reached the same conclusion.[170]

But part of the answer is that politicians and regulators believed the myth of their own making: that goal-oriented mortgage lending was highly profitable. Hence regulators remained in denial as the losses mounted. New York Federal Reserve Vice President William C. Dudley in the fall of 2007, well over a year after the subprime securitization machine had started grinding to an eventual halt, asked: "How did the problems in the subprime mortgage market — with losses that ultimately will probably turn out to be in the range of $100 to $200 billion — lead to such broad market distress?[171] This followed comments by Federal Reserve Chairman Ben Bernanke five months earlier that "we believe the effect of the troubles in the subprime market will be limited, and we do not expect significant spillovers from the subprime market to the rest of the economy or the financial system."[172] Chairman Bernanke had previously publically supported the housing goals, bragging in November of 2006, just before the bubble burst, about the positive contribution of credit allocation to expanding homeownership opportunities and the large gains made in the homeownership rate, particularly among racial minorities.[173]

Yale economist Robert Shiller considers the Fed a victim of irrational exuberance, supporting the theory that credit bubbles can't be identified until after the fact. But Jacobo Carmassi, Daniel Gros and Stefano Micossi (2009, p. 986) point out that the Fed had long implemented a policy – articulated successively by both Chairman Greenspan and his successor Bernanke - of supporting inflating asset bubbles and then providing massive liquidity to slow their deflation when they burst, thus shaping market expectations supporting rational exuberance.

Estimates of actual ultimate net credit loss increased about ten-fold during the ensuing 2 years from Dudley's initial estimate.[174] Within a year of this forecast financial institutions globally had taken a hit to capital of about $700 billion. And the actual write downs and write offs more than doubled during the ensuing 10 months to over $1.6 trillion.[175] But the Fed lacks authority for addressing a solvency crisis so it continued to maintain that this reflected the systemic illiquidity of the system rather than insolvency. If it was only a liquidity crisis it should have been over by year end 2008. As the ability to maintain the myth depended on house prices not falling, that was the focus of Fed and administration policy for the ensuing four years as discussed in the next chapter.

Calling this a "liquidity crisis" provided political cover for the ongoing massive subsidies provided – again opaquely – to fill the solvency hole in financial institution capital. This takes time:

commercial bank loans to Latin American governments in the 1980s, for example, were written off leisurely over a decade.[176] But because of the change to mark to market accounting rules the Fed had much less time than usual to implement a cover-up. These accounting rules were blamed for precipitating the solvency crisis caused by "panicky" sellers, but to the extent there was panic it was investors knowingly invested in a pyramid scheme rationally heading for the exits because only those in the front of the line would get paid in full. In any event most of the $700 billion losses initially recorded by financial institutions in 2008 reflected unrealized mark to market losses.[177] Regulators had lobbied for years to impose mark-to-market accounting for banks in place of mark-to-model as allowed by the then current rules, and this change was implemented in late 2007.[178] The timing couldn't have been worse for the Fed to maintain the illusion of a liquidity crisis. Now they had to disown them.

Investment banks had long used mark to market accounting on the illusion that they only held "dealer inventory" for sale, and hence other measures of value were irrelevant. The concept gained acceptance in the 1980's as a way to measure interest rate risk, but it was flawed even in that application, which required that the yield curve be an unbiased predictor of future interest rates, i.e., a long term forecast of political risk subject to change.[179]

The theory for risky assets was that the opinions of thousands of market participants regarding future default were less biased than that of the bankers who purchased the investment. But in a re-play of the S&L crisis, regulators continued to require mark-to-market write-offs in the virtual absence of any trades.[180] As the book net worth of sub-prime laden bank and investment bank balance sheets was driven down by these marks, making survival questionable, raising capital became increasingly problematic as the bubble deflated. This made it even more difficult for banks and investment banks to de-leverage while recapitalizing.[181] Hence the Fed subsequently did whatever it could to keep financial asset prices as well as housing prices inflated, as discussed in the next chapter.

Mark to market accounting was not a cause of the sub-prime lending debacle or subsequent financial crisis. But it did make the Fed's cover up more difficult.

The "liquidity" crisis inevitably spread to the "shadow banking" market. The Fed has long thought of money market funds as nothing more than regulatory avoidance, and they became a convenient scapegoat. Money markets provide a convenience for retail and small institutional customers, but large corporate customers can fund and invest directly in money market instruments, bypassing money market funds. Some operate on a significant cash deficit, relying on the ability to rollover their own outstanding commercial paper. Others invest directly in commercial paper of other firms, investment banks and SIVs of commercial banks. They may also make direct short term repo loans collateralized by "liquid," i.e. marketable securities to obtain higher yields than available on bank deposits. Hence the shadow banking market ultimately issued bank-like deposits and purchased bank like investments, but without Fed regulation and systemic liquidity support, relying more on the credit rating agencies and staying very short term.

Shadow banks weren't regulated as banks because that's a simple business with nothing much to regulate. They took losses because they relied on SEC approved credit rating agency AAA commercial paper ratings that completely failed to accurately assess the risk of regulated banks and investment banks. This market was not unregulated nor was there evidence of market failure; it was a victim of extreme regulatory malfeasance. But the shadow banking system was not a root cause of the systemic financial crisis.

2. The Fannie and Freddie Spin

Fannie and Freddie advocates have spun a variety of stories as alternatives to our explanation of the incentives facing them to support their exoneration and hence continuation. The first is that Fannie and Freddie were victims of PLSers, blindly following them. There is some truth to that as they were required to follow, but little exoneration. They were industry leaders for most of their existence and the GSEs had led the way around private mortgage insurance underwriting for low down payment loans since 1997. They appeared to lag behind private label sub-prime lending due to the temporary restraint imposed in response to their accounting scandals in late 2004 but, their market share quickly rose to the prior level as soon as the audited accounts were finally released in 2006 and the excess capital requirement was lifted. Internal documents show a policy of regaining the market share lost to private securitizers as their mission regulations required. But it was their market presence that kept the bubble inflated, whether or not leading or following.

Another popular narrative is that the GSEs increased their accumulation of non-goal-qualifying risky loans as well as goal qualifying loans, suggesting "greed" was the problem rather than their housing goals.[182] This view is favored by Weicher, who as assistant HUD secretary for housing and Federal Housing Commissioner was HUD's "mission regulator" at the start of the bubble, argued that Fannie and Freddie management must have been driven by the profit motive because they offered little resistance to the housing goals.[183] This view is also supported by Jaffee (2010) and Thomas and Van Order (2011), but the argument is not very persuasive for several reasons.

First, while the mandated low-income loans had the risk characteristics of "high yield" loans and bonds, they did not have the return characteristics during the sub-prime lending bubble — as other risky loans presumably did — and management knew it. The GSEs had historically experienced higher credit losses on such loans to creditworthy borrowers even in good times, and numerous internal documents at both Fannie and Freddie show that they recognized the shift in risk as the housing boom turned and wanted to tighten standards.

Second, affordable housing goal-qualified lending operated at close to break even in the best of times, but F&F had long cross-subsidized the *deeper* losses on affordable housing loans with profits from other loans, so riskier non-goal qualified lending was expanded this time as well.[184] This explains the move toward increasingly risky lending during this period for loans that were less likely to qualify for their specific affordable housing quota's, but still qualified toward their homeownership goal. As a consequence, during the bubble years of mid-2004 to mid-2007, F&F purchased about 12 million subprime loans that qualified for one or more of these goals.

In retrospect, loans that didn't specifically qualify for affordable housing goals had a slightly higher default rate from 2005-2007 than did the more goal oriented loans. Thomas and Van Order interpret the greater frequency of default on less goal-rich lending during the bubble years 2005 through 2007 as exonerating housing policy, But this was business as usual, only this time they had no choice but to go for broke, and by this time the only such loans available in the marketplace for this purpose were conforming sub-prime. So subsequent losses from the higher risk strategy aren't surprising and private lenders made the same ultimately bad bet for the same reason.

It is true that losses outside F&F were about four times greater that direct F&F losses. This is partly due to the requirement of PMI or in this case second mortgages, but even including losses indirectly related to F&F first liens and FHA loans the GSEs only accounted for about a fifth of all credit losses. PLSers were clearly lending even more recklessly. But this doesn't change the conclusion that F&F's continued market presence facilitated by their agency status kept the PLS market afloat on the GSE-inflated house price bubble until the problem grew to systemic proportions.

The FCIC Report (p. 323) exonerated Fannie and Freddie by noting that "GSE mortgage securities essentially maintained their value throughout the crisis and did not contribute to the significant financial firm losses that were central to the financial crisis." But this is grossly misleading. Fannie and Freddie had promoted their securities to investors globally for at least three decades, and the Chinese central bank alone held over a half trillion dollars in GSE securities in late 2008, making default unthinkable. By mid-summer of 2008 they had reported huge credit losses and their capital and liquidity was depleted - the financial condition was much worse than had been disclosed, as revealed in subsequent SEC lawsuits - and raising equity was problematic, so these international investors wanted assurances. Congress passed the Housing and Economic Recovery Act (HERA) of 2008 on July 30, giving the Treasury virtually unlimited bailout powers. That reassured the holders of senior securities, but spreads over Treasuries on their sub-debt quadrupled in a few months (Kling, 2009, p. 40). The OFHEO and Treasury decided to put Fannie and Freddie into conservatorship on September 4 (FCIC Report, p. 318) and announced this on September 7 in the mistaken belief that this would restore market confidence (FCIC Report p. 320).

3. The Regulators' Spin

In addition to the Fed's spin and the Fannie and Freddie spin, bank regulators provide two explanations of their own. First, it was deregulation and/or lack of regulatory authority over unregulated predatory firms and markets. Second, mission regulation – particularly the CRA – was not a cause and didn't compromise prudential regulation.

Politicians and many analysts argue that deregulation and insufficient regulatory authority removed the constraints on private incentives that were otherwise aligned with producing the debacle. The de-regulation argument is worse than myth because prudential regulators who had the authority and responsibility to stop it actively encouraged such lending for the reasons already discussed, while politicians cheered them on. The only de-regulation related to Glass Steagal restrictions on the traditional underwriting and sales and trading operations of investment banks, which was not a contributing factor. The lack of regulatory authority, e.g., in the CDS market was a moderating influence on the bubble. It was the highly regulated markets that failed.

The FCIC Report's findings actually support this conclusion, i.e., that F&F and bank regulators displaced but failed pervasively to replace inherent private market constraints: "place(ing) special responsibility with the public leaders charged with protecting our financial system, those entrusted to run our regulatory agencies...." [185] Regulators had every reason to support the FCIC Report conclusion in spite of its criticisms of regulators as Dodd-Frank had already provided them with tremendously expanded powers with even less accountability. This regulatory mythology and the reasons for it are discussed at much greater length in the subsequent chapters.

As noted in chapter 2 the notion of predatory lending was a political myth spun by advocacy groups to obtain lower rates when extracting credit allocation commitments. Risk-based pricing was used to some extent, but was generally not favorable to lenders due to adverse selection. Premium pricing has always been a sore point among consumers who don't shop around, less so in mortgage lending. The regulatory thesis that lenders preyed on borrowers earning excess profits had little or no merit even in the 1990s, and certainly not during this period. But whether lenders perceived goal oriented loans as potentially profitable in the 1990s or even the first half of the last decade is irrelevant to the situation in 2005 through 2007, when there was no market clearing price for risk taken.

Much has been made about predatory mortgage instruments. What was the egregious lender offense? They allowed borrowers to choose mortgage loans with a lower monthly payment. This generally meant that rather than the nominal principal balance incrementally declining in the early years, it stayed flat – interest only loans – or modestly increased, a process called negative amortization. The genesis of these loans was HUD sponsored research in the 1970s to deal with the effects of inflation on the fixed payment mortgage insured by FHA.

The fixed rate mortgage only protects borrowers from inflation when it is unanticipated: lenders and investors responded to anticipated inflation by raising the required mortgage rate. But a fixed payment mortgage requires paying now for inflation in the future. The rise in the required real – inflation adjusted – mortgage payment during the early years became known as the "tilt effect." HUD funded a study by the Harvard- MIT Joint Center for Financial Studies and published a subsequent book *Alternative Mortgage Instruments in an Inflationary Environment* in 1975 that suggested a variety of alternative mortgage designs. All had one thing in common, a lower initial payment resulting in either no amortization or negative amortization. By the time these ideas worked their way through the HUD bureaucracy inflation was on the decline but FHA's market share had already fallen by 75%.

Interest only mortgages were popular during the 1920's housing boom but disappeared during the Depression. Wells Fargo and Washington Mutual were among the first banks to reintroduce the loans at the start of this century, particularly in areas where house prices had risen the most such as

California, where Golden West S&L introduced the so-called "pick-a-pay" loan in 1982. As the point of such mortgages was to make housing more affordable, most borrowers chose the lowest payment.

While these worked better in an inflationary environment, the credit risk is increased if inflation is less than expected. But as house prices continued rising during the recent housing boom and the Fed, as both the consumer and systemic regulator denied a bubble, such mortgages made sense for consumers and politicians sanctified lenders for offering them to promote political housing goals. The Fed as we now know was quite wrong. The bubble burst, default rates soared and politicians then crucified lenders.

The FCIC Report (p. xvii) concludes: "The prime example (of regulatory failure) is the Federal Reserve's pivotal failure to stem the flow of toxic mortgages." But these loans only had a marginal impact on negative equity and hence borrower default frequency and loss severity. Low cash down payments were the major cause of the house price bubble and subsequent default as well as the resulting severity of loss

Insufficient documentation is an entirely unrelated problem. Many low doc or no doc loans didn't require verification of income, particularly important to the objects of housing policy, many of whom weren't here legally and others with unstable or potentially illegal income. About 70% of the early payment defaults on low-no doc loans involved borrower fraud.[186] These loans were also generally encouraged by the home ownership initiatives of the Clinton and Bush Administrations.

The Community Reinvestment Act (CRA) of 1977 purportedly reflected a concern that local bankers were not lending "enough" to good borrowers in their communities or neighborhoods, which were typically characterized by ethnic and/or racial concentrations. This systemic market discrimination supposedly persisted throughout the last century. During the last decade, while greedy mortgage lenders were originating about 20 million sub-prime loans to borrowers of dubious credit, CRA proponents implicitly argue that lenders would still have discriminated systemically against profitable CRA-qualifying borrowers but for the requirement. This isn't credible.[187]

Commissioner Wallison and Ed Pinto at AEI have examined the entire scope of housing policy and traced back the roots of risky sub-prime lending generally to these policies. AEI is a conservative think tank and Wallison and Pinto are both lawyers. The lead antagonist to this position is David Kim, also a lawyer, affiliated until 2012 with the Center for American Progress (CAP), a liberal think tank. The debate has thus become legalistic and ideological as well as political and personal. Wallison, Pinto and AEI have been bitterly attacked by defenders of US housing policy.[188]

While Wallison and Pinto provide a plethora of evidence in support of the housing policy hypothesis, in the end they can't prove the magnitude of the CRA link to PLS or F&F due to the same data limitations faced by CRA defenders, and the additional observations provided above are admittedly circumstantial because the necessary data to prove the CRA link "beyond any doubt" is lacking. But the more appropriate civil court test of "a preponderance of evidence" has clearly been met. Oonagh McDonald – a well established economist and experienced former British politician, a Labor member of parliament for over a decade, and a regulator as former Director of Britain's Financial Services Authority – who cannot be dismissed as an AEI "free market ideologue" - has also clearly provided that.

Investigators at the Fed and elsewhere have tried for years to determine the effect of CRA lending. Some studies based on 1990's data found little evidence of excessive credit loss, others that CRA did weaken bank safety and soundness.[189] McDonald concluded that the data simply didn't allow any such conclusions because the performance of individual loans used to qualify initially for CRA was never tracked.[190] Agarwal e. al. 2012 use a more limited data base to conclude what every banker already knows, that riskier loans were made specifically to meet CRA targets and that these subsequently defaulted at a higher rate, particularly if securitized.

The debate over the evidence regarding CRA during the last century is entirely irrelevant. From the very beginning prudential regulators used poor grades on CRA assessment reports based on HMDA data to withhold approval for branching and merger applications in response to political advocacy group pressure to extract easier terms for select borrowers. How this got out of hand leading to about $4 trillion of CRA-related commitments coming due between 2000 and 2007 is explained in chapter 2. These new CRA commitments – the majority agreed to by the "too-big-to-fail" banks – required that banks unleash their mortgage banking subsidiaries.

Losses at US commercial banks – mostly those that were TBTF – account for about half of all US mortgage credit losses. Losses on CDOs and second mortgages account for most of this, with losses on first liens accounting for only about 15%. We provide a plausible link between the second mortgages and CDO securities and the massive CRA lending commitments that is consistent with the magnitude and incidence of mortgage related credit losses. CRA proponents ignore both the CRA commitments and the losses of the past decade on seconds and PLS – primarily CDO - securities, instead referring back to the flawed and irrelevant studies of the 1990s.

CRA defenders follow F&F defenders in attributing bank losses to "greed," but this is similarly unconvincing. The main gatekeepers historically –PMI companies – are also for profit shareholder institutions like F&F and banks. They knew from past experience that they were also not TBTF and as monoline insurers they couldn't cross subsidize goal-oriented borrowers like F&F and TBTF banks could, so they resisted the business and generally dodged the bullet. The major difference is that the PMIs are state regulated and not subject to any mission regulation. Bank leverage provides an incentive to go for broke, but not to go broke knowingly making bad loans.

How mission regulation of F&F trumped prudential regulation has been discussed at length. But the same is true of bank regulation. The Fed, our erstwhile systemic regulator – and the FDIC – our erstwhile prudential regulator – both shared CRA enforcement responsibilities, both defended CRA as costless, and both failed massively and chronically during the sub-prime lending debacle. The FCIC Report cites the Fed's own flawed research to exonerate the CRA (p. xxvii). In the end, stopping the bubble would have blown the whistle on political housing policy as well as regulatory failures. Regulators had no incentive to do either, and were subsequently rewarded for their cover up with increased power and responsibility provided by Dodd-Frank.

4. The Academic Economists' Spin

Thousands of the nation's economists are directly implicated in the Fed, F&F and regulatory spin due to the public sector revolving door. Why did academic research overwhelmingly support the FCIC Report? Wallison (2013, p. 165) argues that all of the witnesses were chosen by the chairman, questioned only by him, and used in the Report only as useful. Gretchen Morgenson and Joshua Rosner quote a lobbyist in _Reckless Endangerment_ (2011, p. 76):

I tried to find academics who would do research on these issues and Fannie Mae had bought off all the academics in housing. I had people say to me "are you going to give me stipends for the next 20 years like Fannie Mae will?"

In chapter 6 we argue that the Fed, while more subtle, exerted similar influence over the academic community regarding its actions. But there is more to it than just direct monetary self interest and industry and institution acceptance.

Why do many economists still deny the root causes of the bubble and what can explain the allegiance of economists to multiple complex causes? It is perhaps because they got locked into alternative explanations early on. To quote Leo Tolstoy:

"I know that most men -- not only those considered clever, but even those who are very clever and capable of understanding most difficult scientific, mathematical, or philosophic, problems -- can seldom discern even the simplest and most obvious truth if it be such as obliges them to admit the falsity of conclusions they have formed, perhaps with much difficulty -- conclusions of which they are proud, which they have taught to others, and on which they have built their lives."

It isn't clear why, as knowledge of the credit and house price bubbles became more widespread as the first half of the decade progressed. Paul Krugman, in a long article in the NYT, asks: How did Economists get it So Wrong?[191] Krugman exonerates the Fed: "an economy that went off the rails *despite the Fed's best efforts.*" He further exonerates the GSEs.[192] His conclusion is that economists relied on an unwavering belief in markets and assumption of rationality, which gave way to a failure to regulate. The later assertions are factually incorrect, as is his analysis of the role of the Fed and GSEs, but the assertion of economists' unwavering faith in markets is even more curious. Academic research generally has an inherent anti-market bias in search of "market failures" as classical economics presumes political and public sector intervention isn't subject to failure so it is not surprising that many economists supported the FCIC characterization of private market failures, ignoring as did the Report the extent of public protection and displacement of market discipline with regulation. The vast majority work at public universities – although the so-called private universities are equally government-dependent and often equally biased – and private think tanks. There are only literally a handful of economists at market oriented think tanks – including John Weicher, now at the Hudson institute.

Academic research is also backward looking because that's were the data resides for time series empirical research. Economists generally are rewarded for building hypothetical models of "market failure," then looking for historical data to fit them.

But to the extent that the FCIC Report used academic input, it generally was not empirical. The research made no attempt to distinguish which of the multiple contributing causes cited by the Report is necessary to explain the sub-prime lending debacle. Instead, it resorts to old un-provable economic theories of mass psychology or "mania" – everybody was irrationally exuberant - to explain why the house price bubble kept inflating to such historic levels. Most importantly, it didn't attempt to explain why all of the "market failures" and observed "bad" behavior it presents as contributing factors happened simultaneously, considering their confluence a serendipitous event.

An excellent collection of academic papers produced and published roughly simultaneously with the FCIC Report entitled *the American Mortgage System: Crisis and Reform* edited by Susan

Wachter and Marvin Smith generally starts from the premise that private mortgage markets were in fact private, i.e., unlike Fannie and Freddie not creatures of political and regulatory distortions, and hence implicitly that the observed symptoms reflected independent market failures. The miss-labeling of private label securities markets opened the door for numerous economist models of private "market failure," mostly the informational asymmetry, investor mis-pricing and agency conflict models.

There is plenty of data to fit these models as discussed in Wachter and Smith – and we generally agree with the analysis (CRA being a glaring exception) - but that doesn't prove causality. Our concern is with the typical prescriptions that flow from these diagnoses. For example, in the aforementioned collected works is the previously cited paper by Levitin and Wachter "Information Failure in the US Mortgage Crisis" that provides an excellent description of the informational shortcomings and asymmetries characterizing PLS. But we disagree with the conclusion (p. 245):

"This means that whatever the ultimate reconstituted form of the housing finance market, the regulatory response to the crisis should concentrate on ensuring sufficient standardization of MBS products – and, by necessity, standardization of the underlying mortgage products – to make the disclosure of information about credit risk a meaningful basis for pricing."

This is a prescription to which many economists subscribe on the false premise that the goal of public policy is to save PLS, itself entirely a consequence of GSEs, deposit insurance and implicit guarantees that this prescription would perpetuate. It was government imposed "information" standards that eventually led to agency status. There is no shortage of private market "experts" – ironically mostly the much maligned mortgage and investment bankers - who support such prescriptions as they would directly benefit from them. But undistorted well-functioning markets would likely solve this problem in the public interest in a much different manner, as discussed in chapter 6.

This large literature developed around the proposition first put forward in Greenbaum and Thakor, "Bank funding modes: Securitization versus deposits" (1987) that securitization is an alternative to bank deposits and which will dominate depends on "informational asymmetries" relating to the risk of the underlying loans.[193] Investors in MBS are thought by some to be at an inherent disadvantage because they have less information than the lenders and securitizers. With deposit insurance and agency status ignorance is bliss for senior creditors, but not equity investors. Numerous analysts have concluded that a major cause of the systemic financial crisis of 2008 was that investment bankers purposely made investment grade securities overly complex to trick investors.[194] Some analysts have argued that originators, securitizers, rating agencies and other intermediaries conspired to mislead investors into purchasing securities that were much riskier than the investors were led to believe.

This argument is as old as the securities market itself. Informational asymmetries are the general state of the universe, but buyers typically pay more for good relevant information, so honest sellers have every incentive to provide it. Since the advent of computer tapes on pool data several decades ago regarding the loan origination and servicing data, all funders can have access to the same data as the originator. It is just a matter of what they ask for.[195] Investors in investment grade MBS could have access to the same data as the securitizer but are no more likely to ask for it than are bank depositors or GSE investors: that job has been delegated to intermediaries since the SEC designation of NRSROs and it wouldn't be efficient to analyze the data independently unless and until market discipline is restored. Again, there were few if any at-risk investors facing undistorted incentives.

Economists have made much ado about the complexity and informational asymmetry of PLS and derivative securities - CDOs, squared and cubed. But informational asymmetries are also common for corporate borrowers because corporations are complex - as are corporate bond covenants. This isn't considered an insurmountable problem and investors didn't resist investment grade PLS and CDOs for these reasons, e.g., by demanding more information and a simpler design, because dealing with these issues had been delegated by regulators to the rating agencies. The CDO phenomenon was investor driven due to their perverse regulatory incentives. This is much ado about nothing. The failure of regulatory oversight, especially given the massive conflict of interest between the raters and issuers, isn't!

Some economists argue that investor pricing models caused them to under-price credit risk of sub-prime MBS and the lack of a market to short these investments allowed the magnitude of miss-pricing to grow until the resulting failure was systemic.[196] In our view, there was no collusion among investors in the choice of pricing models, no shortage of shorting mechanisms and no *ex ante* price to charge sub-prime borrowers that could have prevented the subsequent investor credit losses while avoiding adverse selection. Rather, there were few if any traditional at-risk investors in investment grade MBS facing undistorted incentives when pricing credit risk. Those with undistorted incentives road the bubble for what it was worth, and most got out in advance, leaving the loss with regulated investors.

Discrimination by race is implicitly considered to be a pervasive mortgage market failure warranting housing goals. Insurance only allows for pricing the uncertainties of borrower underwriting for collateralized lending. Credit risks that can't be insured can't be priced. There is no substantive evidence that US credit markets systemically under-served or over-priced credit to any politically sensitive borrower group. If anything, origination markets have been overly competitive, resulting in excessive lending, as evidenced by other consumer loan markets and the historically low net US savings rate. US mortgage markets have generally provided the most liberal terms to qualified borrowers among housing finance systems in market economies.

Some allege that the systemic financial crisis was caused by a failure of models to predict a black swan event, a realization that "stuff happens" a lot more frequently than our models predict. House prices always revert to the mean after a credit bubble, which doesn't require more complex modeling. The primary mortgage insurers – not subject to federal regulation or mission goals - obviously understood that and acted accordingly in spite of the advice of politicians and federal regulators.

Economists typically assume that whenever a price index drops precipitously it reflects irrational panicky selling by investors, i.e., a typical liquidity crisis. But there was no irrational exuberance turned to panic that ended the sub-prime debacle. Even the less astute fixed income money managers were aware by 2006 of widespread criticisms of credit rating agencies as reported in the financial trade press at the time and many simply stopped purchasing new issues. Investor perceptions of credit loss changed somewhat gradually over a three year period from 2006 through 2008 when the rating downgrades swept the market, but speculation against the bubble began in earnest in 2005. The speed of the decline simply reflected the switch from regulatory-approved accounting prices to market prices.

Some analysts argue that households and mortgage investors were caught up in a bubble "mania" – a mainstay of economic models of bubbles - but there is little evidence of that.[197] Had they been investing their own cash from savings for down payments, limited or prohibited from cash-out refi's, and provided lenders with recourse, households would undoubtedly have been a lot less "manic" about taking on mortgage debt at these inflated house prices. Had lenders – loan originators - borne the risk of falling house prices, they would undoubtedly have been a lot less euphoric about the bubble as well.

5. The Armchair Moralists' Spin

Market capitalism is motivated by individual self interest, cited by many armchair moralists as the moral failure of capitalism and a root cause of the financial crisis. In *Why Capitalism* (2012, p.5) Alan Meltzer refutes the German philosopher Immanuel Kant's denial of a moral defense of capitalism because "as humans are morally imperfect so are their institutions" by noting that the conclusion "applies as least as much to public as to private officials." We would add "institutions" and based on the historical track record discussed thus far and the conceptual concerns discussed in chapter 6 we conclude that with respect to the financial system it applies *more* to public officials and institutions, a phenomenon best understood and explained by the public choice economists led by the recently diseased Nobel Prize winning economist James M Buchanan.[198] The fault lies not with private individuals pursuing self interest but with politicians and regulators doing so by distorting private incentives. The former is generally consistent with the public interest, the latter fraught with "unintended consequences" – a euphemism for inevitably bad policy outcomes most often motivated by public sector rent-seeking.

Consider just a few of the actions that invoked the greatest moral indignation and outrage during the sub-prime lending debacle:

Investment bankers pioneered CDOs and other complex derivatives that turned out to be a disaster for investors. CDOs lowered the cost of funds to issuers by giving investors what the wanted, allowing investment bankers and their shareholders to profit. The subsequent investor losses stemmed from the multiple distorting regulations affecting their demand. Is it to be the moral responsibility of investment bankers to discern the 'unintended consequences" of political folly and regulatory malfeasance and refuse to serve their customers' interest?

Investment banks are run by traders in pursuit of short term bonuses. They were historically run by investment bankers in pursuit of protecting and enhancing the value of the firm, but volatile trading in GSE securities resulting from monetary and fiscal policy instability and laws against prepayment penalties were instrumental in changing that model, creating a shareholder problem that regulators shifted to taxpayers.

Mortgage bankers and brokers originated loans for un-or-under qualified borrowers and sold them to investors without retaining any "skin in the game." The mortgage banking industry was virtually created to do exactly this starting in 1938 by serving Fannie Mae, and later all of the GSEs, and they were sued by the DOJ if they failed to implement political housing policy with sufficient enthusiasm. Those with a moral objection to such policies could quit and become clerics, but there would always be others to take their place.

There was a systemic increase in fraud and other illegal activities. What was systemic was the increase in the attempts to prove this hypothesis as occurred after the S&L debacle to find political scapegoats. The results were also the same, a waste of taxpayer money and subsequent legal extortion undermining the rule of law (as discussed in chapter 5).

Morality can not and should not be imposed on capitalism beyond pursuit of individual self interest, with no apology necessary for the sub-prime lending debacle. There will always be criminal activity – private and public - but this is nothing compared to the wealth redistribution and destruction caused by opaque and occasionally illegal rent-seeking public policies. Regulatory actions such as making "excessive pay" illegal will just increase the dead weight cost of regulatory and political rent-seeking, the distortions from which were a root cause of the debacle.

6. The Politicians' Spin

Using finance to subsidize borrowers generally ends badly, and there was no reason to believe the US would be any different during the last decade. Some, the author included, have predicted this outcome since the CRA and affordable housing goals were first introduced. Virtually all of the fallacies discussed above and more found there way into the FCIC Report. Politicians wanted to protect the key false tenets of their power and authority: 1. that they can deliver subsidies without costs or consequences, and 2. that political power is necessary to direct the financial system and protect the participants. Focusing on the events immediately before and during the 2008 financial crisis and then confusing the issue with the "multiple complex causes" narrative successfully deflected political blame.

Wallison's Dissent argues that "housing policy was the "sine qua non" of the sub-prime lending debacle. He then describers the other necessary conditions that led to the sub-prime debacle in much the same way we do. Housing policy defenders first miss-interpret the Latin (that housing policy was a necessary, not the only or even a sufficient condition) by generally ignoring the other necessary conditions, pretending that the Wallison Dissent relies exclusively on housing policy. Second, they generally ignore the homeownership goal, defining housing policy as relating only to the affordable housing quotas and CRA. We've explained the fallacies of each of these interpretations. We've provided more detail on the magnitude of regulatory distortions and malfeasance, explaining: first; how and why PLSers went for broke then went broke, and second; how and why F&F would follow them, doing the same thing. We've also explained how the homeownership goal in conjunction with the affordable housing quotas was orders of magnitude more costly to achieve. We explained that losses were deeper on the more goal rich loans and that the hoped for cross subsidies were part of a go for broke strategy to fund housing policy.

Politicians may have ignored warning signals but should have rightly expected regulators to sound the alarm bell before they blew up the global financial system. After the fact, Commissioner Wallison interprets the FCIC findings essentially as a cover-up by a politically appointed committee controlled by democrats investigating political malfeasance primarily – but certainly not exclusively - by democrats, ironic as the commission's findings largely focused on private market *conflicts of interest*.[199]

The success of the political "private market failure" narrative provided the foundation for a continuation of the same bad policies during the four year aftermath of the financial crisis, discussed next. What they should do prospectively is discussed in the last chapter.

Chapter 5: Government Bailouts during the Aftermath: More of the Same

Property damage due to Hurricane Sandy that hit the east coast in 2012 is estimated to be about $50 billion, exceeded only by the damage done by Hurricane Katrina in 2012 of about $100 billion. These hurricanes cost as much as or more than the real net economic costs of the sub-prime lending debacle that occurred between these two naturally occurring events, as the greater nominal losses of the latter event mostly reflected the reversal of illusory past gains. The recovery from hurricanes generally – these two being no exception - begins immediately and adds to employment and economic growth. In stark contrast, the economy hasn't yet recovered from the systemic financial crisis of 2008, with the economic costs of the failure to grow per capita GDP orders of magnitude ten times as great as the original economic loss and the outlook remains pessimistic. Why is that?

The typical news coverage the day after a hurricane contains interviews of victims surveying the damage under sunny skies. Most are shocked by the magnitude of their loss, but resolved to begin the rebuilding process immediately. Both the magnitude and incidence of loss is estimated within days, with disputes between the victims and insured settled by adjusters within months. Everybody moves on. Hurricane Katrina remains controversial because much of the damage could arguably have been avoided had the dikes been built to withstand a category five hurricane, generating much political finger-pointing to avoid accountability for the disaster.

The first difference between hurricanes and financial disasters is that the policies that produce a credit and asset bubble dramatically re-allocate existing wealth. The second difference is that as a consequence of deposit insurance, the banking sector is highly leveraged. Whereas state-regulated casualty insurers maintain sufficient capital and employ risk-mitigation procedures such as globally re-insuring to avoid bankruptcy when paying these claims, highly leveraged federally regulated banks rely on political protection conveyed by being too-big-to-fail. Should bank losses exceed their equity, people may lose confidence in the payments mechanism and withdraw from many forms of economic activity.

The goal of financial regulators and the objective of economic policy generally in the wake of a financial crisis is not to assess political blame for the cause or to worry about the consequences of a bailout for the future, but to maintain confidence in the system in the short term - whether or not it is warranted. This objective is severely hampered by the political objective of avoiding a transparent taxpayer bailout to finance the cost of mis-represented past political policies. Hence the economic policies of regulators and economists generally rely on the same opaque wealth-re-distributing mechanisms of the past to avoid loss recognition and economic collapse.

This helps explain why economists are generally defensive of past political policies such as the housing policies that caused the problem in the first place. But delivering these subsidies opaquely takes years. In this case the diagnosis of private market failures has produced over five years of policies designed largely to cover up for past policy failures while doubling down on the political and regulatory approach to maintain confidence in the system

This is having many unintended long run consequences. Some of the redistribution has relied upon the legal system, undermining confidence in the future administration of the rule of law. This ongoing uncertainty hampers the recovery in numerous ways.

Worse, politics is not exogenous – as economists like to assume – so the less political accountability in the short run the more politicians pursue the sort of policies that caused the problem in the first place. As the short run turns into the long, economic growth continues to stagnate.

The global financial crisis can be said to have started just before the fall 2008 elections in the US, about a year after the recession had started, although the conditions leading up to the financial crisis extended back about a decade. The immediate aftermath of the triggering event lasted several months – roughly through the end of 2008 – when fear and uncertainty dominated the markets, and arguably affected the election outcome. The financial "crisis" was largely contained and markets stabilized before the change of administrations and the economy was on the upswing as the recession ended during the second quarter of 2009, only a few months into the new administration, but the financial and economic recoveries were just getting under way. Then they sputtered.

The recession was steep, like that of 1980-82 or 1920-21, considered another political plus for the new Obama Administration as the recovery and rebound from those recessions was equally sharp. But the aftermath of this one extended for five years as fears about the health of the financial system persisted, resulting in the worst economic recovery from recession since 1882.[200] Depending on one's diagnosis of the sub-prime lending debacle, this was either in spite of or because of the most massive "bailout" ever undertaken in recorded human history.

The financial distress and economic recession stemmed from the same problem. The house price bubble that had created over $7 trillion in illusory wealth would predictably and rapidly deflate. When it did it would cause millions of homeowners to default, reversing the positive wealth effect that had stimulated the prior consumer spending boom. Those defaults could cost financial institutions $3 to $4 trillion in net credit losses reflecting negative mortgage equity, perpetuating extreme financial sector distress and exacerbating the economic recession. Most analysts believe that a weak economic recovery is an inevitable consequence of recessions originating in the financial sector, but Michael Bordo of Rutgers and Stanford's Hoover Institute concludes that this isn't a foregone conclusion.[201] It depends on the magnitude of the financial insolvency and the steps taken to address it.

The new Administration and the Fed launched an activist three-pronged bailout effort to "restore confidence" in the financial system and economy: the first directed at financial institutions; the second directed at homeowners and the housing market; and the third directed at the macro-economy.

In theory the Fed was created to provide systemic liquidity support to the financial system through the discount window. Loans were made discreetly at a penalty interest rate and over-collateralized with marketable investments to prevent lending to insolvent firms and an unnecessary expansion of credit. But this time the administration was given discretion over an unprecedented $23 trillion committed to prop-up an insolvent financial system.

The federal government had a tradition of providing emergency assistance in a crisis, but had avoided compensating individuals or firms for private loss. The multiple efforts undertaken to provide financial assistance to homeowners and prevent or delay defaults, foreclosures and evictions represented unprecedented individual bailouts, with much of the money going to individuals not directly victimized by the sub-prime lending debacle and financial crisis.

Fiscal policy since the Great Depression has bailed out the economy with automatic tax and spending stabilizers. This time an additional unprecedented $1 trillion of deficit-financed federal stimulus spending was newly authorized on top of a structural deficit of that magnitude with both mostly funded by the Fed purportedly to boost the economy but with little transparency or oversight.[202]

These policies were consistent with the diagnosis of a private market failure causing fear and panic and a prescription of confidence-building measures. As such, they were functionally equivalent to those that induced the boom, a "hair of the dog" elixir for a financial sector and an economy in withdrawal. They too had a dramatic impact on the distribution of income and wealth. But that was not the only objection. The economy was not just suffering from a hangover. Productivity was about half the historical average of 3.5%, domestic savings had collapsed and the balance of payments deficit had ballooned. Conservatives argued that what was needed was a transformative agenda to restore incentives to work, save and invest productively.

The Obama Administration was elected on a platform of a transformative agenda. President Obama's chief of staff responded to a question in the context of the formulating the bailout efforts that "You never want a serious crisis to go to waste." a term first used by progressives arguing to enter World War I for its transformative effect on the US economy.[203] His context was similar: "What I mean by that is an opportunity to do things you think you could not do before." The cyclical crisis was used to push through a secular "transformative" political agenda - not unlike that which caused the crisis - while crisis conditions provided cover to use administrative discretion to partisan ends.[204]

This transformative agenda was almost the opposite of what conservatives had in mind. The subsequent political backlash to these public "bailouts" – understandable in that politicians claimed the private sector was entirely to blame for the financial crash and subsequent economic recession - spawned two large political movements: the Tea Party in 2009-2010 on the right and Occupy Wall Street (OWS) in 2011 on the left.

The Tea Party was aptly named after the Boston Tea Party of 1773, during which tea owned by the East India Company – a private monopoly granted a charter by the British Crown – was dumped into the Boston harbor in protest against taxation without representation by an excessively powerful central government. The parallel between the East India Tea Company and Fannie Mae was made decades ago.[205] The Tea Party viewed the sub-prime lending debacle and financial and economic crisis as a consequence of the growth of centralized political power over the financial system and economy and viewed the stimulus spending bailout as more of the same.

OWS was named after the Street in New York City where the NY stock exchange was started in 1792, since a metonym for the centralization of financial power in the hands of a few private "bankers." Their anger was inchoate but at least in part directed at the banking and financial system for exploiting households in the interest of profit, causing the financial and economic meltdown - essentially reflecting the FCIC Report issued in January of that year as well as the Obama Administration narrative – then getting bailed out at the expense of Main Street.

These two political parties were on opposite ends of the political spectrum in their acceptance of populist rhetoric. But both opposed what they correctly perceived as the consequences of crony capitalism that favored the politically connected elite.

When the various elixirs wore off, the financial sector and economy again went into withdrawal, but this time even more addicted. The financial sector meltdown was avoided, but at the expense of even greater potential for moral hazard in the future. The mortgage market has been taken over almost entirely by the federal government but hasn't yet recovered and those unrealized losses of homeowner equity remain a major threat to the US financial system. Fiscal policy cushioned the economy's fall but resulted in stagnation. The unprecedented expansion of the actual and potential money supply and negative real interest rates to finance these deficits hangs like the Sword of Damocles over the economy.

There were no good policy alternatives to the response to the conditions of 2008, but the politically appealing choice of more of the same arguably made the situation worse than doing nothing. The financial markets and economy remain addicted to continued Fed support, hardly a permanent diet to restore health. The housing market recovery remains fragile. This chapter explains why: bailouts of financial institutions, markets and instruments; bailouts of defaulting households and mortgage markets; ongoing distorting taxes, subsidies and regulation; and a continued application of monetarist and Keynesian fiscal policy prescriptions, oppressive regulations and transformative agendas failed to relieve financial distress or restore economic health.

There was nothing new or unpredictable about the 2008 financial crisis. There was nothing new or unpredictable about the failure of the policies in the aftermath, as they represented more of the same.

A. The Anatomy of Public Assistance and Bailouts

It is not unusual for central governments of wealthy market economies to provide assistance, especially in a crisis. As we write this, the federal, state and local governments are providing all sorts of disaster relief in the wake of hurricane Sandy that hit the east coast of the United States following criticism that the federal government didn't do enough in the wake of the prior hurricane Katrina. The US financial markets and economy were surely disasters in late 2008 in need of relief. So what explains the angst from both the left and right over this particular public bailout?

A fundamental issue of the last two US presidential elections and beyond was where to draw the line between market and state and between individual and collective responsibility. Formal private casualty insurance pre-dates democracy and market capitalism. Private insurers provide the appropriate assistance while mitigating moral hazard to avoid encouraging risk-taking and creating dependence.

Collective assistance also predates the modern market economy, e.g., the local welfare houses of Great Britain. Public emergency relief and the financial and social safety net and publicly sponsored insurance programs and enterprises have some similarities to private insurance. They face the same moral hazard as private insurance, as was first recognized by Nobel economist Kenneth Arrow in 1971. But the differences exceed the similarities.

Hence while the public sector uses private sector insurance terminology, there is a recognizable distinction between the two. The term "bailout" has a negative connotation. The political myth is that the public sector repeatedly bails out private business firms and households for privately insurable exogenous loss. More often, the reverse is true: private individuals and firms and their private insurers bear the loss of endogenous systemic risk originating in the public sector. The politically well connected crony capitalists and their firms are the most likely to receive such public bailouts.

Several things were different with the bailout in response to the financial crisis of 2008. The magnitude of the bailout was much greater; it was marginally more transparent, and; it was more transparently and blatantly political. All of this was inherent in the design of the federal financial safety net.

Charles Kindleberger (1978) concludes that such activist intervention increases future moral hazard and hence the amplitude and frequency of financial crises: "the moral hazard that the more interventionist the authorities are with respect to the current crisis, the more intense the next bubble will be, because many of the market participants will believe that their possible losses will be limited by government measures." He was right.

1. Casualty insurance, Catastrophe Insurance and Emergency Assistance

In market economies life and casualty insurance is generally provided by private insurers because these risks are easily diversified. Many of these companies originated as mutual insurance companies, i.e., owned by the policyholders. Whether shareholder or mutually owned, the interests of policyholders as both beneficiaries and owners were generally well aligned.

Private insurers will insure virtually any diversifiable risk. Two common forms of casualty insurance are automobile and homeowner insurance provided in response to and on behalf of owners and/or lenders. Mortgage default insurance is another form of casualty insurance available in the event that the insured should lose his primary source of income. Even life insurance, i.e., "term" insurance that only pays a death benefit, is a form of casualty insurance for the family left without a source of income.

In each case, benefits are paid to compensate for a loss, so long as the insured didn't personally cause it, e.g., by burning down a house, quitting a job or committing suicide. When such payments are made by private insurers, there is generally no political backlash over the fairness of private insurance benefits or call for public compensation of the voluntarily uninsured. Compensating private loss resulting from a casualty caused by a public sector failure may be appropriate in specific circumstances, e.g., when a public safety vehicle is ruled at fault in an accident. This is merely a diversifiable risk that a public body may be big enough to internally diversify and hence self insure. An uninsured mortgage default, foreclosure and eviction due to job loss is lamentable, but generally no more so and no more deserving of a public bailout when in good company, e.g., during a recession. As politically and emotionally appealing as compensating individual households and businesses for an insurable but uninsured loss is, the public sector should and generally has avoided compensating the uninsured (Obamacare care being a glaring exception)..

Most publicly sponsored insurance plans share several features of private insurance plans: they charge premiums and pay claims, and; the insurer is subject to the moral hazard. But public insurance schemes don't match the private insurance model as the differences exceed the similarities: most of the insurer's capital is implicit (government backing) and "free," the insurance is mandatory for both the insured and insurer (for solvent firms) and hence the insurer is a monopoly; the insurer generally doesn't price risk - the insured is either eligible for insurance at a fixed price or closed and liquidated, and; the risks are highly correlated and hence not subject to the "law of large numbers" required for diversification.

Why do governments get into the business of insuring privately insurable exogenous risks? Mostly they believe they can opaquely socialize risk, a euphemism for making the public pay without knowing it. This is another form of delivering subsidies through finance and is financed in the same opaque manner - with capital subsidies, i.e., tax and uncompensated risk-bearing as previously discussed. This allows politicians to distribute benefits in politically beneficial ways with no obvious transparent cost.

This introduces lots of potential distortions. For example, the single premium favors riskier institutions, the original reason why S&Ls refused to participate in deposit insurance until they got their own lower cost insurer. As another example, when the insurer fails – often reflecting the endogenous systemic risk of government policies - politicians are unlikely to recognize their culpability by providing a budgeted capital infusion. So the insurer will increase the premium prospectively on the less risky survivors. This requires that they have a monopoly and that the insurance is mandatory, driving out private competition. To compensate the insured, regulation will promote cartelization e.g., by consolidating e.g., banks (or medical providers) into TBTF firms to increase their franchise value.

The appropriate public policy is that which most closely resembles normal private insurance in competitive markets, but the conflicts between and among politicians and regulators relative to that benchmark make that problematic. If they were willing to stay within those limits there would be no point to sponsoring public insurance in the first place. Parenthetically, there is no economic role for government in "health insurance" or "retirement savings" schemes other than to provide subsidies through finance. Whether governments should require a minimal level of private retirement savings to mitigate future moral hazard of public assistance and the human trait – particularly common among politicians - of excessively discounting the future is another matter.

At first blush catastrophes such as natural disasters may appear to be an exception because they are uninsurable, e.g., hurricane insurance among homes in Florida, New Orleans or more recently the northeast. Automobile casualty insurance is again instructive. The loss of a vehicle can be catastrophic for an individual family, e.g., in the case that it is necessary to their livelihood, but government doesn't typically require collision insurance – that's up to lenders when applicable. The public doesn't typically compensate the uninsured for such a loss (although at one time it was deductable from federal tax liability). But laws and regulations, including vehicle safety inspections, mitigate the chances of a loss. Similarly, even hurricane risk is diversifiable across geography and insurance types, and is easily re-insured nationally and internationally. The same is true for earthquake and tsunami risk, even for power plants in Japan. But the most important component is risk mitigation, e.g., building codes that require roofs be anchored down to prevent houses from collapsing in high winds, the lack of which was the source of most destruction historically in Florida.

Public disaster relief also compensates victims. The difference is that it doesn't typically compensate for privately insurable risks. In theory, the purpose is to mitigate public health and safety hazards. So for example the public expects government to provide emergency food, shelter and sanitation in the wake of damage from a major natural disaster such as a hurricane. The public benefits justify the budget costs, which may be spread widely among taxpayers and smoothed over time rather than formally insured. But even such disaster relief by the federal government invites moral hazard in state and local risk-mitigation policies.

2. Endogenous Systemic Political Risk

Hurricane Katrina illustrated the difference between private insurable loss and public disaster relief, as private casualty insurers compensated individual homeowners while federal relief compensated mostly government. But even Katrina illustrates the difference between exogenously caused disasters and endogenous systemic political risk. Public policy is primarily responsible for mitigating exogenous natural disaster risks to the extent feasible. The Katrina loss was not due entirely to the hurricane, a class three, but to the lack of ultimate political accountability due to the US system of diffuse political power and responsibility. The corps of engineers of the US government had accepted the responsibility to build the levees to withstand a class 5 hurricane and US – not local - taxpayers had provided the funds to do so, but these funds were subsequently diverted by state and local politicians to other purposes. When the storm hit, state and local politicians subsequently failed to move people out of harm's way before the levees flooded. It was a disaster primarily caused by state and local politicians who then diverted political accountability to the federal government. The ensuing political arguments arguably delayed the recovery.

The wildfires that hit San Diego about twice a decade, destroying thousands of homes and killing dozens of people, are another example of endogenous systemic political risk. They typically start on federal land hundreds of miles away, winds and negligence sweep them to San Diego, and local fire ordinances and mis-management contribute to the conditions for systemic destruction. But private individuals and their insurers pay for most of the damage.

Katrina also illustrates the moral hazard of public protection: why was the federal government subsidizing households to live below sea level in the first place? Private insurance doesn't cover flooding to mitigate the moral hazard, and local building codes historically prohibited building in a flood plain prior to the introduction of the federal flood "insurance" program in 1968. The objective of federal flood insurance was to dramatically reduce the public expense of bailouts in the wake of flood-induced catastrophes.[206] Instead, those now living in a flood plain get both federal "insurance" benefits – paid by both premiums and taxpayers - and public disaster relief. Government insurance and regulation created the expectation of a public bailout in the predictable event of a catastrophic loss, inducing more households to build in previously off limits flood plains.[207]

Third, Katrina raises questions about who got bailed out and who paid for it. Were the victims more deserving of benefits to compensate for their private loss because the government subsidized them to live in the flood plain in the first place? What level of government should have been responsible and accountable for mitigating systemic risk? What level for paying for the bailout? The more distant the government, the less is accountability and greater is moral hazard.

Hurricane Katrina also highlights another political fallacy. Many see the silver lining in the "jobs created" in the aftermath and the boost to GDP reflecting the publicly financed and privately insured rebuilding. But what's being rebuilt is lost wealth, as reflected in the increase in public debt and private (insurance company reserves) liquidated to fund the rebuilding. On net, there is a permanent loss of the return to the destroyed assets, as the rebuilding doesn't reflect a net addition to the capital stock. GDP measures spending, not household well being.

The more recent hurricane Sandy illustrates the fallacy of spreading the risk widely to the public. The outrage of state politicians over a delay in $61 billion in federal subsidies over and above the emergency assistance or public cost can only be described as pigs feeding at the trough.[208] Perhaps loans to the state at a penalty rate, fully collateralized by future federal grants, modeled after the Fed discount window, is a better way to go.

3. The Financial Sector Safety Net: The Source of Systemic Risk

How does the financial sector safety net fit into this discussion? It started with Fed liquidity support in 1913 followed by deposit insurance in 1934 and Fannie Mae secondary market "liquidity" support in 1938. Explicit US Treasury backing was rejected in each case, but each warranted federal regulation.

The Fed's rationale for providing liquidity support – historically the only Fed bailout - evolved from protecting large banks (chapter 1) to protecting the payments mechanism from systemic risk to mitigate the effects of financial crises on the real economy. According to the Board of Governors of the Federal Reserve System (2001):

"systemic risk may occur if an institution participating on a private large dollar payments network were unable or unwilling to settle its net debt position. If such a settlement failure occurred, the institution's creditors on the network might also be unable to settle their commitments. Serious repercussions could, as a result, spread to other participants in the private network, to other depository institutions not participating in the network, and to the nonfinancial economy generally."

No one questions the potential benefit of a lender of last resort in a systemic liquidity crisis as providing liquidity to solvent firms avoids the unnecessary costs of fear and panic, but there are several problems with this. First the assumption that the private sector can't make the distinction between solvency and liquidity is more often than not false. According to Kaufman and Scott, (pp. 377-378):

"The evidence indicates that problems at one bank or at a group of banks do spill over to other banks in general, but almost exclusively only to banks with the same or similar portfolio-risk exposures and subject to the same shock. There is little if any empirical evidence that the insolvency of an individual bank directly causes the insolvency of economically solvent banks or that bank depositors run on economically solvent banks very often or that, when they do, they drive these banks into insolvency."

Second, the Bagehot rule unfortunately doesn't prevent bail-outs of insolvent firms. Central bank authorization to issue paper money when faced with a systemic liquidity crisis has since Bagehot's time in the 19th century been to provide virtually unlimited funds to prevent panic. To prevent the provision of liquidity from bailing out otherwise insolvent firms and mitigate the moral hazard that would result, Bagehot required that such lending was to be fully collateralized, e.g., by posting collateral marked to market and discounted, and at penalty rates to discourage borrowing to re-lend at higher rates - arbitrage – and insure that claim-holders would be even worse off for having taken such loans.[209] There was no exception made in these rules for firms that were victims of systemic risk originating in the public sector as a result of public policies. The authority of the US Federal Reserve, outside the umbrella of political oversight, is so limited.

That's also the purported rationale for deposit insurance, but the role of central banks predates deposit insurance by several centuries. Bagehot developed his rules before the advent of deposit insurance, numerous markets for liquidity such as Fed Funds, and the information technology revolution. This notion that sophisticated investors in the private sector can't make the distinction is a bit dated as financial firms are more transparent, and even with bankruptcy pending debtors in possession are able to make relatively quick lending decisions, assuming *they* have access to liquidity. Moreover Bagehot recognized that the need for a central bank lender of last resort function was not inherent but rather reflected the legally fragmented system of banking that in the US gave rise to the need for deposit insurance.[210]

As Mayer (2001, p. 121) noted several years before this last crisis, when the Fed makes large loans the market is more likely to interpret that as a sign of insolvency, and since the Fed by law takes the best collateral at a discount, this causes the most sophisticated investors to attempt to get their money first. Moreover, what the Bagehot Rule failed to recognize was that such over-collateralized borrowing, while not in the interests of owners (or creditors) in liquidation, may well be in the interest of managers who go for broke, then go broke, which is exactly what banks did. That is, because markets aren't fooled by Fed liquidity lending to plug a solvency hole, a solvency bailout *causes* the panic.

While most of the firms that borrowed from the Fed during the most recent crisis generally didn't pay a penalty interest rate, they surely would have been willing to do so. Most asserted that they were only illiquid, but some were in fact deeply technically insolvent: the Bagehot rule doesn't discourage the demand for funds from firms going for broke or going broke, especially those with federal deposit insurance backing their liabilities. Noted central bank expert Andrew Sheng argued in 1990 that: "when bankers come to the central bank for liquidity help it is no longer liquidity assistance (that's needed), but a question of insolvency."[211]

Deposit insurance was initially introduced purportedly to "protect the little guy," from bank failures, an anachronism in an economy with sufficient money market funds invested in Treasury securities (a proposal discussed in chapter 6). Why do banks fail? According to Kaufman and Scott (p. 380):

"the direction of causation appears to be primarily from downturns in the macro-economy and the stock market (asset price bubbles) to increases in bank failures."

In other words, banks fail due to endogenous systemic political risk at the local, regional, and most often the federal level, not visa versa.

Deposit insurance differs from private insurance in all the ways discussed in section 1 above: most of the FDIC capital is implicit (government backing) and "free;" the FDIC insurance is mandatory for both the insured and insurer (for solvent firms) and hence the FDIC is a monopoly; the FDIC generally doesn't price risk - the bank is either eligible for insurance at a fixed price or closed and liquidated, and; the risks facing the FDIC insurance fund are highly correlated due to endogenous political factors.

Politicians bear the ultimate responsibility for mitigating the sources of systemic political risk – primarily by curbing excessive fiscal deficits (of which GSEs are a part) – as well as by providing oversight of the Fed and other bank regulators, particularly the FDIC. The Fed is often implicated in creating systemic risk by fueling asset bubbles, with banking regulators implicated in allowing the excessive leverage. The FDIC also fosters TBTF by closing small banks that don't threaten the insurance reserve while keeping the large banks open to "grow out of their problem" subsidized with greater franchise value.

The Fed has the strongest incentive to bail out insolvent firms for several reasons. First, in keeping with its role of countercyclical monetary policy as "Bank failures …are likely to exacerbate the magnitude of the downturns that caused them."[212] Second, the Fed is supposed to avoid financial crises in the first place as the systemic market regulator. Third, if a bank does subsequently fail the Fed has sufficient capital to protect itself, passing the resulting loss on to the FDIC, thus avoiding accountability. That's probably been the Fed's strategy for some time. When US National Bank of San Diego failed in 1973, this resulted in the largest FDIC loss to date in spite of an asset base of only $1.3 billion. When Franklin National failed the next year, the Fed had $2.3 billion of collateral for a $1.7 billion advance. Hence the Fed's quest for secrecy is understandable.

For the most part we can't really tell if the Fed has been lending to insolvent firms, as we only know of it when the rescue fails. Most rescues likely succeed as the Fed and FDIC provide ongoing implicit subsidies in the form of "franchise value." When too far gone to save, the Fed transfers the losses to the FDIC who in turn passes it on to healthy banks by raising the FDIC fee.

Even though the Fed still technically has no authority to fill a solvency hole, the Fed has no cost of funds so this requirement isn't easily enforced. Moreover, as former Fed Chairman Paul Volker stated:

"There isn't a developed country in the world in the 1980s and early 1990s that did not run into a banking crisis. I don't know of any of those countries that didn't act to protect the banking system with assistance whatever the law said."[213] Where would the Fed draw the line lending to insolvent banks? Even though the Fed still has no authority to lend to insolvent firms, it generally did so. Apparently willing to lend to Lehman, the Fed has lowered the bar to lending to and bailing out virtually worthless firms if they are large, complex, interconnected institutions, i.e., TBTF or systemically important firms (SIFs).

The financial system safety net isn't designed to protect competitive financial firms from endogenous systemic political risk: their shareholders are usually wiped out. It isn't designed to protect small savers: the value of their deposits is routinely inflated away. It is designed to avoid political and regulatory accountability. This favors politically well connected crony capitalist firms and workers, as well as wealthier households who have more options to protect themselves from political risk, e.g., by diversifying into other assets such as commodities and among sovereign political jurisdictions.

While it is easy take great comfort in the concept of a public lender of last resort, the Fed and other financial regulators all have a strong incentive to lend to insolvent firms in a crisis, expanding its safety net while postponing the debate over moral hazard for a rainy day. There is never a good time to say no. This creates moral hazard not only among financial institutions and households, but by politicians as their regulators deflect blame for the consequences of past endogenous systemic political risk. The resulting moral hazard has ironically but not surprisingly been a primary source of subsequent systemic failure.[214]

FHA remains today a government sponsored mutual insurer, not – like Ginnie Mae – a government agency. FHA/Ginnie Mae provided the safety net to the housing market in the aftermath of the financial crisis. Since the government doesn't guarantee FHA and Ginnie Mae doesn't guarantee credit risk, Ginnie Mae securities aren't explicitly guaranteed any more than those of F&F were. But of course the market has been led to believe they are guaranteed. How did that happen? HUD has taken the legal position that as the HUD Secretary is responsible by statute for maintaining FHA in an actuarially sound condition, congress – taxpayers – are required to pay for the HUD Secretary's malfeasance. Hence regulation implies complete taxpayer liability for $4 trillion in securities.

Why does regulation convey protection and hence lead to moral hazard? Because, according to Meltzer (2010, p.35) "No Treasury Secretary should be expected to opt for failure in the middle of a crisis." Meltzer (p. 47) cites research concluding a need for "constitutional restrictions on the power of regulators.

The Fed, William Poole in particular but Chairman Greenspan as well, had long argued that Fannie and Freddie represented the biggest systemic risk to the global financial system.[215] Why? Because government monopolies not subject to market discipline have the potential to get seriously off track before the entire market eventually collapses. Public regulation and protection cause systemic risk; market discipline mitigates it.

B. The Great Depression and Great Recession: History Repeats Itself

If economists are to be socially useful, the most important thing they can do is advise politicians how to avoid another Great Depression. The prescription depends on the diagnosis, and as we noted in chapter 1 Fed Chairman Bernanke is an expert in the Great Depression as were the macroeconomic fiscal advisors to the Obama Administration. Chairman Bernanke accepts the Friedman and Schwartz (1963) monetary explanation, i.e., that in response to the plummeting velocity of money the Fed should have increased the supply commensurately to avoid deflation.

Writing at the same time as Friedman and Schwartz - some four decades before the sub-prime debacle - Murray Rothbard, economic historian and "dean" of the Austrian School, in *America's Great Depression* (1963) provides an explanation of the Great Depression that mirrors our explanation of the Great Recession of 2007-2009 discussed below, how government intervention - not the business cycle - caused the Great Depression. More recently, in 2007 Amity Shlaes provided a popular version of Rothbard's Austrian School view *A New History of the Great Depression* in *the Forgotten Man*. Austrians would agree with monetarists that the decline in money velocity was a problem, but attribute the decline in confidence leading to the decline in velocity to FDRs policies and even those of the Fed.

The events leading up to the Great Recession as well as those pursued in the aftermath mirror those of the Great Depression in many ways, with similar results. Looking back over the last eight centuries Reinhart and Rogoff conclude that financial crises generally originate in monetary inflation to fund public fiscal folly. This comes as no surprise to the monetarists or Austrians.

Writing in 1963 Milton Friedman in a Monetary History of the United States writes:

"Far from being a failure of free market capitalism, the Depression was a failure of government. Unfortunately that failure did not end with the Great Depression...In practice, just as during the Depression, far from promoting stability, the government has itself been the major source of instability."[216]

In the same year, Rothbard concludes his book with these last two sentences;

"The guilt for the Great Depression must, at long last, be lifted from the shoulders of the free-market economy and placed where it properly belongs, at the doors of politicians and bureaucrats and the mass of "enlightened" economists. And in any other depression, past or future, the story will be the same."

The cycle of bad policy, cover up and double down as evidenced by the sub-prime lending debacle, the FCIC Report and the Dodd Frank legislation are nothing new: indeed, Friedman's diagnosis and Rothbard's prediction would suggest they are chronic. Moreover, Rothbard's prediction accurately characterizes the diagnosis and the monetary/Keynesian prescription implemented by the Obama Administration. That makes his take on the Great Depression worth another look. At the time, the alternative system to market capitalism was socialism and its political manifestations of fascism and communism, with a centralized political concentration of power supplanting market processes. That debate remains equally relevant today as well.

1. The Great Recession and the Great Depression

The standard historical depiction of the roaring 20's characterizing economic policies as laissez faire economics and inflation as non-existent would at first blush seem to have nothing in common with the massive federal economic interventions and monetary expansion at the root of the sub-prime lending debacle of the last decade. But just as alcohol although illegal fueled the social craze of the times from the shadows, federal intervention in money, credit and labor markets fueled the economic boom in opaque ways.

Rothbard's 1963 examination of the 1920's through Austrian eyes finds the same symptoms and root causes as we find for the financial crisis that led to the Great Recession. For Austrians, business cycles reflect the reaction to government – central bank or Treasury – distortions to money, i.e., typically inflationary increases in the supply that cause business to mis-allocate resources to insufficiently productive investments. His conclusions were echoed by a few economists of the Depression era but widely rejected by most.

By 1924, the Fed stopped giving even lip-service to countercyclical monetary policy by announcing that "the Federal Reserve supplies the needed additions to credit in times of business expansion and takes up the slack in times of business recession." But it didn't exactly take up the slack either, lending freely at below market rates when business slowed (p. 67).

The total money supply increased an average of 7.7% during this period, sufficient to fuel inflation. This was largely driven by regulatory arbitrage: the reserve requirement on demand deposits was 10% to 13% (7% for country banks) with little interest paid – illegal for national banks prior to the Fed and subsequently prohibited by the Fed for all banks. For time deposits – at the time essentially callable as demand deposits - it was only 3%, with higher interest freely paid. Banks convinced their customers to switch, which they did at a record rate as the total growth of bank deposits grew by over fifty percent, all in time deposits. But S&L (time) deposits grew even more, by about 225%, fuelling a mortgage lending and housing boom (pp. 51-55). Moreover, the increase in time deposits was greatest for the TBTF banks of the day, i.e., 450% for the Reserve City Banks in New York and Chicago.

The Fed was trying to inflate for several reasons beyond the traditional inflationist demands of farmers, miners and others: first, to ease Britain's return to the gold standard, which they stubbornly insisted be at the pre-war price; second, to alleviate the 1920-1921 recession. It did this by ignoring Bagehot's fundamental rules for central bank lending of lending only to solvent institutions and only at a penalty rate, instead discounting unlimited offers of bankers' acceptances at below market rates. Prices didn't rise excessively during the 1921-1929 period, but the spurt in productivity during this period due to technological advances would have substantially lowered them.

Housing was not the only asset bubble to result. Lending by the Federal Land Banks – created in 1916 by the federal Farm Loan Act – was accelerated at subsidized terms. In addition the War Finance Corporation initially created to finance war exports and subsequently de-activated in 1919 was reactivated in 1921 to lend to farmers. To prevent this cheap credit from driving down farm crop prices, numerous policies were adopted to cartelize the industry and mitigate "speculation" in the futures markets (pp. 125-133).

The stock price bubble - fueled by low margin requirements and plentiful cheap credit – probably inflated stocks the most as inflation causes the greatest optimism in capital spending. Nevertheless through 1929 President Hoover encouraged the Federal Reserve to make credit plentiful and "talked" stock prices up, as did his predecessor. The Fed did its part. Even though its charter didn't allow for directly discounting broker margin loans, it discounted other assets while reducing the collateral requirement on these loans from the prior market limit averaging about 100% to only 10% or less (p. 68).

Tax policy also contributed to the stock market boom by discouraging sellers. The capital gains tax imposed in 1921 on gains not held for two months was intended to be especially onerous to discourage "speculation." Senator Glass introduced legislation to impose an additional 6% sales tax on short term gains, the threat of which was enough to discourage sales (pp. 90-91).

Keynesians generally see the causality running from financial to economic crises. For example, Robert Hall of Stanford begins his often cited 2010 JEP article (2010):

"The worst financial crisis in the history of the United States and many other countries started in 1929. The Great Depression followed. The second-worst struck in the fall of 2008 and the Great Recession followed."

The Great Depression is often blamed on the stock market crash of October 1929 - the equivalent to blaming the Great Recession on the failure of Lehman Brothers - but the Depression had already started in the US in July 1929 and in Germany the prior year, so a global downturn was well underway, and the market realization of the coming adjustment didn't start until the infamous stock market crash of October 29, 1929. In spite of massive Depression-related lending losses, especially for farm and housing loans, the banking crisis didn't occur until almost *four years* later, after the wave of bank failures.

Why were more than ten thousand banks closed or taken over? Deflation increases the value of financial instruments, but the resulting economic dislocations leading to default reduced bank assets more than liabilities. Rickards (2012, pp. 171-172) argues that "the Fed failed utterly" as a lender of last resort: but as it was smaller banks that failed and the Fed was established for and owned by big banks a more cynical explanation is that *it* succeeded.

2. Hoovers 'Laissez Faire" New Deal Intervention

To the Austrians, the subsequent bust is a necessary and unavoidable curative to the prior interventionist policies that led to the boom, which requires a complete absence of further government intervention. But Herbert Hoover, elected to the presidency in 1928, was anything but the laissez faire proponent of political myth. He was in fact indisputably the most transformative interventionist president to that time (pp. 107-143) and arguably the most ever in relative terms, with the possible exceptions of his successor President FDR or more recently President Barrack Obama. He had worked as a business executive, investor and mining engineer all across the globe including Joseph Stalin's Soviet Union, and was very much taken up with the collectivist ideas popular at the time. This started during his war time public service, and was particularly evident during the period 1921-1929 during his stints as Commerce Secretary under both Presidents Harding and Coolidge, where he demanded and got a role in all economic policy matters, especially during the recovery from the 1920 to 1921 recession (p. 108).

Perhaps due to his experience as a miner and later as the war official responsible for food production, Hoover was very much sympathetic to the seemingly inconsistent demands of these industry constituents for both inflation and "price stabilization," the latter a government supported floor against falling prices, i.e., the deflation required by the gold standard to cure booms.

His employment policies were even more progressive, as he believed that it was the government's role to "create" jobs and to pay a "living wage" as well. Throughout this period he supported government public works to create jobs and numerous policies to raise wages, particularly through unionization, while providing public assistance to the unemployed (pp. 107-109).

His policies weren't adopted in response to the 1920-1921 recession, from which the economy rapidly recovered, but gradually became policy over the period prior to his assuming the presidency in early 1929, largely through his influence. When the depression began a few months after he took office, he responded with would now be characterized as the most massive Keynesian deficit financed government spending stimulus effort ever (although Joseph Stalin deserves more credit for his thinking at that point than does John Maynard Keynes). Measuring "fiscal stimulus" in Keynesian terms, budget deficits after 1929 grew at the fastest peacetime rate ever during Hoover's first term, higher even than the subsequent deficits of the first two terms of the subsequent FDR administration.

Public works was not a new approach but to that time had been mostly implemented by the states. Hoover subsidized their efforts while adopting the progressive martial metaphor of the prior war decade – likely highly appealing to an engineer – of "mobilizing resources" to attack joblessness with public works. Job stimulus efforts went beyond public works, targeted to specific industries e.g., to stimulate the distressed construction sector. But he still maintained his high wage policy, bragging during the presidential campaign of 1933 that he had raised American real wages to be "the highest in the world" (p.185).

These wages were in fact about 40% higher than the market clearing wage reflecting labor productivity, making American labor globally uncompetitive. In response, Hoover pushed for protectionism, arguing for higher tariffs in 1929. This resulted in the Smoot Hawley tariff passed in 1930, raising the tariffs to the highest level in American history, above those even during the time when the federal government had relied exclusively on duties and tariffs for all federal funding (p. 186).

To make American goods attractive, American banks were encouraged to lend - and foreigners to borrow from them – at cheap loan rates. To do this, the Fed had to maintain the inflationary policy it had followed prior to the onset of the depression. German banks, in particular, borrowed heavily, generally against the advice of their bank regulators (p. 148-149).

The protection of "American" jobs didn't end with foreign labor employed in foreign countries. Beginning in 1930 Hoover attempted to eliminate immigration of able bodied workers by restricting it to dependents. This Bill again failed in 1932, but by then Hoover had accomplished the objective by administrative fiat (pp. 178-179).

Hoover also reduced unemployment roles indirectly by providing unemployment relief, which encouraged people not to work. Subsidized higher education, another Hoover initiative, also had this effect. Limiting hours worked and work sharing also "created' jobs" to reduce unemployment (pp. 185, 191)

In summary, Hoover's term was the most radical progressive agenda to date: higher taxes for the rich, greater "relief" for the poor; government sector job creation: high wages to maintain high consumption and high tariffs to protect jobs; anti-immigration; federal deficits and monetary inflation; price-fixing and industry cartelization.

But the centerpiece of Hoover's New Deal was the attack on Wall Street and the financial system. He blamed Wall Street "speculators" for causing the stock market crash, and tried to prevent speculation in the stock and commodities markets (p.178). His administration undermined the rule of law and lender property rights and supported states in the same effort with moratoria to prevent foreclosure and bankruptcy (p.186).

He also implemented credit allocation, expanding lending to farmers through the Federal Land Banks and later home borrowers through the Federal Home Loan Banks. In addition, he established the Reconstruction Finance Corporation to allocate credit to the banking sector, industry, agriculture, and local governments.

Hoovers policies prevented rather than enabled the adjustment to the misallocation of resources of 1921-1929, and his depression-fighting policies made the problem worse. Banks failed at an accelerating rate as a result of the policies of the prior era, but as previously discussed in chapter 1 there is no evidence that the public couldn't distinguish the insolvent from the solvent banks. Some households were increasingly converting bank deposits to cash in anticipation of their failure, prompting some states to declare "holidays" at the insistence of generally insolvent banks.

3. Roosevelt's "New" New Deal

Hoover's New Deal policy was a complete disaster, resulting in the election of FDR. Hoover warned during the election campaign that FDR's platform was radical, ironic as nothing in US history had been quite as radical as Hoover's progressive policies. FDR ran on a balanced budget platform in 1932 and 1938. What Hoover meant was that Roosevelt would take his policies even farther. The "new" New Deal of FDR's first three terms was in fact mostly a doubling down of the Hoover New Deal, with even more devastating results.

Hoover did maintain the gold standard at the official price of $20.67, but foreign investors recognized the inflationary effects of Hoover's policies and increasingly converted deposits to gold, which under the gold standard would require a deflationary adjustment in the US, as had past economic recessions. But the election of FDR panicked domestic depositors as FDR advisors had openly proposed going off the gold standard, essentially defaulting on the real value of deposits. (p.186). Shortly after the election, there was a run on deposits in favor of Fed notes backed by gold and personal monetary gold holdings, increasing money in circulation by about 20%. It appears that the only thing depositors had to fear was FDR. Some banks lobbied for a federal "banking holiday" to buy time (p.187).

Fears of foreign and domestic depositors were well founded, as FDR labeled them "hoarders" - as had his predecessor - and defaulted. Foreign holders would receive gold at the new higher price of $35 an ounce, a default – wealth confiscation - of about 40%. Domestic depositors were similarly defaulted upon, but in addition were no longer allowed to hold gold except for personal or manufacturing use. Thus the inflation of the previous 12 years was recognized by inflating away the value of bank deposits.

The Depression itself was characterized by a destructive deflation. Fed Chairman Bernanke subsequently blamed the Great Depression on the shrinkage in the money supply not just because of the Fed (chapter 1) but because the gold standard limited monetary expansion. But Rickards (pp 237-240) disputes this, noting that the stock of gold in the monetary base increased during the Great Depression, putting the blame for the shrinkage in the money supply from this gold base entirely on central bankers.

FDR then caved to the pressure of weaker banks to declare a national banking holiday. National banks had no desire to join in as they were stronger and more liquid – partly as a result of security trading operations – and opposed the bank holiday, but they too were forcibly closed (pp.187-188) to provide credibility to the policy.

FDR also strengthened Hoover's restriction on the labor supply and high wage policy. The National Labor Relations Act of 1935– the Wagner Act – to promote unionization was the first major tool to keep wages high, still the union goal.[217] The Davis–Bacon Act of 1931 predates the Wagner Act. It requires all federal government construction contracts, and most contracts for federally assisted construction over $2,000, to include provisions for paying workers on-site no less than the "locally prevailing" (union) wage and benefits paid on similar projects.

FDR campaigned on a platform of taking Hoover's military metaphors for marshaling the resources of the economy by promising to re-create Wilson's "war socialism." The most important component of this strategy was the recreation of Wilson's War Industries Board as the National Industrial Recovery Act, which established the ironically mis-named National Recovery Administration (NRA) that subsequently set national prices and production quotas (Goldberg, pp. 30-31). The Hoover military metaphor eventually turned to reality, i.e., the removal of the most productive males from the work force drafted into the army in his third term and the wartime deficit spending, disputed as a cure for depression (Goldberg, p.52) and in any event a cure that was hardly better than the disease. In economic policy there were more similarities than differences between the US and its subsequent fascist enemies.

4. The Austrian Laissez Faire Response to Recessions and Depressions

The Austrian approach to recessions is to do nothing to "interfere with the market's adjustment process." That includes doing nothing to undermine lender and investor property rights and lender foreclosure. The logic behind this recommendation is that market incentives will correct the prior distortions and dislocations in the *fastest* and *fairest* way possible, and that the political impulse is to interfere with the required adjustment.

The Austrians may have disagreed with Schumpeter – who was from Austria - about the origins of cycles, Schumpeter staying with the standard business cycle model. But Schumpeter's process of "creative destruction" required an Austrian laissez faire response to recessions and depressions, which improves economic efficiency and productivity after the recovery. Destruction implies job loss in the short run but the creation of more productive jobs prospectively, where productivity is defined as the value consumers ultimately put on labor's share of the final goods and services.

Doing "nothing" runs against the political grain. Rothbard summarized the historical political response and prediction of future political response to recession and depression in 1963 (p. 15) thusly:

1. Prevent or delay liquidation. Lend money to shaky businesses, call on banks to lend further, etc.
2. Inflate further. Further inflation blocks the necessary fall in prices, thus delaying adjustment and prolonging depression. Further credit expansion creates more mal-investments, which, in their turn, will have to be liquidated in some later depression. A government "easy money" policy prevents the market's return to the necessary higher interest rates.
3. Keep wage rates up. Artificial maintenance of wage rates in a depression insures permanent mass unemployment. Furthermore, in a deflation, when prices are falling, keeping the same rate of money wages means that real wage rates have been pushed even higher. In the face of falling business demand, this greatly aggravates the unemployment problem.
4. Keep prices up. Keeping prices above their free-market levels will create unsalable surpluses, and prevent a return to prosperity
5. Stimulate consumption and discourage saving. We have seen that more saving and less consumption would speed recovery; more consumption and less saving aggravate the shortage of saved-capital even further. Government can encourage consumption by "food stamp plans" and relief payments. It can discourage savings and investment by higher taxes, particularly on the wealthy and on corporations and estates. As a matter of fact, any increase of taxes and government spending will discourage saving and investment and stimulate consumption, since government spending is all consumption. Some of the private funds would have been saved and invested; all of the government funds are consumed. Any increase in the relative size of government in the economy, therefore, shifts the societal consumption-investment ratio in favor of consumption, and prolongs the depression.
6. Subsidize unemployment. Any subsidization of unemployment (via unemployment "insurance," relief, etc.) will prolong unemployment indefinitely, and delay the shift of workers to the fields where jobs are available.

These, then, are the measures which will delay the recovery process and aggravate the depression. Yet are the time-honored favorites of government policy, and, as we shall see, they were the policies adopted in the 1929-1933 depression, by a government known to many historians as a "laissez-faire" administration.

Hoover's Treasury Secretary Andrew Mellon advised President Hoover to "liquidate labor, liquidate stocks, liquidate farmers, liquidate real estate… it will purge the rottenness out of the system. High costs of living and high living will come down. People will work harder, live a more moral life. Values will be adjusted, and enterprising people will pick up from less competent people."[218] Additionally, he advocated weeding out "weak" banks as a harsh but necessary prerequisite to the recovery of the banking system. This "weeding out" was to be accomplished by refusing to lend cash to banks (taking loans and other investments as collateral), and by refusing to put more cash in circulation. He also advocated spending cuts to keep the federal budget balanced, and opposed fiscal stimulus measures.

As President, Herbert Hoover generally ignored this advice, as did his successor FDR.

After eight years in office FDR's Treasury Secretary and Mellon's successor Henry Morgenthau lamented:

"We have tried spending money. We are spending more than we have ever spent before and it does not work....After eight years of this administration we have just as much unemployment as when we started...and an enormous debt to boot!"[219]

To quote Raymond Moley, Former advisor of Franklin D. Roosevelt:

"To look upon these programs as the result of a unified plan was to believe that the accumulation of stuffed snakes, baseball pictures, school flags, old tennis shoes, carpenter's tools, geometry books, and chemistry sets in a boy's bedroom could have been put there by an interior decorator."

Historians laud FDR for being willing to try anything and everything: perhaps he would have been more successful had he tried doing nothing!

5. The Contemporaneous Competing System to Market Capitalism – Socialism/Communism

An integral and inseparable part of the philosophical foundations of democracy is limited government, the reason being most self-evident in its twentieth century political polar opposite, communism, the competing political ideology at the time of the Great Depression (and its close but despised cousin, fascism).[220] The two key attributes of communism are government ownership of the means of production and an equal distribution of income, which required the virtual elimination of individual freedom. The role of government in a "market democracy" was initially limited to the funding and distribution – but not the production - of public goods to minimize the sacrifice of individual liberties. With individual liberty comes personal responsibility.

Hoover and FDR saw themselves as transforming capitalism to temper its harsher characteristics without changing economic systems by substituting some collective for individual responsibility, i.e., not a bailout but limited handouts. The primary reason for limiting government was as Alexis de Tocqueville warned that in the extreme the majority would substitute income redistributed from the minority for work and productivity, what we have called an incentive conflict and moral hazard (Meltzer, p. 32).

The initial list of "public" goods was small. Public roads are a good example: private contractors build them but public use fees and taxes pay for them. Some things have been added, e.g., clean air as a result of pollution. Other things could be dropped as a result of technological advances, e.g., smart chips in cars could easily replace public road finances with a use tax. The five-fold increase in the relative size of the public sector discussed in Part E below cannot be accounted for by a rise in public goods. Rather, it reflects political incentives often rationalized as a form of income redistribution.

Early popularizers of collectivist proposals essentially argued that the increased efficiency of man-over-market-driven decisions – socialism or communism over market capitalism - was worth the loss of individual freedom, and redistribution would raise the entire populace up. Others, most notably Hayek, argued otherwise.

Nikita Khrushchev, first secretary of the communist party, first evoked the image of "shovel-ready" projects in 1956 when he told visiting western diplomats "we will take a shovel….and we will bury you." The shovel connotation was a claim to greater economic efficiency, and the Soviet Union delivered on his promise of out-producing the US.[221] Obama Administration economic advisor Larry Summers has Keynesian stimulus in his genes: two uncles have Nobel prizes in economics. One, Paul Samuelson, spread the Keynesian religion as a "neo-Keynesian" through the best selling introductory economic text for about four decades. In that book, Samuelson predicted that Khrushchev was correct - that the Soviet Union would bury us - right up until shortly before the Soviet Union went bankrupt.

Samuelson was not alone. America's CIA had agreed, impressed by the quantity of the Soviet GDP. But the problem was not its ability to produce; rather it was the *value* of what was being produced. Without a price mechanism in the public sector – virtually their entire economy - there was no way to direct resources to those activities that produced the most value, i.e., where they were the most productive. The extreme inefficiency led to complete and widespread economic collapse. By the time the system failed in 1989, workers in the Soviet Union were "fully employed" but the value of the final product for about half of what they made was not worth the value of the non-labor inputs to make it.[222] Put differently, paying half the population to stay home rather than work at government-created jobs would have benefitted their society.

The experience of the last century has proven Hayek correct, as people other than those at the top of the socialist hierarchy have generally faired worse economically over the last century under socialism than those at the bottom of a market economy because the inefficiency of central planning destroys wealth more than it redistributes it, dragging the entire populace down. Hayek focused on the inability of planners to have sufficient information in *The Fatal Conceit* (1988). His much earlier work *The Road to Serfdom* (1944) - the title inspired by the writings of Alexis de Tocqueville, author of Democracy in America (1835), on "the road to servitude" explains the required loss of personal freedom as even the gulag and murder of 100 million people proved insufficient to mitigate the disincentive to provide productive work.[223]

More recently most developed countries have turned to democratic socialism, relying on a surplus from the productive market-oriented private sector to finance a public welfare state. Finding the optimal balance is an experiment in progress. Economic growth starts to suffer when the size of the public sector exceeds about 20% and the current travails of the US and Western Europe illustrate the extreme trade off when the public sector exceeds about forty to fifty percent. Using a crisis as a rationale to expand the public sector has been an ongoing economic failure.

C. The Wall Street Bailout: Systemic Liquidity Support becomes a TBTF Bailout

When facing a major conflagration, that's not the time to worry about spilling a little water. That's the reason the Fed and Treasury get a pass on the actions taken during the second half of 2008, even if they did previously provide the fuel. Now that the fire is out, a re-examination of their actions is warranted, especially given their culpability and incentive to cover up.

Even the Austrians would agree that providing liquidity to solvent but illiquid firms avoids the unnecessary costs of fear and panic on the *assumption* that the private sector can't make the distinction between solvency and liquidity but the public sector can and will, the Fed's original role (which they took over from the private sector, specifically JP Morgan). But the problem in the wake of the sub-prime debacle was solvency, not liquidity, caused in part by the Fed previously flooding the market with excessive credit, a chronic problem. That's not a reason not to provide plenty of fresh water in an emergency, but as it is a source of future risk it shouldn't come cheap.

While the Fed is legally prohibited from bailing out insolvent firms that has historically not been an inhibiting factor. The historic political and regulatory solution for banks has been to delay loss recognition while continuing to provide public subsidies opaquely over time by providing "liquidity" and franchise value that allows firms to grow out of their insolvency. Accounting for loans at historical cost is what had historically allowed delayed loss recognition.

As the sub-prime lending debacle was funded mostly with securities that were required to be marked to market – some would argue at prices below the value of future cash flows – the insolvency was more transparent this time. This accelerated loss recognition requiring a somewhat more accelerated rescue. So the political goal was to bail out insolvent financial firms as quickly and opaquely as possible with regulatory complicity until solvency could be restored.

The least distorting solution to a solvency crisis is to liquidate and/or restructure and recapitalize the failed firms, establishing a terminating "bad bank" to liquidate the bad assets. The Resolution Trust Corporation (RTC) formed as a government entity with a formal budget to liquidate the bad assets of S&Ls in the 1980s is a precedent. In that case, no attempt was made to compensate the owners – largely mutual shareholders – for losses incurred as a result of federal laws and regulations, particularly the prohibition against adjustable rate mortgages. This made it impossible to recapitalize the industry, a public policy objective of the time.

The banking industry couldn't be sacrificed like S&Ls had been. Politicians had no intention of making the cost of political housing policy transparent and imposing them directly on taxpayers this time around either. At the same time, the depth of the solvency hole increased the costs of a political cover-up. The bailout would inevitably favor politically TBTF financial institutions to avoid financial contagion, a largely untested regulatory hypothesis – at the expense of greater moral hazard.

The bailout was only partially successful politically, raising political ire focused on the wrong bailouts. It is impossible to judge its success at avoiding a worse financial crisis as the counterfactual is speculative. I did further politicize the financial system

Section one describes the consequences of using liquidity tools and franchise value to fill a huge semi-transparent solvency hole. Section 2 describes how the politically motivated opaque TARP bailouts and handouts distorted and continue to distort the financial system and the economy.

1. Panics and Financial Sector Liquidity Support: Opaque Bailouts

It was professional private speculators who finally burst the bubble in mid 2007, and professional money managers who purportedly "panicked" in response to the insolvency. By October 2008 US financial institutions had already recorded $700 billion in losses and the market seemed to understand the magnitude of the solvency crisis

Beginning in December of 2007 the Fed launched several initiatives, the first being the Term Auction facility, to pump liquidity into the system. But even as it lowered interest rates, the Libor spread - an index of private bank borrowing rates - continued to rise. Taylor attributes this to the inability to assess counter-party risk due to opaque balance sheets of potentially insolvent firms.[224] Libor could have provided such a market signal, but was self-reported and subsequently revealed that firms perceived as riskier reported lower than their actual Libor offers. The Fed had a desire to see the Libor rate spread remain low to confirm their liquidity diagnosis, so it is not the least bit surprising that the Fed did nothing at the time in response to the widespread knowledge of the practice.

Numerous Fed officials continued to deny the extent of the solvency crisis from mid 2007 until the spring of 2008, issuing much lower loss estimates. In this crisis the Fed – and Chairman Bernanke in particular –denied the bubble *right up to the end,* spinning the story that this was more of a traditional liquidity crisis. Policymakers, particularly Fed Chairman Bernanke and Treasury Secretary Paulsen, remained relatively sanguine and un-involved in the massive de-leveraging that was being attempted until they were faced with the possible failure of Bear Stearns that spring.[225] To avoid a likely bankruptcy in this case, the Fed provided a $29 billion loan against reportedly highly questionable collateral to virtually bribe and cajole an acquisition by a bank, JP Morgan, as the Fed had never lent to an investment bank.

There is no plausible explanation for the Bear Stearns bailout other than to cover for prior monetary policy and regulatory failures. The forced sale by the Fed was unprecedented, and a Bear Stearns failure arguably didn't directly threaten the payments mechanism or real economy the way Lehman's failure subsequently did. The Bear Stearns bailout undoubtedly exacerbated moral hazard as Lehman Brothers failed to downsize and reportedly rejected suitors in the expectation of a better deal from the government.[226] The "Greenspan put" – the moral hazard created by the bailout in the wake of the 1998 failure of hedge fund Long Term Capital Management (LTCM)[227] – had a decade later become the "Bernanke put."

Parenthetically, no good deed goes unpunished: four years after forcing Bear Stearns onto JP Morgan, the government sued JP Morgan for losses on loans funded by Bear Stearns-issued mortgage bonds during the sub-prime lending boom! JP Morgan asked for but didn't get indemnification. Taking this legal exposure into account, Bear Stearns probably was not worth the $2 a share JP Morgan initially offered, thought insulting at the time and raised to $10.

Taylor (2009) and Kane (2010) both argue that moral hazard and ad hoc bailouts created uncertainty that was the systemic trigger for contagion rather than the Lehman bankruptcy filing. Allison (p. 164) also blames the panic on "the inconsistence and arbitrariness of government policymakers," creating uncertainty as to who would and who wouldn't be bailed out. Meltzer (p. 35) argues that the Fed's failure to announce a rule for its emergency lending magnified the crisis.

Whether or not it was Lehman's failure on September 15, 2008 that triggered the market collapse is largely irrelevant as Lehman was deeply insolvent and a market collapse was imminent in any event, waiting for any spark to set it off.

Chairman Bernanke subsequently stated that he tried but failed to bail out Lehman, and even with the benefit of hindsight blamed the subsequent financial market crisis on that bankruptcy filing, interpreting the subsequent financial market crash as a contagion response to the failure of a solvent but illiquid firm and concluding that bailing out Lehman Brothers would have avoided the systemic financial system crisis. This is disturbing for several reasons.

First, over four years since the bankruptcy filing Lehman has returned only 18 cents on the dollar, and that understates the depth of their insolvency as it allowed sales in a rebounding market and doesn't count the interest cost of the time delay. To put this in perspective, if 5% capital is required and real capital is only 4% that's a 20% difference. That would be considered a big allowable standard deviation. But in that example Lehman was more than 85 standard deviations from the target capital.

Second, the widely predicted and reported contagion from Lehman's bankruptcy never happened. While the bankruptcy of a trillion dollar firm is inevitably expensive and protracted, the contagion is myth. The largest contagion was purportedly through Lehman's role as a dealer in and guarantor of CDS. But according to Wallison (2013, p. 354):

"all its CDS obligations were settled without incidence, and all of the CDS written on Lehman itself were settled for a cash exchange of only $5.2 billion among hundreds of counterparties. There is no indication that any financial institution became troubled or failed because of the failure of Lehman, and hence no systemic risk arose out of the failure of one of the largest dealers in the CDS market."

The likely explanation is that the Fed didn't prepare for the consequences of the year of de-leveraging and the Lehman insolvency for the shadow banking system, resulting in an avoidable and containable rout when Lehman failed.[228]

Immediately after the Lehman failure, Chairman Bernanke pushed for the bailout of the huge insurer AIG purportedly to avoid a complete market collapse.[229] On September 16, the day after Lehman failed, the FRB of NY created an $85 billion credit facility for AIG. This became the biggest, most intrusive, and incomprehensible and hence most criticized bailout, but it didn't stop there. Goldman Sachs and Morgan Stanley were converted into bank holding companies over a weekend on September 21 2008 to formally extend the Fed's protective umbrella to investment banks and – indirectly – to the hedge funds they had become. Within about two months of the Lehman Brothers failure, more than $7.5 trillion of public money had been committed to the bailout.

The AIG exposure didn't stem directly from investments in mortgage securities. Rather, AIG had written CDS against actual *ex post* credit losses on the super-senior tranches of sub-prime MBS. The CDS was actually written in a small OTS-regulated thrift subsidiary of the holding company. Moreover, the Treasury department that regulated the thrift subsidiary also nominally regulated the holding company. Allowing the thrift to write and the holding company to guarantee this CDS represented a massive regulatory failure that then NY Fed president Timothy Geitner would have inherited from outgoing Treasury Secretary Paulsen. The failure of the thrift subsidiary arguably did not put the AIG insurance business at risk, although it is clear that investors paid for the AIG thrift CDS based on parent's strength.

At the time, the default appeared to be technical in nature. While ultimate potential insurance claims were to be based on realized losses that are still unknown in this case, investment bankers began adding in collateral requirements to CDS contracts several years prior to this. These collateral requirements are related to specific benchmarks: The ratings of the securities being insured, AIG's own rating and the market value of the collateral. All three were distressed relative to the forecasts of default at the time but it was the inability to meet Goldman's collateral calls based on Goldman's own – some say low-ball - marks based on the ABX that put AIG out of compliance with these requirements, not the inability to pay claims, which apparently prompted the takeover. The structure of the bailout of AIG and commitment of over $180 billion of taxpayer funds raises concerns, in part because Goldman Sachs was the biggest counterparty to these contracts.

Shortly after the take-over in November 2008 the FRB of NY purchased $62 billion of deeply underwater mortgage assets *at par* to terminate the AIG insurance payments otherwise due to be paid out to the holders in dribs and drabs over 30 years. This seems like an incredible windfall to the insured parties, particularly Goldman Sachs, who claims it had hedged its AIG exposure and didn't need a bailout in any event. The other major parties were large European banks. The initial concern – AIG's exposure to Lehman – turned out to be false as that was only $6.2 million (Wallison, 2013, p. 154).

Why were Bernanke, Paulsen and Geitner, then president of the NY Fed and soon to be Treasury Secretary responsible for the OTS, bailing them out? Any default on actual AIG payments would have occurred over years, even decades, and only if the market didn't recover. Why didn't the Fed simply waive the collateral requirements for CDS citing a lack of markets for the underlying securities and inaccuracy of the ABX, acting as a re-insurer or guarantor of these payments only if necessary? Better still, why not let the parties of interest argue it out among themselves The counter-argument is that the collateral defaults could have encouraged counterparties to pursue a bankruptcy filing, and the Fed believes it can reduce uncertainty of a potentially lengthy bankruptcy proceeding. But bankruptcy was not in the interest of CDS holders so long as the claims were being paid.

The AIG bailout begs the question why the Fed took over AIG in the first place, especially as there is no evidence of systemic risk? Both treasury secretaries subsequently testified that they had to take over AIG to avoid another Great Depression, but neither offered any evidence why bankruptcy with unlimited systemic liquidity support to the rest of the financial system wouldn't have worked. In this case we had a takeover by the federal government due to a failure of the Treasury Secretary to regulate the thrift subsidiary and holding company seizing the assets of the state regulated solvent insurance company. This precedent calls into question the entire structure of holding company firewalls and political accountability for regulators. Why were Goldman Sachs and Morgan Stanley shareholders offered Fed protection while AIG shareholders – arguably victims of Treasury-OTS regulatory malfeasance – wiped out entirely?

The most likely answer is that most of the AIG counterparties were the large banks that the Fed was created to protect. There have as yet been no credible answers that suggest a limit to such activities in the future. Constitutional challenges to taking the firm from the shareholders have thus far been rejected on technical grounds – and the government shareholders not surprisingly joined in the challenge - but the case filed by long term CEO Hank Greenburg ousted by NY state AG Elliot Spitzer may yet reach the Supreme Court.[230]

Some liquidity support was arguably necessary and costless, and the Fed offered the standard explanation that interconnected markets required that liquidity support be extended to non-banks as well as banks. Forbearance for under-capitalized firms is sometimes appropriate, allowing them to recapitalize, but the limit is insolvency. The Fed never made a case for a solvency bailout. To have done otherwise would have focused attention on the role of the Fed and Treasury in creating the crisis and the tools being used to address it. To not have known Lehman was insolvent is so incompetent as to call into question the premise of regulation. To have known all along and done nothing is regulatory malfeasance. There is evidence of both, but as Napoleon advised "never ascribe to malice that which is adequately explained by incompetence."[231]

2. The Troubled Asset Relief Program (TARP): Crony Capitalism at its Worst

By the end of that fateful weekend in mid-September, the Fed had thrown its protective umbrella over the entire financial system. The Fed had lent or could lend to just about anybody, even if it was on tenuous legal grounds. So why did Paulsen draw up a plan that same weekend for the Troubled Asset Relief Program (TARP)?

The Fed's AIG bailout was legally tricky because AIG was an insurance company, not an eligible Fed member bank. Paulsen drafted a Treasury funded program to purchase "troubled assets" on September 20 and Paulsen as Treasury Secretary and Bernanke as Fed Chairman pressed President Bush to present and Congress to sign the TARP into law several days later on October 3, 2008, which gave clear authority to purchase virtually any asset from virtually any financial firm. The differences between TARP and Fed liquidity facilities were that TARP could unquestionably deal with all financial institutions and instead of lending could buy troubled assets outright from financial institutions. In addition, getting congressional authority provided cover for subsequent political flack should the solvency bailout under the guise of liquidity support subsequently come under attack. President Bush was a lame duck, but the authority was also approved by both presidential candidates.

Paulsen's original three page TARP proposal provided for purchases of up to $700 billion of "troubled" or toxic mortgage assets. The Fed could already lend against this collateral at a discount to market value but TARP would purchase assets at their true value – the discounted value of their cash flows – presumably well above what they could be sold for in a distressed de-leveraging market. The presumption was that the assets were undervalued relative to these cash flows due to "trouble" i.e., illiquidity in the markets. Financing itself at the government rate, TARP would essentially be a Fannie Mae clone.

It was a hard sell politically, with Bernanke and Paulsen telling the President and Congress that the country would experience another Great Depression if this authority was not approved. Congress responded with a bill of several hundred pages allowing the purchase of a variety of distressed assets, but with an unprecedented Office of Special Inspector General for TARP (SIGTARP) with $50 million appropriated to prevent fraud waste and abuse. Federal inspector's general report to the Congress, but are notionally dependent on the heads of the agencies they oversee for most things, e.g., space, access to documents, etc. SIGTARP's purpose was to provide transparency to the cost of TARP assistance. For example, Chairman Bernanke announced that the Fed would be paid in full on its loans after paying off all of AIGs CDS claims.[232] But when the administration announced it had closed the AIG bailout without taxpayer cost, SIGTARP alleged accounting shenanigans to produce this result.[233]

By the time TARP passed, less than two week from the time Paulsen first thought of it, he changed his mind regarding the viability of purchasing distressed assets as he had insisted in his proposal to Congress and scrapped the plan. Valuing cash flows and pricing these securities independent of market prices was highly problematic and extremely risky. Buying them at a significant premium over market would expose the program as a bailout of insolvent institutions and invite charges of cronyism. What he needed was essentially a "bad bank," e.g., like the RTC, but transferring these assets to the TARP at the market price would have resulted in the accounting recognition of the selling bank's insolvency, exactly what they were trying to avoid. The problem was not "troubled" toxic assets per se but the insolvency the defaults would cause.

Plan B was arguably not much better. Banks could no longer recapitalize privately without great difficulty as the year of soothing talk from Bernanke and Paulsen had by now convinced the markets of the opposite, so they settled on a government re-capitalization with the $250 billion Capital Purchase Plan (CPP). But if they selectively bailed out only the insolvent firms, they believed that markets would further penalize these institutions as having been deemed insolvent by virtue of taking the capital from the government, the same way they would interpret Fed loans according to FDIC folklore of the Great Depression. They decided to follow FDRs bank camouflage precedent with bank closings by forcing *all* large banks to accept government ownership while announcing that the funds would only go to the banks that were "healthy and viable". As the terms of the capital infusion were onerous, this had the added benefit of having the good banks bail out the bad rather than transparently and accountably bill taxpayers for the selective bailout of politically powerful TBTF banks.[234] What did the banks do with the money? Little of it was lent out to commercial borrowers as politicians promised. Among other things, they pursued the acquisition of other banks so as to become TBTF.[235]

Again borrowing from FDRs bank holiday to convince retail depositors that the banks that re-opened were sound, Treasury Secretary Geitner announced that the banks receiving TARP capital would undergo "stress tests" to determine capital adequacy. It is doubtful that this fooled professional bank investors or institutional depositors, who were in any event also insured under the TARP

221

Transaction Account Guarantee (TAG) program, which made deposit insurance temporarily universal and comprehensive.

Competitive solvent banks don't much like the idea of the government bailing out their insolvent bank competition. When the S&Ls were rendered insolvent by the mortgage regulations and subsequently the Garn St Germaine go for broke strategies to keep taxpayers off the hook, the FHLB kept the "zombie" S&Ls alive to defer loss recognition at the FSLIC.[236] Many academics and others who took lucrative and risk-less seats on the Board of Directors of such institutions had no incentive to close them, allowing the zombies to keep going broke by offering higher rates on insured deposits than they earned on mortgage loans. Of course, this caused many otherwise healthy low risk institutions to fail in the not so longer run, ultimately resulting in the systemic industry failure as well as the technical insolvency of the FSLIC insurance fund.

The S&Ls weren't Fed members and weren't politically TBTF, so they did. This time the Fed, along with Treasury, was once again in the position to determine winners and losers, and the non-Fed member community banks were in much the same position of S&Ls a generation prior. The Treasury encouraged Fannie Mae and Freddie Mac to issue preferred stock in late 2007 giving purchasers the impression that it was a safe virtually risk-less investment by granting a 20% risk based capital requirement, the same as for their GSE MBS, i.e., they could provide F&F with capital 98.6% of which was financed with FDIC insured deposits. Then about a year later in 2008 when it put F&F into conservatorship Treasury chose to default on that preferred stock. This bankrupted many otherwise solvent small community banks and forced other to sell out to larger banks, some already TBTF. The savings to the US Treasury by defaulting was small, and partly paid indirectly by the FDIC when subsequently liquidating these banks. The message was reinforced: get to be TBTF.

The idea of purchasing troubled assets, purportedly to "kick-start" consumer lending was revived as early as November 2008 with the Term Asset-Backed Securities Loan Facility, or TALF. The idea was that as banks had dramatically scaled back their repo funding for hedge funds and other similar investors, the Fed (FRBNY) would step in, providing $200 billion in cheap loans to leverage purchases of securities backed by car loans, credit cards, student loans or small business loans. But it quickly became a way for banks to divest of toxic PLS as well, with TARP providing financing for as much as 95% of the acquisition price.

As the securities weren't otherwise being traded and prices weren't transparent and TARP loans were made without recourse, the program virtually enticed bond buyers to over-pay in collusion with sellers, and then to subsequently default on the TARP loan. When the head of SIGTARP Barofsky pressed this point (2012, p. 88), he got no sympathy from the Treasury or the Fed, almost an explicit recognition that this was acceptable so long as it worked to the advantage of the selling bank, a backdoor capital subsidy.

The Public-Private Investment Program (PPIP) was a more desperate attempt to get bad assets off bank books at an inflated price without transparently reflecting the Treasury cost. Using TARP funds, Treasury would put up 2/3rds to 3/4ths of the equity in the fund – for one half of the profits. Then using TALF funds, the Fed would essentially provide repo financing with a haircut of as low as 5% and low borrowing cost for purchasing the sub-prime PLS from banks. It was intended to be a deal banks couldn't refuse.

Right from the beginning, TARP's focus expanded beyond the financial system rescue, where the risks of politicized lending and solvency bailouts were much greater and the policy rationale for protecting the financial sector to avoid undermining the payment mechanism and real economy didn't apply. On the one hand, the recession forced many industries into restructuring that was decades past due. For example, virtually all the airlines had gone or soon would go through a bankruptcy restructuring. On the other hand, the auto industry had always sought political protection from competition and a political bailout as a UAW was the major source of funds for democratic coffers.

The recession of 2007 clearly brought the long standing structural problems of the US automobile industry to the fore. It had long cost GM thousands of dollars more to produce a car as their more efficient competitors due to their legacy costs, paying the excessive benefits for the retired and retiring unionized workforce, almost five retirees for every worker.[237] But a $14 billion auto rescue package of *loans* died in the Senate in the fall of 2008. Immediately thereafter, Treasury Secretary Paulsen privately planned to end runaround Congress by using his recently approved TARP authority. In attempting to limit the administration's discretion provided by the three page Paulsen proposal, the 200-page bill Congress ultimately authored to avoid writing a blank check arguably inadvertently actually expanded the definition of troubled asset and financial institutions to virtually anything and any one.[238]

The incoming administration implemented a much expanded auto bailout, advancing about $85 billion overall. Estimates of the final net taxpayer costs range from a low of $25 billion (Treasury Department) to a high several multiples of that when opaque tax benefits are included, in any event the largest industrial or financial bailout ever. GM and Chrysler went through bankruptcy, but the

223

administration dictated the terms in violation of bankruptcy law and procedure. According to Alan Meltzer (2012) there is no evidence that GM would have been closed rather that restructured in bankruptcy court and even if it had been closed that the US manufacture of automobiles would have shrunk, although it would have likely shifted to low cost right to work states (pp. 40-41). But the auto companies weren't restructured in any event: GM still faces bankruptcy, having failed to restructure.[239]

In fact, their bondholders were gouged relative to what a bankruptcy court would have awarded them, as the administration bankruptcy restructuring ignored their seniority by transferring their assets to others, undermining faith in the rule of law.[240] Where did all the money go: mostly to bailing out the UAW and its members.[241] This is most clearly evidenced in the UAW insistence that TARP fully fund the union pensions not just of GM but of the then long since independent and bankrupt Delphi parts maker, while the non-union pensions were handed over to the Pension Benefit Guarantee Corporation where taxpayer subsidies were more transparent and were dramatically reduced.[242]

GM had been a crony capitalist corporation probably since WW II. But the dealers were independent small businessmen, most of who tended to be Republicans. According top Barofsky, a Democrat, it was for that reason, not the corporate restructuring plan, that they were closed. A union bailout was clearly not the Congressional intent of TARP, but once the bailout window was opened, neither the Congress nor the lavishly funded but structurally weak SIGTARP could stop them from going through it.

The auto companies were to some extent victims of other federal policies, but clearly the unions weren't victims as they were the intended beneficiaries of protective policies. The public cost of the TARP bailout of the auto industry, which was according to government data and outside estimates orders of magnitude greater than the long run costs of the entire financial sector bailout. No public purpose was ever credibly identified, and the actions clearly went against consumer interests. The rule of law was undermined – violated – to achieve political ends. That is truly a "great" trifecta achievement, although not in the way it was hailed during the subsequent election campaign.

TARP was successful in saving the largest insolvent banks. Several TBTF banks that were in fact technically insolvent and otherwise arguably should have failed were saved, but there was nothing new about this policy – it was just more transparent. Treasury Secretary Geitner had done this as NY Fed President in the 1990s and continued this policy as the Obama Administration Treasury Secretary.

Based on the available evidence, the AIG bailout did cost taxpayers undisclosed billions. The beneficiaries are CDS holders like Goldman Sacks. Whether that stemmed a systemic financial crisis is unknowable but unlikely. The financial system bailout – from bearing the cost of the regulatory and political policies of the sub-prime lending debacle – was arguably generally in the near term public interest, even if badly miss-managed and excessive. The losses in the financial system mostly related to their following perverse incentives and being victimized by bearing the cost of housing policy, and their failure could have brought down the US financial system. But TBTF financial firms continued to generate economic rents even while being bailed out under Treasury control.[243] The long term costs of moral hazard – virtually always ignored in a crisis – are much greater as a consequence.

The Congress went to great lengths with the unprecedented creation of SIGTARP to make TARP accountable to the public interest. SIGTARP's failure to do so was probably intrinsic and hence inevitable.

D. The Home Mortgage Bailouts and Housing Market Adjustment

Barofsky's tell-all book *An Inside Account of How Washington Abandoned Main Street While Rescuing Wall Street* is an excellent expose from an auditors perspective and hence a bit myopic and mis-titled. The narrative that lenders victimized borrowers during the sub-prime lending debacle is mostly false – they were following political policies that favored borrowers over lenders and savers. Hence Barofsky's complaint against Treasury Secretary Geitner is that TARP focused more on helping financial institutions survive than assisting victimized mortgage borrowers is true, but helping homeowners was arguably never the objective of the so-called homeowner bailout.

Billions were spent on homeowners, but the link between those most harmed by the house price bubble and those receiving aid was tenuous at best. Those most victimized had made the largest down payments at the peak of the house priced bubble and had their equity wiped out were never the target of assistance. Those least victimized were those with no initial home owner equity and hence the most likely to default. With negative equity and a no recourse loan, default was in the borrower's interest, but those households were encouraged to continue paying on a principle balance in excess of the house value to support the bank bail-out effort.

The massive public efforts to help borrowers were in fact more likely to victimize them by postponing or avoiding the shift of trillions of dollars of negative mortgage equity losses to lenders.

225

Borrowers were provided two incentives to avoid default. First, the Fed did everything in its power to keep interest rates low and mortgage rates relatively lower, with GSEs massively assisting in the latter. Second, various programs implemented to help homeowners kept house prices buoyed and borrowers absorbing more loss than had they just defaulted on their non-recourse loan.

This housing boom was extended to eleven years by government policy, so when the boom ended and the bubble finally burst the necessary market adjustment was huge. During the post WWII period, the housing sector rebound has always led the economic recovery. What policies does that imply? A more rapid housing market recovery would mean more housing sector pain in the short run – not only less production but a more rapid and deeper fall in house prices – followed by a quicker economic rebound.

But Rothbard's prediction of the likely political response proved prescient. Monetary policy subsequent to the sub-prime lending debacle was explained as a housing sector stimulus, but the futility of efforts by the Fed and administration to resuscitate housing after an eleven-year boom by keeping interest rates low – and mortgage rates lower – amounted to the same Fed/GSE policies of the sub-prime lending debacle, with the Fed playing both roles this time. The efforts to keep house prices from falling and borrowers from defaulting are discussed in sections 1 & 2. The use of torts to shift losses from investors and borrowers but in the process undermining the rule of law is discussed in sections 3 & 4. The refinancing programs to keep homeowners in their houses – also intended to slow and limit the decline in house prices, is discussed in section 5. Section 6 describes the continued damage done by HUD in pursuit of housing goals. The decline of the housing sector and the nascent recovery either because of or in spite of these efforts and the implications of the difference are discussed in section 6.

1. The Fed Attempts to Bail Out the Mortgage Market and Stimulate Housing

The Fed historically has certainly believed it can and should attempt to prevent or offset market corrections, e.g., of a housing boom gone bust. Its view on housing as the handmaiden of monetary policy four decades ago argued that the appropriate policy was to ease credit during slack times by lowering interest rates to create a housing boom, and to do the opposite in an over-heated economy. Housing construction would bear the brunt of the downturn but the secondary effects of declining demand would be pervasive.

But the Feds historical track record manipulating booms and busts prior to this century is poor, and during the housing boom of the last decade this policy proved disastrous, as the Fed went way beyond normal countercyclical bounds. The Fed's monetary policy during the five years of aftermath has several components. First, it has been the handmaiden of fiscal policy, funding the fiscal deficit without letting interest rates rise (Part E, below). Second, it has spent newly printed money on long term instruments to shift the structure of interest rates, artificially reducing mortgage rates to make home ownership and over-sized houses seemingly cheap. Third, it purchased mortgage securities directly to keep mortgage rates low and house prices from falling further, providing a temporary boost to affordability.

Historically the Fed has purchased short term Treasury securities in its open market operations but over time it got the authority to purchase almost anything. The Feds operation twist was nothing more than a switch to longer duration mortgage securities to lower long term mortgage rates relative to short term rates, i.e., to flatten the yield curve. As mortgage securities have a longer duration, this program overlaps with quantitative easing directed at mortgage markets. QE1 started in November of 2008 with a target acquisition of $600 billion in mortgage backed securities. Two years later the Fed announced QE2 with a target acquisition of $600 billion of longer term treasury securities. Two years after that a third round of quantitative easing QE3 was announced for the purchase of $40 billion of MBS monthly, later raised to $80 billion.

What the Fed purchased was not historically thought to matter much as the entire structure of rates would rise and fall together regardless of which assets were purchased. Typically longer term rates reflect market expectations so by purchasing long term assets and pushing prices up the Fed can arguably shape market expectations of future Fed policy to maintain low interest rates.

Such actions can affect relative security prices in the short run, especially those of distressed assets. For example, the express purpose of recent EU actions in 2012 was to prop up the value of debt issued by southern European countries with massive purchases – and hence bail-out the banks holding that debt. Such purchases are purportedly to be "sterilized" by selling expensive, e.g., German debt. This may well be Nobel Prize worthy, but is doomed to failure in the long run.[244] Greek debt held by banks at par trades for around 17 cents privately. However it does buy time in the short run to provide massive opaque subsidies to the banking system where most needed by providing cheap loans subsidized by taxpayers to guarantee a positive spread on assets, with bank equity returns and hence capital magnified by eliminating capital requirements on government debt.

That's the Fed's policy as well, as the Fed's quantitative easing policy mirrors that of the ECB. QE1 & QE2 had little obvious effect on the economic recovery and even less is expected of QE3. But whether or not intended, the direct effect of quantitative easing and operation twist were to allow domestic banks and international investors – mainly the Chinese, Russian and other central banks – to unload these securities at inflated prices at US taxpayer expense.

2. The GSE Agency Bailouts: FHA/ Ginnie Mae

Prior to the financial collapse, the GSEs provided financing for about half the US home mortgage market. During the aftermath it has accounted for about 95% of new originations. Is this evidence of the need for GSEs in an emergency such as a housing market downturn? Hardly! The GSEs retained their advantages over private lenders, which have increased during this stressful period.

Recent news stories conclude that the record profits reported Fannie Mae and Freddie Mac not only relieve political pressure for their reform or eventual elimination but for deficit reduction as well.[245] Current reported profitability of a government monopoly has nothing to do with the public interest. The only constitutionally authorized monopoly charter was for the U.S Post Office, "profitable" until competition from FedEx and UPS reduced their margins. More pointedly, direct U.S. Treasury capital infusions and the return of Fannie Mae and Freddie Mac dividends have almost nothing to do with the economic costs and benefits of these government-sponsored monopolies.

However, the reported profits, particularly in the case of Fannie Mae, aren't even what they seem. The key feature of generally accepted accounting principles is dual-entry bookkeeping. Fannie Mae recently reported a markup of over $50 billion for a "deferred tax asset" [246] That is, now that they have returned to "profitability," taxes otherwise due to the U.S. Treasury would not be due as a consequence of this "asset" (reflecting prior tax avoidance strategies). The U.S. Treasury doesn't record the offsetting loss in tax revenue as a liability. But that's not all. Being fully backed by the government in conservatorship, Fannie Mae borrowed $50 billion against this book entry without the Treasury recording the debt because the Treasury assumed only 79.9% ownership. Fannie then used these borrowed funds to pay a $50 billion dividend to the U.S. Treasury which Treasury then reports as an increase in income.

Fannie and Freddie have since 2011 been required to collect a penalty fee (or is it a tax – the Supreme Court Chief Justice has not yet ruled) from borrowers forwarded directly to Treasury to finance the payroll tax reduction.[247] The FHFA has made Fannie Mae and Freddie Mac the plaintiff rather than defendant in the bank litigation morass described below, but politicians are directing these funds as well.

The Obama administration took a step toward receivership on August 17, 2012 when it changed the way it treated F&F in conservatorship by eliminating the Treasury dividend and taking all profits instead.[248] That would render a combined F&F the Ginnie Mae of the conventional loan market, a good short term measure but regrettable long-term outcome. The treatment of the almost $200 billion that Fannie Mae and Freddie Mac together have paid to the Treasury as "dividends" while in conservatorship is the subject of 17 lawsuits and has been called "Grand Theft." [249]Worse still, these payouts largely reflect borrowing that the Treasury remains liable for rather than dividends from competitive market earnings.

The level of political risk has increased. F&F have increased the risk to seller/servicers with lawsuits, but these pale in comparison to the political risks of holding mortgages. GSEs provided somewhat of a safe haven from regulatory and legal recourse in an environment of heightened political risk. The reason is that the government is exempting itself from all of the onerous rules currently being applied to mortgage lenders, as discussed in chapter 6.

Of more consequence, they - like the Fed - offered lower mortgage rates due to their ongoing capital subsidies and increased risk profile. When comparing US interest rates in the aftermath of the sub-prime lending debacle to those in other developed market economies, housing economist Jim Shilling found that US mortgage rates were more depressed than their historical average of about 1 percentage point by about 50 percent, i.e., by 1.5 percentage points.[250] Conservatorship didn't change Fannie Mae and Fannie Mac much, but it did reduce payments to rent seekers. Shareholders were wiped out and politicians stopped receiving contributions, but over 90 managers continued to receive annual compensation in excess of $1 million.[251]

The really big change came at FHA!

FHA started going for broke in 2005 and by 2008 was broke. When Congress banned the use of seller-provided down payments in 2008, FHA's share of business with a nominal LTV over 97 percent declined dramatically, but the share of mortgages with LTVs between 95 and 97 percent increased more than enough to offset this. Moreover, part of the disappearance of seller-provided down payments – an obvious euphemism for an inflated price and LTV - has been replaced by down payments suspiciously "funded by relatives" but commonly reflecting unrecorded debt. This is often in the form of a loan, whether formal or not and whether subsequently registered as a silent second or not. Among FHA loans made as late as 2011, there are still almost a quarter where the borrowers did not provide the small required cash down payment themselves.

Congress also passed the Housing and Economic Recovery Act (HERA) in 2008 granting FHA loan limit authority up to 150% of the F&F conforming loan limits. FHA volume exploded as Ginnie Mae financing substituted for F&F securities: Ginnie Mae outstanding securities have doubled to about $4 trillion in the aftermath of the sub-prime lending debacle, doubling the Ginnie Mae capital subsidies (discussed in chapter 4) to about $40 billion annually and continuing to rise in response to FHA's rising market share. At the end of fiscal year 2012 FHA insured about 8 million loans of about $1.1 trillion in loan principal, a six-fold increase in market share over 2005. After the 2007 market collapse FHA increased insurance in force over threefold, from $350 billion to about $1.1 trillion as it continued going broke.[252] As noted in chapter 4, the rise in market share after 2008 came mostly at the expense of prime conventional lenders, with subprime falling from over half to about a third of originations in 2009 and 2010. Further evidence of FHA crowding out prime conventional lenders is reflected in credit scores: by 2011 only about 4 percent of FHA borrowers had FICO scores below 620, while the percent of the highest-quality borrowers—with FICO scores above 720—rose fourfold to 35 percent.

As a GSE FHA can continue going broke indefinitely, but even Fannie and Freddie eventually had to report their insolvency as the price of their sub-debt started to fall. How is it that FHA can report being solvent? According to Wallison and Pinto (2012, p. 2) Congress approved the same present value accounting of 30 years of purely illusory profits for FHA that the SEC approved for sub-prime lenders. This assumption is premised on rising housing prices, as were PLS profits during the sub-prime lending debacle. Following regulatory accounting for private insurance companies, Wallison and Pinto (p. 3) estimate a capital shortfall of about $35 billion as of a year ago, projected to grow by about $20 billion annually.

Since the end of 2007, the FHA's capital reserves have declined from $22 billion to around $4.7 billion in the fall of 2011. As house prices continued falling, further declines eroded the remaining reserves. The FHA's actuaries estimated that seller financing alone cost $14 billion in losses.

Testifying before the Subcommittee on Financial Opportunity of the Financial Services Committee in October of 2009, Ed Pinto of AEI reported a $54 billion insolvency of FHA, in sharp contrast to FHA's rosy estimate of positive value of $2.7 billion. Testifying before the same

Committee in February of 2013, Pinto presented a similar estimate. In addition to the current book capital shortage of $22 billion, future losses of over $30 billion are forecast based on less rosy assumptions than those FHA continues to make.

FHA counts as capital the present value of future gross revenue before credit expense. By any normal accounting standard, FHA should have long since been put into conservatorship. In fact, by fall 2012 FHA announced it had exhausted its reserves and would likely require direct appropriations – a $16 billion taxpayer bailout - to cover future claims.[253] The FY11 Actuarial Review projects a positive economic value for the agency *solely* on the basis of assuming that future business will generate excess revenues sufficient to cover imbedded losses. In other words, the value of Ginnie Mae future subsidies for prime historically conventional borrowers will be captured by FHA instead of new borrowers to offset past FHA losses. As a start, it raised the insurance fee by 10 basis points and made the total premium permanent, no longer letting the insurance expire after five years when borrower's equity reached 22%, taxing new borrowers to pay for old defaults. FHA is taking advantage of the extension of its monopoly provided by HERA to cover HUD's malfeasance.

The recent FHA request for a taxpayer bailout in the summer of 2013 completed the trifecta, Fannie Mae, Freddie Mac and FHA/Ginnie Mae - the government sponsored enterprises (GSEs) - all required a taxpayer bailout due to credit loss.

3. The Securitizer Lawsuit Investor Bailout

The Economist magazine recently reported that bank fines related to the financial crisis will soon top $100 billion. To quote: "Lost in the flurry of payouts is any clear adjudication of what banks have done wrong, and therefore any guidance for setting things right." [254]

The SEC has used its litigation authority to extract subsidies from financial institutions, although little is returned to the purported victims. CDO deals were considered the most offensive because the underlying collateral was made up entirely of lower rated bonds. In 2010 Goldman Sachs settled an SEC suit for $510 million relating to CDOs with no admission of guilt and no finding of wrong doing. Emboldened, the SEC then sued JP Morgan for bonds originated by Bear Sterns, then reached a similar settlement again without any finding of wrong doing or any admission of guilt. The US District Court that rejected this settlement for that very reason was later over-turned for exceeding its authority.[255] In fact, the SEC has failed to convict anybody for defrauding investors and the suits and subsequent settlements smack of lucrative extortion by the government.[256]

Due to its conservatorship charter, the FHFA has taken a much tougher stance against taxpayer losses than has FHA, for which its administrator Edward J. DeMarco has taken a lot of political heat. The basic task has been to limit additional direct Treasury capital infusions. They also pursued an unprecedented $66 billion in mortgage put-backs.[257] But they may have gone too far trying to emulate the SEC's success, as attempts to shift loan losses to the originators undermines the confidence of originators to sell to F&F. The Federal Housing Finance Agency (FHFA) filed a $200 billion lawsuit against 17 of the nation's largest surviving "deep pocket" mortgage lenders in the fall of 2011, in this case naming the individuals.

The lawsuits all relate to publicly offered private label sub-prime mortgage backed securities AAA PLS – not CDOs - purchased by Fannie and Freddie mostly from 2005 through 2007. Mortgage defaults rose, the securities were downgraded and their market price fell, causing mark to market losses at F&F. The suit argues that F&F made the investments based entirely on the representations in the prospectus, these representations proved to be false and misleading, and had the investors known they would not have made them. Implicit in this charge is that the subsequent losses are due entirely to this mis-information. Implicit in the size and scope of the lawsuits is the allegation of a systemic fraud, i.e. that not a few but most of the loans made by most of the major lenders were in violation of the stated underwriting guidelines or other disclosures.

As previously discussed, F&F purchased mostly senior investment grade securities because these not only qualified towards their housing "mission" goals required by HUD's "mission regulator," but also because OFEHO, FHFA's predecessor prudential regulator, required only 20% as much capital as for their whole loan purchases. Fannie and Freddie purchased as much as a third of all investment grade AAA private label securities during some periods, sometimes purchasing an entire issue originated just for them, enabling sub--prime during the peak of the lending debacle. Among the other investors are the very banks that FHFA is suing. Other deposit-financed investors received the same regulatory capital inducement to purchase these securities, and in addition relied on Fannie and Freddie as the lead investor whose expertise was long touted by politicians and regulators, so if Fannie and Freddie were mislead then these investors were doubly mislead.

The courts will likely spend several more years determining the legal merits of theses lawsuits unless firms continue to cave to settlement demands, but it is hard to believe from what's been disclosed in the sub-prime aftermath that F&F didn't know a lot more about the risks than the FHFA court filings indicate, that their motives were the same as those of any investor, or that the named defendants are necessarily the most culpable. Fannie and Freddie wanted to invest in these securities to meet their mission goals, and more accurate or descriptive disclosure could have inhibited that. If the gnomes of Freddie Mac – a reference to their old advertising campaign - truly didn't know, Fannie and Freddie stockholders may be wondering how their CEOs at the time, who received hundreds of millions of dollars in compensation, could have been so naïve or arguably incompetent not to smell a rat. But management has successfully rebuffed disgorgement of past compensation.

The courts routinely have to deal with such deep pocket lawsuits. While it is certainly appropriate to pursue such cases *on the merits* what is different in this case is that government housing policy promoted the origination and sale of these mortgage loans, the F&F regulator provided irresistible incentives for F&F to invest in these securities to meet housing policy targets, and now it is the regulator of Fannie Mae and Freddie Mac that has filed the lawsuits. As a consequence one branch of government has to rule against another. The courts might have subsequently reject the loss-shifting, concluding that F&F knew after all, but by then issuer fear of such suits may have undermined future securitization. So the firms settled in the fall of 2013 for about $5 billion.

4. The Servicer/Lender Lawsuit "Homeowner" Bailout

The lack of recourse of US mortgages has historically been of little significance as the net lender loss on a mortgage with a 20% down payment in a stagnant or rising market generally was not worth the legal cost of collecting the shortfall from the borrower. This changed dramatically during the sub-prime lending debacle. The borrowers that were victimized the most were those that invested substantial savings: those that put down little or nothing didn't have much to lose and many came out of the sub-prime debacle financially ahead. Similarly, the borrowers who chose a standard fixed rate mortgage fared worse than those who paid less principal.

Borrowers who defaulted on their loans likely lived rent free during an extended foreclosure period as compared to those who paid regularly. Those offered a bribe – forbearance and cheap monthly payments – were made temporarily better off, but subsequently frequently re-defaulted. Unless house prices no longer reverted to the mean, home owners with negative equity were just throwing good money after bad by making mortgage payments. In a role reversal, many borrowers wanted to default because lenders had a lot more to lose than they did. Borrowers who can pay have little incentive to do so when others in similar circumstances pay little or nothing, so paying the mortgage moved from the borrower's first to last priority.

In normal times, foreclosure imposes costs on lenders and loan servicers as well as borrowers and both generally lose when foreclosing on a property. Borrowers bear all loss including accrued interest and penalties up to the cap at total borrower equity due to the lack of recourse in most states, a protection unique to US borrowers among mortgage systems in advanced economies. When the potential borrower loss equals or exceeds the borrower's equity, borrowers are highly motivated to provide the "deed in lieu" of foreclosure to minimize their costs, or to sell the home for less than the mortgage principle, i.e., a "short sale." Lenders typically lose money on foreclosures owing to their "cost of carry", renovation, management and marketing costs, providing an incentive to forbear when there is a good chance the borrower will recover. The servicer loses the ongoing servicing stream of net income and their foreclosure processing costs almost always exceed their servicing revenues.

Hence it has historically been in the mutual interest of borrowers, lenders and servicers to avoid unnecessary foreclosures. A streamlined foreclosure process is similarly in their mutual interest, a consequence of which is generally cheaper mortgage credit in the 27 states with non-judicial foreclosure where the process is much quicker and costs and outcomes were historically highly predictable.

Foreclosure favored borrowers over lenders due to the negative borrower equity of sub-prime lending and lack of recourse. Delayed foreclosure in judicial foreclosure states where eviction takes twice as long allowed occupants a longer period of living rent free. Making matters worse, there were some additional exceptions to these incentives with sub-prime lending favoring borrowers. First, due to securitization the servicers' incentives weren't always aligned with that of their investors, who may have benefited from rapid foreclosure at the servicer's expense. Also, among investors there were sometimes differential impacts, e.g., a particular class of security could benefit from accelerated cash flow even when due to default while another class bore the credit loss. Of more consequence, many servicers – or their affiliated bank - continued to own the "first loss" second mortgage, potentially putting their interest as investor in conflict with their responsibility as servicer on the first mortgage to foreclose on behalf of the first lien holder. The net result was that servicers had much less incentive to foreclose on defaulted first mortgages than was historically the case because that would have required a write-off of the second as well (Chapter 4).

Foreclosure statistics bear this out. The average foreclosure time doubled during the aftermath of the sub-prime debacle and in many states tripled.[258] Post foreclosure evictions and repossessions slowed down. More significantly, the foreclosure process was generally started much later than was historically the case. Nevertheless the foreclosure wave was massive and politicians at the state and federal level entered the fray. In addition to pressuring lenders not to foreclose, politicians have generally supported legal initiatives to slow or stop foreclosures. Economist and NYT columnist Paul Krugman declared that all such lender foreclosure rights are "ill-defined" and hence need to be abrogated with new rights "created" (*ex post*) by government politicians (NYT 10/14/2010). Krugman cites "a man" who purportedly lost his house even though it had no mortgage as evidence of a systemic attempt by lenders to inappropriately confiscate much of the nation's housing stock.

Lenders were overwhelmed with the sheer volume of foreclosures and some resorted to what plaintiff lawyers subsequently called "robo-signing," a phenomenon where processors certified they had personally read documents when in fact they only reviewed them while relying on the advice and opinion of others (something politicians apparently never do). There were numerous studies at the federal level, e.g., by HUD and by the OCC with participation of the other financial regulators. Numerous problems with paperwork processing and documentation issues at the front end of loan closing due to the multiple parties involved in securitization were uncovered with recommendations for servicing improvement, but none of these studies found a systemic attempt to defraud borrowers who were current on their loans or to foreclose inappropriately.[259] Robo-signing was stupid, providing a bonanza for plaintiff lawyers and some benefits to defaulted borrowers by stretching out the foreclosure process.

It worked. The proportion of homes in foreclosure in judicial foreclosure states rose from 45% in 2007 to 65% in 2012 as a result of the significant judicial delays. Not surprisingly, the rebound in house prices occurred in the non-judicial foreclosure states, providing strong evidence that the efforts to postpone foreclosures also postponed the housing market recovery in those states.[260]

All fifty state Attorney Generals apparently wanted in on the bonanza. Servicers and lenders were accused of vastly excessive foreclosures. The wave of contentious litigation went well beyond normal bounds by casting doubt on the rights of mortgage lenders, investors and servicers. After years of litigation with no victims identified, no evidence of a systemic attempt to defraud borrowers provided and no borrower loss identified, the servicers settled on $25 billion in *borrower* compensation.[261] The compensation formulas were unrelated to any findings of fault and allocated politically, disproportionately to California.[262] But almost a year after the settlement only $1 billion had been targeted to aid borrowers – and these borrowers were not in any way identified as victims of these or any other servicers or lenders - with most of the rest of the money going directly into state coffers as general revenues.[263] It was a political scam, a "foreclosure shakedown" the cost of which goes well beyond the $25 billion extortion payment as it undermined the rule of law.[264] But the servicers – deep pocket TBTF banks all – turned this to their advantage by negotiating write downs on first liens held by investors ahead of the second liens they held in portfolio.[265]

5. The Refinancing Bailout

With roughly 25% of all mortgage borrowers under water during the last four years, policy generally focused on providing incentives not to default. The primary incentive was cheap mortgage financing. Former Fed Vice Chairman Alan Blinder (WSJ, Oct 20, 2011) and Former Treasury Secretary Larry Summers (Washington Post and Financial Times, Oct 24 2011) argued for refinancing the nations mortgage stock at the Fed-induced low rates - the Freddie Mac 30 year fixed rate hovered around 3.5%-4% for most of 2012 and closed at about 3%- as a way to both avoid foreclosures and stimulate the economy, a win-win policy.

Refinancing long term mortgages when rates fell was never meant to be an automatic "right" that makes it a good policy to extend the current rate to all borrowers. Borrowers increasingly exploited a feature originally meant to facilitate households moving without taking their mortgage with them. Borrowers like fixed rate pre-payable mortgages for the same reason lenders don't: borrowers have a heads I win tails you lose position that lenders can't effectively hedge. The borrower got the lower rate but if funded long the lender got stuck with high cost funding when rates fell, or if funded short when rates rose. These costs generally got passed on to savers, but in the case of the savings and loan (S&L) industry, the shareholders were wiped out after the fiscal deficits of the 1970s caused interest rates to rise to double digit levels, eroding the value of their fixed rate loans.

Refinancing has always put the lender – the loan originator – in conflict with both the servicer and investor, who each lose the longer revenue stream. The servicer can protect that revenue stream by keeping the loan servicing contract on the re-financed loan if the borrower doesn't go elsewhere. But the borrower's gain on refinancing is the investor's loss. Moreover, refinancing played a role in fueling the housing bubble by allowing borrowers with little or nothing down to refinance teaser rate mortgages at the time of reset, often taking cash out to capitalize on the house price bubble.

It is hard to see how the current "government determined" 3% thirty year fixed rate pre-payable mortgage is a good investment. Even if inflation remained steady at zero for the next thirty years, the real return to savers after loan servicing, credit default and deposit administration or other funding costs would be well below historical levels. And if it merely averaged zero, with historical volatility, then the "refinancing" option would result in a steeply negative average real return to savers. But even that is highly unlikely as high inflation seems all but inevitable if and when the economy recovers as a consequence of Fed monetary policy, rendering such loans virtually worthless. This was the genesis of the S&L industry failure.

Refinancing in the aftermath of the sub-prime lending debacle still required that the borrower and property re-qualify. That was somewhat problematic for many borrowers due to the recession, and even more problematic for many properties due to negative equity, precisely the borrowers lenders wanted to prevent from defaulting. To address that problem, the Home Affordable Refinance Program (HARP) was established by the FHFA in March of 2009 to allow loans held by Fannie or Freddie with payments current and an LTV as high as 125% - and later without limit - to refinance without mortgage insurance, with Fannie Mae and Freddie Mac absorbing the previously insured risk. As a further lender inducement, they were granted a safe harbor against recourse on the original loan, a big deal given FHFA's subsequently hyper-active legal division. HARP refinanced first and second homes, and investor as well as owner properties, reflecting its true intent to avoid foreclosure losses.

The Home Affordable Modification Program (HAMP) was formed the month before HARP. The key difference is that while the borrower could be current, he could also be delinquent, in default, foreclosure and/or bankruptcy. In addition, the loans do have to be below the F&F maximum, but they don't have to be owned by F&F. Hence unlike HARP, HAMP takes additional distressed loans onto the F&F balance sheet.

HAMP monthly expense was generally less than an equivalent rental. Nevertheless, 70% of the loans modified under HAMP in 2009 re-defaulted within 12 months.[266] What the Obama Administration really wanted - and exerted enormous pressure on FHFA to provide - is for principal to be written down to only 80% of the current house value. That's what the Home Owners Loan Corporation (HOLC) required of lenders in the Great Depression before acquiring their loans and assuming all the remaining risk.

Every study FHFA did showed that while principle write-downs would indeed reduce the rate of re-default, the cost of moral hazard – borrowers not otherwise seeking modification would do so – swamped the foreclosure savings. According to Core Logic, 85% of underwater borrowers remained current on their loans, but would have no incentive to do so if default provided them a principal write-down. The moral hazard risk was too extreme. Homeowner negative equity was about $1 trillion dollars in the spring of 2012 including second mortgages and that could have about doubled had house prices fallen all the way down to their long term historical mean or beyond.[267] The Treasury Secretary offered to partially fund these losses transparently, but the opaque losses to F&F would still have been large. This is born out by the HOLC experience: in spite of turning down more applications than it accepted the subsequent foreclosure rate exceeded 20% even with an average of two years forbearance. HOLC was reportedly "costless" to the government in the same way that Fannie Mae and Freddie Mac were, with misleading accounting and hidden subsidies.

By the last quarter of 2012 the rate of first time foreclosures started down, but the rate of re-foreclosure remained stuck at 50%.[268] The financial sector was taking on losses faster than the mortgage modifications could bail them out. As the year ended, the Administration proposed expanding the refinancing programs to include all households, not just those with F&F loans and those with positive net equity.[269]

Then the Fed's policy to re-inflate the house price bubble finally kicked in, as prices rebounded sharply in 2013.

6. The HUD Lender Lawsuits

On the one hand, there are virtually no barriers to entry for mortgage origination and discrimination in hiring mortgage originators has never been asserted, so there is no contemporary record of systemic illegal discrimination on grounds of race or sex. On the other hand, there are still huge disparities among the races (less so among the sexes) regarding jobs, income and wealth. There is no question that sound borrower underwriting will have a "disparate impact" due to this. As previously discussed, such proof is problematic as the result itself is considered proof of racial prejudice not subject to analysis, and the cost of a legal defense is generally crippling. The alternative to litigation is to err on the side of leniency and sign DOJ quota agreements when required to do so.[270] The fact that discrimination lawsuits for foreclosure on disparate impact grounds rival those for discrimination in lending also strongly suggest the foundation for a finding of discrimination based purely on race remains an opaque way of allocating unbudgeted subsidies.[271]

In the Magner case, a group of landlords in Saint Paul alleged that city officials targeted rental properties for housing code violations, causing rents to rise and having a disparate impact on the primarily African-American tenants. The Eighth Circuit Court in Minnesota upheld the landlords' claim, even though there was no evidence that the city intended to discriminate. The DOJ intervened in support of disparate impact on appeal, but when it became evident that the Supreme Court would most likely rule against disparate impact, essentially bribed the cities of Minneapolis and Saint Paul to drop the appeal or face HUD's retribution. [272]

This is precisely the type of policy at the root of the sub-prime lending crisis and HUD is doubling down. In February of 2013 HUD issued a new rule applying disparate impact to the racial mix of all private housing projects, ignoring the cost benefit analysis requirement of such a regulation by asserting that such a regulation has no costs.[273] In June 2012, Representative Scott Garrett (R-NJ) introduced an amendment to the Housing Appropriations Bill that would prohibit HUD from formalizing disparate impact in housing regulations, reflecting its interpretation that the Fair Housing Act prohibits housing practices that have a disparate impact on those who are part of a protected class.

In the fall of 2013 the suit by the Mount Holly Township against the Mount Holly Gardens Citizens was also dropped just prior to a Supreme Court hearing, preserving this form of extortion.[274]

7. The Housing Industry Bailout: Mortgage and Housing Market Adjustments Delayed

Housing construction has always been an interest sensitive and hence boom-bust business. The housing industry adjusted to these boom/bust cycles. Small contractors would shift from new construction to remodeling and rehabilitation (some of which goes unrecorded) and by using more temporary lower skilled workers (some of which is unskilled labor from across the border). Construction workers generally saved more during boom periods to cover lean years (or returned home), but the government safety net of unemployment insurance reduced the need to save. Parenthetically, public unemployment schemes have resulted in tremendous moral hazard in the construction trades, as most beneficiaries now remain formally unemployed until benefits run out, but are reportedly rapidly hired thereafter, resulting in cross-subsidies from employed workers and taxpayers. This is particularly true in construction trades where workers can take odd jobs for unrecorded cash.

Housing markets have to work off excess inventory produced during boom periods before they can recover and production can resume to normal levels. That requires that housing production and prices decline to equilibrium levels or below before rebounding. The house price decline makes housing more affordable. This adjustment takes years and there isn't much that policymakers can do to avoid it. Attempts to stimulate housing jobs after a boom bust cycle has been a consistent loser since the Great Depression, especially when pursuing policies to keep the housing bubble inflated.

Nevertheless, fiscal policy attempted to mitigate the inventory and price adjustment. The first tax credit for housing was provided in the 2008 American Housing Rescue and Foreclosure Prevention Act. This was followed by an $8000 tax credit for first time home buyers in the 2009 fiscal stimulus bill. First time home buyers were hardly financial victims of the sub-prime lending debacle. Most of the tax credits went to people who would have bought anyway the next quarter or shortly thereafter, so in that sense it didn't inhibit the housing market adjustment. But $9 million went to prison inmates, including 240 who were serving life sentences (Meltzer, p.39). It just threw good taxpayer money after bad and if house prices subsequently fell victimized those buyers that had previously avoided buying at bubble inflated prices.[275]

In chapter 4 we reported that housing policy during the housing boom resulted in an additional 4.2 million additional single family (1 to 4 units) houses being constructed, roughly four years of normal production from 1995 through 2007, implying a 30% increase in single family houses during the construction boom. From 2008 through 2011, single family starts averaged about half their historical level, and the home ownership rate fell back to its historical level, so that implies an excess stock of about 2 million units remaining at year end 2011. Multifamily housing starts (5 or more) fell short by 520, 000 units for the period, about two full years of production, implying a total increase in production of about 27% due to housing policy. From 2008 through 2011 average production was only about 1/3rd the historical average, adding another 600,000 units to the shortfall. By year end 2012 the cumulative 2008-2012 shortfall in total housing construction about offset the cumulative increase during the boom years.

Also, in chapter 4 we reported that housing policy inflated the value of the single family housing stock by about 75% over and above the rise in the physical stock of housing and the GDP deflator, which implies a decline in house prices of about 43% (75%/175%) from their peak level to get back onto the trend line. Using Shiller data on existing home sales from chapter 4 Figure 1, the required decline is closer to 50%. According to the FHFA data, house prices declined by only 22% from April 2007 through April 2011 before rebounding. The Case Shiller composite 20 index peaked in April 2006, and then bottomed out down 34% by January 2012.

The faster prices fall the more rapidly the housing market will adjust, although new production won't proceed before the excess inventory is absorbed. Much of this adjustment required the conversion of owner to rental housing. During 2012 multifamily housing starts rebounded sharply, approaching their average of the last decade. Single family housing starts rebounded less in percentage terms but more in absolute terms. So peak to trough for production took about four to five years, not long by historical standards, especially given the magnitude of the structural adjustment necessary. Housing affordability has been restored, but that is largely due to the Fed's negative real interest rate policy. Based on long term production trends, there may still be a combined excess inventory of single and multifamily houses of as much as a million units.

Whether this is the beginning of a strong rebound or a temporary blip to a weak market remains to be seen. In March 2012 when housing prices began rising there were still 4 million households in default and an additional 2 million households delinquent.[276] The rise in prices turned housing equity positive for 1.3 million households, according to Core Logic, but by the second half of 2012 the number of all households with a mortgage with negative equity was still 10.8 million or 22.3% and the percent with five percent or less equity was 27.3%.[277] In the absence of the Fed's zero interest rate policy, house prices could have significantly further to fall. For example, noted forecaster A. Gary Shilling recently predicted a further 20% decline in house prices before rising again.[278] That could cause massive additional foreclosures, repeating the experience of the last 5 years and prolonging the recovery of the financial sector. As late as the first quarter of 2013 economist and housing forecaster Robert Schiller was less than sanguine about the housing recovery.[279]

Who benefited from the boom/bust housing cycle? Huge political constituencies developed around the GSE originate-to-sell housing finance mechanism of mortgage origination and funding in the US. Those in the construction industry mostly moved demand forward, building houses five to ten years earlier than they otherwise would have. Working off the excess inventory of larger detached single family houses – a misallocation of investment – is about half complete and could take a decade or longer. Real estate brokerage did the same regarding sales and brokerage commissions. Several groups held on to past gains and got even more. Mortgage brokerage, for example, continued to benefit from the Fed fueled refinancing boom in the aftermath. And political patronage continued in the aftermath as a consequence of the legislative threats embodied in, e.g., Dodd-Frank.

Homeowners generally didn't benefit from the temporary house price bubble: it's still the same house on the same land providing the same shelter. Of course households that cashed-out and become renters realized a gain when house prices rose above the rental equivalent, offset by the loss of the purchaser and/or lender. Sellers of land – inflated entirely as a consequence of public policy similarly reaped permanent gains at the expense of new home purchasers and/or lenders. The net long run public cost of these policies depends on the extent to which such gains were consumed, and if saved, how productively they were invested.

E. Bailing Out the Economy: The Monetary and Fiscal Policy Bailout

The conflict between short term elixirs and long term cures was most evident in the prescription for the macro economy. Macroeconomics is a relatively new post Depression "Keynesian art." The two macroeconomic tuning tools are monetary and fiscal "policy." At its core monetary policy stimulus consists of selectively debasing the currency without the public's full awareness to induce work and spending for its short term effect, generally with little regard for the long term consequences or political accountability. Fiscal policy stimulus consists of politicians spending taxpayer money often unproductively and generally unaccountably by borrowing or printing it - transferring the burden to the future – to induce a "multiplier" effect.

Their origins reflect a real or imagined economy in which fear of the future causes households to save but fear also makes business reluctant to invest, causing a decline in aggregate demand. The temporary monetary and fiscal elixirs are meant to restore optimism and economic growth, with benefits far exceeding costs. Macroeconomics isn't a "hard" science like physics, where the physical world is a constant and only our understanding of it changes. Not only is the historical understanding of the economy subject to constant revision, but the economy is dynamic so the understanding of economists easily becomes outdated.

Macroeconomic advisors employ mathematical models to formulate policies to "fine-tune" aggregate economic activity purportedly by stabilizing business cycles. But every economy is different and any given economy behaves differently at different points in time and under different conditions, so even the most careful estimates of past parameters aren't always useful in predicting future behavior. Estimates of secondary effects, such as the long term consequences of increasing debt, are particularly problematic and typically ignored.

But monetarist and Keynesian countercyclical policies to fight a recession are a central banker's and politician's dream, making their use potentially indiscriminate and counterproductive when used in the wrong circumstances and applied in the wrong way, e.g., to reinforce the crony capitalist "big business" and "big labor" tendencies of past policies. The incoming Obama Administration quickly formed a team of Keynesian macro-economists to develop a fiscal stimulus plan in early 2009. The primary fiscal stimulus is embodied in the American Recovery and Reinvestment Act, commonly referred to as the Stimulus or the Recovery Act, signed into law on February 17, 2009. This was followed by a legislative and regulatory agenda to "transform" the economy, a by product of which was to be a plethora of new "high paying" jobs. Fed Chairman Bernanke had been appointed by President Bush, but his "New Keynesian" approach to monetary policy meshed perfectly with the Obama Administration's Keynesian approach to fiscal policy.[280] In fact, Rickards (2011, p. 181) reports that both the monetary and fiscal policies were hatched in the 1990s by two Princeton professors, Bernanke and Paul Krugman, the uber-liberal Keynesian and NYT columnist.

The policies certainly didn't achieve the goal of putting people back to work, as fewer were working as of the 2012 election than as of the 2008 election and in generally lower paying jobs. Conservative critics of these policies charged that the economy would have long since recovered on its own but for these policies. Liberal defenders argued that the financial crisis was too severe, the recession too steep and the policies too weak to foster an economic recovery. The debate over the diagnosis and prescription of the Great Recession mirrors the ongoing debate over what made the Great Depression Great.

The common characteristic of the entire transformative agenda was to supplant market prices, wages and processes with political goals, regulatory rules and bureaucratic processes. And the agenda targeted about two thirds of the private sector for transformation: health, energy, and finance while simultaneously expanding the public sector's approximately 40% share of GDP. The tools used to achieve this transformation were in large part the same tools used to create the sub-prime debacle. And the public costs were similarly opaque. Politically, this agenda couldn't have passed without the political narrative of the root causes of the financial crisis as market failure, which is why the correct diagnosis represented such a threat. No one can say for certain that an alternative policy focused on restoring long run economic growth would have worked better in the short run, but the fundamentals are worse now.

Section 1 provides a historical context for the Obama Administrations macroeconomic policies. Section 2 discusses why the fiscal stimulus failed to reduce unemployment to the target level and now threatens a downward economic spiral. The proposals for an infrastructure bank are discussed in section 3. Section 4 discusses the merits of Fed financial sector interventions to finance the deficits and to selectively inflate certain asset classes to stimulate consumption through the wealth effect, leaving the median household broke.

1. The Historical Context of US Macro-economic Policy: Cyclical and Secular Trends

In the Schumpeterian view, business cycles occur naturally as part of a market adjustment process. The period 1869 -1929 was one of rapid if somewhat rocky growth of the US economy. As Meltzer (pp.68-69) points out, during this period the gold standard was pro-cyclical, relying on disruptive unemployment to bring about the required adjustments, more frequent but short. Schumpeter's process of "creative destruction" that generally occurs in the downturn was temporarily painful but served a useful purpose as businesses and households took the opportunity to reassess business practices, down-sizing or even going out of business, increasing productivity during the recovery and beyond as it did in this period of tremendous productivity growth.

Whether you believe in the Schumpeter (business) or the Austrian (public) origins of business cycles, historically governments didn't – and arguably couldn't - do much about them. But the presumptive political myth since the Great Depression is that the downturn is caused by private market imbalance and the public policy objective has been to cushion the amplitude of business cycles in order to mitigate the consequences on worker employment as a means of stabilizing their consumption above some minimal level to cushion the effect of the gold standard adjustment process using what has since been called Keynesian stimulus. From the micro level, the conservative concern with over-extending the social safety net, e.g., with unemployment insurance, welfare, housing, public jobs, etc., has been moral hazard, i.e., their effect on labor force participation, work effort and household saving. Austrians are also concerned with the redistributive effects of deficit-financed government spending funded with printed money and their depressing effect on economic growth and wealth creation.

Up until and through the Great Depression, state, local and the federal government tried to balance the budget when faced with declining revenues by cutting expenditures (Meltzer, p.103). The better way is to set average expenditures over a boom/bust cycle to average tax revenues over the same cycle, running deficits during the bust and surpluses during the boom, providing so-called "automatic stabilizers" to economic activity, the same way those businesses not in the process of a market correction respond.

Since the Depression Keynesians have argued for going a step (or more) further, increasing spending more during slack periods and presumably curtailing them during a subsequent boom. The central bank as the handmaiden of fiscal policy is generally expected to finance such expenditures. Keynes focused on the "stickiness" of wages, e.g., the inability to reduce real wages particularly in the unionized British coal industry as a reason for using inflation - created by government spending financed by printing money - to lower real wages over the deflation required by the gold standard.

In the US the Davis Bacon "prevailing" wage has since the Wagner Act of 1935 generally been interpreted as the union wage, which often is as much as twice the local wage, particularly in rural areas. State and local employees are mostly unionized and often include project labor agreements (PLAs) in public contracts issued to private vendors that require union wages even for non-unionized employees. Numerous other laws and regulations from minimum wage to trade licensing inhibit labor market adjustment and declining real wages. The Keynesian solution to lowering real wages with inflation generally hasn't worked in the longer run as unions caught on to this slight of hand decades ago and the market followed.

Currency markets anticipate future inflation, reducing the exchange rate and labor costs up-front until other governments respond in kind. Hence monetary policy can under certain conditions temporarily counter the effects of other regressive factors, but this can delay or avoid beneficial structural adjustments.

The tremendous growth in the relative size of the public sector since Schumpeter's time makes it the more likely source of economic cycles than private business, as the Austrians argued and discussed throughout this book with respect to the sub-prime lending debacle. When the Great Depression hit the federal government accounted for less than 4% of GDP, and the combined state, local and federal share was 8%. Now that share is five times higher.[281] As the government sector has grown to comparable size – it's about 40% of the economy and government regulations over the other 60% private sector are pervasive - government policies are as or more likely to be the source of macro-economic fluctuations than are so-called normal business cycles.

Governments are like business in one respect. When times are good, e.g., a boom fueled by capital gains tax revenues as in California in the early part of the last decade, they expand wildly. But when the boom turns to bust, they don't adjust! Raising taxes in boom times was equally part of Keynes prescription, ignored in practice. This has contributed to the secular increase in the relative size of the total government sector since the Great Depression.[282] This has also contributed to the relative increase in the size of government debt, as debts incurred in bad times more often than not aren't paid down in good. Moreover, state, local and federal productivity declines when the bust period isn't used for creative destruction, even as the public sector continues to grow.

Virtually all of the planned economies have fallen into bankruptcy and adopted some form of a market economy on their way out, while the older market economies have become mixed public/private economies. In Western Europe the public sector is often the larger partner whereas in the US the private sector is generally considered the more dominant, although some analysts have recently disputed that based on the government control over the private sector. Sweden grew its public sector earlier than most, and then resorted to market oriented policies when economic growth collapsed, as did Germany a decade later.[283] But in the US this secular political trend has continued to favored public sector growth and - as this reflected politics rather than productivity - reduced aggregate economic growth.

2. Government Spending and Regulation: the Stimulus and Beyond

The eleven year housing boom not only produced a bust requiring a massive housing sector adjustment, it sustained many other industries and government services that were likewise enabled to postpone the painful process of creative destruction. In other words, the cyclical boom masked structural problems. The Fed and Administration attempts described above to mitigate the residential housing sector adjustment were counter-productive, just as they had been in the past.

Most would agree that in certain situations of inadequate aggregate demand appropriately targeted federal stimulus spending could conceptually provide countercyclical support with the benefits outweighing the long run costs. Few would argue with automatic stabilizers in the fiscal policies of government, for example. But US Treasury deficits topped $1 trillion dollars for each of the four years of the first term Obama presidency, almost $6 trillion overall, and well beyond the limit of automatic stabilizers. There are two related questions. First, did this situation call for a big fiscal stimulus to offset the consequences for aggregate GDP of the required structural adjustments?

Second, was the stimulus spending likely to be designed with the benefits exceeding the long run costs?

There is no evidence that the Administration ever considered the first question, accepting the implicit Keynesian assumption that this was a normal business cycle with insufficient demand due to the housing bust that government spending could cushion or off-set. All Keynesian macro models show some short term impact on GDP: there is little political demand for advisors or models that predict otherwise. It appears that the Obama Administration chose advisors with the biggest multipliers, well out of the mainstream for these conditions (Rickards, 184-188).

With respect to the second question, Keynes's famously dismissed concerns with the long run consequences of his policies, e.g., government debt, arguing that by then we are all dead (he died soon thereafter at age 63). More seriously, the implicit assumption is that the debt burden can be inflated away without significant worrisome long term consequences. In Keynes defense, he also warned against being the "slave of some defunct economist".

The fiscal policy stimulus of the Obama Administration was led by his National Economic Council head Larry Summers and Council of Economic Advisors Chairman Christine Romer and the monetary policy stimulus was led by his Fed Chairman Ben Bernanke, the latter two both renowned experts on the Great Depression, but apparently with a much different interpretation of its causes than that of the Austrian economist Murray Rothbard, and hence a different interventionist prescription. Larry Summers was a neo-Keynesian, following in his uncle's footsteps: Paul Samuelson famously (and erroneously) predicted that postwar cuts in government would mean "the greatest period of unemployment and industrial dislocation which any economy has ever faced."[284]

Appearing in late 2008 at a Joint Economic Committee hearing several months before becoming Obama's top economic advisor, Larry Summers testified that the economy needed immediate fiscal stimulus that should be timely, targeted (to lower income), and temporary (presumably to avoid moral hazard and government crowding out). Summers didn't include "productive" on his list of requirements, the Keynesian assumption behind the recommended policy of paying people to "dig a ditch and fill it back in" being that they would otherwise be idle and the effect would be temporary in any event, and it would lead to multiplier effects.[285] To be timely, the stimulus plan was initially billed as an investment in "shovel-ready" projects, invoking the Khruschev metaphor relating to the quantity and cost of output rather than value. That problem is inherent in the political allocation of resources and often ignored when a short run stimulus to total spending is the objective.

At the time the stimulus bill passed, the focus was on public infrastructure. The American Society of Civil Engineers gave America's infrastructure a grade of D, i.e., either functionally obsolete or structurally deficient. Public infrastructure investments in the US were historically the most carefully designed to be productive (although corruption was often rampant, e.g., Boston's "Big Dig").

But that begs the question, why hadn't these needed repairs and upgrades to public infrastructure long since been funded? It was not for lack of resources. As the size of government grew, the quality of public infrastructure - arguably the most important state and local government responsibility - declined from state of the art a half century ago to its current eroded condition. A similar problem occurred in other public sectors such as public schools. The reason is that money is fungible, especially in government. That is, tracking the flow of specific revenues and expenditures doesn't reveal what is being funded. Some governments actually stole infrastructure funds from special trust funds designated exclusively for that purpose. But the far bigger problem was that general revenues were diverted from traditional infrastructure investments to pay for other things, mostly rising labor costs, which had approximately doubled relative to their historical relationship to private labor compensation costs even as public employment continued to expand.

There was another complicating factor to the second question, the conflict between the goals of counter-cyclical fiscal stimulus and those of the secular transformative agenda. The President was correct that the transformative agenda would create millions of new jobs, but critics were also correct that this was also by design a job-killing agenda, eliminating millions of jobs in the "transformed" sectors. Real GDP would rise not due to increasing productivity as traditionally measured but to the increasing costs of meeting political goals, which implied *ceteris paribus* a decline in aggregate real wages. Hence real wages could only be raised for some, e.g., those subsidized green jobs, at the expense of others. The transformation could generate high paying – not necessarily highly productive - jobs in health care, green energy and among public sector regulators, but not enough to exceed the jobs destroyed.

That's the context in which the Obama Administration pursued the fiscal stimulus to "jolt" the economy and "jump-start" a recovery from the 2007 to early 2009 recession. President Obama recognized the conflicts between the goals of Keynesian stimulus and the transformative agenda, but still chose to proceed with both simultaneously.[286] The magnitude of fiscal stimulus rivaled Hoover's massive increase in federal deficit spending in relative terms.

But the TARP auto bailout already under way should have been a red flag that the transformative agenda would come first and political constituents would be at the forefront in the design of any spending package. Creating the maximum number of net new jobs at market-clearing wage rates to buoy consumption, for example, conflicted directly with the "transformative" agenda of supporting high paying and where possible union jobs, especially those in the public sector. The 2009 Stimulus Bill kept under a trillion dollars for political palatability was crafted by democratic congressional leaders in about two weeks with the demands of its constituents in mind. At republican insistence the stimulus included some tax cuts intended to stimulate private investment expenditures as the decline in aggregate output was entirely due to the decline in private investment (Hall, pp. 3-4).

In the end only 10% of stimulus funds were actually allocated for public infrastructure and most of that went for maintenance. Construction was cut from the plan for not being sufficiently female, although most of the job losses to that point were disproportionally male.[287] The stimulus was directed to *socially desirable* investments, particularly those that were "green." "Cash for Clunkers" for example was originally proposed as a green "public policy trifecta" by former Fed vice chairman Alan Blinder to stimulate the economy, improve the environment and help the poor.[288] He was correct in a way as it was a trifecta. It helped the poor in the same way as seeding a hurricane devastates squatter camps, destroying cheaper old cars and causing the used car price to skyrocket. "Yuppies" bought newly produced cars, but mostly trucks and SUVs manufactured in polluting plants. Some vehicles were produced domestically, but many were partly or totally produced in foreign countries. Parenthetically, it worked out well for those people owning a first or more likely a second home in a golf course estate who received a tax credit for their golf cart, making it virtually free at US taxpayer expense.

In theory higher employee costs means fewer jobs, so, for example, FDR's public works programs paid a fraction of Davis Bacon wages to generate more jobs. But the Obama Administration high wage policy was – following Hoover - imposed across the board to the entire labor market. At the low end the minimum wage was raised three times from 2007-2011. At the high end, the stimulus funds were directed toward largely unionized public sector work force. Funds were distributed to the private sector without suspending high Davis Bacon or PLA wage requirements, for example. In 2013 it was supportive of the union sponsored initiative to more than double the wages paid at fast food chains.

In addition, unlike in the Depression, the high wage policy was complemented by extending unemployment benefits and the welfare state, linking aid to not working. Other methods were employed to reduce labor force participation such as increasing subsidized student loans to encourage a return to school. According to a recent article by economist Arthur Laffer the value of subsidies for a single mother of two is $45,000 annually and the implicit marginal tax rate kicks in at $9000 and rises to 67% at $14,000 and 100% at $29000 of before tax earnings.[289]

In fact there were only two requirements for stimulus spending. First, could the spending be linked however tenuously to labor compensation, hence a reported job "saved or created" however temporary or productive? Second, was the object of such spending arguably sufficiently productive to avoid political embarrassment? Not all of it was a total waste, but the return will likely be well below the average soviet return on investment (around -4% to -8% real according to World Bank and IMF estimates). But much of this came at the expense of more productive jobs, even in the short term (Rickards, p. 188).

In reality the Obama Administration "transformative" policies weren't all that new, mirroring those of the Great Depression. Policies universally supported increased wages and reductions in the labor supply; the depth and breadth of anti-business regulations and the promise of more such regulation to come mirrored those of Hoover and FDR; support for free trade was replaced with protectionist rhetoric and practice, and; credit was allocated through government directed finance to "socially desirable" investments in people and business.

The stimulus added to total economic *spending* on GDP, which was one short term political goal. It lowered the unemployment *rate,* another short term political goal. And it could take credit for saving or creating the high paying jobs directly linked to it. But the rise in nominal GDP didn't necessarily reflect greater value, only the higher cost of doing business and at the end of the first Obama term the combined net result of the stimulus and other "transformative" labor policies was *fewer* people employed and those that were employed earned *less* than they did four years before. The overall effect on employment was what economic theory would predict. About half of the precipitous drop in labor force participation and hours worked from 2007-2011 – the largest contraction since the Great Depression - has been tied to income transfers for not working.[290] The rest can be attributed to the high wage policy as business expansion substituted capital for high cost labor.

Whatever the political explanation, the result was the same: competitive markets were replaced by crony capitalism. Former VP and democratic presidential candidate turned green energy lobbyist Al

Gore earned $100 million lobbying the Obama Administration for green energy subsidies.[291] (This was followed almost immediately with another "Gory" $100 million payday for the sale of a TV station to Al Jezerra, valued based on his political clout.[292]) Political preferences replaced the revealed preferences of households in the marketplace. On the one hand, that's the prerogative of a democracy. On the other, it doesn't appear to have been an informed choice on the public's part: when gas prices doubled – an explicit transformative green energy goal – the political response was not to explain why they should be "happy" to pay higher gas prices to fund green energy, but to blame oil companies for price gouging and profiteering.

The political response was a federally funded initiative started in 2012 for the US to adopt the approach of Bhutan - not coincidentally one of the poorest countries on earth – to measuring Gross National Happiness.[293] The results may not be as welfare state proponents expect: in a study done in 2003 by the OECD when the European welfare state was at its peak 57% of Americans reported being "very satisfied with their life" whereas only 14% to 17% of the respondents in France, Germany and Italy responded that way (Meltzer, p. 26). But it would presumably eliminate Blinders enthusiasm for destroying the capital stock, i.e., cash for clunkers.

The Dodd-Frank bill was clearly transformative for the financial sector. It made all the root causes potentially worse. During the first term, the Obama transformative agenda also studiously avoided transforming Fannie Mae and Freddie Mac, reducing their portfolio somewhat but only by expanding their guarantee program even more.[294]

The stimulus bill partially offset some of the negative consequences of the "transformative" agenda on labor markets in the short run, but that doesn't mean it was better than doing nothing. Carmen Reinhart and Kenneth Rogoff *This Time is Different* (2009) argued that financial crises originate with excessive debt financing public spending. The sub-prime crisis of the last decade certainly fits that description with F&F considered public. Moreover, Michael Lewis in *Boomerang* 2011 relates a discussion with Kenneth Rogoff on the US fiscal deficit subsequent to the end of his data base in 2007, indicating that as a consequence of the monetary and fiscal policies in the aftermath of the sub-prime crisis the US is near the point of fiscal crisis (Lewis, p. xii). Reinhart and Rogoff, in their subsequent 2011 study "Growth in a Time of Debt," found that from 1790 to 2009, once a developed or developing country – including the U.S. – exceeded a 90% debt-to-GDP ratio, economic growth slowed by nearly 2% annually for nearly a decade with accelerating inflation. The stimulus put the U.S. ratio above 100%. This time isn't any different.

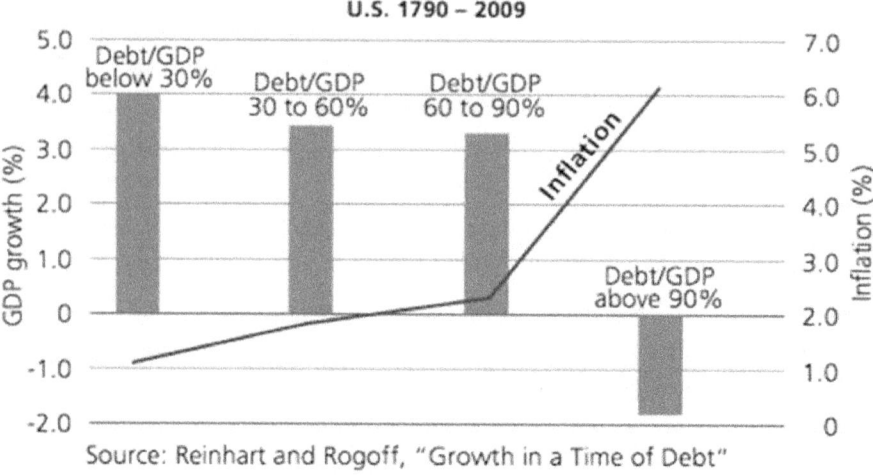

Chart 1

This led the credit rating agencies – previously excoriated by the Obama Administration for overly optimistic ratings on mortgage securities – to downgrade US Treasury securities. Upon the second downgrade, the government responded by suspending a lesser known rating agency for 18 months for what were characterized as "filling out forms wrong," sending a signal to the others that their franchise value would be eliminated if they didn't play along.[295] This was quickly followed by a massive suit against S&P brought in February 2003 alleging securities fraud rating PLS almost a decade prior. Moodies, which was considered equally "optimistic" rating PLS but didn't downgrade US Treasury securities, was not sued.[296]

The Keynesian interpretation of why the economic recovery didn't occur is much different. In his article "Why Does the Economy Fall to Pieces after a Financial Crisis?" (2010) Robert Hall of Stanford blames the continuing economic distress on "financial market frictions." This seems unlikely in the wake of the Fed's massive financial system rescue of institutions, instruments and markets and ongoing Fed efforts. Lack of demand due to continued fear and uncertainty is the more likely culprit. In 2011 former Fed Chairman and macroeconomic expert Alan Greenspan noted that by his measure business's willingness to re-invest free cash flow into their business had fallen to its lowest peacetime level since the tail end of the Great Depression, attributing this lack of demand to increased risk due to "government activism."[297]

3. A National Infrastructure Bank, Once Again

President Obama's Labor Day infrastructure initiative in the fall of 2010 combined some appealing business tax proposals with a national infrastructure bank. This proposal languished, but shortly after the Economist magazine reported that bank fines related to the financial crisis would soon top $100 billion, former President Bill Clinton recommended that the bank fines be used to fund a permanent infrastructure bank.[298]

The first proposal for an infrastructure bank at the Bretton Woods meetings in 1944 by the senior American Treasury official Harry Dexter White - formally the International Bank for Reconstruction and Development – was further developed by his British counterpart John Maynard Keynes whose main interest was in lending to governments to expand the public sector.[299] But Keynes argued that the proposed "World Bank" as it came to be called was really a fund whereas the proposed International Monetary Fund was really a (central) bank. There is more than nomenclature at issue here. Banks have a fiduciary responsibility to get repaid with interest whereas "funds" may invest or give grants. What White – a communist and top Russian spy during WWII – had in mind for the World Bank was primarily funding postwar Soviet reconstruction.

That was no doubt necessary then, as are additional US public infrastructure investments today. The issue is whether this is a good way to raise and spend public money.

Clinton's recommendation reflects his political genius. Democrats and the Obama Administration have long supported public infrastructure investments as an economic stimulus, and former Obama Administration advisor Larry Summers has recently proposed ignoring the deficit in the short run in favor of greater public spending on infrastructure.[300] Republicans have generally been supportive, particularly recently as a way to stimulate jobs.

The problem is the lack of accountability in the prioritization and procurement of public investment projects due to conflicts between economic and political objectives. This was anticipated by Keynes's American critics, who saw the World Bank as a form of "economic imperialism" in spite of his assurances that it would only lend at a penalty rate of interest to avoid competing with private lenders. In practice, the World Bank lends at deeply subsidized rates and more often than not repays itself by making additional loans financed by government (primarily US) backed borrowing.

Politics already often trumps economics in the US, as with the California bullet train to nowhere. The Obama Administration continues to withhold approval for the private $5 billion Keystone Pipeline in deference to environmentalists. Job stimulus is more political than economic and entirely malleable, e.g., the President now personally claims the pipeline will only create 50 jobs, about what the Administration claims for each new food stamp recipient. When politicians do "create" jobs, they usually seek to maximize labor cost, requiring union representation, Davis Bacon wages and/or project labor agreements. The current deterioration of the nation's public infrastructure is more a reflection of the diversion of taxes - even dedicated trust fund revenues - by state and local governments from capital to labor than an insufficient revenue base.

The proposed funding source is even more problematic. Inexplicable tort settlements (well, extortion is the most plausible explanation) are to be the permanent funding source of an infrastructure bank?

The World Bank may be the most politically perfect, i.e., the least accountable government institution ever created. Hence an appropriate formal name for the proposed infrastructure bank is the National Bank for Reconstruction and Development and former President Clinton is the ideal choice to be its first president.

4. Monetary policy: the Handmaiden of Fiscal Policy

The Fed was the primary tool in all three prongs of the Administration's program. It bailed out financial institutions. It bailed out the housing and stock markets. And it financed the federal government's fiscal stimulus and then some. The Fed targeted effective demand in a variety of ways.

First, real interest rates have remained negative, the Fed Funds target rate has remained at or near zero since 2008 and the Fed announced in September 2012 and again a year later that it would remain there for the foreseeable future. This makes marginal projects feasible and attractive, but through year end 2013, almost five years after the recession officially ended, business investment still failed to respond.

Second, the Fed attempted to stimulate household spending. Regardless of what bonds the Fed purchased, the first goal was to inflate stock prices (and other assets including bonds and real estate) to generate a 'wealth effect," e.g., to make households feel wealthier than they really are so that they would spend more. Most agree that the Fed has been successful in temporarily keeping stocks inflated, some by as much as 25%-50%.[301] A 2011 study found the wealth effect to be insignificant. There is no effect for incomes below $130,000, and a barely measurable effect of .004 of the rise in wealth above that.[302]

This is the same wealth effect the Fed and GSEs created during the sub-prime lending debacle by inflating house prices. How well did it work for households? The Fed policies to discourage household savings were complemented by the secular increase in federal entitlements: households were entitled to mortgages with little or no down-payment, retirement payments and medical care without saving. Household savings rates fell from about 12 percent of GDP historically to almost zero during the last decade, most likely as a long run consequence of such policies (discussed at greater length in the next chapter).

The Fed release in June 2012 showed a 38% decline in the median net worth of US households from 2007 through 2010 from $126,000 to only $77,300, a level last seen in real terms in 1992. This was mostly due to a partial deflating of the house price bubble, which affected the median household more than the mean as the rich had alternative assets. But that understates the problem in several key ways. First, it doesn't count the household share of existing federal liabilities of $140,000 per household to pay past debts. Economists typically don't deduct this on the strange theory that "we owe it to ourselves" and hence can default, little consolation to the mean household who is now broke. This exclusion doesn't apply to foreigners in any event. The share that is owed to foreigners that grew in constant dollars from only $6 thousand in 1992 to almost $50 thousand per household in 2010.

Second, while their remaining financial assets were valued at a 5% real interest rate in 1992. The Fed-induced asset bubble generates no real interest, indicating a much lower real value at the historical rate of return. According to the Flow of Funds data of the Fed, households hold over $8 trillion in non-checking certificates of deposits. Assuming that the real rate of interest offered was about 4% instead of the current rate of about zero, that's $40 billion in interest payments annually. In a paper done almost four decades ago, the author calculated the incidence of this implicit tax on depositors.[303] The rich have numerous alternatives to deposits and the poor don't have much savings, so this "tax" falls mostly on the middle class. Those who still have savings living off the interest and dividends – mostly the fixed income elderly - suffered the most from the Fed's subsequent long term zero interest rate policy. Holders of long term debt instruments are at much greater risk as inflation will lock them in to even lower real yields and can render their investments virtually worthless.

About 75% of the lost wealth in the Fed survey related to lost homeowner equity. But house prices had only receded back to about their 2003 level by 2010, still well above their historical norm. Hence the median American household was almost broke and deeply indebted (and to make matters worse with a one in five chance of being un-or-under employed). This is all the more ironic as the central bank mission has historically been promoted as "mobilizing savings" (Mayer, p.58).The rest of the regression appears to be because while aggregate household saving only trended toward zero during this period, the median household was not saving, but was in fact going deeper into debt. The mean household wealth fell only half as much as the median, an indication that higher net worth households continued to save and invest, but-non pension aggregate household saving has been negative since the mid-1980s in the US (see chapter 6, Exhibit 3). That may explain why inflated stock prices don't seem to be having the desired effect on household consumption they once did.

The Fed's monetary policy efforts arguably were single mindedly pursuing full employment from 2000 on, and the Fed has promised to continue doing so through 2015. Unarguable is that the growth in the monetary base is unprecedented, to compensate for an equally unprecedented drop in the velocity of money since the Great Depression. The Fed grew its balance sheet by roughly $4 trillion during the first five years of the first term Obama, on average financing about half and in 2011 and 2012 more than three fourths of the Obama administration deficits.

Rickards (2011, p.182) summarizes: "Here was Bernanke's entire playbook – keep interest rates at zero, devalue the dollar by quantitative easing and manipulate opinion to create fear of inflation…America had become a nation of guinea pigs in a grand monetary experiment, cooked up in the Petri dish of the Princeton economics department" (with Paul Krugman and Alan Blinder).

This raises four fundamental questions: First, why did the Bernanke Fed pursue such policies, beginning in 2000? Second, why were these massive unprecedented Fed interventions such a macroeconomic failure? Third, having bailed out the financial system and funded the deficit, why isn't the Fed – a private bank-owned entity – bankrupt? Fourth, why didn't inflation accelerate and the dollar plummet on the global market?

The answer to the first question goes back to chairman Bernanke's explanation of the sub-prime lending debacle as fueled by a global savings glut, i.e., the Chinese using the proceeds of a trade surplus to invest in dollar financial assets instead of goods. Whether the Yuan was undervalued or the dollar overvalued is a matter of perspective. Moreover, the "beggar thy neighbor" political choice of dollar devaluation is a political expedient to the much less politically attractive policies of increasing productivity and reducing real wages to increase exports.

The financial institution bailout worked less effectively than otherwise due to the efforts to cover-up the real purpose of filling a solvency hole. The macroeconomic stimulus can't overcome fear with Obama Administration policies depressing money velocity and investment. Even Fed Chairman Bernanke recently argued that monetary policy couldn't compensate for "fiscal and regulatory uncertainties," essentially agreeing with his predecessor.[304]

The Fed *is* bankrupt, solvent only under government accounting rules: it doesn't mark to market so the portfolio losses are postponed. The Fed, like the GSEs, went for broke then went broke. It has no cost of funds, and in 2010 the Fed suspended payments to Treasury indefinitely, allowing it to use the retained earnings to cover losses as they occur. This is similar to the GSE subsidies, but even more opaque.

The fourth answer is a bit more complicated. Some analysts argue that changes in definitions are masking a mild inflation that is being under-reported. Others forecast inflation reaching 100% within a few years.[305] The Fed has done nothing to allay long run inflation fears and its actions are certainly scary. International dollar investors – most pointedly the Chinese – don't want the dollar exchange rate to fall, but foreigners are already reducing their US debt exposure and shortening maturities so they can exit even faster.[306] We are in the illusionary period is when money is first distributed and interest rates stay low. The price of nominally denominated assets stays high, and commodity prices rise in response to the inflationary policy, particularly due to Chinese demand as a substitute for Treasury securities. US farmland is at a similar historic peak. Hoisington Investment Management attributes the rise in commodity prices to the Fed's quantitative easing and the failure of aggregate demand to expand to this rise in commodity prices.[307]

This situation is extremely unstable. The Fed has been paying interest on excess bank reserves held at the Fed, essentially bribing them not to lend. If they do, the money supply would expand (due to fractional reserve banking) and inflation could quickly get out of control. Normally bond markets would have responded by now to the inflation threat. The foreigners that helped fund the sub-prime lending debacle mostly got paid back, and those that funded part of the stimulus want to be repaid with positive real interest in the long run as well. If and when they demand this the interest on the federal debt due to the rising inflation premium would quickly absorb a significant share of federal revenues, leading to a debt spiral. The rising mortgage rate could produce another wave of homeowner defaults sufficient to again threaten the financial system. Rather than withdraw reserves, the Fed may be forced to flirt with hyperinflation.[308] This doesn't sound like a risk worth taking for taxpayers, but may make short term sense to term-limited politicians and public servants.

The Treasury can still sell securities because the dollar remains the world's reserve currency, the euro is in trouble and the last thing EU leaders want is a rising currency against the dollar, and the Chinese continue to pursue a cheap Yuan policy.

Can the Fed avoid inflation? Not all Fed officials think so. Richard Fisher, President of the Dallas Federal Reserve, recently stated:

"It will come as no surprise to those who know me that I did not argue in favor of additional monetary accommodation during our meetings last week. I have repeatedly made it clear, in internal FOMC deliberations and in public speeches, that I believe that with each program we undertake to venture further in that direction, we are sailing deeper into uncharted waters. We are blessed at the Fed with sophisticated econometric models and superb analysts. We can easily conjure up plausible theories as to what we will do when it comes to our next tack or eventually reversing course. The truth, however, is that nobody on the committee, nor on our staffs at the Board of Governors and the 12 Banks, really knows what is holding back the economy. Nobody really knows what will work to get the economy back on course. And nobody – in fact, no central bank anywhere on the planet – has the experience of successfully navigating a return home from the place in which w e now find ourselves. No central bank – not, at least, the Federal Reserve – has ever been on this cruise before."[309]

F. An Austrian Approach to the Aftermath

The long term secular threats to the US economy are arguably much worse today than they were four years ago. Thirty years of labor force participation has been reversed. Un-and-under-employment is at a post-WW II high. The monetary and fiscal policies employed represented another dose of the same Fed easy money and politically directed credit elixir that caused such a painful withdrawal in the home mortgage market and housing sector in the first place. The Financial markets remain addicted to the Fed's support. Political risk in mortgage lending has reached and arguably exceeded Great Depression heights. Lenders remain uncertain of the application of the rule of law. The housing market is now totally reliant on the GSEs. Household wealth has been devastated and households are broke when considering just the debt owned to foreigners. Even most of the intended beneficiaries of political housing policy are worse off for the experience. They have been made dependent on political promises of entitlements that can't be kept.

It is not unreasonable to ask if this was the best we could do. If government wishes to see a depression ended as quickly as possible, and the economy returned to normal prosperity, what course should it adopt? As an alternative to his description of what politicians *would* do, what did the Austrian Rothbard recommend they *should* do? "The first and clearest injunction is: *don't interfere with the market's adjustment process*" (emphasis is in the original, p. 14). Would this have worked better? Would this have been less "fair"?

1. The Austrian Prescription

Rothbard clearly agrees with Treasury Secretary Mellon's prescription for the Great Depression described above and would have recommended that prescription in the wake of the sub-prime lending debacle as well.

After the 2012 elections, a panel of top economists criticized the Obama Administration for not eliminating the overhang of mortgage debt – negative borrower equity – much more rapidly. Several former Obama economic advisors agreed, arguing that the Administration should have been much more aggressive with principal reduction, i.e., borrower debt forgiveness. Having the banks pay isn't what Mellon had in mind. His purpose in liquidating real estate was to weed out the weak banks, recapitalizing the financial system much earlier. Real estate *was* liquidated during the Great Depression, albeit at a slower pace due to the forbearance efforts of the HOLC and the political and judicial delays previously discussed.

This could also have worked for the Great Recession. Conceivably, had foreclosures proceeded at their historical pace with maximum political and judicial encouragement, the amount of foreclosures through 2012 would have been achieved several years earlier, potentially by the end of 2010. How might that have changed things? House prices would have reached their bottom that much sooner, facilitating a return to normalcy in real estate brokerage and mortgage lending that much sooner and fostering greater household mobility. How do we know this? Because that's what eventually happened in the non-judicial foreclosure states where foreclosure was much faster, and this didn't happen elsewhere.[310] The homeownership rate would have fallen that much quicker, as houses were purchased by limited partnerships and converted to rental that much earlier. But housing production would not have been accelerated any sooner as the inventory overhang would have remained.

This would have accelerated bank losses and hence failed bank resolution. The major obstacle to raising new bank capital was the political bank bashing rhetoric and practice, as Dodd-Frank punished banks (and other financial institutions) and created uncertainty regarding future profitability. Assuming that hurdle was overcome – by compensating banks for losses where appropriate - Hall's "frictions" in the financial system to the extent they were real could have been lubricated much earlier. The more rapid adjustment in the real estate and banking sector would have had numerous benefits. But would avoiding the Great Recession been one of them?

Mellon's recommended "liquidation" took longer than necessary, but did eventually occur. The Depression didn't end. While Keynesians focus on the frictions in the supply of credit by the financial system, conservatives focus on the reluctance of business to invest. Eliminating Hall's "frictions" earlier would have been beneficial in several ways, but in our view would not have improved the demand for private capital spending, the only component to fall in the Great Recession, which has yet to recover.

In fact, proponents of publically financed principal reduction weren't advocating a faster recapitalization of the financial system or a recovery in capital spending. Their goal was to boost the consumer spending of homeowners with negative equity, the same goal as the Fed pursued through other means by maintaining the illusion of equity by inflating house prices. This is just another version of "stimulus" taxing savers to reward spenders in the name of Keynesian multipliers. Treasury Secretary Geitner's only lament was that wide-scale principal reduction – which would have in many cases exceeded the limit of bank equity and debt and hence been financed by taxpayers - was politically impossible.[311]

These Keynesian policies have not yet worked this time, and their track record in the US economy is mixed, but doing nothing goes against the political impulse. Most academic macro-economists still reject Austrian laissez faire policies in favor of Keynesian intervention. We note that the goal of most academic macro-economists – the vast majority of who work at public institutions – is to advise politicians. The demand for advisors who advise that politicians are more likely the problem than the solution for financial and economic distress is generally limited to libertarians and a few republicans.

Economists turned businessman (e.g., John A. Allison) or political reformers are more likely to favor a less interventionist or "activist" government role.

Whether an Austrian policy of benign neglect would have worked better is a hypothetical question, but Polish economist Leszek Balcerowicz who grew up under Soviet domination in Poland and hence was not steeped in US Keynesian economics believes it would have for the reasons we discussed here. As a crisis manager Balcerowicz has few peers. When communism fell in Europe, he pioneered "shock therapy" to build a free market while avoiding hyper-inflation. In the late 1990s, he included a debt ceiling into his country's constitution, handcuffing free spending politicians. As the Polish central-bank governor from 2001 to 2007 he pursued tight money policies that avoided a credit boom and bust.[312] As a result, Poland largely avoided the troubles plaguing the rest of Europe, which with the exception of Germany has pursued loose monetary and fiscal policies.

2. Is Austrian Laissez Faire Unfair?

Why do virtually all economists reject the Austrian analysis and laissez faire policy prescription? Goldberg (2012, p. 83) explains that the opposition of most American economists to a policy prescription of benign neglect is historically rooted in a concern that it is "unfair" or worse:

"Richard Ely, the leader of the University of Wisconsin progressives during their heyday and founder of the American Economics Association…was the foremost lay leader of what was called the "Christian socialism" or "Christian sociology movement." "…that rejected laissez faire economics as sinful and cruel."

That unfairly miss-characterizes the laissez faire ideology. Austrians support competitive markets, but dispute how best to provide them. They don't necessarily reject transparent public cyclical or secular protection and/or subsidies, but only within limits sufficient to mitigate moral hazard and other incentive distortions. The main conclusion of the prior chapters is that the distortions were bigger, more pervasive and came earlier than proponents of a bigger public role generally recognize.

A key requirement for the credit-financed goal of a 65% and subsequently a 70% homeownership rate was that in the event of default the house was repossessed. This requirement is no less fair in a recession than a boom. None of the individual homeowner bailouts can be justified on grounds of fairness. The social safety net for such people isn't motivated by fairness but empathy and compassion as well as social stability.

The political housing policy was not fair to taxpayers, consumers or savers, costing them trillions of dollars. It often was not fair to the intended beneficiaries who were stuck with mortgages greater than the value of their house. The policies in the aftermath were more of the same. It is impossible to determine the net incidence of the costs and benefits of housing policy, any more than it is to determine the same for any of the other opaque income redistribution policies implemented in the name of social justice, and it is certainly not possible to identify the net effect of all these policies cumulatively. Not surprisingly, losses of this magnitude are not likely to be distributed evenly, fairly or transparently.

What is certain is that the policy-induced housing boom and the subsequent bust represented a dramatic redistribution of income and wealth. In the US, income redistribution generally penalizes savings: e.g., during the sub-prime crisis those who made the largest cash down payments at the peak of the house price bubble lost the most in the crash. In addition socially directed credit allocation resulted in a reduction of aggregate national wealth by discouraging savings and directing it to less productive – hence less valuable – investments. The net financial losses of trillions of dollars fell largely on savers and taxpayers – two largely overlapping cohorts.

But political wealth redistribution and destruction doesn't necessarily favor the less politically powerful poor. The indirect costs of recession generated by the housing market crash fell on the un- and-under employed. As noted above, the Fed's prior policies have wiped out the wealth of the median household. Dylan Grice of Societe Generale attributes the current political angst to the inevitable currency debasement and resulting prospective erosion of what wealth still remains.[313]

We are unaware of any economic argument that the massive wealth re-distribution and reduction caused by housing policy complemented with regulatory malfeasance that led to the sub-prime lending debacle was "fair." Similarly, the bailout was not motivated by fairness and there was much that was unfair about it. Whether an Austrian response to the Great Recession – a sharper downturn and quicker rebound - would have been any less "fair" is also debatable. The consequences of continued wealth destruction won't be fair to many. Fairness is a red herring justifying bad policy to cover up prior bad policy.

Chapter 6: the Long Run Policy Prescription

The need to align incentives should be clear from our analysis of the sub-prime lending debacle. But how do we create the right incentives for financial firms? In three words: require sufficient capital.

Two years prior to the FCIC Report and a year before Dodd Frank, Jacobo Carmassi, Daniel Gros and Stefano Micossi wrote the following abstract for their article "The Global Financial Crisis: Causes and Cures" (2009):

> "The massive financial instability of 2007–08 was, in the main, the result of monetary policy. Regulation compounded this error by allowing excessive leverage and maturity transformation by banks. Innovation did contribute to reckless credit expansion and investments, but without lax money and excessive leverage, reckless bets on asset price increases would not have been possible.
>
> Therefore, a repeat of this instability could be avoided by correcting these two policy faults There is no need for intrusive rules constraining non-bank intermediaries and financial innovation. The main message is: *keep it simple*." (Emphasis added)."

In his recent book *Act of Congress* (2013), Robert Kaiser lauds Dodd-Frank as a political masterpiece. It is the opposite of simple, the most complicated financial legislation in world history. Remarkably, it does virtually nothing to prevent excessive credit expansion or leverage. Hence it is not at all surprising that economist Ed Kane, the dean of financial regulatory critics, calls Dodd-Frank "An exercise in denial and cover-up" (2011). A simple policy blueprint may not be a political masterpiece or even politically viable – my task is to present policies to help us avoid repeating our past failures.

The reduction or elimination of monetary policy discretion would help us avoid credit bubbles. Separating subsidy from finances would limit housing bubbles, We can reduce moral hazard and avoid financial crises by raising capital requirements and eliminating regulatory arbitrage, scaling back and restructuring deposit insurance to alter the incentives that arise from a depositor safety net, enacting capital market regulations that apply capital requirements consistently and promote more efficient markets, eliminating TBTF crony capitalism while promoting competition and market discipline, and restoring traditional down payment requirements on mortgage loans.

Did past regulation fail? In the most comprehensive book-length critique of the US regulatory system to date, Barth, Caprio and Levine's (BCL) Guardians of Finance (2012) attributes the systemic financial crisis to "a colossal failure of regulation."[314] If anything, this understates the problem with regulation. The failure was not only colossal, but also chronic. Regulators not only "allowed" bad lending, but in many ways induced it. This regulatory fix would *de facto* eliminate binding housing quotas, regardless of one's view regarding their relative contribution to the past crisis.

In their broad historical study of *Why Nations Fail*, Acemoglu and Robinson (2012) find that a centralized political authority is a key to why nations succeed, as an enabler of markets and growth. This is entirely consistent with the exceptions to the Founder's limits on centralized powers and with our finding regarding the initial rationale for the extension of powers and introduction of federal enterprises over the past century, to facilitate commerce in financial securities.

Why nations fail is that such centralization of power ultimately leads to a crony capitalist system of rent-seeking that favors politicians and the political elite - generally including economic advisors - at the expense of the public, such as the one described here. Unfortunately there are no good historical examples of politicians and bureaucrats voluntarily ceding political power. Bureaucrats face strong incentives to avoid reform of their own institutions that would limit their power and politicians will not require reform and accountability or reform their own political oversight structures until the voting public demands reform.

Despite the massive government efforts to sway public opinion, voters generally distrust the cycle of political intervention, political failure, political cover up, and policy doubling down but have thus far been powerless to stop it. What is needed to reform the system is a clear political agenda, but voters need to be careful what they wish for. A desire to avoid systemic crises is appropriate and justified but a complete financial safety reduces economic efficiency and promotes stagnation. Some stability may be desirable, but complete stability is the source of the problem, not the solution. Balancing on this line is both politically and economically difficult, if not impossible, for politicians and bureaucrats. Because of this, only well-functioning markets have historically discovered the best balance between stability and efficiency. It is not in spite of but because of the process of creative destruction and the liquidation of existing firms that markets can produce this balance. This holds true across all firms, including public enterprises and agencies.

It is a political illusion to believe that the US can go back to the housing finance system of the last three decades of the twentieth century, enjoying the benefits but this time without the costs. To pursue it would be delusional. To do so while expanding public contingent liabilities would be more so, with extremely unfortunate consequences. Restoring household savings incentives is the new *sine qua non* of US housing finance.

It is time to seriously consider scaling back or eliminating the institutions that precipitated this crisis. As we approach HUD's 50th anniversary, its future role – particularly in supporting home ownership through housing finance - should at a minimum be limited. The 100th anniversary of the Fed is an appropriate time to have a serious debate about its future role and accountability. So long as federal deposit insurance persists, what's needed is not more but better regulation, which requires that political and regulatory incentives and accountability are re-aligned to the public interest while being scaled back to a manageable level. Greater reliance on market discipline is required to mitigate systemic risk. Fixing mortgage capital markets without anesthetizing them with federal guarantees is part of this solution.

The results of these simple but politically problematic reforms will be disappointing unless domestic savings – not more Fed money creation – is restored and allocated by markets – not politicians. After all, economic growth enabled households to achieve the American dream of home ownership, not political promises.

A. Are There Lessons from Mortgage Finance Systems in Other Developed Countries?

Before the US housing finance system crashed, the issue was whether other countries should adopt the US hybrid model.[315] Now the issue is what the US can learn from the experience of other countries.

The work by Hendershott and Villani (1983) previously cited described how the US housing finance system developed entirely in response to US laws, regulations and taxes. The same is likely true of other developed countries, so it is not surprising that financial sector housing policy is somewhat unique to each. But what can we learn from others about repairing the US housing finance system?

Regulation did not eliminate housing cycles or housing price bubbles, but it did moderate them. Regulation also did not eliminate the occasional solvency crisis, although these were similarly moderated. Some countries are reviewing and reforming their regulatory environment in the wake of the sub-prime lending debacle, but it is clear that the balance between market and regulatory discipline generally worked better elsewhere.

Several comparative studies, e.g., Lea (2011) and Bardhan, Edelstein and Kroll (2012) in the aftermath of the sub-prime lending debacle note striking differences between the US and virtually all other developed housing finance systems. They find that the role of the GSEs and government insurance was much greater and regulation was much worse in the United States; the US had easier lending terms and required less household saving; the US had a wider range of mortgage instruments, with much greater reliance on fixed rate mortgages, and; the ability to deduct mortgage interest paid from taxable income is extremely rare.

1. Deposit versus Capital Markets: Regulation

The relative balance of deposit and capital market funding generally varies by the financial depth and relative age of a country's population, as retirement savings generally flow toward capital markets. The UK and other countries that inherited the British System still largely rely on deposit-funding (as did the US prior to the rise of the GSEs) and lenders hold mortgages on their balance sheet rather than sell them. The Northern European capital market covered bond model is also a retail bank model as all issuers are regulated banks, i.e., commercial, savings, cooperative or mortgage. The market share of mortgage banks – more comparable to finance companies in the US – has been declining in favor of more diversified issuers. Unlike US securitization, all covered bonds are accounted for as a financing with recourse to the issuer, which is regulated and well capitalized. The Danish system is distinct in that it issues a bond in a series for each mortgage, facilitating the borrower's re-purchase of their own mortgage. This effectively allows borrows to cancel their own mortgage by paying it off below par when rates fall.

Only Canada has a system akin to FHA and Ginnie Mae with issuers issuing federally guaranteed pools of government insured mortgage loans, although Japan has a somewhat similar system of guaranteed securities. But there is nothing comparable to the public/private Fannie Mae and Freddie Mac, and there is no conflict between housing goals and prudential regulation in the Canadian system. Canadian regulation and supervision is part of a unified regulatory structure unrelated to any housing agency. All of these countries with a market economy have a single regulator held politically accountable only for maintaining safety and soundness of the financial system. There is no evidence of regulatory arbitrage or housing mission regulators trumping prudential regulation.

2. Savings for Down Payments and Borrower Underwriting

Home lending in all market economies consists of two related processes. First, lenders underwrite the borrower's ability to repay from income. Second, they encourage repayment by requiring an up front cash investment with additional borrower recourse in the event of default. Historically, the US relied more on the latter, i.e., a mortgage was more of a collateralized loan than a personal loan. The advantage of this was that granting a loan was depersonalized: many lenders never met a borrower in person. This was particularly important in the US where race-based discrimination was historically of concern. With depersonalized lending, the borrower did not encounter substantial social stigma for default, foreclosure or eviction, the cost of which was predictable and manageable for lenders.

Among developed economies, minimum down payments range from 20% to 30% and virtually all countries have some variant of recourse beyond that. Only Canada and the Netherlands have a public mortgage insurer remotely comparable to FHA. Most other countries require significant personal savings, although some provide direct taxpayer-funded subsidies for down payment savings.

During the last decade, the US simultaneously had the lowest down payment and the weakest underwriting requirements. No developed economy had significant sub-prime lending, either with respect to underwriting or down payments, comparable to the US. Regulators presumably discouraged lenders while recourse discouraged borrowers. No country has ever experienced anything near the frequency or the severity of default as the US in the aftermath of the sub-prime lending debacle. Some countries experienced a large rise in the household debt to GDP ratio during the last two decades, but none as great a rise as the US. Nevertheless, all countries experienced a fall in household savings. As this occurred well prior to any potential house price bubble "wealth affect" it most likely reflects the substitution of government unfunded promises of future benefits - entitlements - for household savings, as discussed in the last section below.

Figure 1

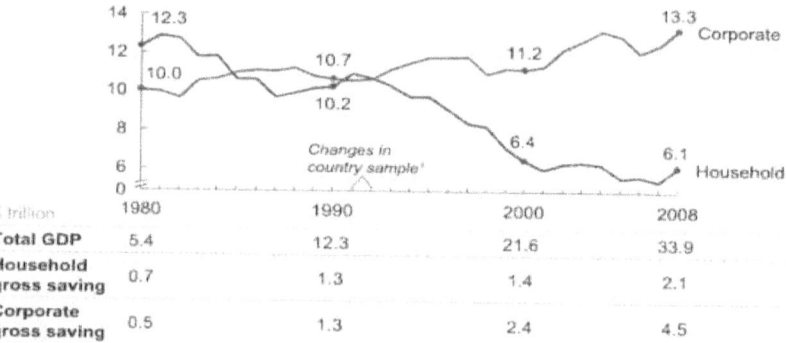

3. Fixed Rate Mortgage Lending

Only two countries provide fixed rate mortgage financing to borrowers. These are France (where one can obtain 15 to 20 year mortgages with a prepayment penalty) and Denmark. However, this financing is not very abundant in either country. Ninety percent of loans in Denmark since 2005 have been (mostly one year) adjustable loans, while adjustable loans now account for two thirds of the stock.[316] In neither case must short term deposits finance them, as was historically the case for federally chartered S&Ls. Furthermore, government does not "promote" fixed rate lending.[317] Banks issue covered bonds with cash flow generally matched to the bonds. There is no prepayment penalty in Denmark as loans are either assumed or the bonds are bought back at a market price. In this way, Danish borrows hold a slight advantage over US borrowers when paying off low rate loans in a high rate environment (although if such loans are prepaid often, the price of Danish bonds often will not fall much below par). There is nothing comparable to the US system of interest and prepayment risk management, which initially spawned the derivatives market.

4. The Mortgage Interest Tax Deduction

Most developed countries do not allow the deductibility of home mortgage interest. But the "tax loophole" is not the deduction; it's the failure to tax "imputed rent" from homeownership, i.e., the value of rental services the homeowner receives. This tax is imposed only in the Netherlands, Denmark, Belgium, and Switzerland where interest is appropriately tax-deductable.[318] However, this has never been seriously considered in the US because the political, conceptual, and methodological problems of taxing farmers for consuming their home grown food – as the US has done – are much greater for homeowner imputed rent (taxed at low rates where taxed in any event).

Lea finds evidence of a higher rate of growth in the mortgage stock in countries with mortgage interest deductibility.[319] There is little cause to believe this effect to be a significant factor in the US sub-prime lending debacle because few sub-prime borrowers paid enough taxes to take advantage of the deduction while still qualifying for housing goals. While taxing imputed rent is a worthy topic to be considered in the context of overall tax equity, fairness, and efficiency, it is not a realistic or desirable reform due solely its effect on the financial system.

The Treasury Department views all income not taxed as a tax-expenditure loophole to be closed, and the biggest of these is the home mortgage interest tax deduction. The National Commission on Fiscal Responsibility and Reform reports estimated lost tax revenue of $130 billion. Most economists have long argued that the MID diverted too much capital away from more productive investments

But just removing the mortgage interest tax deduction rather than taxing imputed rent is a revenue raiser that exacerbates economic distortions. Whether the tax code favors homeownership relative to rental is questionable. Whereas few if any subprime borrowers got any benefit as homeowners, they would have benefited as renters from accelerated depreciation and likely a plethora of federal, state and local tax credits for low-income housing as well. Businesses similarly have a plethora of tax "breaks" as the Treasury would define it. But the biggest distortion is that middle aged households who are now being forced to pay for Obamacare to subsidize the elderly aren't generally able to avoid the tax, whereas the elderly can avoid the tax increase by just selling off e.g., taxable bonds to pay off mortgage debt.

B. Separating Subsidy from Finance:

This section addresses the role of HUD and the GSEs in subsidizing through finance.

Given the potential risks, sustainable lending inherently means discriminating against at least some of those seeking credit. The function of underwriting is to screen potential borrowers and allocate limited funds to those most likely to repay. The likelihood of repayment is difficult to determine but some indicators may include income, wealth, borrower behavioral characteristics, and/or the quality and safety of the real estate collateral provided. Prudential regulation is supposed to protect lenders from type one statistical errors - accepting borrowers who will default - with the aim of preventing losses to insured depositors or the insurance fund. Competition among lenders in well functioning markets mitigates type two errors, i.e., of lenders systemically rejecting stronger credit risks in favor of weaker ones. US credit markets have historically been extremely competitive, and there has never been irrefutable evidence of home mortgage markets failing systemically in this regard, such failures providing the typical economic rationale for credit allocation.

The FCIC Report spends only ten of its 662 pages addressing social lending mandates, concluding that "these (housing) goals only contributed marginally to Fannie's and Freddie's participation in those (risky) mortgages."[320] But even if you find our refutation of this argument –shared mainly by AEI and McDonald - unconvincing, it remains the case that no other developed country with a market system of housing finance super-imposes credit allocation to inner cities to prevent urban decay, and none failed in the same way. However, it is under such context that both the community reinvestment and affordable housing goals administered as credit allocation arose and continue.

The HUD and Treasury Report to Congress entitled "Reforming America's Housing Finance Market," offers a similar narrative to the FCIC report. It blames the subprime lending crisis on poor consumer regulation, inadequate financial institution regulation, complex securitization, inadequate capital, and inadequate loan servicing. The HUD/Treasury Report supports greater transparency and better targeting of affordable housing support – as it always has – but like the FCIC Report it explicitly rejects the notion that social housing goals played a role in the financial crisis and does not specifically recommend their elimination. Mortgage related capital regulations were – and still are - entirely politically determined, reflecting the political commitment to home ownership and the belief that achieving this goal would be free or close to free.

The implicit assumptions behind GSE and other policies that allocate funds to weaker borrowers with little or no prior savings are that the benefit of the lender's franchise value will off-set the cost and that the supply of funds available to US mortgage borrowers is infinitely elastic. If this was true, such policies could not crowd out better qualified borrowers. The first assumption proved false during the sub-prime crisis and the second assumption is no longer realistic, as will be discussed in Part F below.

1. The Future Role of HUD

The joint HUD/Treasury Report represents a break in tradition. The Treasury historically supported transparent markets and HUD supported social credit allocation. HUD was created during the Great Society initiatives under the premise that bad housing leads to urban decay and hence better housing leads to urban development. How has that worked out? To quote Milton Friedman:

"The Department of] Housing and Urban Development has done an enormous amount of harm. My god, if you think of the way in which they have destroyed parts of cities under the rubric of eliminating slums . . . there have been many more dwelling units torn down in the name of public housing than have been built."

- Milton Friedman, Interview, Hoover Institution, February 10, 1999

While noting that HUD is and has been a general failure, whether the federal government has a legitimate role to play in housing and/or urban affairs to the extent of requiring a cabinet level bureaucracy is beyond our current scope. Its comparatively small budget of about $50 billion annually has it to stay under the radar of those who would eliminate it. To put HUD's budget in perspective, the value of the home owner tax mortgage interest tax deduction is in the range of $100-$150 billion, the same order of magnitude as housing subsidies delivered through finance. HUD cannot influence Treasury over the former (which go to higher income households in any event, not HUD's low income clientele), so its attention is naturally drawn toward finance subsidies for the same reason bank robber Willie Sutton said he robbed banks: because "that's where the money is." This gives HUD an outsized impact relative to its political accountability.

Off-balance sheet capital subsidies worked to the advantage of politicians, bureaucrats, shareholders and management so it was intevitable that politicians and HUD would eventually over-reach. It should have been obvious that home ownership goals could not be financed with capital subsidies alone, but neither HUD nor F&F appear to have made that calculation or considered the consequences of a mis-calculation of the magnitude that produced the sub-prime debacle for which HUD has never been held accountable. HUD's role in ending discrimination should be eliminated altogether as that is DOJ's job.

The HUD/Treasury Report makes no mention of reforming HUD, which retains some authority over U.S. housing finance policy. It implicitly rejects the notion that housing finance regulation has become politicized and feigns support for a robust private market for housing finance. Home ownership goals should be abolished as a matter of sound housing finance policy.

Dodd-Frank stripped HUD of its F&F oversight, a good idea coming a bit too late to avoid several trillion dollars of credit loss. But the same conflict between housing goals and prudential regulation latent in HUD's responsibility for Ginnie Mae and FHA is now evident, with similar consequences as FHA is now predictably insolvent. Responsibility for prudential regulation of these agencies needs to be transferred out of HUD, if it isn't already too late.

HUD will undoubtedly refocus on "affordable housing." This is a broad umbrella that encompasses many policies. It is likely that that set of promulgated policies will largely revolved around newly produced housing financed with federal, state and/or local tax credits and tax exempt financing. Often this is provided by specific "urban development" authorities. These schemes all involve delivering subsidies through finance, and the subsidies are often captured by owners of land and existing housing as this increase in demand drives up housing costs.

An alternative option is to directly deliver HUD's section 8 subsidies to borrowers to subsidize rent on existing housing. This is a better idea, although the vouchers – currently limited to the jurisdiction of public housing authorities for historical and political reasons – should be portable across jurisdictions to subsidize rents nationwide. This would increase flexibility and mobility, with the added benefit of reducing the need for HUD's local and regional bureaucracies. Of course, greater reliance on the earned income tax credit would allow the bureaucracy to be eliminated.

2. The Future Role of Fannie Mae, Freddie Mac, Ginnie Mae, the FHLBs and the FHFA

The long and enduring list of "benefits" relative to "costs" of GSEs a testament to political and GSE propaganda, remarkable for inevitably and inherently crony capitalist monopolistic firms. The benefits fall into two categories: the political benefits arising from the control over credit allocation, opaque subsidies and political patronage and the economic benefits arising from government correction of a purported market failure.

The housing finance components of the recommendations in the introduction - replace the GSEs and current secondary market regulations with enabling capital market regulations that avoid regulatory arbitrage - are generally consistent with the Recommendations of the President's Commission on Housing in 1982, the Obama Administration Report of 2011 Option 1, and the American Enterprise Institute's "principles of reform."[321] While the Administration's Report supports a winding down of Fannie Mae and Freddie Mac, Options 2 and 3 propose alternative guarantee mechanisms in times of "crisis" and for "targeted" borrowers that go well beyond the government backing and social mission initially conferred upon Fannie and Freddie that led to their subsequent failure. That presumably explains both their expanded role while under Obama Administration conservatorship, and also the head butting with the FHFA Administrator who for the most part stuck to the FHFA mandate of protecting taxpayers while resisting the subsidy expansion in spite of continual political demands that he be fired.[322]

GSEs came about as a politically expedient way to bypass laws and regulations. They possess no special powers other than the externalities conveyed by their implicit government credit guarantee, the source of all incentive conflicts. They don't save or alter the characteristics of national savings, so they don't influence the demand for or the supply of long-term securities such as fixed rate mortgages. They don't provide liquidity, but instead provide marketability: they trade at a more narrow bid ask spread than other bonds, hardly the rationale for a government guarantee that some believe. Their absence may be bemoaned by traders and speculators but not necessarily investors who ultimately determine borrowing costs.

We noted in chapter 3 that there was a worldwide shortage of highly rated paper driven entirely by regulation. There is a large demand for liquid instruments, but that can certainly be met with the $17 trillion of US Treasury debt outstanding and GSE securities aren't "liquid" in any event. Some claim they mitigate financial panics. In reality, they are the source of systemic risk giving rise to those very same panics. Others say they are no worse than commercial banks backed by deposit insurance. However, we need banks (with or without deposit insurance), not GSEs.

Additionally, there is a GSE-justificatory myth that investors require a federal credit guarantee. That certainly has not been the case historically, even for Ginnie Mae securities. In fact, they never asked for such a guarantee: investors and money managers make their living earning a risk-adjusted spread. If their assessment of mortgage securities is that the spread is not worth the risk, then that implies mispricing usually associated with excessive political risk. A federal guarantee is just an anesthetic for the root problem of political credit allocation that has extreme side effects.

Another enduring myth is that the GSEs remain necessary for hedging. Fannie Mae's constituency has historically been under-capitalized mortgage bankers. Rather than raise sufficient capital to bear the price risk due to changing interest rates from the time they originate a loan to the time they sell, they have historically hedged this risk. There are a variety of ways to do this, discussed below.

The FHLBs - GSEs with comparable capital subsidies - are not yet insolvent but would be if not for excess collateral seized at the FDIC's expense. Their advances have fallen in half and they are now making unsecured loans to technically insolvent Eurozone banks. Most recently, they replaced Bank of America as a correspondent bank when Bank of America exited the market because of the risk. This mission creep and "go for broke" strategy is reminiscent of F&F during the sub-prime crisis. The individual FHLBs could potentially each become a totally privatized covered bond issuer, with a name change as well. Preferably, they would be sold to a private bank.

Option Two, to insure access to credit "during a housing crisis" and/or "in times of stress" — at actuarially sound premiums — sounds harmless. Yet it is not a credible promise. Fed Chairman Bernanke made the case to retain the GSEs to cushion housing cycles. However, that is the job of the Fed, which has acted like a GSE as described in Chapter 5.[323] Policymakers always face political pressure to make both findings (and there are always academics willing to provide support for a finding of a credit shortage or market stress). True actuarial premiums are virtually never charged for reasons discussed in Chapter 5, yet even if they were charged more often, such lending would still undermine the private sector while distorting the market.

Appropriate capital requirements eliminate capital subsidies and hence the ability to fund housing goals, rendering these GSEs obsolete. Capital subsidies go way beyond actuarial soundness, as discussed throughout, and the costs become evident only when failure is recognized. The federal government has never run an actuarially sound unsubsidized insurance system for very long: what's the point if the private sector can do it at the same price? Moreover, there is no way to effectively limit the guarantee. It was investors, not the government, who conferred agency status in the first place.

Option Three is a virtual rehash of the Fannie and Freddie structure from their creation to the end of the last century, with private insurers backstopped by a federal "pool insurer." The intellectual merit of the concept is that as the government is the most likely source of the catastrophe, it should provide the bailout. It always has the option to bail out the market without establishing a permanent enterprise to do so, but as described in the last chapter the footing of such bailouts is on a slippery slope of moral hazard. The objections are the same as for Option 2.

The FHFA was not so much relieved of HUD interference as it was created as an offspring, maintaining the HUD DNA by inheriting the housing goals along with the prior HUD staff to enforce them. Whether this bureaucratic transfer will mitigate the inherent conflict between these goals and prudential regulation only time would tell, but it is not worth the risk. The goals should go immediately and FHFA should go as well when the entities it regulates are fully liquidated.

While liquidation will work, privatization will not. No physical or human capital is lost in liquidation and there are no good economic reasons for crony capitalist firms. If there really are positive externalities to the organizational structure, then the markets will organize to realize them within the regulatory constraints mitigating TBTB. Hence there is only one rationale to "privatize" the existing enterprises: to maintain opaque subsidies and protect the existing rents flowing to politicians and their constituents.

How do we know this? Because Fannie and Freddie had already been privatized! Markets conferred agency status in spite of government protestations to the contrary. History shows that once introduced, rent-seeking grows because competitive private market cannot survive public competition.

3. Privatize FHA

As F&F have been somewhat limited in conservatorship, the systemic risk has been shifted to the FHA, which is now deeply technically insolvent as a direct consequence. The FHA request in 2013 for a taxpayer bailout completes the trifecta, Fannie Mae, Freddie Mac and FHA/Ginnie Mae - the government sponsored enterprises (GSEs) - all required a taxpayer bailout due to credit loss. This loss was reported in fact that FHA counts as capital the present value of future gross revenue before credit expense, i.e., is severely undercapitalized as were Fannie Mae and Freddie Mac. Like them, the US Treasury forgoes the tax on the return to this implicit capital and pays no after-tax return to the government or mutual policyholders. FHA failed for the same reason: this capital subsidy proved insufficient to cover the costs of its housing mission.

Ginnie Mae passes the credit risk back – to a government "sponsored" insurer (FHA) – and the interest rate risk forward – to investors in Ginnie Mae mortgage backed securities (MBS). Historically Fannie Mae and Freddie Mac MBS differed only in their reliance on private mortgage insurance (PMI). The initial reason for GSEs was to bypass the state and local barriers to issuing and trading mortgage securities nationally, barriers long since removed facilitating privately issued MBS.

FHA joined the sub-prime lending debacle late because the FHA commissioner – who was also the Fannie and Freddie "Mission Regulator" - pushed the cost of political housing policy to Fannie and Freddie, who then used their monopoly status to push this risk onto the PMIs and three subsequently failed.

The operation of FHA during the first term of the Obama Administration undercuts the assertion that the federal government can permanently run an insurance program in an actuarially sound manner without taxpayer risk. The future health of the FHA will greatly depend upon insuring a significant share of higher-quality borrowers. The FHA's current forecast depends heavily on its assumption that its percentage of borrowers with FICO scores above 720 will remain at least 22 percent in future years. In other words, as with Fannie Mae in the 1980's, FHA wants to grow out of insolvency by using its subsidies to crowd out private competition. This is the only path to solvency and it is what we've called "going for broke" while private firms subject to competition go broke. FHA plans to end the private market with massive Ginnie Mae capital subsidies, a play we have seen before with Fannie Mae. In the past, it ended tragically for S&Ls and the mortgage market.

Government enterprises are exempt from government rules for the private sector: that's why politicians start them in the first place. FHA is to be exempted from the onerous "qualified mortgage" rules. Moreover, Ginnie Mae gets all the GSE capital subsidies available to F&F and a bit more with no payment to Treasury, all of which are passed through to FHA. These subsidies cost $50 billion annually. So, when FHA shows losses, it's over and above these subsidies. "Actuarial" subsidies are just the tip of the iceberg.

Private mortgage insurance companies are numerous and, but for FHA, we could expect more multiline insurers. They are state regulated in multiple states. FHA represents a source of systemic risk. Private mortgage insurance both mitigates and diversifies the underlying risk of individual mortgages and state regulators are less politicized than FHA's HUD oversight without the associated taxpayer capital subsidies. Greater reliance on PMIs and pool insurers transfers this risk from the

GSEs, but it remains concentrated in a few firms, posing a systemic risk as several mortgage and pool insurers failed in the last cycle.

FHA and Ginnie Mae should join F&F under a single regulator - the FHFA for now - and be phased out along with F&F and the FHLBs. FHA could theoretically be sold and recapitalized as a private mortgage insurer without the advantages such as Ginnie Mae funding. As it is already insolvent this would have to be part of a liquidation and reorganization as a new company without the name or the residual risk portfolio, which would remain for HUD to manage and liquidate.

C. The Role of the Fed: Past, Present and Future

The Federal Reserve is the most powerful federal bureaucracy and the most criticized in the FCIC Report. The Fed provided the excessive credit that the GSEs and PLSers channeled to sub-prime mortgages, and is thus a central character in our narrative. Suppose Morgenstern and Rosner, authors of the Fannie Mae expose *Reckless Endangerment*, 2010 (Freddie Mac largely got a pass due to its relative youth) were to take on the Federal Reserve System with a comparable expose, beginning with a comparison of the Fed to Fannie Mae. [324]

Both are/were owned by the customers they serve (commercial banks for the Fed, mortgage banks for Fannie Mae). Fannie Mae began paying shareholders dividends and raising its stock price, but in the early days it provided benefits to shareholders indirectly. These benefits came mostly as a sure source of funds at favorable rates. The Fed pays a statutory dividend to member banks of 6%, but the indirect benefit of Fed protection has an even bigger impact on the share price of banks – the Fed's "owners" - than do the dividends. This is especially true for those banks that are TBTF; after all, protecting them was the Fed's initial mission. Also, the Fed provides bank services on behalf of its shareholders, e.g., check clearing that private business would otherwise provide at a higher market price: Fannie Mae never took over mortgage servicing but is a master loan servicer.

Both the Fed and Fannie Mae argue that they are private. However, they also argue that they are public whenever it suits their goals. They both purchased land/headquarters buildings in the nation's capital Washington DC to establish their status as political enterprises and exercise political influence. Both then refused to pay taxes to the District of Columbia on grounds that they were public entities. But they are both exempt from any normal public discipline, e.g., they don't rely on a congressionally approved budget.

While neither faces the discipline of congressional appropriations, it is also true that neither enterprise is subject to market discipline: Fannie Mae raises all the money it wants at the Treasury borrowing rate, whereas the Fed owes no principle or interest as it merely "prints" the money it needs. Fannie Mae uses the money to buy mortgages to support housing policy. The Fed historically bought Treasury securities to support public fiscal goals although in the aftermath of the financial crisis it bought trillions of dollars of mortgage securities to support housing policy as well.

Both use privilege to create enormous bureaucracies that court political protection of their institutional prerogatives. Fannie Mae spent tens of millions of dollars to re-write its own history, convincing the public it was indispensible to the workings of a mortgage market that historically worked better without it. It likely got the idea from the Fed, which has used its virtually limitless resources to do the same. Fannie Mae spent tens of millions of dollars courting the goodwill of economists. They also got that idea from the Fed, which hires more economists than any other domestic public/private organization in the US and has long hosted conferences at posh resorts to woo other economists who then publish generally favorable opinions of Fed actions.

The Fed Chairman Bernanke supports keeping Fannie Mae as a "countercyclical policy tool," even though it has historically been pro-cyclical in support of mortgage banks. Similarly the Fed's stated public mission has been countercyclical monetary policy, but it too has more often than not operated pro-cyclically in support of commercial banks. Writing several decades before the subprime debacle, Rothbard (p.82) argued that the Fed was in fact created to fuel bubbles, bail out the banks when they burst and keep markets from adjusting in the aftermath.

The real irony is that due to Fannie Mae's extreme leverage, it faced strong go for broke incentives that contributed to the sub-prime lending debacle. When it did eventually go broke, Fannie Mae became indispensible. Having (once again) provided the funds for the housing bubble, the Fed also became indispensible in the aftermath, with Fed management facing the same go for broke and go broke incentives as Fannie Mae management when bailing out insolvent institutions. By market accounting standards, the Fed went broke as well, but like Fannie, it gets enormous ongoing, opaquely funded taxpayer subsidies and is subject to no external accounting rules or bankruptcy constraint. Neither management has paid a price for their failures.

As discussed in Chapter 1, the Fed's original purported role was to provide an "elastic currency" by acting as a lender of last resort, lending to solvent but illiquid banks during a systemic liquidity crisis. As with Fannie Mae, a political case was made upon the Fed's initial chartering in response to a prior "crisis" having little to do with the real objective of credit expansion. As with Fannie Mae, there were lots of reasons to fear it would make matters worse.

Unlike the Fannie Mae secondary market facility, the US already had (not particularly successful) experience with central banks. As with Fannie Mae, the Fed's mission was expanded with each failure as politicians doubled down. The Fed expanded to three primary missions; monetary policy, systemic liquidity support and prudential regulation, but has taken on other non-core missions as well, such as consumer protection, to broaden its political base. Like Fannie Mae, who went well beyond their charter by expanding from a broker/dealer to a housing bank, the Fed has gone well beyond its charter by bailing out politically powerful insolvent institutions. As with Fannie Mae, Fed reform advocates say they want to keep the best while getting rid of the rest, ignoring the political economy of mission creep.

Intervene, fail, cover-up, double down, and mission creep. This is the story of Fannie Mae, but is it also the story of the Fed? The Fed's mission under Chairman Bernanke has grown to: 1. control over the nation's money supply and *determination of the structure of interest rates*; 2. bailing out *insolvent* but systemically important firms; 3. *market* regulator and *systemic* protector; 4. providing full employment, and: 5. funding massive fiscal deficits. The Fed's political independence is only warranted arguably for their role in monetary policy, and even then only for modest discretion in the pursuit of price stability. It nevertheless keeps secrets with regard to all five activities to avoid accountability.

The Fed's "budget" (what it decides to spend on itself) is now over $5 billion. The Fed employs over 22,000 employees. When it comes to protecting its bureaucratic power, the Fed – like Fannie Mae - has one advantage over all others, including the executive and legislative authorities: it enjoys the benefits of a taxpayer-funded budget while not being accountable to anyone but it. According to Milton Friedman, central bankers have two shared objectives with politicians: "avoiding accountability on the one hand and achieving public prestige on the other" (as quoted by Mayer, p.94). The Fed, as currently structured, is too powerful, totally out of control and completely unaccountable for its widespread and chronic failures. Just as Acharya, Richardson, Von

Nieuwerburgh and White (2011) concluded for Fannie Mae and Freddie Mac, the Fed is *Guaranteed to Fail*.

The Fed's unlimited power and lack of accountability have been recurring themes of financial writers. These problematic elements have been attacked from the populist left in William Greider's *Secrets of the Temple: How the Federal Reserve Runs the Country* (1989), from the more conservative right in Martin Mayer's *The Fed* (2001) and from the market-oriented Austrian School in Murray N. Rothbard's *The Case Against the Fed* (1994). The problem has become significantly worse during this century. Now, as we approach the Federal Reserve's 100th anniversary, it is time for these issues to be seriously re-considered.[325] At a minimum, it is time for another National Monetary Commission as called for by Selgin, Lastrapes and White in "Has the Fed Been a Failure?" (2011).

Although the Fed has argued otherwise, its three contemporary missions of monetary policy, systemic liquidity support and financial regulator can and should be considered independently. In addition, the role of progressive consumer regulation needs to be separated from the role of prudential regulation. The Fed's role as systemic regulator is addressed separately in Part E below.

1. Monetary Policy: Discretion, Rules or Metals?

Printing money was not the initial role of central banks. The primary mission of the oldest central bank, the Bank of England, was to maintain the convertibility of paper notes into gold at a fixed price (Mayer, p.62). While there is no fixed definition of a "gold standard," gold had been used as a medium of exchange and store of value for five millennia. The United States minted gold coins during the "classical gold standard" of 1870 to 1914, a period of modest deflation and rapid economic growth, but it did not formally join the international gold standard system until 1890. The gold standard was in fact created, implemented, and enforced by private individuals for their mutual benefit and, as it turns out, for society at large. It required no public intervention or administration.[326]

Rothbard (p.46) argues that commercial bankers created the Fed to remove the strict requirements of the gold standard to contract in response to balance of payment shortfalls in order to keep a bubble inflated. Economic stability and growth was the objective of hard money supporters, therefore proponents of an inflationist Fed had to assume that hard money mantle in order to achieve sufficient political support for creating another central bank in the US. The creation of the Fed represented an inflationist victory over hard money advocates, but it was not until the Great Depression under FDR that the public could no longer convert their Fed notes to gold.

Current Fed Chairman Bernanke, a scholar specializing in the Great Depression, agrees with the assessment of Friedman and Schwartz in their *Monetary History of the United States* 1867-1960. He blames the Depression on the Fed's tight monetary policy, really a failure to target negative real interest rates to compensate for the dearth of investment demand.[327] The failure to increase the money supply by enough to offset the decline in money velocity is often explained as the consequence of a political turf battle: the New York FRB – long the power center of the system under the leadership of its President Benjamin Strong – tried to do so but was rebuffed by the Board of Governors in Washington DC, the same Board of Governors that centralized power in the wake of Strong's death in 1928. While Austrians dispute the causality attributed to the money supply - they would have addressed the structural adjustment problems directly - the shift of power to Washington DC and Milton Friedman's work in the 1960's put the debate over "monetary policy and monetarism"– open market purchases of Treasury securities to adjust the quantity of money and control the pace of aggregate economic activity - front and center.[328]

Milton Friedman had long been the Fed's biggest critic regarding monetary policy, arguing that a simple rule would have performed much better than the Fed's much-protected and vigorously defended discretion. More recently, John Taylor has argued that the Great Moderation" of the 1980's and 1990's resulted from following simple rules rather than discretion, a policy from which the Bernanke Fed seriously deviated (chapter 4).

How well has the Fed done in its primary mission of maintaining price stability? From Selgin, Lastrapes and White (p. 3):

"The Fed has failed conspicuously in one respect: far from achieving long-run price stability, it has allowed the purchasing power of the U.S. dollar, which was hardly different on the eve of the Fed's creation from what it had been at the time of the dollar's establishment as the official U.S. monetary unit, to fall dramatically. A consumer basket selling for $100 in 1790 cost only slightly more, at $108, than its (admittedly very rough) equivalent in 1913. But thereafter the price soared, reaching $2422 in 2008 (Officer and Williamson 2009). ….most of the decline in the dollar's purchasing power has taken place since 1970, when the gold standard no longer placed any limits on the Fed's powers of monetary control."

The Humphrey-Hawkins Full Employment and Balanced Growth Act of 1978 is remembered for creating the Fed's dual mandate of price stability and full employment. The law's other directives -

that the federal government rely on private enterprise to achieve full employment, encourage balanced growth in production, and promote a balanced trade and fiscal budget - are rarely mentioned by politicians and are generally forgotten. Interestingly, it also specifically prohibits any "discrimination" in credit allocation when achieving the Act's goals.

Most monetary analysts understand that the Fed cannot simultaneously pursue two fairly contradictory goals with one policy tool. However, this dual mandate has been a boon to the Fed, as the dual mandate ensures that the Fed can never be held accountable for its failures. If it fails at accomplishing one goal, it can blame its failure on its pursuit of the other goal. Failure to achieve either is attributed to the inconsistency between its goals. As a result, the dual mandate has politicized monetary policy, leading Texas Congressman and inflation hawk Ron Paul to introduce the Sound Dollar Act in 2012 to restore the single price stability mandate.[329]

A benign interpretation of the Fed's perceived mission is really to maintain steady economic growth by smoothing out business cycles. But as discussed in the last chapter, business cycles represent a natural and necessary market correction. Moreover, this inflation didn't occur while mitigating boom/bust cycles. The reality is that the Fed is more often than not the cause: it facilitates growth even when driven by an excess of credit, then tries desperately to maintain growth in the wake of the ensuing market correction. Arguably the most important thing the Fed could do to achieve the H-H Act goal of private sector employment in the long run is maintain price stability, but in the short run price stability often conflicts with that goal.

The real contemporary purpose of central bank power over fiat money is to fund the government by purchasing government debt in the market. The Fed got its start by funding the British and French war effort in WW I and the later American war effort by doubling the money supply. In 2011 it financed over three fourths of the Treasury deficit, a pace it maintained in 2012.

But the Fed-planned changes in the money stock redistribute wealth from those holding depreciating assets to those receiving newly-created money. This is the Austrian concern discussed in chapter 5. The Fed's argument for secrecy is based on this redistribution, limiting gains to speculation ahead of Fed actions.

The Fed argues for independence to protect the public from politicians. Could Fed monetary policy possibly have been more politically accommodating, less successful or less publicly accountable? The Fed's political independence depends upon the political bidding in the first place.

Independence is a convenient political fiction, although few go as far as Zimbabwe did in throwing their "independent" central bank chairman off the bridge when he took his "independence" too seriously. When things work out well, politicians get the credit; when they don't, they blame the central bank and its managers. Most studies of the Fed find that it has generally been more accommodating when the Chairman is up for reappointment.

Other countries are looking to supplant the dollar as a store of value. Not surprisingly, the IMF has been leading the effort to replace the dollar. Joseph Stiglitz has proposed a scheme of using SDRs, IMF paper money, exclusively. The IMF has suggested that SDRs could be issued by the World Bank and other regional development banks, ironic as these institutions are the purest form of financial pyramid schemes, relying on new debt to refinance old.[330] Other fiat currencies will not be any more viable. However, some country or group of countries will likely develop a commodity or metals based currency to eventually replace the dollar. The dollar's continuing strength reflects the current weakness of the alternatives. As Barry Eichengreen points out in *Exorbitant Privilege* (2011) the inertia to change is great, but current monetary and fiscal policies may leave international traders with no other choice.

Monetary economists could probably reach some consensus on a monetary rule to achieve price stability - metals based or not – that out-performs the Fed's discretion. Meltzer (pp. 68-69) does not favor a return to a full gold standard because it was pro-cyclical and relied on unemployment to restore equilibrium. But even under our current system of open market purchases, we don't need the Fed to conduct monetary policy: Teddy Roosevelt's Treasure Secretary Leslie Shaw ran open market operations out of the Treasury before the Fed was created.[331] The Bureau of Printing and Engraving is in the Treasury Department. In fact, the US Treasury printed its own currency (silver certificates) until 1968.

2. Moral Hazard Run Amok

If the entry point of the Fed story is the immediate aftermath of the systemic financial crisis, then it is easy and generally appropriate to laud the role of the Bernanke Fed. David Wessel of the Wall Street Journal's book *In FED We Trust: Ben Bernanke's War on the Great Panic* does exactly that. Simon Johnson, a former IMF chief economist and renowned expert on monetary affairs, also believes the Fed remains necessary as a traditional "lender of last resort" in a crisis. The as-yet-

283

unanswered question is how the Fed or Treasury can signal the existence of this safety net – the Treasury's line to Fannie and Freddie was miniscule – without engendering serious moral hazard.

The Fed and Treasury argued that bailouts of solvent firms should be opaque to prevent banking runs. According to FDIC folklore, when the Resolution Finance Corporation (RFC) was required to make its loans to banks public in 1932 – before deposit insurance - it encouraged depositor runs on those banks.[332] Others, e.g., Taylor, argued for transparency so that markets could properly discipline insolvent firms.

What did Dodd-Frank do to address this complete lack of accountability? It extended the Fed's direct lending authority to include all large complex enterprises, including hedge funds. But it also established a quick resolution authority to pay creditors quickly to purportedly avoid a systemic crisis.[333] This eliminates creditors as a source of market discipline, putting the entire burden on shareholders and regulatory capital requirements. Why pay all creditors 100 percent, as the Fed did for Goldman on AIG CDS? Until TBTF banks are allowed to fail, the markets will not believe we have reached the end of TBTF.

Do we need a central bank to make loans? The US Treasury provided the liquidity backstop for Fannie Mae. The Fed's only comparative advantage as lender of last resort is opaquely providing subsidies to insolvent institutions.[334] Should the Fed or any branch of government have the authority to lend to insolvent banks, investment banks or hedge funds that it deems large and inter-connected without congressional budget authorization or administrative authority? What is a reasonable limit on the taxpayer subsidy and the degree of insolvency?

The Troubled Asset Relief Program (TARP) passed in 2008 included a Treasury loan program with essentially the same charter as the Fed, e.g., to provide liquidity to solvent institutions. So what is the difference? The Treasury has to be nominally politically accountable for issuing debt, and in this case the creation of the Special Inspector General (SIGTARP) provided greater transparency of taxpayer cost. Of course, TARP was administered as bailouts. The Treasury ignored the legal limits of its authority and acted to bail out political benefactors, as previously discussed in chapter 5. But SIGTARP at least revealed some of the Treasury's obfuscation and much more was revealed in the numerous, subsequent, tell-all books, in comparison to the Fed's ongoing secrecy.

The Treasury also used the Exchange Stabilization Fund created in 1934 and chartered exclusively to stabilize the dollar at the new price of $34 an ounce as a slush fund in the most recent crisis. This has also been the case in prior crises, with little Congressional objection. The recent and prior series of bailouts were accused of being politically-driven, but the Congress has shown little inclination to demand accountability.

Nevertheless, the currently-structured Fed should not be the lender of last resort. It is inherently unaccountable and has every political and bureaucratic incentive to maximize short term bailouts without regard for long run moral hazard. The Treasury hasn't historically been much better, but a system could be designed for the provision of loans at a totally unsubsidized rate, including capital subsidies. All subsequent losses would require direct Congressional appropriations to insure political accountability. A super SIGTARP could be empowered with bureaucratic independence – reporting only to the Congress - to implement strict accounting and disclosure rules.

These loans should be senior are is private "debtor in possession" loans for firms in bankruptcy, but subordinate to all prior claims of government agencies, particularly the FDIC, since overcollateralization just shifts the taxpayer cost. Since the FDIC bears the cost of resolving insolvent banks even without collateral, it should have a vote – potentially a veto - on emergency lending to keep insolvent banks open. To speed up the normal liquidation process and avoid unnecessary economic disruptions, reimbursement up to a maximum loss limit for various creditor classes could be paid immediately with seniority reflecting the debt covenants and residuals paid as the liquidation proceeds.

3. Eliminate the Consumer Financial Protection Bureau (CFPB)

The Fed has also accumulated various consumer protection responsibilities. These include Rulemaking, Enforcement, Community Affairs, and Consumer Education. Consumer Education dates back to the 1968 Truth in Lending Act. The original objective was to combine points and fees into a single, comparable interest rate, the APR. However, consumers generally ignore it.[335] Rulemaking covers unfair or deceptive practices as well as CRA and related regulations that are then enforced at banks under Fed supervision. The Community Affairs Division is essentially another community action group designed to encourage local bank lending.

These activities were at best a distraction and at worst a conflict of interest, involving the central bank in direct credit allocation in violation of Humphrey Hawkins. The Fed took little interest in these powers at first, but any expansion of authority without accountability was eventually embraced. As in most things, responsibility for regulating CRA activities was diffuse, with the FDIC in the lead.

Consumer regulation has now been vested in the Consumer Financial Protection Bureau (CFPB) within but separate from and not accountable to the Fed.

That the second half of the Dodd Frank legislation' title is the "Wall Street Reform and Consumer Protection Act" is as misleading as the first half. President Obama proposed the CFPB almost two years before the FCIC Report on the causes of the financial crisis.

What was the egregious lender offense that required the creation of the CFPB? Allowing borrowers to choose mortgage loans with a lower monthly payment. This generally meant that rather than the nominal principal balance incrementally declining in the early years, it remained flat – as in interest-only loans – or modestly increased, a process called negative amortization. HUD sponsored research in the 1970s to deal with the effects of inflation, as discussed in chapter 2. This led to the genesis of these loans. Herb and Marion Sandler, CEO and President of Golden West S&L introduced the so-called "pick-a-pay" loan in 1982. Interest only mortgages were popular during the 1920's housing boom but disappeared during the Depression. Wells Fargo and Washington Mutual were among the first banks to reintroduce the loans at the start of the century, particularly in areas of the greatest house price increases, such as California.

As the point of such mortgages was to make housing more affordable, most borrowers chose the lowest payment. As house prices continued to rise – making home ownership less affordable – and the Fed, as both the consumer and systemic regulator denied the house price bubble, such mortgages made perfect sense for consumers. Politicians sanctified lenders for offering such products. The Fed was quite wrong. Default rates soared and politicians then crucified lenders.

The downside to negative amortization for loans with little or no initial borrower equity was that the loans were quickly submerged. But really, these loans only marginally increased negative equity, borrower default and loss severity: No sub-prime and few alt-A loans allowed negative amortization. Teaser rates became particularly common for sub-prime loans, but most borrowers refinanced before the rate rise and adjustment to the fully indexed rate didn't increase the rate of default. Furthermore, most borrowers with option ARM chose the lowest payments, but the rise in default was not related to the scheduled rise in monthly payment.[336]

As reported in chapter 3, the lack of cash down payments was a greater cause by orders of magnitude. Down payments on subprime loans for home purchases fell from a reported ten percent in 2003 to zero from 2005 through 2007. Payments on Alt-A pools fell from ten percent to five percent. Further, many notionally five percent down payments were so-called "3/2 down payments" where borrowers report that a "gift" will appear at closing to cover the 3 percent share, when in fact that money often comes from an unrecorded loan or a loan that was recorded after the mortgage credit check was complete. Low down payments were the major cause of the house price bubble.[337] They were also by far the major reason for default and were responsible for the resulting severity of loss.[338]

The qualified mortgage (QM) requirement of Title XIV of the Dodd-Frank Act requires a lender first determine that the borrower has a reasonable ability to repay the loan, with fines, civil liability, and potentially class action liability for a failure to do so. This reflects the narrative that unethical lending practices were the cause of the financial crisis. However, the Act's author, Congressman Barney Frank, amended the bill on the House floor to state that the CFPB can issue regulations modifying the QM "upon a finding that such regulations are necessary or proper to ensure that responsible, affordable mortgage credit remains available to consumers in a manner consistent with the purposes of this section."[339]

QM essentially provides a safe harbor. Mortgages originated within these guidelines are less likely to incur regulatory wrath and invite subsequent legal challenges.[340] A "safe harbor" is viewed by lenders as essential in the wake of the waves of litigation and recrimination, but this issue too has become politicized. In early 2013, after years of intense lobbying, the new CFPB issued regulations for QM. In deference to affordable housing advocates, the definition included loans demanding no borrower savings for a down payment and had no meaningful underwriting requirements. Loans with negative amortization were excluded. Within weeks of promulgating the regulation, the acting CFPB head was encouraging lenders to lend outside of the QM guidelines.

The focus on loan products was part of the political and regulatory effort to deny and cover-up the political origins of the crisis. The CFPB incorporates the fallacy of the federal government as the consumer protector and the schizophrenia of the political treatment of lenders, especially by the Act's authors. Responsibility for mortgage instrument design and credit risk mitigation has been taken away from the prudential regulator and lender to a consumer advocate as political mission regulation has once again trumped prudential regulation. The inevitable consequence will be regulations limiting consumer choice.[341]

Dodd-Frank nominally removed the responsibility for consumer protection from the Fed, a step in the right direction. But it then created the CFBP, an enormous leap backward. There can be only one reason for the unprecedented decision to house it within the Fed but outside the Fed's authority. That is, like the Fed, it has virtually unlimited funding over and above all the funding for the existing federal, state and local consumer regulators and protectors with no Congressionally approved budget, and in spite of nominal Congressional reporting requirements was designed to be unaccountable to anyone or anything, certainly not consumers. As expected, the CFPB quickly became over-bearing, terrorizing the mortgage lending industry.[342]

The various proposals for reform include replacing the Director with a five person Board, providing a Congressional appropriations process, and giving prudential regulators veto power over CFPB rulemaking. These proposals, all necessary but not likely sufficient, have all been stymied by House Democrats.[343] The enormous costs of operation will be dwarfed by the lenders' regulatory compliance costs, with little net consumer benefit and a potential loss of choice to show for it. It was a bad idea reflecting a misdiagnosis of sub-prime lending and should be abolished.

D. Reform Bank Prudential Regulation: Keep it Simple

Eliminating the GSEs and other forms of credit allocation, and reforming (or eliminating) the Fed will go a long way toward mitigating politically and regulatorally fueled asset bubbles. Yet the moral hazard incentives of deposit insurance that drove PLS would remain.

Had capital been required in relation to risk according to historical market norms, the sub-prime lending debacle would not have occurred. That it was not required was due entirely to regulatory intervention, as bank and F&F regulators made several key mistakes. First, the minimum capital levels were set much too low. Second, the risk-based rules didn't adjust for increasing loan risk. Third, off balance sheet financing bypassed the regulatory minimum, reducing net capital requirements to only about 1%. Fourth, the traditional 20% cash down payment or private mortgage insurance was replaced with lightly capitalized second mortgage securities on increasingly risky loans while continued cash out refinancing during the house price bubble further depleted borrower equity.

Hence the solution is obvious and simple. But this begs the question: Why didn't they require sufficient capital? Unlike with Fannie and Freddie, there is no evidence of direct political interference in the ability of PLSers to reduce the capital requirement for mortgage securities to a fraction of the transparent bank risk-based capital requirement of 4% although this may well have been so that banks could meet their $4 trillion CRA commitment. PLS leverage appears to be mostly the result of incompetence.

The good news is that this is amenable to a simple regulatory fix. The bad news is that regulatory reform is politically problematic. In the absence of more substantial reforms the best alternative is to reduce or eliminate deposit insurance. Whatever the historical merits and distortions, we don't need fractional reserve banking and deposit insurance to provide safe demand deposits and a reliable medium of exchange for the economy.

Section 1 describes the simple deposit insurance regulatory fix. Section 2 provides a simple market alternative.

1. Mitigating Moral Hazard: Regulating Federally Insured Banks in the US

As long as deposit insurance continues to enjoy strong political support in the US regulators will have to be held accountable for mitigating moral hazard. Addressing the first problem requires consolidating all bank regulatory responsibilities into the FDIC and all oversight responsibilities into a single congressional committee. The second problem requires regulatory reforms to mitigate moral hazard behavior that could put depositors and their backers at risk.

Regulation of depository institutions originated in state and then federal chartering. It was only later that federal deposit insurance added another overlapping layer to the chartering authorities. The panoply of bank regulators reflects the sordid history of overlapping authority for bank chartering and prohibitions on branching that was a cause of early bank panics and financial market volatility and the political turf battles that produced it. The result of the US centralization is best described by Johns Hopkins professor Steven M. Teles (2012, p. 1) term, "kludge":[344]

"The term comes out of the world of computer programming, where a kludge is an inelegant patch put in place to be backward compatible with the rest of a system. When you add up enough kludges, you get a very complicated program, one that is hard to understand and subject to crashes."

Teles's description of American policymaking as a series of kludges reflecting this diffusion of power and responsibility applies to the role, structure, and political accountability of the Fed and other financial regulators. It was a kludgocracy from inception, and has only become worse.

Regulatory arbitrage is the biggest problem of kludgeocracy and needs to be eliminated. This requires eliminating arbitrage between loans and securities, as well as between banks, GSEs, and their replacement capital financing mechanisms. Some of the regulatory arbitrage occurred within a single regulator. For example bank risk-based capital rules administered by the FDIC weighted mortgage loans 50 percent and the same loans held as securities at half that. But most of the regulatory arbitrage occurred across bank regulatory boundaries. This was particularly true of the CDS market. For example BCL provided a withering attack on the Fed for providing capital relief for CDS, an entirely appropriate rule so long as the CDS writer posted an equivalent amount of capital. That was the responsibility of AIG's thrift regulator, the OTS under Treasury, which failed to do so.

That the two regulators did not coordinate policies does not require a third, and oversight has proven ineffective. To prevent regulatory arbitrage, all regulation of explicit or implicit beneficiaries of deposit insurance or the federal protective umbrella should be put under a single regulatory entity. There should not be more than one federal regulator of banks. The FSLIC was consolidated into the FDIC in 1989. The thrift regulator, the Office of Thrift Supervision (OTS), moved to the Treasury in 1989 and was subsequently merged by Dodd-Frank into the OCC in 2011, still within Treasury. The OCC is twice as old as the FDIC dating back to the introduction of national banks, but the FDIC is responsible for the insurance fund guaranteeing the deposits of those banks. As a result, it should be the survivor. The National Credit Union Administration (NCUA) should also be consolidated into the FDIC along with credit union insurance.

Senator Dodd pushed for a single regulator as part of Dodd-Frank. He was supported by the soon-to-retire Deputy and acting OCC Director John Walsh, who called it "an idea worth dying for." Former FDIC Chairman Sheila Bair has recently come out strongly in favor of abolishing the OCC and consolidating bank regulation within the FDIC.[345] The Obama Administration, the Fed and the new Comptroller opposed this.[346]

There are (at least) four complementary ways for the FDIC to mitigate moral hazard: require more capital, eliminate regulatory arbitrage, provide market based regulation, and reduce loan and investment risk. The consensus solution thus far provided by most bank regulatory analysts is to minimize the cost of taxpayer backing for the FDIC by imposing and enforcing significantly higher and more transparent capital requirements on insured banks. Basel III takes one step in the right direction by providing for significantly higher capital requirements, but entirely within the context of politicized risk-based capital rules. How much capital should banks hold? Not enough encourages moral hazard but too much stifles competition and unnecessarily increases borrower costs. The problem is not just determining how much capital to hold for risks, but measuring it accurately and applying that capital requirement uniformly. The substitution of legislatively and bureaucratically determined rules for an active competitive insurance market increases the likelihood that such requirements will be set either too low (as in the past) or too high (as is possible prospectively).

The Basil I 50% risk weighting was justifiable for mortgage loans with at least 20% cash down or private mortgage insurance down to 75% LTV with strict underwriting based on historical experience during periods of stable or rising housing prices, yet it was woefully insufficient for sub-prime loans. Many banks making portfolio loans with 4% risk-based capital failed in the aftermath of the sub-prime crisis, and second mortgages performed even worse. Based on historical experience, loans without 20% down or PMI should be subject to at least a 100% capital weighting.

Under the proposed Basel III capital framework, residential mortgages guaranteed by the government or its agencies would maintain a zero risk-weight for those unconditionally guaranteed and 20% risk-weight for those conditionally guaranteed. All other mortgages would be divided into two categories depending on loan-to-value ratios. A category 1 mortgage has a risk weighting of 35% to 100%, while category 2 loans (including home equity lines of credit, first liens with balloon features, delinquent loans, and more exotic adjustable-rate mortgages) would receive risk-weightings of 100% to 200%. But risk-based capital will not work without a continual re-assessment of loan risk and the associated risk-weightings, imposition of loan loss reserves, and more judicial use of existing "cease and desist" orders where appropriate for unusually risky loans.

US regulation has failed not just because it is more extensive and costly than in other market economies, but primarily because the conflicts of political incentives are greater. Political accountability that promotes both stability and competition requires that political reform precede regulatory reform. In the US, this requires not only eliminating overlapping regulatory responsibilities of various entities but also vesting oversight for insured institutions in one Congressional committee, held transparently accountable for regulatory failures.

The next most important step is to eliminate the potential for assets to return to the balance sheet, or to capitalize them as if they never left. Regulators will still have to guard against bank off-balance sheet leverage and excessive bank leverage provided to non-banks such as that which leveraged private mortgage securities excessively. The elimination of SIVs and other implicit put contracts is relatively straight forward. The more recent massive attempts to put back defaulted loans under representation and warranty contracts launched by federal agencies are largely extra-legal and hence more problematic. In Section E we argue loans financed in capital markets should remain on the lender's balance sheet as a "financing" for accounting purposes, resolving that potential problem.

Finally, establishing appropriate loan loss reserves is an essential component of regulatory capital requirements. Mayer (p.105) quotes Andrew Sheng's 1990 reflections on his experience with the Malaysian central bank:

"Bankers have a tendency to sit on a problem until it becomes too big to handle." Sheng cites a rule of thumb derived from Spanish experience by Aristobulo de Juan in 1985: "Loan loss provisions by external auditors tend to be double those made by bank managers. Bank examiners would double the provisions made by the auditors, and in a liquidation situation, loan losses would turn out to be double those estimated by the bank examiners." [347]

Gerard Caprio Jr. and Lawrence H. Summers add bleakly that: "both political and economic forces lean towards supervisors keeping silent about problem banks until net worth is already negative."[348] And this assessment was well before the sub-prime lending boom! Bank examiners would require additional reserves if supported by FDIC leadership, although that does not mean the bank examiners and auditors are always right. Allison (pp. 152-153) concludes that bank examiners have pro-cyclical assessments: always too optimistic when times are good, and too pessimistic when times are bad.

Two former regulators Eugene A. Ludwig and Paul A. Volker "Bank Reform Takes One Flawed Step Forward" wsj, Jan 18, 2013, suggest projecting future credit losses to establish a "rainy day" fund.[349] It was not the lack of a rainy day fund that contributed to the sub-prime crisis, but the opposite. Securitizers' models forecasted both credit losses and projected net income on retained interests over thirty years and predicted nothing but sunny days ahead. They were able to borrow against that present value to generate cash, keeping the house price bubble inflated for several additional years – just as in the sub-prime lending debacle of the 1990s. The only problem is that this time it made the resulting financial crisis systemic when it burst. The credit premium in the yield is supposed to compensate for future loss, but accelerating the "loss" without accelerating the gain" is also misleading. Allowing or requiring accountants to predict the future is a step backwards.

Banks are risk intermediaries and no discussion would be complete without mentioning the need to regulate other forms of risk exposure. The central issue, however, is what levels and types of risk are acceptable. While this is generally beyond our scope, most of the focus has been on Glass-Steagall's historic separation of traditional investment banking activities, once repealed and now under reconsideration because risky mortgage securities were held in proprietary trading accounts. As discussed in Chapter 4, underwriting, distribution and broker/dealer activities have not historically represented undue risk and did not substantially contribute to this crisis. But hedge fund risk and private equity risk – recent bank and investment bank activities– historically employing much less leverage than allowed for banks, was a contributing factor, and should be prohibited. In principle the Volker Rule is a reasonable way to reduce bank risk by eliminating "proprietary trading". Unfortunately, it is incredibly complex and has proven problematic to codify. This could very well weaken rather than strengthen banks. Moreover, these separated entities will once again represent counterparty risk to the banking system, inviting regulation in lieu of market discipline. The Volker rule should be abandoned and the present value accounting rules – comparable to those promoted by Ludwig and Volker above – should be abandoned as well.

Regulator incentives need realignment. The FDIC should be *held accountable* for protecting the insurance fund. Kane (2009, pp.109-110) provides a medley of ways to improve regulatory incentives. For example, regulators could have long term deferred compensation plans, like the investment bank partnerships of the 1970s. Finally, the FDIC's mission statement could be improved upon.[350] It is written in bureaucratese, without mention of competition, innovation, or cost-benefit analysis.

One example of a possible mission statement improvement can be found in the European Union's adoption of the Capital Requirements Directive (CRD) on January 1st 2007. It was designed to ensure the financial soundness of credit institutions (banks and building societies) and certain investment firms. The CRD framework incorporated in Basel II introduced the simple concept of three concrete "pillars": minimum capital requirements, additional capital against risks not covered in Pillar I as determined by regulators and management, and improved market discipline by requiring firms to publish certain details of their risks, capital, and risk management.

The United Kingdom went a step farther. In addition to the CRD reliance on market discipline, the FSA follows three principles of good regulation: proportionality, i.e., strict cost benefit analysis prior to all regulatory actions, innovation, i.e., encouraging multiple and novel ways to meet regulatory requirements, and competition, i.e., promoting international competitiveness and domestic competition.[351] The FSA mission statement focuses on prudential regulation but does not include "financial stability" as a goal, as the Bank of England does.

The CRD and FSA approach is worth emulating in the US as it focuses on what is important while eliminating all the distractions. The mission statements of US erstwhile *prudential* bank regulators bear more resemblance to the *progressive* missions of the Fed or even HUD. The FDIC Strategic Plan 2008-2009 adopted in December 2008 and released in 2009, after the financial crisis had peaked, promised *increased* emphasis on community reinvestment and low income lending. Defenders of CRA respond that banks would have made the bad loans in any event. The mission statement should not be otherwise cluttered with progressive consumer regulation that would provide the FDIC with a credible excuse for failure, undermining accountability for subsequent prudential regulatory failures.

The FDIC mission statement should emulate the CRD and FSA focusing on only two things:

1. sufficient capital: minimum requirements, additional risk based capital, and market discipline.
2. good prudential regulation: cost-benefit analysis, innovation, and competition.

Still, these reforms are all backward looking, addressing the distortions that gave rise to the last financial crisis. The key to success of regulatory reform is greater reliance on market discipline. There is a large literature on how to improve regulatory incentives by pricing deposit insurance to market requirements as an alternative to raising the capital requirement. But the FDIC is not subject to the same adverse selection as a private insurer due to its monopoly and mandatory requirement for participation and fee payment. Its efforts may work for a while, but regulators and politicians have neither the incentives nor the information to set market prices correctly. Risks should be hedged in the market, not just priced with models.

Federal deposit insurance replaced prior private and state attempts that generally failed due to moral hazard and lack of diversification from systemic risk. An alternative at the time was to provide private re-insurance, best limited to catastrophes. There are innumerable ways to provide market monitoring of insurance risk with multiple private insurers. The contract renewals among private insurers could be staggered to reveal changes in the perceived risk to the fund, for example. Contracts could be issued to re-insure specific TBTF banks, providing an independent market assessment of risk. Banking analyst Bert Ely has proposed a private variant on deposit insurance with the primary insurance cross-guaranteed by the participant banks (as is done now by the FDIC) and the catastrophe risk re-insured privately.[352]

Lowering the tax on capital and raising the tax on debt - the deposit insurance fee – would reduce the incentive to over-leverage. Markets and management could help decide the amount of capital necessary to support risk. Some analysts would create a derivative debt instrument specifically designed to foster speculation against an increasingly risky firm as a market indicator of risk, e.g., a convertible preferred bond or stock that converts to common equity when capital falls below a certain level. Changes in the price of such instruments – if actively traded – could act as an early warning indicator for regulators.

These steps are intended to reduce bank failures, but what happens when they occur? As noted in chapter 5, federal insurance does not operate like private insurance. To keep the costs of bailouts opaque, they are paid *ex post* by enhancing "franchise value." When this does not work, the costs are typically shifted forward with a higher mandated insurance premium. This penalizes successful firms or households for good behavior. When such costs are large, as they were with regard to the recent sub-prime lending crisis, it uses the legal system to accomplish its goals.

This political cover-up can occur only because of monopoly pricing and the continued franchise value subsidy. All funds not recoverable from the offenders should come from the US Treasury. Capital injections to the insurer/regulator should be budgeted currently. The current process for budgeting loans as provided in the Federal Credit Reform Act of 1990, amended in 1992 to accrue all future credit costs of federal lending, is a small step in the right direction but the costs of Treasury loans should include all costs, including risk and foregone taxes.

2. Rolling Back or Eliminating Bank Deposit Insurance

Deposit insurance is not the only nor necessarily the least controversial way to mitigate bank runs, but the moral hazard concerns regarding deposit insurance weren't an issue for most of the first half century, before the expansion of deposit insurance coverage that made it virtually universal. The use of off-balance sheet entities implicitly extended that coverage while the Fed's view of interconnected markets and systemically important firms (SIFs) extended it further until the limits to protection - if any – were no longer visible to risk-takers.

Protection increased the depth and breadth of the financial safety net, which continually expanded due to regulatory and political incentives until temporarily made universal by the Transaction Account Guarantee (TAG) in 2008. Protecting individuals in the financial sphere inevitably leads to protecting the enterprises with which they do business. Oftentimes, this is the primary objective in the first place. Once protections are introduced in a market economy the trend is very difficult to reverse, as the battle to let TAG expire at the end of 2012 revealed. The outcome of that policy was increased protection, less competition and growing moral hazard risk.[353]

Kane (2011, Table 2) cites seven major conflicts of interest between regulators and the public interest, characterizing the result as a cycle of denial and cover up. Rather than reform, regulators and politicians double down with additional protection, regulation and political control. Each extension has unleashed increased moral hazard, repeating the cycle. How can this cycle be broken?

Whether deposit insurance has been successful in other countries is difficult to assess because the costs of the safety net aren't generally readily apparent. But in the wake of the systemic failure of the savings and loan industry during the 1980s and the failure of the regulatory reform passed as a result of the most recent crisis, it is reasonable to conclude that extensive deposit insurance in the US over the last three decades has caused more harm than good.

The deposit insurance safety net – increased by TARP to $250,000 and extended during the crisis to investment banks and their on balance sheet proprietary trading account hedge funds – eliminated the charade that it sought to protect the "little guy" rather than the banks. The current deposit insurance limits protect the relatively wealthy. Insurance limits can easily be reduced to protect individual retail savers without providing the currently quasi-universal coverage. Insurance could be limited to its pre-1980 level of $40,000 adjusted for subsequent inflation, and limited per household. This would provide substantial but finite coverage while avoiding incentives to break the deposits into parcels below the limit and broker them. Individuals could purchase additional private insurance if they so desired. Even without these restrictions, as Alex Pollack notes, full insurance for all household time and savings deposits still only amounts to 30% of total deposits.[354]

Moreover, there are a lot of reasons not to be sanguine about the required regulatory reform. First, while addressing the problems that caused the sub-prime bubble is necessary, this does not necessarily address the causes of the next crisis. Second, the magnitude of political and regulatory changes necessary to make deposit insurance work is enormous. Third, politicians have shown no inclination towards comprehensive or substantial piecemeal reform. Dodd-Frank went in the opposite direction. If the FDIC cannot be held accountable for regulating capital and loan risk to mitigate moral hazard and firms cannot be shrunk below the TBTF and SIF thresholds, then publicly backed deposit insurance as currently provided is not viable.

It is at least worth noting that deposit insurance is no longer necessary to protect small or even large depositors. This leaves aside the question of whether it ever was necessary. Money market funds provide the benefits of bank demand deposits without the liquidity and credit risks while virtually eliminating the monitoring problem. Eliminating deposit insurance in favor of money market funds would transfer responsibility for financial adjustments from politicians to market participants. Admittedly, this is probably overly optimistic. Nevertheless, after eliminating deposit insurance and allowing several large bank failures, this policy would be more credible.

Money market funds were historically invested entirely in liquid US Treasury securities, reflecting the arbitrage between market rates on Treasury securities and regulated deposit rates while avoiding the minimum Treasury purchase requirements imposed on small investors. This investment strategy eliminated the need for systemic liquidity support and confidence building necessary for bank deposits backed by limited reserves. But when this source of arbitrage revenue was eliminated by deregulation, the funds eventually bought GSE securities and highly rated -- typically AAA -- commercial paper as well. This decision was based on the theory that prices of these securities could not change very much based on credit deterioration over their short (typically 30 day) life span. The financial crisis immediately spilled over into the "unregulated" shadow banking industry due to their extensive funding of Lehman's AAA commercial paper, which proved that theory false. This was really a minor blip in an otherwise stellar industry record: even the failed Primary Reserve Fund eventually paid 99 cents on the dollar.

Another alternative to limit FDIC risk exposure is to have banks issue money market accounts backed only by relatively risk free assets, as in the shadow banking system. Money market funds holding only Treasury bills or close substitutes would not need insurance. They would essentially be "banks limited to real bills," an idea popular in the 18th Century. There is about $16 trillion in US Treasury debt outstanding and over $20 trillion of US Treasury and government backed securities. The combined US time and savings deposits in all US financial institutions is only about 60% of that, and only about 40% of that total is in demand deposits. Arguably, only demand deposits should be guaranteed, and only a share, e.g., half, to protect the payments mechanism. There is a more than sufficient volume of assets for such accounts that this could meet all legitimate needs for risk-free deposits without fractional reserve banking supplying them.

AAA paper only adds about another trillion dollars to that supply. Some funds could include AAA CP with proper disclosure and/or public insurance at a nominal fee. All depository institutions could offer such accounts alongside uninsured certificates of deposits backed by the bank only. Parenthetically, while the need to regulate the money market industry has been dramatically oversold, regulating and guaranteeing money market accounts in lieu of bank deposit insurance is an idea worth considering. Issues regarding regulation are under discussion, but the reality is the need is low and the public exposure is lower still.

E. Mitigating Systemic Risk: Rely on Market Discipline

The 2,600 page Dodd-Frank Act and the 100,000 pages of implementing regulations is the most comprehensive and complex financial regulatory regime ever undertaken. Its promise was to eliminate systemic financial risk. Even if regulatory incentives were perfectly aligned with mitigating systemic risk, the system complexity would make regulation an endless effort doomed to failure. Yet the Dodd Frank approach is the byproduct of misaligned incentives, offering much worse outcomes.

Chapter 5 argued that politics-induced fiscal profligacy and financial regulation is the primary source of endogenous systemic risk while market discipline has been the historic solution. Dodd Frank did little to address the root causes of the 2008 financial crisis. Our diagnosis of the 2008 financial crisis and the work of others, such as Carmassi, Gros, and Micossi, find no fault with non-bank institutions, instruments, and markets. The primary problem in those markets arose due to SEC regulatory malfeasance regarding investment banks. The simple solution was more capital, the same as for banks. Capital requirements are well understood by market participants, so accepting insufficiently capitalized loans, investments, guarantees and/or other forms of counterparty risk is not the sort of chronic error market participants typically make,.

Why has US prudential regulation systemically failed? The financial safety net was introduced to protect "the small depositor" from financial crises. Further regulation and additional financial crises due to excessive leverage followed, then even more regulation due to the extension of the financial safety net. This vicious cycle is a recipe for ever-increasing complexity increasing both the frequency and severity of systemic failure. Dodd-Frank's additional regulation of firms, instruments, and markets will further stifle market discipline, institutionalize systemic risk, and likely lead to systemic collapse that could well result in a more permanent nationalization of the financial system.

That market discipline alone would have served the public better can be inferred, although not proven. Yet it is clear that having been replaced with government policy, market discipline alone can hardly be considered to have *failed*. Robust speculative markets are the ultimate arbiter of individual judgment and a primary source of market discipline. Speculative shorting has been around for centuries and played a vital role in disciplining markets. At the same time, regulators and politicians have generally opposed it because it has exposed substantial political interference and regulatory malfeasance, as evidenced by decades of restrictions imposed on short sellers.

The US system worked best with a faux-regulatory system reliant on market discipline for mitigating systemic risk while enabling a modicum of regulatory and political rent-seeking. Speculative derivatives instruments and markets have always been the primary tools to mitigate systemic risk, stymied opaquely during the sub-prime lending debacle by GSEs and TBTF financial institutions.

Dodd-Frank constrains the last vestiges of market discipline, putting in its place a regulatory regime doomed to failure. The incentive conflicts that produced this approach are discussed in section 1. Section 2 discusses the incentive conflicts inherent in Fed and Treasury responsibility for mitigating systemic risk. Section 3 discusses the problems with TBTF and SIFs and why the Dodd Frank Orderly Liquidation Authority (OLA) will produce unintended consequences the opposite of the purported purpose. Section 4 discusses the incentive conflicts with the new non-bank instrument and market regulation that will exacerbate rather than mitigate systemic risk.

1. Conflicting Incentives Among Politicians, Regulators, Economists and the Public

The financial systems of market economies developed prior to any public regulatory institutions. Participants relied on contractual arrangements and private monitoring. The US had and still has many means of private self-regulation which predate public regulation. For example, the stock exchanges generally regulate the behavior of its firms and investors. The US also relies on private corporate auditors regulated by the industry-operated Financial Accounting Standards Board (FASB).

Historically, the reason private monitoring worked is that it was arranged to be in the interests of all parties to comply. It was not perfect but was self-correcting because all market participants had an incentive to protect the mutual benefits of a well-functioning market. This mitigated systemic risks.

Capitalism provides greater incentives for compliance than alternative systems (Meltzer, p. 5). Nobody likes to admit mistakes, even to themselves. But as any CEO or CFO of a publicly traded company who has faced irritated investors on a conference call can attest, investors will sell your stock short while they are still on the phone if you fail to promise credible remedies.

Competitive markets subject to effective market discipline offer the greatest public benefit of a market economy. Why do politicians, regulators, and most economists resist effective market competition and discipline in favor of regulation, ultimately leading to a regulatory spiral? The simple answer is that it provides those individuals with abundant rent-seeking opportunities.

Politicians initially introduced regulation to "protect quality" by maintaining market standards and "promote stability" by limiting competition. This resulted in cartels that erected barriers to competition, - recognized as early as 1776 by Adam Smith in *The Wealth of Nations* – that facilitated political rent-seeking.

In many countries, including the US, prudential regulation eventually becomes a tool of financial repression. Deposit rate ceilings in the 1960s and 1970s are one example of this. The current misuse of risk-based capital requirements to subsidize profligate governments in Europe and the US is just one more recent example. But this is hardly new behavior: state owned banks were required to purchase risky state-issued railway bonds to finance the crony capitalists of the late 19th century.[355]

Financial firms will often try as best they can to protect themselves from political risks by avoiding lending to politically powerful borrowers altogether, but politicians may require it. Financial repression uses "carrots" (e.g., capital subsidies) as well as sticks (e.g., housing "goals", a euphemism for quotas) to achieve its ends.

Regulators are often charged with promoting "stability." This means regulators avoid the failure of favored firms for which politicians may hold them accountable. The "Progressive Era" dramatically expanded high regulatory barriers to entry that often stifled competition, giving rise to the cartelization of industry. The Fed was created during this era largely in response to the banking interests of the Morgans and Rockefellers who sought the same cartelization in banking as in their other enterprises (Rothbard p.48). In finance, politicians and regulators historically intervened specifically in the interest of "stability supporting banks growing until they are SIFs that are TBTF."[356]

The irony is that avoiding containable failures allows risks to build to a systemic threshold. This can be observed outside of finance as well. For most of the 20th century, the US Forest Service repressed all naturally-occurring fires. They eventually realized that when a fire did occur, they had provided the conditions for a conflagration. The Forest Service now follows a policy of a controlled burn of small, naturally-occurring fires.

As Karl Popper, an Austro-British philosopher and professor at the London School of Economics, long ago explained, "In an economic system, if the goal of the authorities is to reduce some particular risks, then the sum of all these suppressed risks will reappear one day through a massive increase in the systemic risk and this will happen because the future is unknowable." The sum of the risks in an economic system over time is a constant. The only question confronting economists is whether we should prefer to take our risk in small doses or in a massive injection.[357] It is not surprising that deposit insurance experts Kaufman and Scott ask "What Is Systemic Risk, and Do Bank Regulators Retard or Contribute to It?" and conclude that bank regulators indeed contribute.

Regulatory agencies are theoretically designated "independent" to maintain the aura of incentive compatibility, but this is a charade in practice. Politicians and regulators may be loath to liquidate financial institutions that fall victim to bad macroeconomic policy, e.g. the technical insolvency of the S&L industry and Fannie Mae due to sharply rising interest rates, or bad regulatory policy, e.g. the failure of bank regulators to prevent undue risk exposure on loans to Latin American governments.

Competitive markets require creative destruction that is inherently unstable, producing many minor shocks to avoid less frequent but larger shocks. Creative destruction also destroys existing political rent-seeking opportunities, causing politicians and regulators to actively resist such processes.

Regulatory policies and laws will not prevent the expansion and perpetuation of the kludgocracy. As we've seen, regulators will go beyond their legal limits to bail out firms even without political pressure. The Independent Agency Regulatory Analysis Act introduced in the summer of 2012 sought to improve agency accountability and require rigorous cost-benefit analysis. This was a potential step in the right direction and, not surprisingly, universally opposed by regulators.[358] But politicians have not yet been held accountable by voters for holding a similar kludgeocracy accountable, so this law is not likely to be successful in addressing the entire problem.

As noted in Chapter 4, economists are thought to generally favor competitive markets but have strong career scholarly publication incentives to make market failure arguments. Moreover, economists are not immune from rent-seeking, as discussed in the previously cited Fannie Mae expose *Reckless Endangerment*. In addition to exploiting market failure publication opportunities, economists will have ample opportunity to test out their latest economic theories with potential policy implications as political advisors. Chaos and complexity theories for example are fascinating but of questionable application to the last systemic failure. Chaos theory argues that "stuff happens" - but we argue the bad stuff didn't just happen; it was in response to distorted incentives. Complexity theory argues that "the bigger they are the harder they fall – like dominoes" - but we argue they didn't just get big and important on their own; it was as a result of political and regulatory policies.

Regulatory experts Barth, Caprio and Levine provide a typical regulatory prescription in *Guardians of Finance*: first implement re-regulation and then impose additional external oversight. More specifically, they propose a Sentinel – a panel of economic experts – to guide politicians and regulators. However, the shadow regulatory committee has existed for decades and exposed most regulatory failures. The Sentinel may provide ample rent-seeking opportunities, but the Dodd-Frank Financial Stability Oversight Council (FSOC) has already hired hundreds of economists.

Long run stability was promoted by adherence to the rule of law and known legal limits on the power of politicians to intervene during volatile times. Now, the safety net is the source of the very systemic risk it is supposed to protect the public from. If the financial system becomes too big, too complex and dominated by SIFs as a result of government policy, chaos theory predicts systemic risk will increase exponentially. At that point, public regulation is indeed a Sisyphean task.

2. The Fed's Role as Systemic Regulator

Central banks are not typically involved in regulation. Through the mid 1950's the Fed's regulatory role was mostly limited to monitoring bank collateral in the context of administering the discount window to prevent lending to insolvent institutions. The FDIC supervises Fed non-member state banks and the Comptroller of the Currency national banks. The Fed is the primary federal bank regulator for the approximately 900 state member banks. In addition, it is directly responsible for supervising about 5,000 bank holding companies (BHCs).

The Bank Holding Company Act of 1956 attempted to address the bypassing of the Glass Steagall restrictions on branching and on non-bank activities such as investment banking or commerce. Banks could form a holding company that owned multiple banks in different states. Activities not permitted for the bank, such as investment banking, were conducted in the holding company. As a BHC could own a state chartered bank in one state and a federally chartered bank in another, the Fed was then assigned the task of regulating the their activities, a typical kludge patch.

But that did not end the regulatory arbitrage. After all, the Fed was not the primary bank regulator. Banks had always held the option of choosing between a state charter and a federal charter. In the 1960s, the state-federal competition increased as the OCC began allowing banking activities that the Fed would not allow even for the holding company. Fed Chairman Arthur Burns once described the US system of competing and overlapping bank regulation as a "competition in laxity."

The net result was that BHCs could do many things that banks could not. In addition, Congress had exempted single-bank holding companies from the Act. At the time, these were mostly small community banks. In response, the number of BHCs grew from 117 when the law passed to 783 by 1968, accounting for a third of all deposits due to big banks' exploitation of this legislative loophole. The 1970 BHC Act Amendments required holding companies to divest of all activities except those "so closely related to banking or managing or controlling banks as to be a proper incident thereto" and left the interpretation and enforcement to the Fed.

Holding companies are generally a source of strength for banks. Rather than pay cash dividends to shareholders, the BHC invests in presumably productive assets. If such investments fail, there is no recourse to the bank. If they succeed, they are a potential source of recapitalization if the bank experiences difficulties. But there are also a variety of ways that banks can subsidize BHC activities and cover losses, for example, through transfer pricing for mundane activities such as data processing or providing bank support for off balance sheet risks.

As the Fed's conflicts with the OCC over BHC authority festered, its conflicts with the FDIC also grew. As regulator of state member banks, the Fed could keep insolvent banks open by lending at the discount window. As insurer, the FDIC footed the bill when they closed an institution as Fed advances were over-collateralized. Mayer (2001, p.39) summarizes the resolution to this conflict proposed in the 1970s:

"Through this period, think tanks and presidential and congressional commissions kept proposing new systems to get away from the divided supervision of the banking industry, most commonly a Federal Bank Commission that would take over the regulatory and supervisory powers of the OCC, the Fed, and the FDIC, and perhaps the state agencies as well. There was not much support for giving the job to the Fed. J. L. Robertson wrote to Senator William Proxmire of Wisconsin in late 1974, "[I]n my opinion, based on forty years experience in the field of federal bank supervision, including twenty-one years as a Governor and seven years as Vice Chairman of the Federal Reserve Board, the merged supervisory function should not be vested in the Federal Reserve System. The function of formulating and implementing monetary policy and the equally important and coordinate function of supervising banks and bank holding companies cannot be performed by one agency without seriously compromising the effectiveness of each function."[359] Fed governor Jeffrey N. Bucher chimed in: "[W]here the same agency has both the responsibility for monetary policy and a major role in bank regulation and supervision, conflicts of objectives may arise... Examiners should be insulated from any possible temptation of the monetary authority to use supervisory powers to implement monetary policy and they should be at all times free from evaluating certain loans differently from others".[360]

These conflicts were not addressed and did not improve with time. By 1998 there were seventy-eight financial regulatory agencies in the US (Mayer, p.40). In 1999 under Chancellor Gordon Brown the role of the 300 year old Bank of England was reduced to one goal and function: price stability. All regulatory functions were shifted to the Financial Services Authority (FSA) that already regulated all other financial services. The need for consolidation was obvious and the Bank of England had not been considered the survival candidate.

But the Fed's political power had been on the ascent during this period, just like that of Fannie Mae and Freddie Mac. The Fed was revered under Paul Volker in the 1980s and Alan Greenspan was viewed as the savior of financial markets after the crash of 1987. Greenspan was called a "maestro" (Bob Woodward, 2000) and a "magician" (Mayer, 2001). Rather than recognize the conflict, the Fed argued that regulation was the primary central bank role, with monetary policy a secondary adjunct (Mayer p. 40). When the Gramm-Leach-Bliley Act of 1999 finally removed the last vestiges of Glass-Steagall, under relentless lobbying from Chairman Greenspan, it designated the Fed as the "umbrella supervisor" of all financial holding companies.

Mayer describes the Fed's turf battle as a victory of the economists over the lawyers, which he supported as a step towards market discipline (p. 48). While a laudable sentiment, it was uncharacteristically naïve on Mayer's part to assume that economists supported market discipline. The Fed predictably diffused regulatory and political accountability while contributing to regulatory arbitrage fostered by the primary regulators. There was no move toward market discipline.

The last financial crisis was caused by excessive credit expansion and regulatory failure. The failure to resolve the inherent conflicts of interest among the multiple federal banking regulators ranks second as an underlying regulatory cause only to the failure to appropriately regulate Fannie Mae and Freddie Mac. The Fed rightly gets most of the blame in the FCIC Report, but this additional failure has yet to be addressed.

Wherever this responsibility is assigned, it should not be with the Fed or Treasury. But the Dodd-Frank solution to the problem of systemic risk - the Financial Stability Oversight Council (FSOC), not only chaired by Treasury with the Fed in a lead role as vice chair, but with representatives from eight prudential regulators and the Senate - does just that. The Fed and Treasury share the role of market regulator with authority over all large, complex financial institutions, including hedge funds. It is, as one central banker noted, like "putting the monkeys in charge of the bananas."[361]

This FSOC has already housed hundreds of economists in the Treasury, which seems more likely to entrench the political mantra "nobody could have seen this coming" than to act as an early warning system.[362] The FSOC has ignored the risks of the Treasury's fiscal deficits, the related Fed's ballooning balance sheet and the potential consequences of unwinding it. Will the economists' modeling efforts help?

"Staying with the above ideas, consider that all the quantitative models and statistical techniques like "value at risk" will prove to be hopelessly wrong when true volatilities re-emerge (as they always do!). And when that occurs, who doubts that many financial institutions will, once again, find themselves in the line of fire."[363]

If politicians were serious about limiting systemic risk in the future, they would eliminate regulatory responsibility for managing it, along with the hundreds of systemic risk regulators hired to provide political cover, thereby restoring market discipline.

3. Regulating Firms: Ending TBTF and SIF

Because policymakers in the US and elsewhere promoted bank consolidation over competition, there were more bigger and more integrated financial firms that were likely technically insolvent during the 2008 financial crisis. The worst evidence of moral hazard was found at the TBTF banks, including Citibank, WaMu, B of A, Wachovia, and the TBTF investment banks such as Lehman Brothers and Morgan Stanley. The GSEs also faced enormous moral hazard. All of these firms took excessive risks with excessive leverage. Whether they were all deserving of rescue is highly questionable. Nevertheless, it is difficult to refute the accusation that bailouts were more likely for the politically powerful than the technically solvent.

There is no evidence of economic advantages to the multi-trillion dollar, virtually unmanageable mega-banks. The primary reason for promoting TBTF is to hide the costs of regulatory failure and resolution. Currently, the cost of resolution when regulators fail is put on the remaining institutions, penalizing safe and sound banks and their customers for the losses of profligates and the failures of regulators. This is incredibly distorting, as demonstrated by the WaMu bailout of uninsured depositors. The FDIC – in a break from traditional practice - paid un-insured depositors in full and transferred the bill to the more senior bondholders. This caused the price of the bonds to plummet. The stock followed the bonds, making recapitalization impossible. The losses were then partially passed on to JP Morgan to be financed with additional future franchise value.[364] This cross-subsidy process is the same game housing policy played with F&F, leading to their eventual problems.

This political cover-up can occur only because of monopoly pricing and the continued franchise value subsidy. Since the public ultimately pays for regulatory failures, the costs should be imposed directly and transparently. This would arguably provide full political accountability. All funds not recoverable from the offenders should be provided by the US Treasury. Capital injections to the insurer/regulator should be budgeted currently. The current process for budgeting loans as provided in the Federal Credit Reform Act of 1990, amended in 1992 to accrue all future credit costs of federal lending, is an improvement over many alternative processes but the costs of Treasury loans should include all costs, including risk and foregone taxes, as discussed in Chapter 2.

During the aftermath of the 2008 financial crisis regulators forced numerous mergers. This created even more TBTF SIFs. Dodd-Frank then codified SIFs by specifically defining firms that were systemically important financial institutions (SIFIs). This definition is so broad as to include all TBTF firms and any other that the Fed wishes. To the monkeys at the Fed, most firms look like bananas. This grants the Fed broad regulatory authority. It also conveys to the market that firms designated as SIFIs are deemed too politically powerful to be allowed to default.

If the FDIC cannot reverse policies promoting TBTF, it is better that such banks be strong and well-diversified. However, more capital requires enhanced profitability. Universal banks – those engaged in traditional investment banking activities of underwriting, sales, and trading, i.e., market making – were stronger than small commercial banks during the Great Depression as a result of those activities. But this also would have made them SIFIs - virtually impossible to regulate without very high capital requirements. Former FDIC Chairman Sheila Bair defends Dodd-Frank, arguing that it puts TBTF institutions in a penalty box of higher capital requirements. Because Dodd-Frank actually identifies the firms designated TBTF and SIF while stating they will not be allowed to fail, the entire regulatory burden is put on the historically politicized determination of capital requirements. But regulators have always facilitated regulatory capital avoidance in the past, so it is not clear what is different this time.

Politicians think they have already eliminated TBTF in Dodd-Frank. For evidence of this, look no further than "Financial Markets are Crazy to Expect Future Bailouts" by former congressman Brad Miller.[365] Mark Calabria of the Cato Institute argues that Dodd-Frank allows regulators sufficient discretion to ignore constraints now that they have more bailout power than prior to the ACT.[366] Convincing market participants that TBTF is dead presents a bigger challenge, as markets believe SIFs will be protected one way or another.

Dodd-Frank contains a provision for Orderly Liquidation Authority (OLA) which allows regulators to take over virtually any SIFI and liquidate it to make the creditors whole. The purported premise is that bankruptcy takes too long, although that argument originally related only to transactions balances requiring immediate resolution. This is a small part of the total. Moreover, based on past experience, especially with TARP administration and the rest of the 2008 bailout, there is no reason for market participants to believe that this authority will be implemented other than in a political manner. Hence firms should strive to achieve SIFI designation. The markets will readily accept their implied federal guarantee and generate the revenues necessary to pay additional political rents, exacerbating moral hazard.[367]

Some observers, most notably former Fed Director and now FDIC Vice Chairman Thomas Hoenig argue for breaking up the large TBTF firms.[368] As the current TBTF firms are a Frankenstein-like creation of public policy, there is reason to be less than sanguine that a regulator-designed break-up will mimic the consequences of market discipline and provide well diversified, efficient financial firms that counterparties can adequately assess and shareholders can effectively manage. The first step toward smaller competitive firms is to stop sponsoring and encouraging financial enterprises that are TBTF and risky for market speculators to "short" due to political protection. The massive regulatory burdens and mechanisms of Dodd-Frank are exacerbating the trend toward industry cartelization and TBTF institutions.

4. Regulating Instruments and Markets

The SEC was established in 1934 in the wake of the stock market crash in order to shift blame for the asset bubble from the Fed to "market manipulators." Until the 1970's, it focused on corporate disclosures for publicly traded stocks. Whether the stock exchanges could have done this more efficiently is an open question, since much of the information SEC attorneys demand often is not helpful to investors. Moreover, the SEC was negligent to the extent of accusations of complicity in the Bernie Madoff pyramid scheme.

The expansion of SEC regulatory purview since the 1970's has been mostly disastrous, as discussed in prior chapters. BCL devote 11 pages (pp. 100-111) critiquing the SEC's role in designating NRSROs and setting policies (particularly capital requirements) for consolidated supervised entities, and regulating over-the-counter (OTC) derivatives. Recommendations for a functioning financial sector include: the elimination of the NRSRO designations; the end of SEC capital requirements, which are mostly a responsibility of the FDIC in any event and; the termination of its role in present value accounting, a major contributor to the PLS debacles of the 1990's and 2000's.

The SEC's only role in OTC derivatives was related to the NRSRO designations for ratings of the CDS writers. BCL devote another ten pages excoriating policymakers for not granting Brooksley Born, Chairwoman of the Commodity Futures Trading Commission (CFTC), the authority to regulate CDS in 1999, viewed by many at the time as a typical regulatory and political turf battle. Is the BCL criticism warranted? The CDS was arguably the most successful market innovation of the decade. It helped burst the housing bubble when regulators failed to do so. It is for that reason that the FCIC Report criticizes CDS, blaming the messenger for exposing fiscal profligacy. (BCLs' arguments here undermine their "Sentinel" recommendation substituting the guiding hand of economists for that of the market).

The CDS market did not fail in the aftermath of the 2008 financial crisis, as Wallison (2013) amply demonstrates. The problems identified at the time related not to the lack of regulation but to the regulatory arbitrage between bank regulators, purportedly resulting in too little capital posted by the issuer, particularly AIG, who used corporate parent guarantees as a form of capital. Even in that case, things worked out well for the buyer. Even Bernanke and Geithner now deny that the contracts were under-capitalized, announcing that after paying off CDS in full the AIG bail-out was costless.[369] Since banks write most CDS, the FDIC should regulate them and impose appropriate and uniform capital requirements on the writer with commensurate relief for the purchaser.

The derivatives market started with interest rate swaps to hedge fixed-rate prepayable mortgages. Virtually all of the problems of the derivatives market have been associated with home mortgages and most of the problems arise from regulations requiring pre-payment without penalty for fixed-rate mortgages. The notionally-$600 trillion derivatives market was created to, and still mostly does, shift interest rate risk of political origin relating to political support of the fixed rate mortgage.

In response to the purported CDS market failure, Dodd-Frank regulation *centralizes* derivatives trading – creating a new systemic risk by centralizing it in a single exchange – and imposes regulatory restrictions on traders that will inevitably be politicized when they bet against public policy, as they did in the sub-prime debacle. This problem should be addressed at the source. Dodd-Frank derivative regulation should be unwound. Derivative design and trading, for speculating as well as hedging, should instead be encouraged as the last vestige of market discipline.

Many developed economies have a single regulator focused exclusively on prudential regulation with effective supervisory oversight. In Britain, for example, even though they are (unfortunately) abolishing the Financial Services Authority (FSA), a single new agency will still have sole responsibility for all prudential regulation of financial firms, including banks, investment banks, building societies, and insurance companies. Should all the non-bank regulators be consolidated into one, like the FSA of the past decade? It is probably an idea worth considering in order to prevent new sorts of regulatory arbitrage and stymie systemic risk. It should report to a single Congressional Committee on Financial Regulation with no other responsibilities, such as "Housing" as at present.

Should non-bank regulation be combined with bank regulation? One reason why consolidating bank regulation with the regulation of other non-bank financial institutions is a bad idea is that banks are different from all other financial institutions by virtue of deposit insurance. On the other hand, the main reason to consolidate into one financial regulator with a single political oversight committee is to minimize the extent to which additional rent seeking drives the regulatory reform process. Most of the "deregulation" narrative was cover for the underlying turf war over the distribution of economic rents among competing politicians; that's a main theme of Robert Kaiser's *Act of Congress* (2013), ironic as it was written in support of Dodd-Frank. Additionally, consolidation might be more practical, since US banks have now become universal banks with an undefined scope of activities, including some non-bank activities. If deposit insurance is replaced by MMMFs, then both bank and non-bank regulation should definitely be consolidated.

F Restoring Mortgage Capital Markets

What is necessary to restore private mortgage capital markets? Not much, other than the steps discussed above. Most of the enabling legislation and regulation already exists. Left undone are several specific laws and regulations mostly related to setting appropriate capital requirements.

The mortgage lending S&L industry has been mostly absorbed by commercial – mostly universal - banks, which cannot and should not fund the entire stock of residential mortgages on their balance sheet with deposits. So the issues are: what should capital market instruments and institutions look like and how do we transition from GSEs? Complicating these issues is Dodd-Franks mortal sin, the creation of the Consumer Protection Financial Bureau (CFPB).

1. Private Label Securities (PLS) and Private Covered Bonds (PCBs)

Capital market investors generally take risks in equity markets but not debt markets, investing mostly in government debt or that of very highly rated companies with easily monitored leverage. The high yield bond market in the US transferred the risk of medium sized companies from banks to capital markets. However, it is relatively small - a potential source of capital funding for banks or mortgage finance companies but insignificant relative to the size of the mortgage market and past F&F financing. High yield bonds have extensive covenants mitigating risk and the issuers have publicly traded stock, making ongoing monitoring of their risk feasible by tracking the stock market.

In the US, the GSEs who retain that risk accounted for the lion's share of the mortgage capital market. Officials at Treasury and FHFA have worked with F&F to develop proposals for risk sharing bonds to allow private investors to participate in credit risk. These apparently have run afoul of CFTC rules regarding the use of swaps to hedge the interest rate risk.[370] Senior-subordinated securities and collateralized debt obligations efficiently transferred risk from issuers, but the risks were not always transparent to the mostly regulated and government-backed investors if other taxpayer-backed lenders leverage these investments as appears to have been the case. Thus far this small investor base mirrors that of the market's sub-prime predecessors. But new F&F issues are in any event a way to save them, not a way to faze them out.

Transferring primary first loss mortgage credit risk to third party capital market investors has never really worked. Internationally, covered bonds are virtually risk free and issued by government-backed and/or regulated entities with borrower recourse. Private securitization under the REMIC legislation relied, in principle, on credit tranching to pass risk on to those most able to bear it. In practice, it was funded almost entirely by regulated investors that depended on regulator-sanctioned ratings, with almost all the securities rated AAA/AA indicating *ex ante* that there was virtually no risk. This was generally consistent with bond investor behavior.

Initially, the first-loss mortgage securities were retained by the originator. The reason was not investor aversion to credit risk per se, but rather the agency conflict between loan originator and investor. Prior to PLS, third party investors mostly purchased senior participations in whole mortgage loans. But Fannie Mae and later Ginnie Mae created a mortgage banking industry dependent on them and in need of "sales treatment." This meant these first-loss securities were sold, sometimes at deeply discounted prices.

The private market of truly "at risk" non-bank investors in investment grade securities is mostly imaginary and will remain so unless and until both the SEC designation of credit rating agencies and the reference to credit ratings is eliminated in risk-based capital rules. While regulators are attempting to eliminate reliance on credit rating agencies, as required by Dodd-Frank, it is not clear what will take their place.[371] In any event, investors - not issuers - need to pay for ratings, with credit rating agency regulatory oversight if they are to retain their privileged status with the SEC. Simultaneously, bank regulators need to prevent regulatory arbitrage of capital requirements between loans and securities as pre-requisites to market discipline.

Even if the SEC ratings designations were abolished, would there be any third party at-risk investors that would invest in securities with significant primary mortgage credit risk without facing distorted incentives? The largest investors in mezzanine mortgage debt during the last crisis were hedge funds, mostly representing state and local government retirement fund assets with seriously distorted incentives. To fix their incentives, state and local pension funds would need to cut their assumed earnings rate about in half – making transparent a funding shortage measured in the trillions of dollars - and stop their going-for-broke strategy. This does not seem very likely, and so the distortions in this market are not likely to change soon, nor are hedge funds likely to price primary mortgage credit risk efficiently.

This is one reason why the new issue private MBS – the PLS – market remains moribund in spite of Chairman Bernanke's "Cunnard Line" attempts to inflate prices.[372]

So, what is the next step? The alternative that has received the lion's share of political focus is a resuscitated private label securitization market. These efforts inevitably lead back to the taxpayers bearing the risk. The better focus would be on the European covered bond model, a variant of the FHLB model in the US.

The Senate's Corker-Warner GSE reform bill of 2013 is contingent on the introduction of a new federal guarantor. The protections in the proposed Federal Mortgage Insurance Corporation (FMIC) in Corker-Warner – investor coverage down to 90% (Fannie Mae and Freddie Mac historically had a minimum borrower 20% cash down payment or only as little as 5% with or private mortgage insurance coverage private insurance down to 75%). The FMIC would essentially recreate a new GSE just like the old.

Federal Reserve Chairman Ben Bernanke endorsed this scheme based on the switch from implicit guarantees to explicit insurance, arguing that policymakers could lay out "rules of the game" with details, for example, on how a potential government insurance fund would charge premiums to private-sector participants.

"If the government does play a role then it should be fairly compensated," Bernanke said. "Instead of having an implicit guarantee that it ended up having to make good on, like the [Federal Deposit Insurance Corp.] or some other similar institution it should receive some kind of insurance premium."[373]

This Fed endorsement represents an about face as the Fed had long argued that Fannie and Freddie guarantees posed systemic risk to the U.S. financial system and under Bernanke expanded its guarantor role internationally.[374]

By pretending to treat the guarantee problem as actuarial rather than political, Corker-Warner can garner the support of all the traditional lending and housing lobbies that historically supported Fannie Mae and Freddie Mac, with bipartisan support making it politically feasible. But political feasibility isn't the requirement for successful economic reform. This Bill is wrong on several levels.

First, federal government guarantees are the opposite of insurance. Insurable mortgage credit risks are those that can be mitigated with upfront loan underwriting with the remaining *independent* default risks actuarially priced based on the "law of large numbers." The implicit guarantee – implicit because it was inferred by Wall Street rather than granted by Congress – was really a market "assurance" that the federal government – primarily the Federal Reserve – would avoid macroeconomic catastrophes, such as housing bubbles, i.e., systemic risk of widespread mortgage defaults as occurred in the Great Depression.

Second, the government has no inherent comparative advantage in the insurance business. It achieves monopoly status due to its implicit opaque subsidies, allowing it to dole out political favors. As a "federally sponsored" mortgage insurer the FHA, for example, is allowed to have a fraction of the capital of a private insurer, saving the cost of capital. As the private returns to capital are heavily taxed, FHA also receives substantial tax benefits. Moreover, federal monopolies can generally charge higher prices to new purchasers as FHA does whenever it gets into trouble in spite of these subsidies.

Perhaps US mortgage capital markets should look a lot more like their older Northern European counterparts. There, the originating lender, typically a bank, retains virtually all of the credit risk. Covered bonds were first used by Prussia's Frederick the Great to finance the rebuilding of residential and commercial real estate in the late 1700s. After the mortgage securitization market shut down and the Treasury Department put Fannie Mae and Freddie Mac into conservatorship in 2008, the Treasury published a white paper suggesting covered bonds as an alternative. Covered bonds are a simpler capital market funding vehicle, less distorted by taxes and regulations than PLS in the US.

The closest US counterpart to the Northern European covered bonds are the Federal Home Loan Bank (FHLB) securities. FHLBs have issued trillions of dollars of notes and bonds collateralized by their mortgage holdings over the past three quarters of a century without missing a single payment and currently have over $500 billion debt outstanding. Private-label covered bonds are not necessarily that much different, but do not feature the implicit federal backing enjoyed by the FHLBs that provides them their current AAA rating or the same inducement of moral hazard. The primary distinction is that, like MBS and MBBs, covered bonds designate a specific loan collateral pool and put the burden for pricing and managing mortgage credit risks on the originating bank/finance company and their investors in equity and unsecured debt where it can be more effectively priced and monitored.

Any community bank should be able to issue a covered bond, as the collateral cover will be the most important factor in evaluating the default risk and determining the credit rating. PCBs essentially expand a bank's funding source beyond deposit funding, to potentially longer maturities at a much lower issuance cost than private-label securitization (once standardized with shelf registration) and virtually eliminate the prior concern with excessive PLS credit ratings. Intermediate banks may evolve as bond issuers to diversify the credit risk of community banks, producing something like a private FHLB system or potentially a private pool guarantor.

Today mortgage brokers and mortgage banks also play a significant role in Europe. In the US, where mortgage bankers have historically had a large share of the originating and servicing market, selling primarily to GSEs and funding with PLS, they are likely to divide into brokers (originating for others) and regulated finance company security issuers that retain servicing.[375] Banks may divest of their mortgage banking units to limit exposure to "deep pocket" seeking lawsuits.

2. Eliminating Regulatory Arbitrage within Banks and Between PCBs and PLS

As regulation crowds out private market discipline, both PLS and PCB are more accurately categorized as "regulated bank" rather than "private market" solutions. Hence the policy focus should be on appropriate bank regulation, in particular eliminating the potential for regulatory arbitrage between alternative capital market funding vehicles when accessing capital markets. Covered bonds are a financing, so the capital requirement should be the same as required under bank risk-based capital rules for whole loans held by banks.

The covered bond capital requirements should be the same for finance companies as for banks. Why regulate finance companies? Because the lion's share of the capital structure will be funded with senior PCB debt, whether or not rated or purchased by regulated investors. As a result, finance companies should have the same capital requirement as banks when selling comparable debt. The primary difference is that investors in finance company covered bonds will rely only on external auditors to determine the adequacy of reserves and to maintain appropriate collateral without regulatory supervision of the underlying loans.

Any additional over-collateralization pledged to covered bond holders would have to be fully capitalized, either directly or with an enforceable capital call, e.g., from a bank holding company. Otherwise, covered bonds are a form of regulatory arbitrage if depositors and the FDIC have less collateral in the event of liquidation than for, e.g., whole loans financed with deposits. The inability to establish rules to accomplish this objective has proven to be the major obstacle to the covered bond bill introduced by Congressman Scott Garrett, Chairman of the House Financial Services Subcommittee on Capital Markets and Government-Sponsored Enterprises in July 2010 but should not prove an insurmountable barrier once F&F's un-capitalized competition is eliminated.[376]

Excessive investor over-collateralization requirements generally reflect a lack of confidence that regulators will monitor the quality of bank capital and of loans, e.g., not requiring sufficient loan reserves or banning certain types of lending like sub-prime. This reflects the historically poor track record as evidenced by the previously discussed Indy Mac case. Tighter underwriting guidelines, higher down payments, borrower recourse, and improved loan performance in the future can address this.

Net regulatory capital requirements for PLS and PCB financing for a comparable mortgage pool should be identical for the same reason, as well as the same for banks as for other issuers. That is, if a 50% risk weighting is required for mortgage loans with at least 20% cash down or private mortgage insurance down to 75% LTV, and a 100% weighting otherwise, that should be reflected in the covered bond capital requirements as well. Regulatory capital for covered bonds issued by banks is more transparent than for PLS while the originator retains the credit risk and the loans are subject to examiner review and hence to loan loss reserves. These are major points in their favor. Assuming PLS capital requirements are transparent and require the securities to be classified as a financing for GAAP accounting purposes, PCBs will likely have a competitive advantage over PLS in the marketplace reflected in their financing cost, although both could flourish.

Policymakers are off to an inauspicious start implementing a new framework for capital market financing. The Obama administration's Treasury Department Report correctly identifies regulatory arbitrage as a contributing factor to the financial crisis and recommends eliminating it prospectively. This has been said before, but with little follow-through due to regulatory and political conflicts.[377] Dodd-Frank required securitizations to retain the "riskiest" 5% retained interest, consistent with the recommendation above for loans with 20% down or PMI coverage. The Dodd-Frank 5% risk retention rule would eliminate "asset sale" accounting treatment for PLS if implemented as intended. But there has been extensive lobbying both before and after the Act's passage to once again render the capital requirement meaningless.

Before the bill passed, the legislation exempted "qualified residential mortgages" (QRMs) from *any* retained capital requirements. But the insanity did not stop there. A political battle ensued over whether risk retention applies to first loss or any tranche, e.g., the least risky, making this requirement meaningless. This would re-introduce "asset sale" accounting and "present value" accounting, the two main contributors to the PLS lending debacles of the past two decades, and make the risk retention rule ineffective.

After the bill passed, the capital *exemption* to the risk-retention rule for QRMs was interpreted by all six prudential regulators to mean loans with a 20% cash down-payment. The CFPB, lobbied to exempt about half the mortgage market to avoid a "disparate impact," rejected the 20% down payment requirement.[378] After the CFPB issued the toothless QM rule in early 2013, Fed Chairman Bernanke weighed in with the opinion that the QRM rule should be the same as the QM rule.[379] Bernanke wanted no capital requirement for securities funding loans with zero down payment.

When the regulations were issued in late August 2013, QM and QRM were combined with neither requiring any borrower down payment. This eliminated 98% of all mortgages from any borrower or securitizer capital requirement. Adding insult to injury, the "risk retention" rule was expanded to include any risk, not just "first loss." The affordable housing lobby pushed the risk envelope beyond even that of the prior decade.

Bank, GSE and private-label securitization regulations that relate to borrowers – the qualified mortgage and qualified residential mortgage rules – should restore the original Fannie and Freddie requirement of a minimum *cash* down payment of 20% or mortgage insurance down to a 75% loan-to-value ratio, eliminating the use of purchase money seconds in lieu of insurance.

3. How Mortgage Markets Can Price and Hedge Risk Efficiently

Banks can finance fixed-rate mortgages with PCBs using both long-term financing and derivatives to hedge duration risk. PLS passes prepayment risk on to the investor more easily and more completely. However, they require investor loan servicing for unpredictable monthly cash flows, a significant burden for some investors.

The 2013 Nobel Memorial Prize in Economic Science was awarded to Eugene Fama for his theory that markets efficiently price financial instruments. The caveat is that this doesn't apply to loans and securities priced by undercapitalized government-backed lenders, the source of the irrational exuberance cited by co-winner Robert Shiller that led to the home price bubble. Higher capital requirements for federal mortgage lenders, more stringent QM and QRM requirements for borrowers and a heightened reliance on private markets will help keep taxpayers from paying for future bailouts. Prospectively, any borrower subsidies to meet housing goals should be explicitly budgeted and targeted to homebuyers so well-capitalized markets can efficiently price and manage both credit and interest rate risk.

Credit default swaps efficiently transferred risk from the regulated government-backed banking system, but were often written by even less well regulated banks, e.g., AIG's Treasury-regulated thrift subsidiary that wasn't required to post the requisite capital.

Speculators can play the key role in mitigating systemic risk given the right instruments efficiently priced and actively traded. The CDS market was thin and prices were not a good leading indicator of rising credit risk during the last crisis. A liquid market for credit-linked futures could contribute to more transparent and efficient credit risk pricing as Treasury futures have for interest rate risk.

One popular GSE myth is that they remain necessary to hedge mortgage banking pipeline risk. The under-capitalized mortgage bankers originally hedged mostly in Treasury futures and options markets because these were the most liquid. Essentially an originator could buy a Treasury "put," which would change in value by approximately the same amount as the mortgage. A synthetic Treasury put - selling Treasuries forward and buying a call - was generally more liquid and cheaper.

Mortgage bankers often believed that the price of Treasury securities was not well correlated with the price of agencies due to the pre-payment feature of the mortgages underlying F&F loans, a minor factor during the short life of a production hedge. Mostly what they perceived as less than perfect correlation was imperfection both in their hedge strategies and in their inability to accurately predict the extent to which loans in their pipeline would fail to close (fall out of their pipeline). A forward market – called To Be Announced (TBA) developed in which F&F securities could be sold forward before they had been created. This required standardization following rules for "good delivery" administered by the Securities Industry Financial Markets Association (SIFMA). While mortgage bankers bemoan the potential loss of an F&F TBA market, there is nothing about this process that requires participation by a GSE or a federal guarantor.

4. The Implications for Fixed Rate Mortgage Lending

Fixed-rate mortgage lending incorporates two types of interest rate risks: the loss for lenders using short-term debt when rates rise and the loss for maturity-matched lenders due to the free borrower prepayment option when rates fall. In addition, a falling rate environment is typically associated with rising credit losses as house prices often fall as well. During the last decade, Fannie and Freddie's strategy of buying back mortgage-backed securities with short-term debt didn't result in interest rate losses due to the Federal Reserve's low interest rate policy, but their credit losses skyrocketed.

The common cause of both the S&L and GSE systemic failures was the fixed rate mortgage. Firms that borrow short and lend long without hedging are guaranteed to fail when interest rates raise enough, as savings-and-loans and technically Fannie Mae did in the 1980s. Deposit-based lenders can use interest rate swaps and/or futures markets to transfer the interest rate risk of fixed rate mortgages, but the availability of swaps is limited by the availability of long-term fixed rate liabilities, down about 80% as a share of financial liabilities since the 1970s in response to high and volatile interest rates according to the Federal Reserve Flow of Funds Accounts.

Options are used to manage the risk of mortgage loan commitments prior to closing, but MBS has proven to be the only effective way to transfer lender prepayment risk for closed loans. The free borrower prepayment option remains an un-hedgable investor risk.

The continued existence of fixed rate mortgages in the US is often attributed to the GSEs, who either successfully hedge in the derivatives market or in extremis pass losses to taxpayers. GSEs have mythical powers only due to government accounting and political spin. Fixed rate mortgages will remain available to those borrowers willing to pay the appropriate risk premium. Private markets won't eliminate fixed rate mortgage lending but borrowers – rather than taxpayers – will have to pay for the risk.

5. The Transition to Private Securities

Originators and investors will not commit to private mortgage finance until convinced GSE competition and mis-pricing of risk is gone for good, so all the GSEs and implicit credit subsidies must be credibly and permanently eliminated prior to transitioning to a market-oriented integration of housing finance with the "private" regulated banking system that protects the FDIC. This may be the best political opportunity for reforming housing finance regulation since President Kennedy's Chairman of the Council of Economic Advisors Gardner Ackley first called for reigning in the GSEs in his 1963 Report of the Council of Economic Advisors. At the same time, it may also be the worst economic environment since then for doing so.

The housing market and economy are in their worst shape since 1963 and the GSEs continue to deliver massive unbudgeted subsidies to home borrowers. The problems are compounded by the Federal Reserve's suppression of mortgage interest rates at artificially low levels. In addition, the litigious attempts to shift the cost of the sub-prime mortgage debacle *ex post* have created legal and regulatory ambiguity that further discourages private mortgage finance. Few investors believe that the federal government will ever withdraw its implicit backing. Moreover, the perceived political risk – from which the GSEs have been exempted - is currently too great to attract sufficient investors without such assurances.

Hence a return to competitive private markets requires both confidence building measures to reduce political risk and an ironclad sunset on Fannie Mae and Freddie Mac. Numerous technical issues concerning a managed liquidation would undoubtedly arise, but none likely would prove insurmountable. A first step toward gradual liquidation would be to re-impose the traditional PMI requirement and prohibit future debenture issues for new business. That way all future MBS issues would have private capital behind the credit risk while passing the interest rate risk on to investors, as was traditionally the case. The second step would be to explicitly guarantee the entire stock of outstanding debt and MBS - by now indisputably backed by Treasury in any event - and include it in the deficit calculation. A third step could include calling or swapping this debt and issuing Treasuries: this might give greater control of the underlying mortgages to the enterprises, thereby assisting in the foreclosure and liquidation of the remaining assets. Fourth, all new MBS should be explicitly capitalized with Treasury preferred stock, with Treasury liability limited to that capital investment.

It goes without saying that both the liquidation and prospective future mortgage system should be designed to minimize long-term taxpayer expense. But current expense has never been transparently budgeted. Requiring transparency reform does not increase the current "budget deficit." Simply recognizing the existing liability is a major obstacle, and its lack of recognition is likely a not-so veiled attempt to maintain the status quo, a tactic that worked spectacularly to prevent Social Security reform a decade ago. [380] Mortgage rates on appropriately capitalized private mortgage backed debt will be higher, reflecting the lack of an implicit subsidy. To the extent that this debt also includes a large political risk premium that is not easily addressed by new confidence-building laws and regulations, the Fed should target large-scale asset purchases toward these securities for subsequent sales.

In short, there are not any market constraints to a transition. The smoothness of transition is not dependent on either the housing market or economic recovery, but enabling regulation and certainty regarding GSE withdrawal from the market. Banking regulators are already working on Basil III implementation, so the GSEs can be taken off the table and put into liquidation once again or, more likely, allowed to unwind through pre-payment until market conditions warrant. Passing a re-drafted version of Congressman Scott Garrett's bills would furthermore enable private mortgage capital markets to start up immediately.

Senator Garrett recently introduced the Private Mortgage Market Investment Act, a complement to the covered bond legislation and one of numerous bills he has introduced to help re-start the private mortgage capital market. The bill contains three main sections relating to transparency, standardization, and the rule of law intended to help spur private lending as F&F are phased out. He has also repeatedly submitted the companion covered bond bill.

Market-makers want "standardization" of mortgage backed securities (MBS) to facilitate trading. The primary motivation for trading both private and GSE MBS has historically been to speculate on pre-payment. PLS would facilitate the transfer of this risk from banks to investors/speculators more easily than PCBs. But government-imposed standardization limits innovation and risks a return of agency status to impose it.

Congressman Garrett's concern that the rule of law needs re-enforcing is well founded because mortgages lenders feel they are under siege.[381] The dearth of private mortgage finance in emerging markets is a reminder of just how dependent a market system of housing finance is on a sound, predictable legal system to provide an enabling environment and on the absence of public sector competition. This enabling environment was hard-earned in the US. However painful foreclosure was during the Great Depression, the ensuing changes clarified and strengthened lender rights, resulting in predictability in the meaning and application of laws and regulations that have been a tremendous boon to mortgage borrowers ever since. Political risk during the Great Recession has been worse than that of the Great Depression and is still increasing.

Thinking ahead strategically is generally a good business practice. But the FHFA is largely an interim regulatory solution, pending future resolution of the GSEs. Should they design mortgage capital markets and the future of housing finance, the stated task of their recently-adopted strategic plan?[382] Ultimately, they are designing and implementing secondary market infrastructure.[383] Both of these initiatives provide the FHFA with a yet-to-be-assigned long-term role. Such actions will likely be a political obstacle to subsequent regulatory reform.

G. Sources and Uses of Funds for Mortgage Finance

A well functioning market system not only allows households to compete for mortgage credit, but also encourages households to save for a down payment. These savings add to the total credit pool. Unresponsive or under-responsive governments - predominantly those of previously-centrally-planned economies – generally have high "forced" household savings rates allocated mostly toward (state owned) business, whereas politically responsive governments, e.g., the US and much of Europe, have much lower net savings rates. However, the latter have favored the allocation of a much larger share to household investments, although the US is an exception in its required down payment savings and some others have actively encouraged savings generally.

During the GSE era, the US had the latter household allocation without the former savings as down payment requirements continued falling until they became negligible. This created a downward spiral, as the more savings fell the greater the "need" for credit allocation. During the middle of the GSE era home mortgage credit was increasingly funded with domestic household retirement savings. But during the last decade as much as a quarter to a third of US home mortgage credit was funded directly by foreigners investing in GSE securities – that they thought to be direct Treasury debt substitutes – or in mostly AAA rated private label securities. This trend was unprecedented and unsustainable, with major implications for the availability and sources of US mortgage credit in the future.

1. Sources and Uses of Funds for Home Mortgages 1960-2010

Under the original S&L "closed" model of housing finance, most of the funds for mortgage lending came directly from households saving for a down payment. Exhibit 1 illustrates the basic savings trends discussed in previous chapters. Domestic savings, mostly in deposit institutions, was more than sufficient to fund home mortgages through the 1960's and 1970's, although in the 1970's the GSEs transferred (mostly) deposit funds from credit deficit to credit surplus areas created via the interstate – and later interregional - restriction on branch banking. The trend of tapping wholesale savings sources accelerated as retirement savings grew much faster than financial institution insured deposits and money market funds during the 1980's and 1990's. Unlike in Europe, US securities laws prevented banks from issuing mortgage backed securities, such as covered bonds, nationally to access this wholesale saving supply.

The fixed-rate liabilities of life insurance companies were a good match for Ginnie Mae passthrough securities backed by fixed-rate mortgages that historically could not or were not refinanced when interest rates dropped. Whereas in 1970 about 70% of long term savings was in fixed nominal life contracts and pension annuities, by 2000 that percentage had dropped to only about 10% according to the Fed's Flow of Funds accounts. This reversed the excess demand for fixed income securities. Pensions, unlike life annuities, were generally adjusted for inflation and grew much faster partially as a consequence of the high and volatile inflation of the 1970's after the dollar was de-linked from gold in 1971.

Exhibit 1

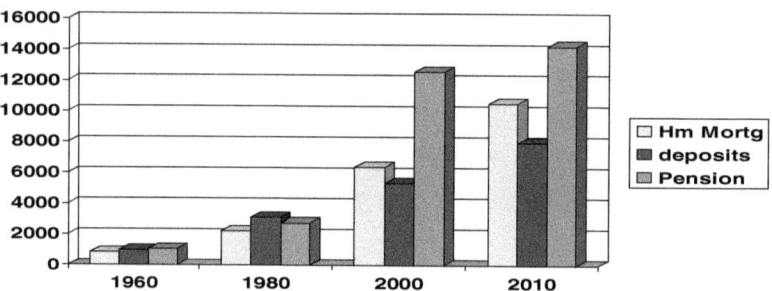

The use of mortgage insurance in the 1950's and 1960's reduced initial down payment requirements - and hence household home owner equity - somewhat, but the value of the mortgage stock remained about one third of the value of the housing stock as illustrated in Exhibit 2. This rose a bit with the beginning of the GSE era in the 1970s even though house prices rose more in value during that period, largely due to the ease of refinancing arising from restrictions on pre-payment penalties and due to the advent of cash-out refinancing. This trend persisted during the 1980's and 1990's with the growth of second mortgages, especially home equity lines of credit, and accelerated during the last decade with interest-only and negatively-amortizing loans. All of these trends reduced the accumulation of so-called "forced" savings due to loan amortization. This resulted in a huge increase in mortgage debt relative to the value of the housing stock without much change in the homeownership rate.

Exhibit 2

Added Leverage has not delivered long-term gains

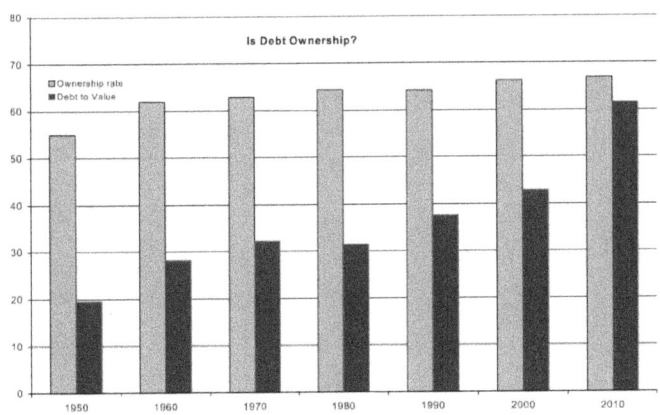

Not only did households use every available tool to cash out homeowner equity during the last three decades, but the remaining homeowner equity caused them to save less in other ways as well due to the "wealth effect" that encouraged greater consumption. Rising house prices don't increase real household wealth, but households that mis-perceived the rise in house prices as a permanent increase in real wealth reduced savings and increased consumption. As shown in Exhibit 3, household accumulation of savings other than for retirement was negative during the last quarter century, turning positive only after the financial crisis as lenders wrote off defaulted debt, encouraged by the temporary personal income tax exemption on the defaulted household's imputed income (i.e., reduced debt and hence increased wealth).

Exhibit 3

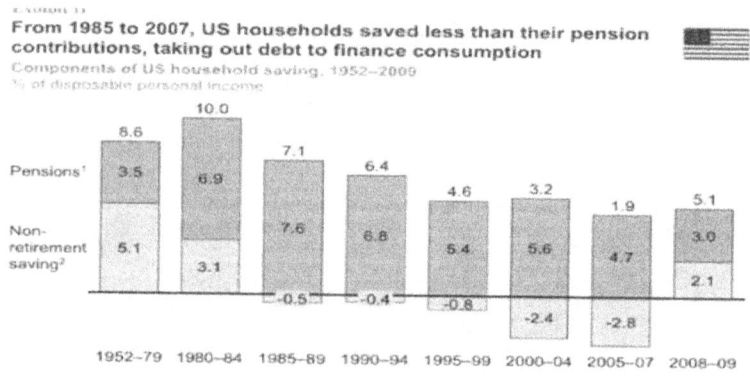

From 1985 to 2007, US households saved less than their pension contributions, taking out debt to finance consumption

Components of US household saving, 1952–2009
% of disposable personal income

1 Includes public and private pension plans, 401(k) plans, and individual retirement accounts, does not include Social Security withholdings
2 Other saving calculated through the change in household assets less liabilities, excluding retirement saving.
SOURCE: Bosworth & Bell (2005); US National Income and Product Account; US Federal Reserve Flow of Funds Accounts; McKinsey Global Institute

Another way to look at this is that US households borrowed instead of saved, enabled by readily available mortgage credit. The US household saving rate, low even in comparison to other developed economies, continued falling during the 1980's and 1990's as households took on ever-increasing debt. Household debt as a fraction of GDP more than doubled from about 60% to over 130 % by the peak of the last house price bubble, as illustrated in Figure 2.

Figure 2

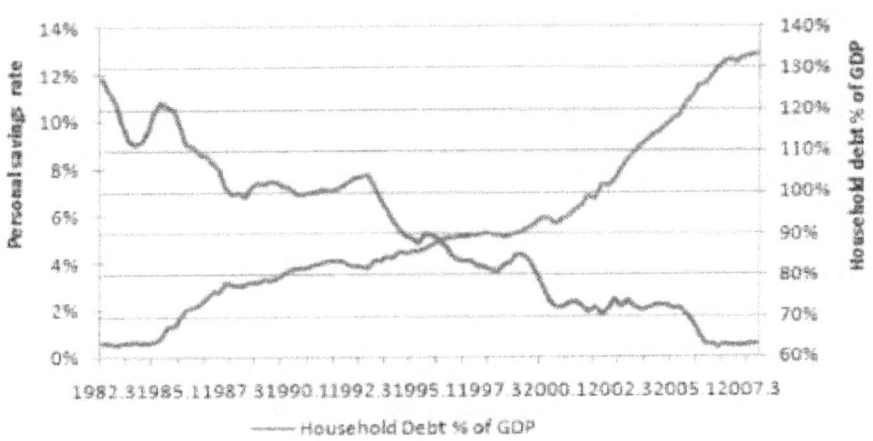

Over the last decade, the stock of mortgage assets approximately doubled while the stock of pension fund assets grew by only about 40%. US net savings shortfalls spilled into global capital markets where GSEs borrowed significantly and PLS funding also followed. Table 1 illustrates the US progressively providing less credit internationally during the 1980's and 1990's. It also shows the US acceleration during the last decade to net debtor status with a flow reversal of almost $11 trillion. As noted previously, the global distribution of GSE MBS contributed to the globalization of a national systemic financial crisis: the US financial system was further integrated with those of other countries. As can be inferred from Exhibit 1 in Chapter 4, this reversal to net foreign borrowing represents most of the capital surplus available globally.

The US stock of financial credit liabilities approximately doubled from year end 2000 to year end 2010 while the percent of that stock held by foreigners increased by about 25% to roughly a third of the total. This was largely a result of foreign central banks (primarily Chinese) and other investors purchasing US Treasury and GSE debt. China has not only scaled back purchases, but gone short-term as well.[384]

	Table 1	Flow of Funds		
		Rest Of World		
	1960	1980	2000	2010
Total Assets	41	489	6873	17419
Agency-GSE				
Public		7	116	669
Private		2	232	408
Total		9	384	1077
Total Liabilities	65	675	3611	9985
Net US Surplus/Deficit	25	186	-3262	-7,434

2. Prospective Sources and Uses of Funds for Home Mortgages 2010-2030: Crowding Out

The potential future source of funds for housing is from household domestic deposits, capital market savings, and foreign savings. The competing uses are business investment, government borrowing, and foreign borrowing. Only a few small countries with their own currencies, e.g., Hungary, borrow internationally directly to finance housing. There is no good reason for a country the size of the United States to fund home mortgages internationally, as in the past, and several good reasons not to do so. From the perspective of foreign investors, individual home mortgage borrower risk is the last thing a foreigner should want to underwrite due to the political risks posed by foreign entities implementing foreclosure and eviction. Foreign investors did not foresee this risk for GSE securities and demanded that they be explicitly guaranteed by the government when in default. International creditors generally fund governments first and businesses second.

But it makes no difference whether households borrow domestically or internationally to the overall availability of funds. US housing finance policy has for decades been premised on a global surplus of savings and hence infinite supply of domestic mortgage credit. The new reality is an extreme global shortage. It is unhealthy for the business sector, historically a net borrower, to invest less than it saves; household savings is essentially non-existent among the western market economies; net global savings is shrinking rapidly, and the current trends of public sector demand for funds swamps available domestic and foreign sources of savings. Mortgage borrowers are typically near or at the back of the queue in credit-short countries for several reasons. First, governments typically want to allocate more to business to offset the negative consequences of anti-growth policies. Second, long-term housing finance easily becomes overly-politicized in a credit-short environment, discouraging lenders from rationing by price or by quality.

Household savings has been in decline for decades in other advanced economies - Japan and the euro area – as in the United States, all with aging populations. All have been living off the excess precautionary savings of emerging markets, particularly China (see Exhibit 1 in Chapter 4) in the short run. The excess savings in surplus nations mirrors their current account surplus. Foreign borrowing financed an average of $1 trillion annually of the US savings shortfall over the past decade (Table 2), mostly financing US federal deficits. This has been falling and is likely to continue to fall if not as a result of the policies of current account deficit nations such as the United States, then as a result of the domestic consumption policies and investment strategies of the surplus nations. Nevertheless, at the same time that both US political parties promoted policies to end the current account deficit – and hence the supply of foreign savings – there was little or no off-setting decline in the federal government demand for funds.

The life cycle hypothesis popularized by Franco Modigliani in the 1950's would have predicted large growth in the stock of retirement savings over the last few decades in industrialized countries to be drawn down by the baby boomers as they entered retirement starting at the end of the last decade. Medical insurance is generally considered a form of casualty insurance because people require a lot more care in old age, when their income is lowest, and it is inextricably linked to life cycle savings for old age. The most reasonable explanation as to why the anticipated savings bulge did not occur is that unfunded public health and retirement promises served as substitutes for private savings.

Social Security was introduced and administered as a pay-as-you-go welfare scheme in 1935 using language usually associated with retirement plans, a ruse that continues to this day. Private retirement plans in the US are required by the federal government to be essentially fully-funded. The amount of savings required depends primarily on the retirement age of the beneficiary relative to life expectancy the promised benefits, and the return on investment. Public funds are also generally expected to be fully-funded but are exempt from assuming a realistic rate of return. Using highly improbable rates of return has resulted in public pension underfunding of about $5 trillion.[385]

Politics expanded the federal entitlement promises of the purportedly self funding pay-as-you-go pyramid system until the cumulative difference between the future revenues under the current tax structure and the future benefits as currently promised is estimated to be on the order of $100 trillion, the current "unfunded" federal liability. Had the same advance funding laws been applied to these entitlements, as private pensions the current required fund would be about $50 trillion - the Trustees estimates about $38 billion using somewhat less realistic assumptions - discounted at the Treasury yield used for Social Security. To put that in perspective, US household wealth is currently about $65 trillion. This additional funding would have nearly offset the dramatic decline of household savings over the last three decades and provided a slight baby boomer life-cycle-driven bulge to the savings trend depicted in Exhibit 3 above.

At that time Social Security was introduced the minimum age to receive benefits was 65, when male life expectancy of a 35 year old was under 60 years and for a new borne was 46 years. 65 remains the official age to receive full benefits, but male life expectancy has increase by two thirds to 76 years old and most recipients start receiving Social Security benefits at 62 years old since the benefit structure discourages work, especially after 65. The initial Social Security benefit is tied to the beneficiary's wage level and indexed to inflation, as measured by the CPI-W for urban wage earners.

It is the substitution of the pay-as-you-go Social Security and Medicare welfare system for private household retirement savings – initially financed by 46 taxpayers for each recipient, now three for each recipient, and soon only two - and the explosion in the scope, depth, and duration of benefit promises that has created the unfunded Social Security and Medicare/ObamaCare liability of $100 trillion.

Early estimates from the 1960's showed a 50% decline in private savings in response to Social Security benefits, but as the real value of Social Security benefits increased and households came to believe that the 1982 reforms resulted in a funded system, the offset might well have grown to 100% as demonstrated by the decline in household direct retirement savings.[386] Aggregate net savings in other developed economies arguably fell – when they too should have been rising to fund the baby boom - for similar reasons relating to the welfare state.[387]

It is arguably too late for today's elderly to do much of anything about their financial situation, already stressed by the effects of the Fed's negative real short-term interest rate policy on their savings. Cuts in elderly entitlements will cause them to draw down their own personal savings faster, reduce bequests to their children, and depend more on others, who are in bad shape from the last financial crisis. The Fed release in June 2012 showed a 38% decline in the median net worth of US households from 2007 through 2010. This was a decrease from $126 thousand to only $77.3 thousand, a level last seen in real terms in 1992. At the same time, their share of *existing* federal liabilities – the present value of the tax already due - is $140 thousand, almost $50 thousand of which is owed to foreigners. But the present value of the contingent future liabilities owed by younger households for current entitlements going mostly to elderly households is at least five times that. The state and local retirement benefits seemingly modestly under-funded at the typically assumed 8% rate of return essentially represent an additional unfunded intergenerational entitlement in today's zero interest rate environment of potentially another $50,000. That's roughly a million dollar bond, which helps explain why economic activity is going underground.

H. Final Comments: Restoring Economic Growth

The past saving shortfall obviously reduced investment and economic growth well below potential. This is water over the dam at this point. Now compound interest works in reverse: the consequence of past underfunding is reduced future consumption estimated at $100 trillion. The three current options to "save the system" are cutting entitlements, raising taxes, and/or borrowing the money, none politically appealing.

The two legislative centerpieces of the Obama Administration; Obamacare health insurance reform and the Dodd Frank financial reform both passed in 2010 avoided the hard political choices. The $100 trillion unfunded entitlement liability is essentially the same as the unfunded housing liability but on a much larger scale. Both policies favored consumption over savings and both did or will cause a systemic crisis.

Financial firms – especially the large impersonal insurance companies and banks– were ripe for political demonization as many people have their individual gripes, but greed doesn't wash as an explanation of the purported crises. Many health insurers are non-profit and health insurance has historically been less profitable than other forms of insurance. Private bank shareholders lost about $2 trillion as a result of home mortgage defaults on loans made during the housing boom. Nevertheless large health insurers and banks willingly accepted demonization as the price for political protection; crony capitalism works for demons and demonizers alike.

The progressive "Great Society" social safety net policies of the 1960s to provide access to adequate health care and decent housing - reasonable goals for a wealthy society - morphed into much more ambitious universal health care and home ownership goals. At issue is how to pursue these more ambitious goals without undermining those policies that made society sufficiently wealthy in the first place.

The right approach - carefully targeted transparently budgeted subsidies - was politically problematic from the start due to the "massive" $25 billion "guns (Vietnam War) and butter (Great Society)" federal deficit in 1968. So the costs were made opaque in two ways: first, by shifting costs to other borrowers and insurance customers; and second, by passing unrecorded liabilities on to future generations.

Beginning in the 1960s the new Department of Housing and Urban Development (HUD) started socializing costs and risks by using FHA low down payment mortgage insurance programs, subsequently expanding this approach to include Fannie Mae and Freddie Mac as well as private banks. This created a "moral hazard" of excessive risk-taking that ultimately turned the American dream into a nightmare, causing these government sponsored entities to fail resulting in a global financial crisis. The systemic failure of the financial system reflects this risk-socialization.

Medicare introduced in 1966 similarly socialized the cost and risk of health care insurance. Medicare engaged in price setting to keep transparent budget costs down, shifting insurance costs and risks. And as with home ownership goals, Medicare drastically reduced the need for household savings – in this case for old age medical expense. As with Social Security, there never was public saving to fill the ironically mis-labeled Medicare Trust Fund.

Politicians created both crises and the subsequent cover-up - the addition of approximately one hundred thousand pages of new regulations for each - will make things worse. Obamacare has already failed fiscally because the young didn't need a government subsidized college education to figure out the "tax" for becoming insured – cost shifting from the elderly - and the relatively free ride provided by the guarantee of insurance for previously existing conditions.

Cutting entitlements while raising taxes caused economic collapse which led to social unrest in Southern European countries, where they have been forced to mostly rely on borrowing. Pressuring the Germans and other official lenders, such as the partially US-funded IMF, to lend money spreads the pain while pressuring the European Central Bank to print it delays the pain, at the cost of prolonged economic stagnation.

US politicians think we can avoid this fate by growing out of the problem, but it is not clear why they believe this. The prospects for growth were not very good to begin with according to economist Robert Gordon, who believes that the low trend rate of private sector productivity growth in the US since the 1960's will inevitably worsen due to factors beyond political control.

But federal policies of the last four years have significantly dimmed growth prospects. Economists Carmen Reinhart and Ken Rogoff (2011) found that since 1790 once the US or any country exceeded a 90% debt/GDP ratio, economic growth slowed by nearly 2% annually for a decade. It is already above 100% as a result of the massive deficits of the past four years. Making matters worse, the cost of additional federal regulatory burdens is estimated at almost a half trillion dollars annually. Cutting entitlements and raising taxes will further discourage savings and productive investment.

Raising taxes on the "rich" only raises pennies on the dollar and most of the tax increases will fall disproportionately on saving and investment. Moreover, while the tax code is ripe for "reform" the quest for revenue will likely make current distortions worse. Cutting the mortgage interest deduction, for example, will tax the already-stressed middle-aged at the expense of the retired elderly who typically have one, and often a second vacation home, debt free generating untaxed imputed rent.

The influx of younger immigrants historically attracted by jobs has deferred the US day of reckoning relative to Europe, but the debate over comprehensive reform has focused on how to limit work visas while expanding eligibility for government programs. Even if economic growth were to double from the current anemic rate of about two percent – economically problematic even with an equally politically problematic policy reversal – significant entitlement cuts would remain necessary.

As in Europe, the Fed is already printing most of the money to finance the current deficit. Foreigners are reducing their US debt exposure and shortening maturities so they can exit quickly in response to the inevitable inflation to come, and they will no longer have the excess savings to fund the prospective deficits even if they were willing.

The US is rich enough that it does not have to throw grandma from the train or impoverish its elderly. Politicians will have to venture beyond reasonable entitlement cuts and tax increases to avoid decades of stagnation and inflation, likely much worse than the stagflation of the 1970's. Even the most ambitious pro-growth policies will fail without generating sufficient savings. Entitlement and tax reform should restore individual incentives to work longer and save more. The threshold for not paying taxes should be dropped from the current median income household to the bottom quintile. In return, there should be liberal tax credits for down-payments and tax-free health and individual retirement savings accounts that will work in conjunction with phasing the younger generation out of the unfunded federal entitlement pyramid scheme altogether.

If federal policy continues to punish formal savings, it is quite likely we will see evidence of financial system avoidance, with rebar jutting out of smaller dwellings.[388] Down payment accounts – similar to individual retirement accounts – are the simplest way to encourage savings for "the American Dream." The threshold for paying federal income tax should be lowered, with non-refundable tax credits to stimulate savings. If a household is too poor to pay any federal income tax, subsidizing their home ownership is probably not a very good idea.

The anticipated return to pre-war unemployment levels was not avoided by growing but by shrinking government. It is no coincidence that the tremendous post-World War II economic growth was accompanied by a dramatic rise in home ownership. Economic growth provided the necessary income, but the employment was provided almost exclusively by new firms. The initial start-up capital for most new businesses was not typically provided by venture capital funds, private equity funds or venture "angels' but by borrowing against homeowner equity. That was the market solution to incentive conflicts.

Most of the euphemistically labeled "under-developed" economies place a disproportionate bureaucratic emphasis on housing relative to the size of their economy, even as they discourage savings and allocate credit away from consumers. Their potential home mortgage borrowers have a plethora of consumer protections – foreclosure is problematic and eviction unlikely – but generally have very little reason to save or access home mortgage credit, often accompanied by weak property rights. Again, these are not unrelated events.

America's experiment with home ownership was vast and created many political constituencies. It is easy to lose sight of the conditions under which both the economy and the home ownership rate grew. Private home mortgage finance was a key part of the growth engine that created the contemporary American middle class.

The lack of political fiscal restraint that allowed the sub-prime credit bubble to inflate to systemic proportions pales in comparison to the currently inflating bubble of US Treasury debt.   Economist and former central banker Jerry Jordan in his recent paper "Fix Fiscal First," (2012) refers back to James Madison's efforts to imbed fiscal discipline into the US Constitution. Madison's ultimate safeguard - a constitutionally-required reliance on currency backed only by gold and silver – did not last.

The US has thus far been able to print money to finance fiscal profligacy in the virtual absence of domestic saving by exploiting its position as the global reserve currency. However, it holds this position based not on merit but the lack of alternatives in the short term. That is because other central banks are also trying to compensate for bad policies regarding taxes, spending, labor, trade, and business. The net result is that they all inflate simultaneously. Analysts often characterize politicians as "kicking the can down the road" but this does not truly convey the consequences of delaying the inevitable. In the 1960's, the advice of the mechanic in a popular commercial for Fram Oil Filters was "you can pay me now (about $2 for a new filter) or you can pay me later (about $1000 for a new engine)."

Despite political claims to the contrary, we do not have another generation to wait before dealing with the problem. Ultimate discipline will once again most likely be provided by the market. When it comes, it will once again most likely be abrupt and devastating. And with certainty, politicians will once again wail that "nobody could have seen this coming."

Footnotes

¹ e.g.; *Meltdown,* Regnery (2009) by Thomas E. Woods, a senior fellow at the Ludwig von Mises (a leader of the Austrian School) Institute, *Financial Fiasco,* Cato (a free market think tank) (2009) by Johan Norberg and later *Guaranteed to Fail, Fannie Mae and Freddie Mac and the Debacle of Mortgage Finance,* Princeton University Press (2011) by Viral V. Acharya, Matthew Richardson, Still Von Nieuwerburgh and Lawrence J. White, with Austrian sympathies.

2 Gerald P. O'Driscoll Jr. concludes "Government regulations concentrated bank reserves in major cities, with the result that the economy was subject to panics and bank runs (which were rare in other countries), culminating in the Panic of 1907. Instead of fixing the problems of the national banking system, however, lawmakers led by the progressive president, Woodrow Wilson, created a central bank, the Federal Reserve System." In "Debunking the Myths About Central Banks," Wall Street Journal, February 28, 2013, for an in depth discussion

3 See Johnson, Simon and James Kwak, 13 Bankers, Pantheon Books, 2010.

4 See by Murray N. Rothbard, The Case Against the Fed (2012) p. 46.

5 See Milton Friedman, and Anna Schwartz, in A Monetary History of the United States: 1867-1960, Princeton University Press, 1963

6 See Ben Bernanke, "Conference to Honor Milton Friedman," University of Chicago, Chicago, Illinois, November 8, 2002.

7 See Murray Rothbard, America's Great Depression, Von Mises Institute, 1963.

8 See J. Friedman, "A Crisis of Politics, Not Economics: Complexity, Ignorance and Policy Failure," Critical Review, 21, 127-183, 2009.

9 See Martin Mayer, the Fed, The Free press, 2001, pp 153-155 for this discussion.

10 See Edwin Kemmerer, the ABC of the FRS (1922), p. x.

11 See Alex Pollack, Alex, "Why Canada Avoided a Mortgage Meltdown," AEI, March 2010.

12 See Friedman, 2009, p 166.

13 See Michael Perino, The Hellhound of Wall Street, the Penguin Press, New York, (2010) for an in-depth discussion of the Pecora Commission.

14 See Charles Calomiris, Charles W and Eugene N. White, "The Origins of Federal Deposit Insurance" in the Regulated Economy, Goldin and Libecap ed., 145-190, 1994.

15 Congressional Research Service (CRS), 1966, pg A1.

16 See Kent Colton, "Housing Finance in the United States: The Transformation of the US Housing Finance System," Harvard Joint Center for Housing Studies, 2002 pg 2.

17 See Hyman for this discussion, p. 145)

18 For a more in depth discussion, see Franklin Allen, James Barth and Glenn Yago, Fixing the Housing Market, Prentice Hall, 2012, PP 25-32"Origins and Development of Savings and Loan Associations1830-1930.

19 See Bodfish and Theobold, Saving and Loan Principles, 1940.

20 Reported in Herzog, p. 7.

21 See CRS, 1966, p 3.

22 For a general history, see Thomas Herzog, "History of Mortgage Finance with an Emphasis on Mortgage Insurance," Society of Actuaries, 2009.

23 See Colton, 2002, pp 4-5.

24 See Kerry Vandell, "FHA Restructuring Proposals: Alternatives and Implications," Housing Policy Debate, 6, 299-393, 1995, Table 1.

25 See William Silber, William L, "Why Did the Bank Holiday Succeed?" FRBNY Economic Policy Review, 19-30, July 2009, p 20.

26 See Franklin Allen, James Barth and Glen Yago, Fixing the Housing Market, Milken Institute, Feb. 2012, p. 35 for a discussion of the bad debt deduction.

27 Survey of Mortgage Lending Activity, U.S. Department of Housing and Urban Development, various years.

28 See Congressional Research Service, Congressional Research Service, Federal National Mortgage Association, January, 1966.

29 This paragraph is taken from Ed Pinto, "FHA: 60 years of Mission Failure," American Banker feedback, Dec 26, 2012.

30 CRS, 1966, p 44,

31 See Herzog, p.24.

32 Any firm could sell to Fannie Mae, but virtually all the sellers were mortgage bankers. The minimum stock subscription was establish in law and varied from a stiff 3 percent of loan principal, lowered to 2 percent then in 1965 to 1 percent

33 See Canner and Passmore [1994; page 884].

34 In the early 1970s a similar requirement was implemented for S&Ls.

35 See Patric Hendershott and Kevin Villani, "Escrow Accounts and the Value of Mortgage Servicing Contracts," Journal of Financial Services Research, 1994, 59-76.

36 See Raghuram G, Fault Lines: How Hidden Fractures Still Threaten the World Economy, Princeton University Press, 2010 for a discussion of tail risk.

37 More sophisticated investors made decisions based on the ex ante "option adjusted" spread, but few looked back to measure gains and losses relative to this benchmark.

38 This discussion is from Michael Lewis, Liars Poker, 1989; pages 88-89.

39 See Franco Modigliani and Merton Miller, "The cost of capital, corporate finance and the theory of investment, AER v xlviii June 1958, #3

40 See Robert Van Order, "The U.S. Mortgage Market: A Model of Dueling Charters." Journal of Housing Research 11, no. 2: 233–55, 2000.

41 The Fannie Mae target is for 1995 in Pinto (2011, p 71) and the Freddie Mac target was during my time there in the early 1980s.

42 See congressional testimony of CBO Director June O Neill prepared by Marvin Phaup, June 12, 1996.

43 See also Helen Thompson, "The Political Origins of the Financial Crisis: The Domestic and International Politics of Fannie Mae and Freddie Mac," The Political Quarterly, 80, January-March 2009.

44 See Joseph Stiglitz, Joseph E., Jonathan M Orszag and Peter R Orszag, Implications of the New Fannie Mae and Freddie Mac Risk-Based Capital Standard, Fannie Mae Papers, March 2002, p 2.

Partnoy, Frank, "How and Why Credit Rating Agencies are Not Like Other Gatekeepers," Legal Study Paper Series, USD, May 2006.

45 See Deborah Lucas, and Robert L. McDonald, "An Options-based Approach to Evaluating the Risk of Fannie Mae and Freddie Mac," Journal of Monetary Economics 53, 155-176, 2006.

46 HUD's general counsel was assigned responsibility for keeping watch on Fannie Mae, which resulted in a subsequent career path to Fannie Mae by several HUD gc's.

47 See John Weicher, "Setting GSE Policy through Charters, Laws and Regulations." In Serving Two Masters Yet Out of Control, Wallison ed. chapter 7, AEI, 2000, p 125.

48 FRB Boston Munnell Alicia H. Lynn E. Browne, James McEneaney, and Geoffrey M.B. Tootell, "Mortgage Lending in Boston: Interpreting HMDA Data," Federal Reserve Bank of Boston, Working Paper WP-92-7, October 1992.

49 Jo Ann s Barefoot, "Navigating the Shoals between Alan and Deval: How do Banks Price for Credit Risk While Avoiding Discriminatory Pricing", ABA Banking Journal, Vol. 88, 1996.

50 After the first lender that was targeted failed while fighting the law suit, others readily agreed to quotas. See Paul Craig Roberts, "Confiscation by Consent Decree", National Review, vol. 46, October 24, 1994

51 After the first lender that was targeted failed while fighting the law suit, others readily agreed to quotas. See Paul Craig Roberts, "Confiscation by Consent Decree", National Review, vol. 46, October 24, 1994.

52 See Patric Hendershott, and James Shilling, "The Impact of the Agencies on Conventional Fixed-Rate Mortgage Yields," The Journal of Real Estate Finance and Economics, 2, 101-115, 1989 for a discussion of the benefit passed through to borrowers.

53 See Wayne Passmore, 2005.

54 Urban Institute Press, Washington DC, 1981.

55 GAO 1990 Government Accounting Office, "Government Sponsored Enterprises: The Government's Exposure to Risks, Washington, DC, 1990.

56 See Edward J. Kane and Chester Foster, 1986, "Valuing conjectural government guarantees of FNMA liabilities" in Proceedings: Conference on Bank Structure and Competition. Chicago: Federal Reserve Bank of Chicago.

57 See George R Ackerloff, Paul M. Romer, Robert E. Hall, and N. Gregory Mankiw, "Looting: The Economic Underworld of Bankruptcy for Profit," Brookings Papers on Economic Activity 24, 1-73, 1993):1-73.

58 See Henry N Pontell., "Control Fraud, Gambling for Resurrection, and Moral Hazard: Accounting for White-collar Crime in the Savings and Loan Crisis," Journal of Socio-Economics, 34, 756-770, December 2005.

59 See Simon Johnson and James Kwak, 13 Bankers, Pantheon Books, 2010, pg.74.

60 See Patric Hendershott and Edward Kane, "Causes and Consequences of the 1980s Commercial Construction Boom," Journal of Applied Corporate Finance, 61-70, 1992, pp 65-66.

61 See Patric H. Hendershott and Edward J. Kane, pp 61-70.

62 FIRREA and insurance regulators required an immediate sale, for which there were no US buyers. Foreign buyers purchased most at prices about 50% of par. The high yield bond yield spreads subsequently covered ex post losses, as expected.

63 The Conference Committee inserted the language at the suggestion of the author as a market with only sellers by rule was bound to tank.

64 See James R Barth, Susanne Trimbath and Glenn Yago, the Saving and Loan Crisis: Lessons in Regulatory Failure, Milken Institute, 2004, and Kevin Villani and John Tuccillo, a History of Savings and Loan Study Commissions, 1978.

65 Patric Hendershott and James Waddell, 119–32.

66 Mike Stamper, the author's long-time friend and colleague, proposed this as a vice president at Ginnie Mae. He was later an executive vice president at Freddie Mac. The author opposed the idea as a HUD economist at the time.

67 RVO foster 1986 Foster, C. and R. Van Order. (1984). An Options-Based Model of Mortgage Default, Housing Finance Review, 3, 4, 351-372, 1984.

68 Patric Hendershott and James Waddell, "Changing Fortunes of FHA's Mutual Mortgage Insurance Fund and the Legislative Response," Journal of Real Estate Economics and Finance, Volume 5, Number 2 (June 1992): pg 12).

69 See Pinto, 2011, p 71.

70 See Pinto, 2011, p 86.

71 According to the Wallison Dissent.

72 See McDonald, 2012, p.82.

73 See McDonald, p.6.

74 A recent study tracked the frequency of CRA loans, finding them more frequent before CRA exams, and subsequent default rates on these loans 15% higher. See Sumit Agarwal, Efraim Benmelech, Nittai Bergman, and Amit Seru, "Did the Community Reinvestment Act (CRA) Lead to Risky Lending?" NBER Working Paper No. 18609, December, 2012

75 See Pinto, 2011, p 108.

76 An article by Joanne Pierson "Navigating the Shoals between Alan and Deval" captures the essential conflict between prudential regulation and credit allocation. As Federal Reserve Board Chairman, Alan Greenspan argued that banks should discriminate on the basis of risk and price accordingly, what Deputy Attorney General of the DOF Deval Patrick argued was discriminatory. See Jo Ann s Barefoot, "Navigating the Shoals between Alan and Deval: How do Banks Price for Credit Risk While Avoiding Discriminatory Pricing", ABA Banking Journal, Vol. 88, 1996.

77 Rajan (2010) forcefully makes this case

78 See Gasparino, 2009, pp 132-135

79 See White (2010) for a complete discussion of the role of credit rating organizations.

80 As discussed in Allison, pp.83-84.

81 These rules were published simultaneously in Nov 2001 by the Fed, FDIC and Treasury Office of Thrift Supervision.

82 See Kling (p. 28) for a detailed discussion of the opinion of the shadow regulatory committee.

83 See Walt Bettinger: Time for Compromise on Money Market Reform - WSJ.com here:
http://online.wsj.com/article/SB10001424127887324352004578132770453306616.html?mod=ITP_opinion_0

84 See H&V (2012) for an expanded discussion.

85 See "Analysis of the Failure of Superior Bank, FSB, Hinsdale, Illinois," GAO 2002.

86 A REIT was like a grantor trust in that it was tax free as long as it was purely an investment vehicle and the earnings were paid out in dividends. Rule changes in the 1990s allowed a REIT to have a taxable operating subsidiary such as a finance company. The residuals were then transferred to the REIT. Of course the price at which they were transferred determined the subsidiary's tax liability, which was subject to abuse.

87 This discussion is largely taken from Mayer, Pence and Sherlund, 2009).

88 Pinto (2011) estimates that over 30% of all loans originated in 2006 had no down payment and many more had as little as 1%-3%.

89 See Glenn Seltzer, "PMI Insurers Owe Many Thanks to Piggy back Mortgages," Mortgage News Daily, November 13, 2007.

90 See Mayer, Pence, and Sherlund, 2009, p 32.

91 See HHS, 2010, p 5.

92 See James R. Barth, Tong Li, Wenling Lu, Triphon Phumiwanasana, and Glenn Yago, The Rise and Fall of the US Mortgage and Credit Markets, John Wiley and Sons, inc. 2009, p 166.

93 See Blundell-Wignall and Atkinson, 2008, p 95

94 Every securitization structure is different and every securitizer employed different leverage techniques, but our assumptions are in the ball-park, illustrating the relative magnitude and difference for different leverage strategies.

95 The various sources are summarized by Van Order and Thomas, 2011, pg 6.

96 See Adrian Blundell-Wignall, Gert Wehinger and Patrick Slovik, Figure 6, page 10.

97 See Simon Lack, Hedge Fund Miracle, John Wiley and Sons, 2012.

98 Hedge Fund Research

99 See Howard Bornstein, Stan Markuze, Cameron Percy, Lisha Wang, and Moritz Zander, "Going For Broke: Reforming California's Public Employee Pension System, Stanford Institute for Economic Policy Research, 2012.

100 See "Defined Benefit Pension Plans, Guidance Needed to Better Inform Plans of the Challenges and Risks of Investing in Hedge Funds and Private Equity," GAO, August, 2008.

101 Countrywide was sold to B of A in the fall of 2007 for about $8 billion. B of A has since closed much of the origination network and servicing foreclosures is estimated to cost about six to eight times that. Ironically, Countrywide became the biggest mortgage banker by uniquely relying on in-house loan originators, but switched to the broker model at the beginning of the sub-prime lending boom.

102 See Ashcroft and Schuermann 2008, pg 31.

103 Again, the pricing assumptions are illustrative and every deal is different, but these profits are not atypical for PLSers.

104 There is sufficient cash flow remaining in this example to structure an excess interest security that could also be pledged as collateral.

105 See Goodman, et.al., 2010.

106 See Viral V. Acharya Matthew P and Richardson, p 203.

107 See Acharya and Richardson, Table 1, page 203 for this data.

108 Taken from Pinto, p. 157.

109 Allison 2012 makes this argument (pp.24-27).

110 See Ben S Bernanke, Speech at the Bundesbank Lecture, Global Imbalances: Recent Developments and Prospects, Berlin, Germany, September 11, 2007.

111 See "Why the Euro Crisis Isn't Over" by Brian M. Carney in the WSJ Feb 23, 2013 available here: http://online.wsj.com/article/SB10001424127887324445904578285503854758408.html?mod=ITP_opinion_0

112 Paul Krugman, "Dubya's Double Dip? The Conscience of a Liberal," New York Times, August 2, 2002, http://www.nytimes.com/2002/08/02/opinion/dubya-s-double-dip.html.

113 See CBO, "Estimating the Value of Subsidies for Federal Loans and Loan Guarantees," August 19, 2004.

114 Between 2001-03 and 2005-06, the share of mortgage originations that were "junk" more than tripled from 10 to 33 percent according to Patric Hendershott, Robert Hendershott, and James Shilling (HHS), p. 5).

115 See the Wallison Dissent, pp 457, 459.

116 See Paul S., Leonard Nakamura and Susan Wachter, "Implications of the Housing Market bubble for Sustainable Homeownership" in Wachter and Smith, pp. 87-111.

117 See Acharya, Richardson, Van Nieuwerburgh and White, p138.

118 Fannie Mae was alleged to have over-stated earnings by $10 billion to increase current year bonuses. Freddie Mac was alleged to have reduced current year income by $5 billion, presumably saving to protect future bonuses. See Helen Thompson, The Political Origins of the Financial Crisis: The Domestic and International Politics of Fannie Mae and Freddie Mac, The Political Quarterly, Vol. 80, No. 1, January±March 2009, pp 8-9.
119 Blundell-Wignall and Atkinson, 2008, pp 82-84

120 See Weicher, 2010, Table 1.

121 See Wallison and Pinto (2010)

122 See Wallison, 2010, pp 6-7.

123 See Weicher, 2010, p 10.

124 See the FCIC Report, p184.

125 See the FCIC Report, pp 179-180.

126 As reported here: http://online.wsj.com/article/SB10001424127887323316804578165750660857958.html?mod=WSJ_article_LatestHeadlines

127 See http://www.larouchepub.com/other/2003/3010ofheo_rpt.html and Blundell-Wignall and Atkinson, 2008, pp 82-84

128 According to Wallison (2013, p.32) the Administration wanted a stronger bill limiting the portfolio, reflecting an ill-timed concern with interest rate risk.

129 This discussion borrows liberally from Mark Calabria, "Fannie, Freddie, and the Subprime Mortgage Market," Cato Institute Briefing Paper no. 120, March 7, 2011, http://www.cato.org/pub_display.php?pub_id=12846.

130 Testimony of Brian Montgomery, FHA Commissioner, before the United States Senate Committee on Banking, Housing and Urban Affairs, Subcommittee on Housing and Transportation, June 20, 2006.

131 Peter Wallison, "Barney Frank: Predatory Lender, WSJ, October 16, 2009.

132 See for example Paul Calem, Christopher Henderson and Jonathan Lies, "Cherry Picking in Sub prime Mortgage Securitization, FRB Phil., July 2010, and

133 This is all from the Flow of Funds Account, FRB.

134 See http://www.fdic.gov/regulations/laws/rules/2000-6750.html S 345.12(T)-a for securities focused on CRA lending.

135 See Peter Wallison, "Deregulation and the Financial Crisis: Another Urban Myth, "AEI, October 2009, p.266.

136 See Carol Loomis, "Robert Rubin on the job he never wanted: The reluctant chairman tells Fortune's Carol Loomis why Citi didn't see the sub-prime mess coming", Fortune, November, 2007.

137 See " Information Failures and the US Mortgage Markets" in The American Mortgage System, ed. by Susan M. Wachter and Marvin M. Smith, University of Pennsylvania Press, 2011

138 This data is taken from the US census bureau for 5 or more units.

139 The chart and discussion are taken from the Heritage Foundation to be found here: http://www.heritage.org/research/reports/2008/04/how-smart-growth-exacerbated-the-international-financial-crisis

140 See http://www.calculatedriskblog.com/2012/11/real-house-prices-price-to-rent-ratio.html

141 See Table B100 line 4 of the Flow of funds data base.

142 View table 7a available here: http://www.census.gov/housing/hvs/data/histtabs.html

143 See Wendell Cox, "The Housing Crash and Smart Growth," NATIONAL CENTER FOR POLICY ANALYSIS, Policy Report No. 335, June 2011.

144 Land prices were obviously depressed as numerous builders liquidated inventory at steep discounts to raise cash.

145 See Kristopher s. Gerardi, Christopher L. Foote and Paul S. Willen, Reasonable People did Disagree" in Wachter and Smith, op. cit.

146 See Cordell, Huang and Williams (CHW) 2011, Table 14.

147 See CHW, Table 15b.

148 See CHW p. 16.

149 See Acharya and Richardson, 2009, p 206.

150 See Sunyoung Park, The size of the Subprime Shock, Korea, 2011.

151 See Wallison and Calomiris, 2008, p 6.

152 See Pinto, 2011.

153 See Calhoun, 2005, p 8.

154 http://www.corelogic.com/about-us/researchtrends/asset_upload_file912_15196.pdf

155 The TED spread, i.e. the spread, the gap between the US Treasury and rate that banks borrowed, quadrupled at this time.

156 UBS, for example, took $19 Billion in sub-prime write-downs in late 2007 and 2008.

157 See Garry Gorton "Questions and Answers about the Financial Crisis", FCIC, February, 2010. He has a graph showing the haircut, i.e. discount to par, on structured assets rising from 1% in mid 2007 to 45% in mid 2009, following their price decline of that magnitude.
158 The ratings agencies were threatening Lehman with a downgrade when they filed, making bankruptcy inevitable.

159 See Gorton, Gary, Questions and Answers about the Financial Crisis, FCIC, Feb 2010.

160 See Edward J. Kane, "Unmet Duties in Managing Financial Safety Nets," Networks Financial Institute, September 2009, pg. 24.
161 See Taylor, 2009, pg. 28.

162 Treasury prices went up, everything else went down, and hence spreads widened. Economists generally point to this as evidence of contagion.

163 See Roger Lowenstein, The End of Wall Street, the Penguin Press, 2010, pp205.
164 The Reserve Primary Fund had paid out 99.04% of assets according to the WSJ, July 17, 2010, B11.

165 See Daniel Kahneman, Thinking Fast and Slow, New York, 2011,

166 See Nassim Nicholas Taleb, The Black Swan: the Impact of the Highly Improbable, Random House, 2007.

167 See Lewis, Michael, The Big Short, WW Norton & Co., New York, 2010 for a general discussion of this phenomenon.
168 By the second half of 2006 there were hundreds of hedge funds shorting the housing market using synthetic CDS. See FCIC Report, p 191-192.

169 See http://query.nytimes.com/gst/fullpage.html?res=9F05E6D91F3DF931A35752C1A96E9C8B63&ref=jameskgalbraith

170 Cynthia Angell, "Housing Bubble Concerns and the Outlook for Mortgage Credit Quality," FDIC Outlook, February 2004, fdic.gov/bank/analytical/regional/ro20041q/na/infocus.html/.
171 Remarks of William C. Dudley, Executive Vice President of the FRB of NY, delivered at the FRB of Philadelphia, Oct. 17, 2007.

172 Remarks made by Federal Reserve Board Chairman Ben S. Bernanke, Federal Reserve Bank of Chicago's 43rd Annual Conference on Bank Structure and Competition, Chicago, Ill., May 17, 2007.

173 Remarks by Federal Reserve Chairman Ben S. Bernanke, Opportunity finance Network Annual Conference, Washington, D.C. November 1, 2006.

174 See Barth (2009, pg103) for the trend of rising estimates.

175 See Blundell et al, 2009, Table 2, page 11.

176 See Meltzer, 2012, p.

177 See Barth, et. al. p 109.

178 FASB 157 was phased in November 15, 2007 requiring mark to market accounting.

179 Thrifts used several ways to measure interest rate risk: regulators preferred duration gap analysis. Mark-to-market was really a discounted cash flow analysis based on the theory that the yield curve is always an unbiased predictor of future interest rates, hence showing thrifts to be technically insolvent by 1980. But this prediction proved to be terribly wrong, as interest rates fell in several years to reverse the calculated industry insolvency.

180 GAAP was modified somewhat at the end of 2008, but it was too late by then.

181 See Gorton 2008, p63-65.

182 Jaffee (2010).

183 Weicher (2010).

184 Thomas and Van Order (2011) conclude from this that the housing goals didn't contribute to the financial crisis. David Min at the Center for American Progress does the same in … as does Richard Green in…

185 FCIC Report, p. xxiii.

186 See Tyler Cowen NYT January 17, 2008.

187 See George Benston, "The Community Reinvestment Act: Looking for Discrimination That Isn't There, Cato, October 1999.

188 See for example the characterization of Wallison and Pinto as "unscholarly" and the recommendation that the AEI to be abolished here: http://delong.typepad.com/sdj/2012/12/richard-green-on-joe-nocera-on-why-we-would-all-be-better-off-without-the-american-enterprise-institute.html

189 See for example Jeffery W. Gunther, Safety And Soundness and the CRA: Is their a Conflict?" Economic Inquiry (ISSN 0095-2583) Vol. 40, No. 3, July 2002, 470–484

190 See McDonald chapter 1, especially p. 14.

191 Paul Krugman, How did Economists get it So Wrong? New York Times, Sept 6, 2009 available here: http://www.nytimes.com/2009/09/06/magazine/06Economic-t.html?pagewanted=all

192 Available here: http://krugman.blogs.nytimes.com/2013/02/13/marco-rubio-has-learned-nothing/

193 Stuart Greenbaum was at the time a member of the Board of Directors and Chairman of the Finance Committee of ICA, which owned Imperial Savings, the largest securitizer on the west coast at the time. I was CFO.

194 See Gary Gorton, "The Panic of 2007,"FRB Kansas City, 2008.

195 See Cordell, et al p. 22 for a discussion of the data availability.

196 See for example Adam J. Levitin, Pavlov, Andrey D. and Wachter, Susan M., Securitization: Cause or Remedy of the Financial Crisis? (August 27, 2009). Georgetown Law and Economics Research Paper No. 1462895; U of Penn, Inst for Law & Econ Research Paper No. 09-31. Available at SSRN: http://ssrn.com/abstract=1462895

197 See for example Robert Shiller, Irrational Exuberance. 2nd ed. Princeton, NJ: Princeton University Press, 2005.

198 See Donald Boudreaux: In Appreciation—James M. Buchanan - at: http://online.wsj.com/article/SB10001424127887324581504578231932109403950.html?user=welcome&mg=id-wsj

199 One major exception to the political narrative is the Report of chairman Issa's Committee, the US House of Representatives Staff Report, "The Role of Government Affordable Housing Policy in Creating the Global Financial Crisis of 2008, 111th Congress, Committee on Oversight and Government Reform, July 7, 2009.

200 See http://confoundedinterest.wordpress.com/2012/10/16/slowest-recovery-since-1882-homebuilder-enthusiasm-inflation-and-industrial-production/

201 See http://online.wsj.com/article/SB10000872396390444506004577613122591922992.html?KEYWORDS=Rebound+effect+of+deep+recessions

202 See Barofsky, 2012, p. 162 for a discussion of this calculation.

203 See Goldberg, p.50 for this discussion.

204 As quoted by Michael Grabell 2012, p.27, and Peter Wallison, 2013, p.23.

205 See Tom Stanton, 1992.

206 See http://online.wsj.com/article/SB10001424052970204712904578093281955820410.html?mod=ITP_opinion_0

207 For a discussion of federal flood insurance and taxpayer bailouts, see "Taxpayer Deluge" here:
http://online.wsj.com/article/SB10001424052970203707604578090902568526178.html?mod=ITP_opinion_2

208 See Larry Harris in the WSJ January 10, 2013, "Sandy Relief by the (Remarkable) Numbers;
The $61 billion proposal translates to $69 million per linear mile of coastline from Maryland to Maine here:
http://online.wsj.com/article/SB10001424127887324081704578232192273419174.html?mod=ITP_opinion_0

209 See the Economist, The God's Strike Back", Feb 13, 2010 Special insert on the financial crisis.

210 See Gerald P. O'Driscoll Jr., Debunking the Myths About Central Banks: Does an economy need a lender of last resort? Is the Fed really independent? It's time for some rethinking, the Wall Street Journal, February 28, 2013, for an in depth discussion.

211 Andrew Sheng, ed., Bank Restructuring: Lessons from the 1980s, World Bank, Washington, DC, 1996, p.54

212 In Kaufman and Scott, p. 380.

213 Paul Volker, at the FDIC Conference, 1997.

214 See Lowenstein (2010, pp.205).

215 William Poole, "Housing in the Macroeconomy, FRB St Louis, May/June 2003 and the Regional Economist, Federal Reserve Bank of Saint Louis, July 2004.

216 As quoted by Peter Wallison, 2013, p.1)

217 The estimates are that it kept wages 35%-40% higher than the market clearing level.

218 See Hoover, Herbert (1952). Memoirs. Hollis and Carter, p. 30.

219 See Blum, John Morton (1970). Roosevelt and Morgenthau, Boston, Massachusetts: Houghton Mifflin Harcourt. p. 256, LCCN 75096063. OCLC 68158.

220 See for example Johan Goldberg, Liberal Fascism, Doubleday, 2007.

221 Meltzer (p.85) makes the same reference to and interpretation of Khrushchev's comment

222 This is admittedly a rough calculation I made from data supplied to me when working there shortly after the collapse.

223 See The Last Exit to Utopia, 2010 and the Bloodlands, 2010.

224 See Taylor, 2009, pages 15-18.

225 Treasury Secretary Paulsen stated on CNN on March 16, 2008 that "I have great confidence in our capital markets and our financial institutions. Our financial institutions, banks, and investment banks are strong.

226 See Lowenstein (2010).

227 Professor Philip Maymin, a LTCM employee at the time of the failure, argues that the bailout was both unnecessary and unwise here: http://www.americanbanker.com/bankthink/no-financial-institutions-are-systemically-important-1052344-1.html?ET=americanbanker:e12183:2268417a:&st=email&utm_source=editorial&utm_medium=email&utm_campaign=AB_Intraday_090512

228 See Lowenstein (2010, pg 205) for a report on this conclusion based on interviews with Fed officials.

229 See Lowenstein (2010, chapter 12) for a discussion of the sequence of events.

230 See Holman Jenkins, :Was the AIG Rescue Legal," wsj, February 1, 2013

231 As cited in Meltzer, p.33.

232 Chairman Bernanke announced on June 9, 2010 that advances to all the financial firms had been paid back with dividend and interest by then with the exception of AIG, which he said was expected to do the same (WSJ, June 10, 2010, C3).

233 See "AIG, Surprise Money Maker" 8/31/2012 here: http://online.wsj.com/article/SB10000872396390443618604577623373568029572.html?mod=ITP_opinion_0

234 See Allison PP. 172-173 for a discussion of the cross subsidy from healthy banks.

235 Barofsky discusses throughout the inability to monitor bank use of TARP money and the uses to which it was put.

236 See Ed Kane, "Zombies on the Loose: The S&L Insurance Mess," Financier: The Journal of Private Sector Policy, 15 (July 1991), pp. 9-19.

237 See http://articles.nydailynews.com/2009-06-01/news/17929088_1_cost-gm-millions-gm-management-princes and here: http://mjperry.blogspot.com/2008/11/crippling-burden-of-legacy-costs-gm-is.html

238 See Barofsky, p.50.

239 See http://www.forbes.com/sites/louiswoodhill/2012/08/15/general-motors-is-headed-for-bankruptcy-again/

240 See http://mercatus.org/publication/administrations-auto-bailouts-and-delphi-pension-decisions-who-picked-winners-and-losers for the many ways the administration negotiated bankruptcy skirted the law.

241 http://mercatus.org/expert_commentary/americas-taxpayers-lost-big-uaw-bailout

242 See http://www.politico.com/news/stories/1012/82900.html

243 See "Tarp Firms Pay Unchecked" wsj, Jan 29, 2013.

244 See http://www.foxnews.com/opinion/2012/10/12/eu-wins-nobel-peace-prize-is-this-joke/ and the interview with former ECB economist Bernard Connolly "Why the Euro Crisis Isn't Over" by Brian M. Carney in the WSJ Feb 23, 2013 available here: http://online.wsj.com/article/SB10001424127887324445904578285503854758408.html?mod=ITP_opinion_0

245 See: http://www.washingtonpost.com/blogs/post-politics/wp/2013/05/14/deficit-projection-reduced-to-642-billion-cbo-says/

246 See: Econbrowser: How Fannie Mae made its profit; http://www.econbrowser.com/archives/2013/05/how_fannie_mae.html

247 See http://www.americanbanker.com/bankthink/congress-must-stop-using-fannie-and-freddie-as-piggy-banks-1054992-1.html

248 Peter Wallison interprets this as a measure to prevent F&F from returning to the market as private enterprises: http://www.aei.org/article/economics/financial-services/housing-finance/treasury-revision-of-fanfred-payments-seals-their-fate/

249 See: an Unconstitutional Bonanza here; http://www.hoover.org/publications/defining-ideas/article/161456

250 See James D. Shilling, "Three Years After takeover, How Have Fannie Mae and Freddie Mac Benefitted the US Housing Market? July, 2012.

251 See for example Nick Timiraos "High Earners at Fannie, Freddie Draw Scrutiny" wsj, December 9, 2012 available here: http://online.wsj.com/article/SB10001424127887323316804578165750660857958.html?user=welcome&mg=id-wsj

252 See Peter J. Wallison and Edward J. Pinto, "Bet the House: Why the FHA Is Going (for) Broke," AEI, January 2012 available here: http://www.aei.org/files/2012/01/24/-bet-the-house-why-the-fha-is-going-for-broke_144915374900.pdf

253 See tp://online.wsj.com/article/SB10001424127887324595904578119140604024484.html?mod=djemalertMARKET

254 See: http://www.economist.com/news/finance-and-economics/21588928-banks-must-pay-and-comply-even-if-it-isnt-clear-why-or-what-culture-fear

255 New York Attorney General Eric Schneiderman also filed a civil lawsuit against J.P. Morgan alleging widespread fraud by Bear Stearns without naming any individuals.

256 For a discussion of these cases, see http://online.wsj.com/article/SB10001424127887323894704578109090587877784.html?mod=WSJ_hp_LEFTWhatsNewsCollection

257 See http://online.wsj.com/article/SB10000872396390443890304578006482230678780.html?KEYWORDS=no+change+for+fANNIE+AND+fREDDIE

258 See for example http://www.huffingtonpost.com/2011/07/01/home-foreclosure-backlog_n_888655.html

259 See for example http://www.americanbanker.com/issues/177_109/robo-signing-scandal-faulty-documents-compliance-foreclosures-1049941-1.html

260 See for example: http://www.businessinsider.com/michelle-meyer-foreclosure-process-home-prices-2012-12

261 See the analysis of the chief negotiator: http://www.americanbanker.com/issues/177_126/national-mortgage-settlement-robo-signing-servicing-1050542-1.html

262 See http://www.americanbanker.com/countdown2013/news/california-the-state-that-ate-the-national-mortgage-settlement-1055479-1.html?ET=americanbanker:e13584:2268417a:&st=email&utm_source=editorial&utm_medium=email&utm_campaign=ABLA_Daily_Briefing_122712

263 See http://online.wsj.com/article/SB10000872396390444592704578062903822008268.html?KEYWORDS=editoria+what+happened+to+the+25+billion+settlement

264 See "The Foreclosure Shakedowns: Politicians keep looting the banks to pay people who weren't harmed" WSJ, January 7, 2013 available here: http://online.wsj.com/article/SB10001424127887323482504578227781406254380.html?mod=ITP_opinion_2

265 See http://www.ft.com/intl/cms/s/0/da037536-2eaa-11e2-9b98-00144feabdc0.html#axzz2CW4Q6csU

266 Goodman, op cit, p. 2.

267 See http://www.corelogic.com/about-us/news/asset_upload_file365_15650.pdf

268 See http://confoundedinterest.wordpress.com/2012/10/22/housing-recovery-first-time-foreclosures-continue-to-decline-although-50-of-foreclosures-go-into-foreclosure-again/

269 See "Refi Program Expansion Eyed", wsj, December 25, 2012 available here: http://online.wsj.com/article/SB10001424127887323291704578199832047537030.html?mod=ITP_pageone_1

270 Deval Patrick served on the board of directors of ACC Capital Holdings, the parent company of failed sub-prime lender Ameriquest and Argent Mortgage from 2004 to 2006.

271 Having led the suits that forced lenders into racial quota agreements as Deputy AG, Deval Patrick then led the foreclosure discrimination suits as Governor of Massachusetts.

272 See: http://www.americanbanker.com/issues/177_186/pivotal-fair-lending-case-squashed-by-doj-quid-pro-quo-1052999-1.html

273 See HUD's Race-Based Housing: The agency rushes out a rule to sway the Supreme Court, wsj, February 22, 2013.

274 See Review & Outlook: Rigging Antidiscrimination Law - WSJ.com:
http://online.wsj.com/news/articles/SB10001424052702304243904579198144114654908

275 See Grabell, p.169.

276 See the testimony of Laura S. Goodman of Amherst securities before the US Senate Subcommittee on Housing, March 15, 2012.

277 See Core Logic release at: http://www.corelogic.com/about-us/news/corelogic-reports-number-of-residential-properties-in-negative-equity-decreases-again-in-second-quarter-of-2012.aspx

278 See http://advisorperspectives.com/commentaries/millennium_101512.php?WT.rss_f=CommentaRSS&WT.rss_ev=a&WT.rss_a=Seven_Varieties_of_Deflation

279 See Robert Shiller, A New Housing Boom: Don't Count on It, NYT, Jan 26, 2013 available here: http://www.nytimes.com/2013/01/27/business/housing-markets-future-still-has-many-clouds.html?ref=business&_r=1&

280 For a discussion of the new Keynesians, see http://online.wsj.com/article/SB10001424127887323316804578161324169068746.html?mod=ITP_pageone_1

281 See http://chartingtheeconomy.com/?p=409

282 For a discussion on the growth of government, see Thomas A Garrett and Russell M. Rhine, "On the Size and growth of Government", FRB St. Louis, Fan/Feb 2006, pp.13-30.

283 See the article by Swedish economists Andreas Bergh and Magnus Henrekson, "Lessons From the Swedish Welfare State" here: http://online.wsj.com/article/SB10001424052748704535004575348641192320912.html

284 As quoted by George Will, "The Manufactured Crisis of Sequester" Washington Post, Feb. 22, 2013 available here: http://www.washingtonpost.com/opinions/george-will-the-manufactured-crisis-of-sequester/2013/02/22/d22d4466-7c81-11e2-82e8-61a46c2cde3d_story.html

285 Keynes actually added the caveat: To dig holes in the ground, paid for out of savings, will increase, not only employment, but the real national dividend of useful goods and services. It is not reasonable, however, that a sensible community should be content to remain dependent on such fortuitous and often wasteful mitigations when once we understand the influences upon which effective demand depends."

286 See Grabell, p.

287 See for example Michael Grabell, Money Well Spent?, Public Affairs, 2012.

288 See Grabell, p.161.

289 See Art Laffer, "Disincentives Still Crazy After All These Years," wsj Feb. 8, 2013 available here: http://online.wsj.com/article/SB10001424127887324235104578243373468081096.html?mod=ITP_opinion_0

290 See Casey Mulligan, Failure to Stimulate, 2012, summarized here: http://online.wsj.com/article/SB10001424052970204712904578093021310711016.html?mod=ITP_opinion_0.

291 See for example http://usatoday30.usatoday.com/news/health/wellness/story/2012-06-20/gross-national-happiness/56669830/1 and http://ricochet.com/main-feed/Al-Gore-Welfare-Queen.

292 See Holman Jenkins: "Al Gore Is Good at Rent-Seeking (and Microsoft Isn't):Current TV may not have been a success, but the ex-vice president's style of entrepreneurship is in vogue" available here: http://online.wsj.com/article/SB10001424127887323374504578221512505966072.html?KEYWORDS=Al+Gore%27s+sale+of+current+TV

293 http://usatoday30.usatoday.com/news/health/wellness/story/2012-06-20/gross-national-happiness/56669830/1

294 See http://online.wsj.com/article/SB10001424127887324735104578117082930871430.html?KEYWORDS=no+change+in+fannie+and+freddie+nov+2012

295 See http://www.bloomberg.com/news/2013-01-22/egan-jones-lives-to-fight-the-government-another-day.html

296 See Holman Jenkins, S&P and the Lehman Tsunami, wsj, Feb. 8, 2013 available here: http://online.wsj.com/article/SB10001424127887324590904578292112019660782.html?mod=ITP_opinion_0

297 See Alan Greenspan, "Activism," International Finance, Spring 2011)

[298] See: http://www.bloomberg.com/news/2013-11-12/clinton-says-bank-fines-should-fund-u-s-infrastructure.html

[299] http://www.amazon.com/Battle-Bretton-Woods-Relations-University/dp/0691149097/ref=sr_1_1?s=books&ie=UTF8&qid=1384380709&sr=1-1&keywords=the+battle+of+bretton+woods+by+benn+steil
http://www.hoover.org/publications/defining-ideas/article/161456

[300] See: http://www.washingtonpost.com/blogs/wonkblog/wp/2012/10/11/larry-summers-deficit-reduction-isnt-enough-to-drive-growth/

301 See for example "Hoisington Quarterly Review and Outlook" by John Mauldin: http://www.mauldineconomics.com/outsidethebox/hoisington-quarterly-review-and-outlook

302 See "Applied Economic Letters entitled, Financial Wealth Effect: Evidence from Threshold Estimation" by Sherif Khalifa, Ousmane Seck and Elwin Tobing, 2011

303 See Patrick Hendershott and Kevin Villani, "the Distributional Consequences of Deposit Rate Ceilings," in Grant Elements in the Nations Economy, Ball State University, 1977.

304 See " More Fed Bond Buying Won't Let "Animal Spirits" out of the Cage" at
http://online.wsj.com/article/SB10000872396390444812704577611820877493502.html?mod=ITP_opinion_0

305 See David Widemer, John A. Widemer and Cindy Spitzer, Aftershock,, John Wiley and Sons, New Jersey, September, 2011

306 See :http://online.wsj.com/article/SB10001424127887324296604578179730422597100.html?mod=ITP_moneyandinvesting_0

307 See Hoisington Investment Management, Quarterly Review and Outlook' Third Quarter 2012

308 Eugene F Fama discusses this possibility in a recent interview that can be found here: http://www.cfapubs.org/doi/pdf/10.2469/faj.v68.n6.1

309 As quoted by John Mauldin, "The Quest for Certainty", Oct. 2012.

310 See "The States of Foreclosure: Housing prices stabilize when lenders can enforce contracts." Wsj, January 8, 2013 available here: http://online.wsj.com/article/SB10001424127887323297104578175522391676156.html?KEYWORDS=US+house+prices+rebound+in+non-judicial+foreclosure+states

311 See http://www.washingtonpost.com/business/economy/economists-obama-administration-at-odds-over-role-of-mortgage-debt-in-slow-recovery/2012/11/22/dc83f25e-2e87-11e2-89d4-040c9330702a_print.html

312 His views and policies are recounted in an interview available here:
http://online.wsj.com/article/SB10001424127887323981504578179310418828782.html?mod=ITP_opinion_0

313 This is in Popular Illusions. You can find it here: http://www.ritholtz.com/blog/2012/10/memo-to-central-banks-youre-debasing-more-than-our-currency/

314 See BCL, p.3.

315 See for example American Way: Some Take It, Some Leave It", Wall Street Journal, July 12 2004,

316 See Ashok Bardhan, Robert Edelstein and Cynthia Kroll, p.17.

317 Nor were regulators otherwise generally involved in dictating mortgage design to lenders or borrowers.

318 See Lea p.11.

319 ibid

320 FCIC Report, 2011, p xxvii.

321 This can be found here: http://www.aei.org/

322 See for example http://www.americanbanker.com/issues/177_149/donovan-obama-cant-fire-fhfa-demarco-1051528-1.html

323 See Ben S. Bernanke, "The Future of Mortgage Finance in the United States," The B.E.Journal of Economic Analysis and Policy 9(3) (Symposium): Art. 2 2009

324 See Gretchen Morgenson, and Joshua Rosner, Reckless Endangerment, Times Books, New York 2011 for a discussion of Fannie Mae.

325 See "the Gold Standard Goes Mainstream" at http://online.wsj.com/article/SB10000872396390444914904577619383218788846.html?mod=ITP_opinion_0

326 See Rickards, pp. 43-45 for this discussion.

327 See the discussion in chapter 1.

328 See "The Federal reserve: From Central Bank to Central Planner" by professor John H. Cochran here: http://online.wsj.com/article/SB10000872396390444812704577609384030304936.html?mod=ITP_opinion_0

329 See the Article by Columnist George Will at http://www.washingtonpost.com/opinions/george-will-the-feds-mission-creep/2012/10/17/7bf8e96a-1877-11e2-9855-71f2b202721b_story.html

See Rickards (pp.229-234) for a discussion of SDR and IMF proposals.

331 In Rothbard, p. 75 and p. 58 respectively.

332 As reported in Herzog, p. 7.

333 See http://www.realclearmarkets.com/articles/2012/11/01/dodd-frank_and_too_big_to_fail_receive_too_little_attention_99956.html

334 See Simon Johnson, an Institutional Flaw at the Heart of the Federal Reserve," NYT, 6/14/2012

335 Even consumer advocates think it has been counter-productive after four decades. See : http://www.americanbanker.com/issues/177_170/cfpb-mortgage-reform-applies-wrong-fix-to-right-problem-1052322-1.html?ET=americanbanker:e12164:2268417a:&st=email&utm_source=editorial&utm_medium=email&utm_campaign=AB_Intraday_090412

336 See Mayer, Pence and Sherlund PP 35-40.

337 See John Duca, John Muellbauer, and Anthony Murphy. 2011. "Credit Standards and the bubble in US house prices: new econometric evidence." BIS Papers No. 64.

338 See Mark Calabria, "Mortgage Finance and Stability," Harvard MIT Joint Center, page 8, forthcoming.

339 See Dodd-Frank's 'Qualified Mortgage' Was Intended to Be Broad in the American Banker April 2012 available here: http://www.americanbanker.com/bankthink/dodd-frank-qualified-mortgage-was-intended-to-be-broad-1048714-1.html

340 These definitions became part of the 2012 Presidential race, a sure sign of the extent to which the market has become politicized. See http://www.americanbanker.com/issues/177_194/mortgage-lenders-tighten-requirements-ahead-of-qualified-mortgage-rule-1053306-1.html?ET=americanbanker:e12625:2268417a:&st=email&utm_source=editorial&utm_medium=email&utm_campaign=AB_Intraday_100912

341 See http://www.americanbanker.com/bankthink/how-to-loosen-the-qualified-mortgage-straitjacket-1053861-1.html

342 See for example http://www.americanbanker.com/issues/177_190/why-american-express-fine-should-scare-bankers-1053172-1.html

343 A discussion of these proposals can be found here: http://www.americanbanker.com/issues/177_169/what-romney-victory-would-mean-for-banks-1052289-1.html?zkPrintable=1&nopagination=1

344 See Steven M. Teles, "Kludgeocracy: The American Way of Policy, " New America Foundation, December 2012

345 See BULL BY THE HORNS: Fighting To Save Main Street From Wall Street And Wall Street From Itself by Sheila Bair, Free Press, 2012

346 See the American Banker at: http://www.americanbanker.com/issues/177_168/what-ex-comptroller-walsh-really-thinks-about-the-state-of-banking-1052256-1.html?ET=americanbanker:e12119:2268417a:&st=email&utm_source=editorial&utm_medium=email&utm_campaign=AB_Intraday_083012

347 Sheng, "Role of the Central Bank in Banking Crisis," in Downes and Vaez-Zadeh, eds., The Evolving Role of Central Banks, p. 209.

348 Gerard Caprio, Jr., and Lawrence H. Summers, "Finance and Its Reform: Beyond Laissez Faire," in Dmitri B. Papadimitriou, ed., Stability in the Financial System (New York: St. Martin's Press, 1996), p. 406.

349 Available here: http://online.wsj.com/article/SB10001424127887323468604578245421482083936.html?mod=ITP_opinion_0

350 See http://www.fdic.gov/about/mission/

351 See FSA at http://www.fsa.gov.uk/about/aims/principles

352 See for example: http://www.independent.org/pdf/tir/tir_04_2_ely.pdf

353 See "Banking's Fiscal Cliff: Five Reasons to Extend TAG" in the AB Dec 12, 2012 available here: http://www.americanbanker.com/bankthink/bankings-fiscal-cliff-five-reasons-to-extend-tag-1055036-1.html

354 See Alex Pollack, Which Depositors Should Suffer Losses When a Bank Fails, AB, Feb.6, 2013 available here: http://www.americanbanker.com/bankthink/which-depositors-should-suffer-losses-when-a-bank-fails-1056522-1.html?zkPrintable=1&nopagination=1

355 As described in Allison, p.19.

356 See Acemoglu and Robinson, Why Nations Fail, 2012, for a discussion of this process over 15 millennia.

357 This can be found in "The Control Engineers And The Notion Of Risk" by Charles Gave, December 14, 2012.

358 See http://www.americanbanker.com/issues/177_209/banking-regulators-fight-back-against-agency-review-bill-1053952-1.html?ET=americanbanker:e12899:2268417a:&st=email&utm_source=editorial&utm_medium=email&utm_campaign=ABLA_Daily_Briefing_102912

359 Compendium of Major Issues in Bank regulation, Committee on banking Housing and Urban Affairs, U.S. Senate, August 1975, PP 908-9.

360 Ibid, p.926.

361 From the Central Bank of Malaysia Chairman as cited in Mayer (p.103).

362 For an assessment of their easily progress, see: http://www.americanbanker.com/bankthink/the-fsoc-systemic-oversight-or-overlook-1053177-1.html?ET=americanbanker:e12553:2268417a:&st=email&utm_source=editorial&utm_medium=email&utm_campaign=AB_Intraday_100212

363 See http://american.com/archive/2012/october/the-financial-stability-oversight-councils-fatal-flaw

364 See Allison (pp.75-76) for this discussion.

365 American Banker Jan 29, 2013 available here: http://www.americanbanker.com/bankthink/wall-street-is-crazy-to-expect-future-bailouts-1056192-1.html?zkPrintable=1&nopagination=1

366 See "An End to Bailouts", National Review, January 28, 2013 here: https://www.nationalreview.com/nrd/articles/337357/end-bailouts

367 See Wallison (2013, pp.526-528) for a more detailed discussion of the problems with OLA.

368 See for example Arnold Kling, "Breaking up the Banks," National Review, April 5, 2010.

369 It's not very likely they were being truthful, however. See Neil Barofsky, pp. 212-213.

370 See http://online.wsj.com/article/SB10000872396390443768804578036400697837818.html?mod=ITP_moneyandinvesting_1

371 As of this writing the SEC is over a year in default and no rules are pending.

372 QE1, QE2 & QE3 largely attempted to inflate MBS prices.

373 See: http://www.americanbanker.com/issues/178_137/housing-plan-must-be-clear-about-governments-role-bernanke-1060676-1.html?ET=americanbanker:e16145:706024a:&st=email&utm_source=editorial&utm_medium=email&utm_campaign=AB_Intraday_071813

374 See: http://economistsview.typepad.com/economistsview/2008/04/whence-systemic.html

375 See Lea, PP. 7-8 for a discussion of mortgage brokers in Europe.

376 See Lawmakers, FDIC Square Off Over Blueprint for Covered Bond Market American Banker | Tuesday, July 27, 2010 and Alex Pollack http://www.americanbanker.com/issues/176_70/covered-bond-solution-housing-1035798-1.html?ET=americanbanker:e10850:2268417a:&st=email&zkPrintable=1&nopagination=1

377 See for example the FRB study 2000.

378 See http://www.americanbanker.com/issues/177_178/cfpb-opposes-20-percent-down-payment-wont-abuse-powers-cordray-1052643-1.html?ET=americanbanker:e12296:2268417a:&st=email&utm_source=editorial&utm_medium=email&utm_campaign=AB_Intraday_091312

379 See Ed Pinto, "The Devil is in the Details part 2; regulators mull making the QRM rule identical to the CFPB's new QM rule, AEI, Feb 26, 2013, available here: http://www.aei.org/article/economics/financial-services/housing-finance/the-devil-is-in-the-details-part-ii/

380 The individual social security accounts proposed in 2001 would have transferred the Treasury securities on the SS books to individuals, increasing the deficit because the Treasury doesn't record a liability to the SS Trust Fund on the grounds that it doesn't legally owe it.

381 See http://www.americanbanker.com/gallery/mortgage-lending-under-siege-1053860-1.html

382 See http://www.americanbanker.com/bankthink/fhfa-vision-for-securitization-platform-ambitious-laudable-dicey-1053346-1.html?ET=americanbanker:e12641:2268417a:&st=email&utm_source=editorial&utm_medium=email&utm_campaign=AB_Intraday_101012

383 See http://www.americanbanker.com/bankthink/fhfa-vision-for-securitization-platform-ambitious-laudable-dicey-1053346-1.html?ET=americanbanker:e12641:2268417a:&st=email&utm_source=editorial&utm_medium=email&utm_campaign=AB_Intraday_101012

384 See http://online.wsj.com/article/SB10001424127887324296604578179730422597100.html?mod=ITP_moneyandinvesting_0

385 See for example: http://newsandinsight.thomsonreuters.com/New_York/News/2012/11_-_November/Citing_$5_trillion_national_crisis,_Boies_enters_R_I__pension_fray/

386 See Martin Feldstein, http://www.jstor.org/discover/10.2307/1829174?uid=3739560&uid=2&uid=4&uid=3739256&sid=21101296966941

387 See the World Economic Outlook, IMF, September, 2005.

388 In much of the "less" developed world, households avoid the confiscation of wealth by politicians by investing in housing with equity one concrete block at a time, resulting in a permanent state of unfinished construction.

Glossary of Abbreviations

ABS: asset backed security

AIG: American International Group insurance company

ABX: Asset backed securities index

AEI: American Enterprise Institute in Washington DC

AMINET: Automated Mortgage Market Information Network

APR: annual percentage rate calculation

BCL: Barth, Caprio and Levine, *Guardians of Finance* (2012)

BHCs: bank holding companies

BoE: Bank of England

CAP: Center for American Progress

CBO: Congressional Budget Office

CDO: collateralized debt obligation

CDS: credit default swaps

CEA: Council of Economic Advisors

CEO: chief executive officer

CESs: closed end second mortgages

CFO: chief financial officer

CFPB: Consumer Financial Protection Bureau

CFTC: Commodity Futures Trading Commission

CLO: collateralized loan obligation

CLTV: combined LTV

CMO: collateralized mortgage obligation

CPI: consumer price inflation

CPI-U: CPI for urban dwellers

CPI-W for urban wage earners

CPP: Capital Purchase Plan

CRA: Community Reinvestment Act of 1977

CRD: the Capital Requirements Directive of the EU

CRS: Congressional Research Service

DOJ: Department of Justice

EU: European Union

FASB: Financial Accounting Standards Board

FCIC: the Financial Crisis Inquiry Commission

FDIC: Federal Deposit Insurance Corporation

FDR: President Franklin Delano Roosevelt

Fed: Federal Reserve System

FERA: Fraud Enforcement and Recovery Act

F&F: Fannie Mae and Freddie Mac

FHA: Federal Housing Administration

FHEFSSA: Federal Housing Enterprises Financial Safety and Soundness Act

FHFA: Federal Housing Finance Authority, the current GSE regulator

FHLB: Federal Home Loan Banks, Board or System

FHLMC: the Federal Home Loan Mortgage Corporation or Freddie Mac

FICO: Fair, Issac and Co, now a generic term for a borrower credit score

FIRREA: the Financial Institution Regulation and Reform Enforcement Act of 1989

FNMA: Federal National Mortgage Association or Fannie Mae

FRB: Federal Reserve Banks (e.g., NY) or Board

FRM: fixed rate mortgage

FSA: Financial Services Authority

FSLIC: the Federal Savings and Loan Insurance Corporation

FSOC: Financial Stability Oversight Council authorized by Dodd Frank

FT: Financial Times newspaper

GAAP: Generally Accepted Accounting Principles

GDP: gross domestic product

GM: general Motors Corporation

GNMA: Government National Mortgage Association or Ginnie Mae

Gramm-Leach-Bliley (GLB) Act of 1999

GSEs: Government Sponsored Enterprises

HAMP: Home Affordable Modification Program

HARP: Home Affordable Refinance Program

HELOCs: home equity lines of credit

HERA: the Housing and Economic Recovery Act of 2008

HMDA: Home Mortgage Disclosure Act of 1975

HOLC: the Homeowners Loan Corporation

HUD: the Department of Housing and Urban Development

IMF: the International Monetary Fund

IMI: Investor Mortgage Insurance

IO: Interest only securities

IRS: Internal Revenue Service

JEP: Journal of Economic Perspectives

LTCM: Long Term Capital Management

LTV: loan to value ratio

M&A: mergers and acquisitions

MBB: mortgage backed bonds

MBS: mortgage-backed securities

MIT: Massachusetts Institute of Technology

MMMFs: money market mutual funds

M&M: Modigliani & Miller

MGIC: Mortgage Guaranty Insurance Corporation

NAHB: National Association of Homebuilders

NASDAQ: National Association of Security Dealers Automated Quotation System

NCUA: National Credit Union Administration

NRA: National Recovery Administration under FDR

NR: non-rated security

NRSROs: Nationally Recognized Statistical Rating Organizations

NYT: New York Times

OCC: Office of the Comptroller of the Currency, national bank regulator in Treasury

OECD: Organization for economic cooperation and Development

OFHEO: Office of Housing Enterprise Oversight, now defunct

OLA: Orderly Liquidation Authority authorized by Dodd Frank

OMB: Office of Management and Budget

OTS: Office of Thrift Supervision

OWS: Occupy Wall Street movement

PCs: Ginnie Mae pass-through certificates or Freddie Mac *participation* certificates

PCBs: Private Covered Bonds

PLS: private label securities

PLSers: private label securitizers

PMI: private mortgage insurance

PO: principal only securities

QE: Quantitative easing

QM: qualified mortgage authorized by Dodd Frank

QRMs: qualified residential mortgages authorized by Dodd Frank

RAP: regulatory accounting principles

RCA: Regulatory Capital Arbitrage (sometimes risk-controlled arbitrage)

REMIC: Real Estate Mortgage Investment Conduits

RFC: Residential Finance Corporation under FDR

ROE: return on equity

ROA return on assets

RTC: the Resolution Trust Corporation

SDRs: Special Drawing Rights at the IMF

SEC: Securities and Exchange Commission

SF: structured finance securities

SIFs: systemically important firms

SIFIs: systemically important financial institutions

SIGTARP: TARP special inspector general

SIVs: Structured Investment Vehicles

SMMEA: the Secondary Mortgage Market Enhancement Act of 1984

S&Ls: savings and loan associations

S&P: Standard and Poors credit rating agency

SPV: special purpose vehicle for securitization

SS: Social Security system

SS&TG: Securities Sales and Trading Group at Freddie Mac

TAG: Transaction Account Guarantee for deposits

TALF: Term Asset-Backed Securities Loan Facility

TARP: Troubled Asset Relief Program

TBTF: too-big-to-fail

TIPS: Treasury Inflation Protected Securities

UAW: United Auto Workers union

VA: Veteran's Administration

WW: World Wars I & II

References

Acemoglu, Daron and James A Robinson, Why Nations Fail, Crown Publishers, NY, 2012.

Acharya, Viral V. and Richardson, Matthew P., Causes of the Financial Crisis (May 1, 2009). Critical Review, Vol. 21, Nos. 2 & 3, pp. 195-210, 2009. Available at SSRN: http://ssrn.com/abstract=1514984

Acharya, Viral V., Matthew Richardson, Still Von Nieuwerburgh and Lawrence J. White, Guaranteed to Fail, Fannie Mae and Freddie Mac and the Debacle of Mortgage Finance, Princeton University Press, 2011

Ackerloff, George R., Paul M. Romer, Robert E. Hall, and N. Gregory Mankiw, "Looting: The Economic Underworld of Bankruptcy for Profit," Brookings Papers on Economic Activity 24, 1-73, 1993:1-73.

Agarwal, Sumit, Efraim Benmelech, Nittai Bergman, Amit Seru, "Did the Community Reinvestment Act (CRA) Lead to Risky," University of Chicago and National Bureau of Economic Research, October, 2012.

Allison, John A., The Financial Crisis and the Free Market Cure, McGraw Hill, 2012.

Ashcroft, Adam B., and Til Schuermann, "Understanding the Securitization of Sub-prime Mortgage Credit," FRB of NY, March 2008.

Bardhan, Ashok, Robert Edelstein and Cynthia Kroll, "A Comparative Context for US Housing Policy, Bipartisan Policy Commission," Funded by the Mac Arthur Foundation, April, 2012.

Barofsky, Neil, An Inside Account of How Washington Abandoned Main Street While Rescuing Wall Street, Free Press, 2012.

Barth, James R., Gerard Caprio and Ross Levine, Guardians of Finance, MIT Press, 2012.

Barth, James R, Susanne Trimbath and Glenn Yago, the Saving and Loan Crisis: Lessons in Regulatory Failure, Milken Institute, 2004.

Barth, James R., Tong Li, Wenling Lu, Triphon Phumiwanasana, and Glenn Yago, The Rise and Fall of the US Mortgage and Credit Markets, John Wiley and Sons, inc. 2009.

Bernanke, Ben S. "The Future of Mortgage Finance in the United States," The B.E.Journal of Economic Analysis and Policy 9(3) (Symposium): Art. 2, 2009.

Bernanke, Ben S. Speech at the Bundesbank Lecture, Global Imbalances: Recent Developments and Prospects, Berlin, Germany, September 11, 2007.

Blundell-Wignall, Adrian and Paul Atkinson, "The Subprime Crisis: Causal Distortions and Regulatory Reform," OECD, 2008.

Blundell-Wignall, Adrian, Gert Wehinger and Patrick Slovik, The Elephant in the Room: The Need to deal with What Banks Do," OECD, 2009.

Bodfish, Morton and A.D. Theobold, Saving and Loan Principles, Prentice Hall, New York, 1940.

Calhoun, Charles A., "The Hidden Risks of Piggyback Lending," Calhoun Consulting, 2005

Calomiris, Charles W and Eugene N. White, "The Origins of Federal Deposit Insurance" in the Regulated Economy, Goldin and Libecap ed., 145-190, 1994.

Carmassi, Jacobo, Daniel Gros and Stefano Micossi, "The Global Financial Crisis: Causes and Cures," JCMS Volume 47, Number 5, pp. 977-996, 2009.

Colton, Kent, "Housing Finance in the United States: The Transformation of the US Housing Finance System," Harvard Joint Center for Housing Studies, 2002.

Congressional Research Service, "Federal National Mortgage Association," January 1966.

Cordell, Larry, Yilin Huang and Meredith Williams, Collateral Damage: Sizing and Assessing the Sub-prime CDO Crisis, FRB Philadelphia Working Paper No.11-30, 2011

Department of Housing and Urban Development (HUD), 2004, November 2004 Final Rule at Federal Register, Vol. 69, No. 211, November 2, 2004, pp. 63580-63887, which is also available for download on HUD's web site, at http://www.hud.gov/offices/hsg/gse/gse.cfm.

Eichengreen, Barry, Exorbitant Privilege, Oxford University Press, 2011

Financial Crisis Inquiry Commission Report, US Government Printing Office, Washington DC, 2011.

Foster, C. and R. Van Order. (1984). An Options-Based Model of Mortgage Default, *Housing Finance Review*, **3**, 4, 351-372, 1984.

Friedman, J. "A Crisis of Politics, Not Economics: Complexity, Ignorance and Policy Failure," Critical Review, 21, 127-183, 2009.

Greenbaum Stuart I. and Anjan V. Thakor, "Bank funding modes : Securitization versus deposits," Journal of Finance Volume, September 1987, Pages 379-401

Goldberg, Johan, The Tyranny of Clichés, Penguin Group, 2012

Goodman, Laurie S., Roger Ashworth, Brian Landy and Ken Yin, Second Liens: How Important," Journal of Fixed Income, Fall, 2010

Gorton, Gary, "Information, Liquidity, and the (Ongoing) Panic of 2007," *American Economic Review, Papers and Proceedings*, vol. 99, no. 2 (May 2009), pp. 567 - 572.

Grabell, Michael, Money Well Spent?, Public Affairs, 2012

Hall, Robert E., "Why Does the Economy Fall to Pieces after a Financial Crisis?" Journal of Economic Perspectives—Volume 24, Number 4, Fall, 2010, Pages 3–20.

Hendershott, Patric and James Waddell, "Changing Fortunes of FHA's Mutual Mortgage Insurance Fund and the Legislative Response," Journal of Real Estate Finance and Economics, 5, 119-132, 1992.

Hendershott, Patric and Kevin Villani, "Escrow Accounts and the Value of Mortgage Servicing Contracts," Journal of Financial Services Research, 1994, 59-76.

Hendershott, Patric and Kevin Villani, "Housing Finance in America in the Year 2001," in Gau and Goldberg eds.), North American Housing Markets into the 21st Century, North-Holland; pp.181-202, (1983)

Hendershott, Patric H. and Kevin Villani, Regulation and Reform of the Housing Finance System, AEI, Washington DC, 1977.

Hendershott, Patric and Kevin Villani, " The Subprime Lending Debacle: Competitive Private Markets Are the Solution, Not the Problem," Cato Institute, Washington DC, 2011.

Hendershott, Patric and Kevin Villani, "The Subprime Lending Debacle: Competitive Private Markets Are the Solution, Not the Problem," Cato, June 2011,

Hendershott, Patric and Kevin Villani, "The Politically Incorrect View of What Made the Financial Crisis Systemic: Government Housing Policy," Journal of Housing Research 2012, Volume 21, Number 1, pp. 15-48.

Hendershott, Patric and Kevin Villani, "What Made the Financial Crisis Systemic? The Politically Incorrect View of Intervention in Financial Markets," Cato April, 2012.

Hendershott, Patric, Robert Hendershott, and James Shilling, "The Mortgage Finance Bubble: Causes and Corrections," Journal of Housing Research, 19, 1-16, 2010.

Hendershott, Patric, Robert Hendershott, and James Shilling, the Mortgage Finance Bubble: Causes and Corrections," *Journal of Housing Research*, 19, 1-16, 2010.

Herzog, Thomas, "History of Mortgage Finance with an Emphasis on Mortgage Insurance," Society of Actuaries, 2009.

HUD and Treasury, Reforming America's Housing Finance System, February, 2011

Hyman, S., and Marriner S. Eccles, Graduate School of Business, Stanford University, Stanford, 1976.

IMF (2008), Global Financial Stability Report – Containing Systemic Risks and Restoring Financial Soundness, World Economic and Financial Surveys, IMF, Washington DC.

Jaffee, Dwight, "Reforming the US Mortgage Market through Private Incentives," presented at "Past, Present, and Future of the Government Sponsored Enterprises" conference, FRB St Louis, November 2010.

Jaffee, Dwight M. and John M Quigley, "Mortgage Guarantee Programs and the Sub-prime Crisis," California Management Review, 51, fall 2008.

Johnson, Simon and James Kwak, 13 Bankers, Pantheon Books, 2010.

Jones, David, "Emerging Problems with the Basel Capital Accord: Regulatory Capital Arbitrage and Related Issues," Journal of Banking & Finance, 24, 35-58, 2000.

Jordan, Jerry L., "Fix Fiscal First," in Roads to Sound Money edited by Alex Chafuen and Judy Shelton, Atlas Economic Research Foundation, December 2012, pp.107-120

Kane, Edward J., Incentive Roots of the Securitization Crisis and Its Early Mismanagement, Yale Journal, May 2009.

Kane, Edward J., 2010. "Redefining and Containing Systemic Risk," Atlantic Economic Journal (forthcoming).

Kane, Edward, "The Expanding Financial Safety Net; The Dodd-Frank Act as an Exercise in Denial and Cover up," in Susan Wachter and Marty Smith (ed.), The American Mortgage System: Rethink, Recover, Rebuild, Philadelphia: Penn Press, 2011, 271-285.

Kane, Edward J, Gerard Caprio, Jr. and Aslı Demirgüç-Kunt), W "The 2007 Meltdown in Structured Securitization: Searching for Lessons not Scapegoats," World Bank Research Observer, 25, February 2010.

Kaufman, George C., and Kenneth E Scott, "What Is Systemic Risk, and Do Bank Regulators Retard or Contribute to It?," The Independent Review, v. VII, n. 3, Winter 2003, ISSN 1086-1653, Copyright © 2003, pp. 371– 391

Kindleberger, Charles, **Manias, Panics, and Crashes, A History of Financial Crises,** MacMillan, 1978.

Kling, Arnold, "Not What They Had In Mind: A History of Policies that produced the Financial Crisis of 2008," available at: http://papers.ssrn.com/sol3/papers.cfm?abstract_id=1474430

Lea, Michael, "Alternative Forms of Mortgage Finance: What We Can Learn From Other Countries?" in Nicolas P. Retsinas and Eric S. Belsky eds., Moving Forward: The Future of

Consumer Credit and Mortgage Finance, Brookings Institution Press and Joint Center for Housing Studies, 2011.

Lewis, Michael, The Big Short, WW Norton & Co., New York, 2010.

Lowenstein, Roger, The End of Wall Street, the Penguin Press, 2010.

Lucas, Deborah and Robert L. McDonald, "An Options-based Approach to Evaluating the Risk of Fannie Mae and Freddie Mac," Journal of Monetary Economics 53, 155-176, 2006.

Mayer, Christopher, Karen Pence and Shane M Sherlund, "The Rise in Mortgage Defaults," *Journal of Economic Perspectives*, 21, 27-50, 2009

Mayer, Martin, the Fed, the Free Press, 2001.

McDonald, Oonagh, Fannie Mae and Freddie Mac: Turing the American Dream into a nightmare, Bloomsbury Academic, London and NY, 2012.

Meltzer, Alan H., Why Capitalism, Oxford University Press, 2012

Morgenson, Gretchen and Joshua Rosner, Reckless Endangerment, Times Books, New York 2011

Munnell Alicia H. Lynn E. Browne, James McEneaney, and Geoffrey M.B. Tootell, "Mortgage Lending in Boston: Interpreting HMDA Data," Federal Reserve Bank of Boston, Working Paper WP-92-7, October 1992.

Norberg, Johan, Financial Fiasco, Cato, 2009.

Passmore, Wayne (2005). "The GSE Implicit Subsidy and the Value of Government Ambiguity," *Real Estate Economics,* vol. 33, no. 3, pp. 465-486.

Perino, Michael, The Hell Hound of Wall Street, the Penguin Press, New York, 2010.

Pinto, Edward J, "Government Housing Policies in the Lead up to the Financial Crisis: A Forensic Study," AEI, February 2011.

Pollack, Alex, "Why Canada Avoided a Mortgage Meltdown," AEI, March 2010.

Pontell, Henry N., "Control Fraud, Gambling for Resurrection, and Moral Hazard: Accounting for White-collar Crime in the Savings and Loan Crisis," Journal of Socio-Economics, 34, 756-770, December 2005.

Reinhart, Carmen M. & Kenneth S. Rogoff, "Growth in a Time of Debt," American Economic Review, American Economic Association, vol. 100(2), pages 573-78, May, 2011.

Reinhart, Carmen M. and Kenneth S. Rogoff, This Time is Different: Six Centuries of Financial Folly, Princeton University Press, 2009.

Rickards, James, Currency Wars, Penguin Group, 2011.

Rothbard, Murray N., America's Great Depression, Princeton, 1963

Selgin, George, William D. Lastrapes and Lawrence White, "Has the Fed Been a Failure?, Cato, 2011.

Seltzer, Glenn, "PMI Insurers Owe Many Thanks to Piggy back Mortgages," *Mortgage News Daily*, November 13, 2007.

Silber, William L, "Why Did the Bank Holiday Succeed?" FRBNY Economic Policy Review, 19-30, July 2009.

Stiglitz, Joseph E., Jonathan M Orszag and Peter R Orszag, Implications of the New Fannie Mae and Freddie Mac Risk-Based Capital Standard, Fannie Mae Papers, March 2002.

Stiglitz, Joseph E., Jonathan M Orszag and Peter R Orszag, Implications of the New Fannie Mae and Freddie Mac Risk-Based Capital Standard, Fannie Mae Papers, March 2002.

Taylor, John B. Getting Off Track: How Government Actions and Interventions Caused, Prolonged and Worsened the Financial Crisis, Hoover Institution Press, 2009.

Thomas, Jason and Robert Van Order, "Housing Policy, Subprime Markets and Fannie Mae and Freddie Mac: What We Know, What We Think We Know and What We Don't Know," St. Louis FRB Conference, November, 2010.

Vandell, Kerry, "FHA Restructuring Proposals: Alternatives and Implications," Housing Policy Debate, 6, 299-393, 1995.

Van Order, Robert, "The US Housing Market: A Model of Dueling Charters," *Journal of Housing Research*, 11, Fannie Mae Foundation, 2000.

Villani Kevin, How Politicians and Regulators Caused the Sub-Prime Financial Crisis of 2007 and the Subsequent Crash of the Global Financial System in 2008, and Likely Will Again, August, 2010. Available at: http://chicagoboyz.net/archives/14624.html

Villani, Kevin, "The Sub-Prime Lending Debacle in a Word: Capital: Politicians and Regulators Depleted it, Causing a Systemic Financial Crisis" available at http://ssrn.com/abstract=2060562

Von Hoffman, Alexander, "Calling upon the Genius: Housing Policy in the Great Society, part Three," Joint Center for Housing Studies, Harvard, 2010.

Wachter, Susan M. and Marvin M Smith, The American Mortgage System: Crisis and Reform, University of Pennsylvania Press, 2011.

Wallison, Peter J., Bad History, Worse Policy: How a False Narrative about the Financial Crisis Led to the Dodd Frank Act, AEI, 2013.

Wallison, Peter J., "Slaughter of the Innocents: Who Was Taking the Risks That Caused the Financial Crisis?" AEI, Oct-Nov 2010.

Wallison, Peter J. and Charles W Calomiris, "The Last Trillion-Dollar Commitment: The Destruction of Fannie Mae and Freddie Mac, AEI, September 2008.

Wallison, Peter J. and Edward J. Pinto, "Bet the House: Why the FHA Is Going (for) Broke," AEI, January, 2012.

Wallison, Peter J and Edward Pinto, "How the Government Is Creating another Housing Bubble," AEI, November, 2010.

Weicher, John, "The Affordable Housing Goals, Homeownership and Risk: Some Lessons from Past Efforts to Regulate the GSEs," presented at "Past, Present, and Future of the Government Sponsored Enterprises" conference, FRB St Louis, Nov 2010.

White, Lawrence J. "Markets: The Credit Rating Agencies," Journal of Economic Perspectives, 24, 211–26. 2010.

Woods, Thomas E. Meltdown, Regnery Publishing, 2009.

About the Author

Kevin E Villani is currently an executive scholar at the Burnham-Moores Center for Real Estate at the University of San Diego and an international financial and economic consultant.

Villani began his public policy career with the Federal Reserve System in 1974 as a monetary and financial institution economist. He was later Deputy Assistant Secretary and Chief Economist for HUD in Washington D.C. In the early eighties, he served in various capacities at Freddie Mac, including Chief Economist and acting Chief Financial Officer. He then served as an advisor to the World Bank, IFC, U. S. AID and various think tanks in the areas of housing finance, real estate, finance and capital markets, privatization and macro-economics.

From 1985 through 1990 he was CFO of Imperial Corporation of America (ICA). In the 1990s he served as the Vice-Chairman of Imperial Credit Commercial Mortgage Investment Corporation, EVP/ CFO of Imperial Credit Industries Inc. and President/CEO of Imperial Credit Asset Management, and served as a Board member of ICII and its subsidiaries. During this time he was involved in mortgage, commercial and investment banking and risk management and was instrumental in the development and introduction of some of the innovative capital market instruments.

Villani was the Wells Fargo Visiting Professor of Real Estate and Finance at the University of Southern California and has taught at the University of Pennsylvania, Northwestern University, George Washington University, Purdue University, George Mason University, Cleveland State University and San Diego State University. He has written or co-authored over 100 books and articles.